Astronaut Eugene Cernan
and America's Race in Space

The
Last Man
on the Moon

Astronaut Eugene Cernan
and America's Race in Space

The
Last Man
on the Moon

EUGENE CERNAN AND DON DAVIS

St. Martin's Press ⚜ New York

3 1460 00085 1526

Library of Congress Cataloging-in-Publication Data

Cernan, Eugene
    The last man on the moon : astronaut Eugene Cernan and America's
race in space / Eugene Cernan and Don Davis.
        p.   cm.
    Includes index.
    ISBN 0-312-19906-6
    1. Project Apollo (U.S.)—History.   2. Space flight to the moon—
History.   3. Space race—History.   4. Cernan, Eugene.   I. Davis,
Don (Donald)   II. Title.
TL789.8.U6A52435   1999
629.45'0092—dc21
    [b]   98–48206
                                                                CIP

C 334

dou.
5/01

First Edition: March 1999

10   9   8   7   6   5   4   3   2   1

Book design by Bonni Leon-Berman

To Jan and Robin

Contents

For many years, I have wanted to write a book for my grandchildren. I wanted Ashley, Carson, Kaylee, Katelyn, Whitney and those yet un-named who are sure to follow to hear from me this story of what it was like to live out a dream, with the hope that someday they might understand their grandfather a little better. And I wanted to create something special for the many, many people who helped to reach the Moon, for without their commitment, dedication, and personal self-sacrifice, I would never have been able to reach so far, nor would I have had the opportunity to share my story. Although it would be impossible to name them all, I am deeply grateful to each of them.

I want to thank those who critiqued various parts of this manuscript during the many preliminary drafts, particularly my peers, whose insights were invaluable. I hold them all in the greatest esteem. In addition, I will always treasure my friendship with Deke, Al, Roger, and Ron, who, while they were with us, played such significant roles in my life.

Special thanks to my agent, Jane Dystel and her staff, and my editor, Charlie Spicer and the team at St. Martin's Press, who believed in this project, made it happen, then improved it. And to Don and Robin Davis, my co-conspirators, without whom I could never have done it.

Most importantly, I want to thank my family and close friends, whose support and help was so important throughout this long project. Mom and Dad were with me in spirit every step of the way. Dee and Jim gave safe haven while providing background about our growing-up years. Barbara Cernan dug deep into the past to help recall and document long-ago events. Martha Chaffee painfully recalled her family's story and gave reassurance during critical moments. Max Ary, Norma Van Bunnen, and the staff at the Kansas Cosmosphere and Space Center lent timely and invaluable assistance, uncovering documents and film that had lain unseen for more than a quarter of a century. Skip Furlong, Fred Baldwin, and Tom and Carol Short helped steer the story through our early years together. Claire Johnson somehow survived the writing and publishing ordeal with her usual charm and efficiency.

My daughters Tracy, Kelly, and Danielle were a wealth of encouragement when the task seemed insurmountable, and the end of the book was nowhere in sight.

A simple "thank you" does not seem enough for my wife, Jan, who endured the difficult months of my reliving a life of which she was not a part. Her love and understanding made it all possible.

And to everyone who helped put American astronauts on the Moon, where ever you are today, I salute you.

Eugene A. Cernan
Houston, Texas
September 1998

1

Fire on the Pad

FRIDAY, JANUARY 27, 1967, was another balmy southern California winter day with temperatures in the low seventies, but a blizzard might as well have been hammering the North American Aviation plant in Downey. Inside the altitude chamber, where Tom Stafford, John Young and I were buckled into a titanium container not much larger than a kitchen table, there wasn't any air, much less any weather. Time, not snowfall or sunshine, was our concern. The most experienced astronaut crew in the U.S. space program, with five completed missions between us, we were trying to bring a new, untried and stubborn spacecraft up to launch standards, and we weren't having much success.

On the other side of the United States, in Florida's afternoon sunshine, three of our fellow astronauts were conducting similar tests in an identical spacecraft perched atop a giant Saturn 1-B rocket at Cape Kennedy. The world knew Gus Grissom, Ed White, and Roger Chaffee as the crew of *Apollo 1*, and they were scheduled to lift off in less than a month. They weren't having much luck either.

The days of the one-man Mercury missions seemed like distant history, and the two-man Gemini series had proven we could walk in space, rendezvous, and endure long flights. Now the time had come for the start of Apollo, the gigantic undertaking that would realize President Kennedy's dream of putting an American on the Moon, and bringing him back alive, by the end of the decade.

My gut feeling as a test pilot was that as badly as the program needed this flight, the bird simply wasn't ready. In fact, I was amazed that we were so far along the path toward launch with so many things still going wrong. Before Apollo could fly, tens of thousands of parts in both the rocket and spacecraft had to work flawlessly, and so far, they hadn't. But the damned Russians were breathing down our necks, and we were going to force that spacecraft to do what it was supposed to do, even if we had to bend some mechanical and physical laws through sheer willpower. Despite the problems, all signals remained go for *Apollo 1*.

In Florida, the prime crew was atop an empty rocket for what was called a "plugs out" test, which meant that everything was being run as it would be for a real mission, except the Saturn was not fueled. In California, our crew was in a duplicate spacecraft in the middle of a chamber that simulated the vacuum of outer space. The cone-shaped command module had given fair warning that this was not going to be a good day even before I climbed aboard. The forty-pound hatch fell on my foot and I could have sworn the bird had dropped it on purpose, part of its evil plot to keep me, Gene Cernan, from ever flying in space again.

I wormed in through the small hatch, slid onto the middle canvas couch, then moved over to my own position on the right side of the crew compartment. Although spacious in comparison to the tiny spacecraft of Mercury and Gemini, there still wasn't much room in Apollo, and I carefully eased my feet down among a clutter of unprotected bundles of wires. A technician helped buckle me in and attach the hoses to my suit, then the radio in my helmet came alive with a burst of static. While waiting for the others to climb in, I stuck a checklist onto the Velcro that wallpapered the interior of the Apollo spacecraft. We had discovered that the sticky stuff was the best way to keep things from floating around in zero gravity.

Tom Stafford, the mission commander, squeezed through the hatch and scooted into his place on the left side. Finally, John Young, the command module pilot, settled into the empty couch in the middle, and, with the help of the guys outside, hauled the big hatch into place over his head and screwed down the multiple clamps that locked it. The thing was heavy and awkward, a big pain in the ass, and in my case, a pain in the foot as well.

When we were all on board, the cabin was pressurized with 100 percent oxygen, the same way all American space missions were flown. Then the air was pumped out of the altitude chamber to simulate the environment of space, although we were really at sea level, only a few miles from the Pacific Ocean. When the desired pressure was reached, we checked the suit loops, those serpentine hoses which delivered our life-support systems, and verified the ability of the spacecraft to withstand the vacuum of the "space" now surrounding us. The pressure of the oxygen inside the command module was higher than was the vacuum outside, and pushed against the inward-opening hatch, sealing it so securely that a herd of

elephants couldn't have pulled it open. Nobody wanted a hatch to acci-
dentally pop off on the way to the Moon.

Tom, John and I were anxious to complete our work that Friday so
we could peel off the bulky suits, jump into a couple of NASA T-38 jets
that we had parked at Los Angeles International Airport several days earlier, and fly home to Houston. But first we had to finish the test, even if
it took us into the weekend. So we lay there on small couches that looked
like little trampolines and monitored the electronic guts of Apollo.

Our work continued in stops and starts. A leaking hose dripped poison
glycol coolant onto the floor of the spacecraft, and electrical short circuits
disrupted communications with the control booth just outside the chamber. After a few irritating hours, Tom grumbled, "Go to the Moon? This
son of a bitch won't even make it into Earth orbit." Left unsolved, such
glitches could stack one atop another and come back to haunt us. Every
problem we could find and fix on the ground was one less the guys would
have to worry about in space, so we remained locked in our seats, running
endless checks of systems, dials, and switches.

Time was the enemy, the pages falling quickly from the calendar toward
the launch date of February 21.

At the Kennedy Space Center in Florida, Gus Grissom was bitching
about communication problems. "I can't hear a thing you're saying," he
barked to the launch team. "Jesus Christ . . . I said, how are we going to
get to the Moon if we can't talk between two or three buildings?" Gus
didn't mince his words or his actions. As one of the Original Seven astronauts, he had already flown in space twice, and now commanded
Apollo 1. Everyone in the program knew that Gus firmly believed that
when the first American stepped onto lunar soil, the name patch on his
suit would read: GRISSOM. If Gus didn't like something, he let people
know; at one point he had hung a huge lemon on a balky command
module simulator to compare the malfunctioning space-age machine to
a broken-down automobile. Such outbursts added even more color to his
crusty reputation.

Ed White, suited up in the capsule with him, was another celebrity in
the astronaut ranks. A West Pointer and the son of a general, slender and
good-looking and straight as an arrow, Ed had been the first American
to walk in space, just eighteen months ago. The third crewman was a
nugget, a rookie. Roger Chaffee had never flown in orbit, but had so
impressed our bosses that they assigned him a coveted spot on the first
Apollo. Roger was my next-door neighbor and one of my closest buddies.

*   *   *

THE LITANY OF PROBLEMS we were experiencing both at the Cape and Downey had strained the already uneasy relationship between the astronauts and North American Aviation. All of the spacecraft of the Mercury and Gemini programs had come from the McDonnell Aircraft Corporation in St. Louis, and a strong bond of trust had grown between the McDonnell engineers who built the machines and the astronauts who flew them.

The news that North American had won the bidding to be the prime contractor for the Apollo command module had come as a shock to us. We knew the company had a tremendous reputation for building airplanes, but spacecraft were entirely different animals. As the months passed, many of us felt the North American design teams seemed determined to reinvent the wheel rather than build upon what already had been proven to work, an attitude that was difficult to accept in a program that had already endured 20,000 system failures.

In our opinion, they also showed little or no interest in astronaut suggestions. Just because we had already flown in space and would be the pilots to fly their new creation did not make us experts in their eyes. The North American engineers were working under immense pressure and were not about to let some astronaut "wish list" further complicate the program's already staggering costs and tight schedules. The result was more of an uneasy truce than a full partnership between us.

The pair of spacecraft being tested that day, known as Block One models, were never meant to go to the Moon, but only to orbit the Earth. Each Apollo flight would build upon the experiences of those before it and stretch our space bridge a little closer to the lunar surface. The Block Ones were little more than buckets of bolts, but damn it, they were the only buckets we had, and by God, we were going to make them fly!

The Block Two versions, true spaceships that would carry some of us to the Moon, were coming down the line, but would not be ready any time soon, and we desperately needed a launch now. The Russians had put up three unmanned lunar probes in the past year and the space race was scalding hot.

Our work in Downey was only about half done when the disembodied voice of a technician crackled in our headsets: "We're going to terminate the test now and bring you guys down."

Terminate? We groaned in disbelief. There were always hiccups in such tests, "holds" that stopped the clock while something was checked out. We would sit tight and work on other things while the problem was fixed. It might be a few minutes or it might take hours, but it was part of the job.

A "hold" was one thing, but "termination" was something else. No one, especially the crew, wanted to stop a test before it was complete, because the whole thing might have to be run again, which could take us into the weekend. Besides, dumping the vacuum from the chamber, undoing that damned, complicated hatch, and climbing out while wearing our space suits was not easy.

"Why?" barked Tom. We didn't really want to get out. We'd rather hang on, finish, and go home. After several hours of work, the problems seemed to be mounting rather than diminishing. Patience was never an astronaut virtue.

"Tom's got an important telephone call," came the answer. Now that was strange. We never took calls, no matter how important, during a test, but they had already started bleeding air into the chamber.

"Who is it?" Tom pressed. "Tell them I'll call them back."

"No," came the voice. "We've been told to get you on the phone *now*." In minutes, technicians would unlock the hatch and help us out.

As I began to unlock my hoses, my mind raced with possibilities. Maybe something had changed. Something was always changing in the space program. Maybe we had been assigned to be the prime crew on a lunar landing mission. Why not? We had more total hours in space than any other crew in the program, and we were already the official backup crew for the next Apollo flight. But a telephone call about something like that could wait. Whatever it was had to be important.

Hell, maybe our crew was even being tagged to make the *first* lunar landing. Or maybe it was our worst nightmare come true, and the Russians were on their way to the Moon. The only other time I could recall such vagueness had been when we lost two astronauts in an airplane crash just before the *Gemini 9* mission. I kept it all to myself.

I glanced over at Tom, whom we always kidded about going into politics. "Might be your campaign manager, Senator," I said. "Maybe the president is calling," cracked John. Tom, disgusted with the termination, didn't think we were funny.

It took about fifteen minutes for the guys to haul us through the hatch, like pulling sardines from a can. John and I stretched our aching muscles as we walked to the Ready Room while Tom snatched the telephone from the hand of a technician waiting right outside the command module. We didn't bother getting out of the suits because we might have to return to work, and taking off a space suit wasn't as easy as slipping out of a sports coat. John and I relaxed for the first time all day, sipping cups of hot coffee and talking about whether we would get home earlier than usual or have to remain in California and start this test all over again tomorrow.

Tom joined us in about five minutes, his face chalky white. I had shared some pretty hairy experiences with T.P., and knew the man to be totally unflappable, always in control. I had never seen him like this. Before we could ask what was wrong, he stared at us and spoke with a halting voice. "There's been a fire on the pad."

John and I traded quick looks. Fire on the pad? What did that mean? "Are the guys all right?"

Stafford shook his head. "They're dead," he said. "Gus, Ed and Roger are *dead.*"

2

Taps

A NORTH AMERICAN HELICOPTER ferried us to LAX, and without much of a pre-flight inspection we took off in our T-38s, Tom and I flying lead and John on our wing. In the air, we still knew nothing more than we had learned at the Downey plant. "Tom, what did they tell you?" I asked on the intercom as we roared through the late afternoon sky, the Pacific coast and the sprawl of Los Angeles giving way to the broad, empty deserts that stretch across California, Arizona, and New Mexico. The sun was setting behind us, the sky darkening ahead. Below, pinpoints of light blinked on as the edge of nightfall crept over the desert communities. Tom tried to recall the exact words, searching for some new clue, for some meaning in the terse call he had received. All he knew, all he could tell me, was that our guys were dead. Fire on the pad. Until now, such a thing had been inconceivable. It was an hour and twenty minutes to El Paso, where we refueled and flew on, cruising near the speed of sound at 45,000 feet in a zone of stony silence.

We found it difficult to say anything at all. Silently, I harbored a sense of disgust at the way they had died. Others had been killed in the program, but they had gone down in airplane crashes, and everyone figured that someday an astronaut might perish in space. It never crossed our minds that we would lose somebody in a spacecraft on the ground. As pilots, we willingly accepted risks, relying on our training and confidence when climbing into a new plane. If I was going to bust my ass on this job, at least I wanted to be flying, not sitting helplessly on the pad, waiting for something to happen!

These three guys didn't even have a chance to light the engines on that monster rocket. Hell, the thing wasn't even fueled. If it had exploded after liftoff, they would still be dead, and it would still have been a tragedy, but somehow more palatable. Gus, Ed, Roger and the rest of us had chosen to become astronauts in order to take our chances going to the Moon, not to die sitting on the pad. Challenge me to react to a problem, to make a decision, be it right or wrong, but at least give me the fighting chance they didn't get. We always knew we were vulnerable to a host of unknown problems, but a fire on the pad? That was a waste, and something for which we were unprepared.

I didn't know where to take my anger. I couldn't blame anyone, because I didn't know exactly what had happened, and blame wouldn't have done any good anyway. They were dead.

The glow of San Antonio faded behind us as Houston's bright lights rose on the night horizon and we began our descent.

ROGER CHAFFEE HAD BEEN a year behind me in the Naval ROTC program at Purdue, and I really didn't know him during our early years as naval aviators. But when we were both among the fourteen astronauts announced in October, 1963, our lives became linked. When all else fails, line up alphabetically: Cernan, then Chaffee. In the official group photo and on many other occasions, he was right there beside me.

We all arrived in Houston in January, 1964. Roger and his wife Martha, a beautiful young woman who had been homecoming queen at Purdue in her freshman year, had taken a little tan duplex apartment in Clear Lake, southeast of Houston, with their two kids, Sheryl and Steve. My wife, Barbara, our nine-month-old daughter Tracy, and I moved into a rented house on nearby Huntress Lane. As young lieutenants, we barely made 10,000 dollars a year, but soon used a windfall of cash from a publication agreement with *Life* magazine to buy a couple of lots in a new subdivision where we built homes, side by side, a thin wooden fence separating our yards on Barbuda Lane. We moved in within ten days of each other. Roger had the first swimming pool on the block, and I built a walk-in bar in my family room, so we became a gathering place for many parties. Almost everybody in the neighborhood was involved in the space program, and several astronauts were only a stone's throw away. Mike Collins, Jim McDivitt and Dick Gordon were just down the street, and Alan Bean, Buzz Aldrin and Dave Scott were right around the corner.

Roger was a workaholic, and I guess we all were, but off-duty, he had a great sense of humor. We often hunted together, and I always used one of his handcrafted rifles because I never had one of my own. Martha would later give me that .243 Magnum, and it is now one of my most cherished possessions. Only six weeks had passed since our families shared

Thanksgiving dinner at their place next door. That same weekend, Roger and I had gone hunting with golfing legend Jimmy Demaret, and I had gotten airsick in Jimmy's little Beechcraft Debonair on the flight to west Texas. Roger never let me forget it. An airsick space hero? "You gonna barf on the way to the Moon, too, Geno?" As it turned out, some guys actually did. I knew Roger wouldn't, because he had a iron stomach that let him eat a banana-sized jalapeno pepper in two big bites.

At parties, Roger would challenge others to do the "broom trick." He held a broom out in front of him horizontally, stepped over it, wiggled it up behind him and over his head, coming back to the starting position without ever releasing either hand. It was easy if you were sober and somewhat double-jointed, and an embarrassing catastrophe if you weren't. He particularly liked the way it would rile Buzz Aldrin, a natural athlete who was stymied by the simple parlor game. Roger and I had bonded. We shared a dream. We were, in a special way, brothers. And now he was dead.

From the day we reported to NASA, our space careers grew in parallel paths. We shared rental cars, hotel rooms, and often the same airplane. In fact, we were both learning to fill the lunar pilot slot in Apollo. It was a peculiar honor, for the Block One spacecraft did not have the docking capability needed to pair up with the lunar modules that we were to fly to the Moon's surface, and Grumman had not finished building the LEM anyway. So on that January day of 1967, Roger and I were lunar module pilots aboard a pair of spacecraft that didn't even have lunar modules.

On many a Friday night, coming home from a week-long training mission in a T-38 just like the one I was in now, Roger and I would buzz our houses just before turning sharply left, dropping the gear and landing at Ellington Air Force Base. From as far as San Antonio, we would point the needle nose of our plane directly at the driveway separating our houses and roar over Barbuda Lane, shaking the shingles and rattling the dishes at 600 knots. The noisy message let our wives (and neighbors) know that we would be home soon. We would land, jump into our cars, and race down the two-lane Old Galveston Highway, through the single stoplight in the town of Webster at eighty miles per hour and screech up to our houses in less than ten minutes. It was all somewhat illegal, but what the hell, we were astronauts!

Those flybys were in my thoughts as Tom and I started our descent, but this time we avoided the neighborhood as we swept in for a landing and quietly parked the plane on the ramp. It was always a long trip home from California, but this time I was reluctant to see it end. Finally alone, I drove home slowly, overwhelmed by a feeling of inadequacy.

OUR NARROW STREET LOOKED like a parking lot as I arrived, stopped in my driveway, and turned off the ignition. Still wearing my sweat-stained yellow flight suit, I crossed the lawn, thirty-six steps from my front door to Roger's, nodding to a security guard who had taken position to keep away the growing crowd and the press. There was no reason for me to go into my own house, for I knew Barbara would be next door with Martha. The wives in the space program were a special breed and knew what they had to do, for they had been through this sort of tragedy before. All of them shared the same nightmare, that their husbands some-day might not come home, and that a somber official would knock on their door with horrible news.

I gave Barbara a big hug as soon as I saw her, clinging for a long moment to prove to both of us that we were still alive. Then I found Martha and held her tightly in a hug that we both needed so badly. Emotionally empty, I tried to convey physically what I could not put into words. What could I say? *I'm sorry that your husband just burned alive?* Fortunately, I was not the one who had to explain the accident to Martha. That duty had fallen to Mike Collins.

Martha had been in the kitchen, fixing hot dogs for dinner, when Alan Bean's wife, Sue, dropped by unexpectedly. She wasn't alarmed, because it was normal for wives to visit, and Barbara probably would be over in a little while, as soon as she got back from the movies. Yes, traffic seemed to be getting heavy outside, but that was normal, too, since everybody was getting off work for the weekend. Her kids, Steve, five, and Sheryl, eight, were watching TV in the den. As Sue chatted on nervously, Martha wasn't worried about her husband. Roger was in Florida, and wasn't even flying today.

But then Mike appeared at the front door. He wasn't supposed to be there. He didn't fit into the normal routine. When she saw his eyes, Martha realized something was terribly, terribly wrong. It was written all over his face. She knew.

As Mike gave her the awful news, another friend walked into the den and turned off the television set, which would start broadcasting news bulletins soon, and kept the kids entertained by folding the foil wrapper from a cigarette pack into the shape of a duck. After her initial shock, Martha took her son and daughter into a bedroom and haltingly told them that their daddy wouldn't be coming home again. Sheryl at first thought her mother was talking about a divorce, but when she realized that her father was dead, the little girl was overwhelmed by a sense of abandonment. Martha removed a double gold-heart locket she always wore, a present from Roger many years ago, and linked it around the neck of their daughter, to keep her daddy's memory close. Sheryl still wears that necklace today.

I watched the sisterhood go about this awful task of sharing grief, the women showing through their actions that Martha was loved, even as she roamed the rooms in a trance, like the hostess of a party, staying busy to keep from thinking that Roger would not be coming home that night, or ever again. It had to be so damned hard, but I saw her shrug her shoulders, lift her face, wipe away the tears and do her duty, denying reality. She was the wife of an astronaut, and an astronaut's wife kept the faith. She was not allowed to be less than perfect, even in the time of darkest grief. At one point, Martha crossed over through the backyards and made a private telephone call from our house. When she returned by the front, the security guard stopped her, demanding to know who she was before letting her enter her own home.

Deke Slayton, our boss, soon told me to put everything else aside and help take care of Martha. It made sense, because there was not much else to do in a space program that had suddenly come to a screeching halt. Other astronauts were assigned to shepherd Pat White and Betty Grissom through the bewildering maze of adjusting to the highly publicized deaths.

I found there was a down side to Roger's determination to do every-thing perfectly. He ruled his household, wrote all the checks, made all the decisions. Now that he was gone, his wife and children were adrift in a strange sea. Martha didn't even know if there was insurance. Roger had always taken care of those things.

The next few days passed in a blur as I attempted to put my friend's affairs in order and give his family a sense of security. Barbara was at my side every step of the way.

A private memorial service was held at the tiny Webster Presbyterian Church, just off Old Galveston Highway, the white chapel jammed with a shocked community of friends and neighbors. A civilian minister deliv-ered a homily and, as we gathered outside, a flight of T-38s piloted by astronauts zoomed overhead in the Missing Man formation, one peeling away from the pack as they swept over the steeple. This service was just for the home folks, the people who best knew the three astronauts, those who had spent the most important years of their lives working for NASA. Not only did we feel sorrow, but each individual carried a sense of personal guilt, as if we might have done something, anything, to prevent the tragedy that now so impacted our lives.

IT WAS COLD IN the Arlington National Cemetery on the last day of January, particularly for those of us who had come up from Texas. A bitter wind whipped the manes of six dark horses that beat a slow clip-clop tattoo on the winding pathway between the tombstones, pulling the caisson that held the flag-draped coffin of Roger Chaffee. The three horses on the left were ridden by solemn young soldiers, and the three on the right bore empty saddles to symbolize the missing riders. Not one, but three. Gus had been buried at few hours earlier in Arlington, and Ed was buried at the U.S. Military Academy cemetery at West Point. A winter sun shone above banks of high clouds overhead, but this was a black and mournful day, the worst ever in America's space program.

I was in my Navy dress blues and my polished shoes crunched through the frost as we took our places for the brief ceremony. My heart thumped as I studied the grim scene. It seemed all wrong.

Martha squeezed my hand so tightly that it seemed as if our gloves would melt together. The widow was in shock. So was I. So were her children, eight and five, barely aware of what was happening as they sat on cold metal chairs beside their mother. So was Barbara, who had been in bed at the hotel with exhaustion. So were Roger's parents, who had come from Grand Rapids, Michigan. So was Lyndon Johnson, the president of the United States, standing beside the open grave. So was the entire country, because what happened simply should not have happened.

The awful details had emerged over the previous few days. Apparently a spark ignited somewhere in that labyrinth of wiring, and the pure oxygen environment within the spacecraft created a holocaust. The guys fought for their lives, trying to open that goddamned heavy hatch, but died in a matter of seconds, asphyxiated in their suits.

The space program was ill prepared for such a disaster, and now we gathered in Arlington not as space heroes, but as mere mortals, shorn of our cloaks of invincibility, with failure at our feet.

*   *   *

THE CAISSON RUMBLED ALONG, the brisk wind rippling the red, white, and blue flag. The horses walked the twisting mile from where a brief memorial service had been held near the administration building toward the waiting grave, number 2502-F, on the crown of a cold hill, where Roger would rest for eternity next to Gus. The creak of the leather saddles, the rattle of metal fasteners, and the soft hoofbeats provided accompaniment as a military band, marching to muffled drums, played "Onward Christian Soldiers" as a slow dirge. Astronauts were the pall-bearers.

The weather was thirty degrees colder on that bleak Virginia hillside than in Houston as full military honors were rendered for Lieutenant Commander Roger B. Chaffee, who lost his life only a few weeks before he was to become the twentieth American to fly in space.

Martha dried the tears of her daughter, Sheryl, and Roger's father, visibly shaken, laid his hand on his son's cold, steel coffin. President Johnson personally expressed the thanks of the nation, although Martha wouldn't remember it. Lady Bird Johnson and Vice President Hubert Humphrey were performing the same ceremonial task at West Point. Members of Congress, NASA officials, and several hundred more people were gathered at a discreet distance as the flag was removed from the casket, folded into a triangle by a detail of Navy enlisted men, and presented to Martha.

There was a sudden crack of noise as three rifle volleys sounded, and the mournful notes of "Taps" seemed to last forever. Looking up, through the arthritic, winter-bare trees, we saw a flight of Phantom jet fighters thunder by in salute, one peeling up and away from the formation. Now, it was final.

An overwhelming question lay just beyond our circle of grief. Were we here to mourn our loved ones and friends, or were we actually at Arlington to bury the manned space program? From this point on, the dream of sending men into orbit and beyond would be viewed through the prism of the sacrifice demanded. It was a dangerous enterprise and we all now clearly understood what President Kennedy meant when he said our country had accepted this challenge not because it was easy, but because it was hard. He had wanted us to put a man on the Moon by the end of the decade, and now, in the first months of 1967, the first spacecraft that could move us toward that goal lay in ruin. The clock was ticking and we had a long way to go. Maybe what JFK had asked really was impossible.

As I watched my friend being buried, I began to wonder if the deaths of Gus, Ed, and Roger had cost us the chance to walk on the Moon. Was this the end of Apollo?

3

Sold by the Nuns

IT WAS THE NATURE of the early astronauts to be cocky and bold, for you cannot strap into a canvas seat atop a monster rocket and be ready, even eager, to ride it into space without having total confidence in yourself and your ability. A bit of arrogance seemed in order. *I can do anything!* We were competitive to a fault, whether racing our Corvettes around the Cape, pulling elaborate pranks, or tearing across the skies in our T-38s, turning a milk-run flight into an aerial dogfight.

It took a special person to overwhelm us, and Wernher von Braun was just such a man. To the American public, we were shining and daring heroes, but in the presence of *Herr Doktor*, we were mere schoolboys with dreams to fly in space. We were smart. He was brilliant, the man who was creating those magnificent rockets that would take us to the Moon. We furnished the bodies and he furnished the brains.

In a Houston restaurant one evening, where he had gathered four rookie astronauts before any of us had flown, I realized that the big German—almost movie-star handsome, with thick dark hair carefully oiled into place and the burning eyes of a true believer—was much more than a scientist. He was a visionary and a philosopher, perhaps the Jules Verne of our time, able to peer into the future. German scientists usually were regarded as "square corner" people in the extreme: engineers and technicians who strove for straight-line perfection above all things. Von Braun reached beyond that, out to the realm of ideas where the lines are loopy and there are no fences, and he considered rigid formulae to be important only insofar as they could advance his lust for space travel. He was the ultimate engineer, but he was also a dreamer, just what the space program needed, far out in front of what was going on at the moment. Von Braun was the alchemist who could turn science fiction into science fact.

He leaned forward, elbows on the stiff, white tablecloth, dominating us with his stare and confident words. Don't worry about getting to the

Moon, he said, almost casually. A large hand waved aside the problems which were consuming so much time, effort, and money as merely a set of technical matters that would be overcome. Ideas spilled out of him and flowed over us.

My buddies, busy talking to each other about one of von Braun's predictions, faded into the background when he turned that piercing gaze on me. "It's your turn now, Gene," he said. "You must carry on the dream." I must have gulped in astonishment, because he laughed. "You are to be one of the explorers, and I envy you."

I stared in disbelief, wondering whether the man was a real genius or real crazy. The director of the Marshall Spacecraft Center envied me? But it was logical. I was training to eventually fly to the Moon aboard his giant Saturn V rocket, while the only similar experience he ever had was as a kid, when he attached a bunch of skyrockets to a wagon, lit them and went on a wild ride. Von Braun would have to live his dreams vicariously, through our journeys into space.

He adjusted his chair and reached for a small object at the center of the table. "The true importance will come from what you do when you get to the Moon," he said. It wouldn't be enough to just go up, land, and return home. "Lindbergh didn't fly the Atlantic to get to Paris." An exploratory voyage must expand the universe of knowledge, a job without end.

Von Braun nudged a silver-topped saltshaker, as if pushing a toy. "Gene, you are going to need mobility. We will provide a car." In his mind, we would leave the Moon lander, get out, and explore the untracked and unknown dirt of an alien landscape.

Since I was in my mode of respectful worship, I didn't say, "Whoa up there, Wernher. A car? Come on. We're barely able to get a spacecraft into Earth orbit to practice basic rendezvous techniques, and you're saying I'll be cruising the craters in a Moon buggy?" I couldn't imagine this concept. But I said nothing, and it was good that I kept my mouth shut, for on *Apollo 17*, I would do exactly as von Braun predicted, and take a lunar rover on jaunts miles away from my spacecraft.

I HAD BEEN DISTANTLY linked with von Braun's work almost from my birth on March 14, 1934, at St. Anthony's Hospital in Chicago. When I was little, my big sister, Dolores, kept me in line by whispering that I had better be good, because I wasn't really part of the family, and that she had just gone down to St. Anthony's and bought me from the nuns for a couple of dollars.

The fact that Andrew George and Rose Cernan had produced a second child passed unnoticed except for family members and neighbors around our home in the Chicago suburb of Broadview. Other babies, however, did make the news that year. In May, five famous little girls, the Dionne quintuplets, filled a little farm house in Callender, Ontario, Canada. A few months later, an immigrant carpenter named Bruno Richard Hauptmann was arrested for kidnapping and murdering the infant child of aviation pioneer Charles Lindbergh. And I certainly wasn't the biggest event that summer in my hometown, since my birth certificate didn't state that the last man who would walk on the Moon had just been born. No, the headlines went to gangster John Dillinger, who was betrayed by the Woman in Red and shot by g-men as he left a downtown movie theater.

Not much was being printed about events in Europe, where ominous clouds were brewing that eventually would darken the entire globe. Adolf Hitler that year murdered his Nazi Party rivals and gave himself a title the world would come to fear—*Führer*.

Coming of age in Germany during that same time was a unique group of rocket scientists. Their experiments, however, were expensive, too much so for the limited private funds available for esoteric research. So the German generals offered funding, total support, and a secure place to work. The naïve scientists took the deal, dismissing Hitler as a fool who would soon pass from the stage. Von Braun had been right about many things, but he was dreadfully wrong about Hitler, who cared not at all about space exploration. The scientists were swept up to become part of Germany's war effort, and their revolutionary V-1 and V-2 rockets, fitted with explosive warheads, rained down on England.

When the war ended in 1945, Russian and United States forces raced for the rocket base in the coastal town of Peenemünde to grab its treasure trove of scientists, records and hardware. Von Braun and 117 other German rocket experts surrendered to our side, but many others were captured by the Soviet Union. That was the genesis of the space race that dominated my life.

I AM A SECOND-GENERATION American of Czech and Slovak descent. Rozalii and Frantisek Cihlar, and Stefan and Anna Cernan came to America before the start of World War I and, like many Czechs and Slovaks, settled around Chicago.

My mother's family, the Cihlars, from the Bohemian town of Tábor, about 100 miles south of Prague, were considered cultured and talented. My grandfather changed his name to Frank, found work in a coal yard, and courted and wed Rozalii Peterka—a pretty girl who had Americanized her own name to "Rose"—in Braidwood, Illinois. My mother, born in 1903, was also called Rose, and grew into a beautiful, dark-eyed woman depicted in photographs as being slim and smiling in the "flapper" outfits popular in the 1920s. My maternal grandparents both died by the time I was a year old.

Whereas the Czechs, such as my mother's family, were considered among their homeland's elite, Stefan and Anna Cernan were peasants from a hardscrabble Slovak mill town called Vysoká nad Kysucou, some two dozen miles south of the Polish border. Stefan stood only four feet eleven and one-half inches tall and weighed but 120 pounds, but it was he who gave me the gift of determination and the strong will needed to succeed against all odds.

He came to the United States first, and brought his bride, Anna Lucan, to these shores at the age of twenty-two. She gave birth to my father, Andrew, in 1904. They later had a second son, my uncle Steve, the American version of Stefan. Grandpa Cernan took a job in a coal mine and put away enough cash to buy a little home on Hoyne Avenue, on the south side of Chicago. But his lungs, battered by the suffocating work, forced him to make another change, and in 1930, he and Grandma left Chicago for the clear air on a farm in the north woods of Antigo, Wisconsin.

It was almost as if they had not just moved to another state but had emigrated back to the Old World. In Chicago they had the conveniences of industrialized life, such as electricity, running water, and a coal-burning furnace. On the farm, such things did not exist and frugality was a way of life. If something needed to be done, they did it themselves. I would one day touch the future and live an existence found only in science fiction, but as a youngster, trudging up the mile-long gravel road from the mailbox to my grandparents' farm was like making a trip backward in time.

Grandpa Cernan, tiny and gnomish, had thick muscles lacing his arms, and helped only by his two horses, Dolly and Prince, he cleared eighty acres of land, piling up the huge rocks and stumps yanked from the rich dirt to make room for rows of corn. When my dad tried to bring electricity to the farm, Grandpa adamantly refused. What could electricity do that he couldn't? And some people wonder where I got my stubborn streak.

Behind the closed doors of the two-story farmhouse, my smiling Grandma, a classic Old-World peasant woman who wore long dresses and a babushka on her head, ruled a neat kingdom. Doilies on the solid, massive furniture were always clean, almost sterile, as were the floors. Boots came off before coming inside. At nights, as a pendulum clock ticked away on the wall, we read by kerosene lamplight and listened to platter-sized polka recordings on a windup Victrola, while on a wood-burning kitchen stove, Grandma would create miracles. With a butcher knife, she would cut strips from a roll of homemade dough, boil them into noodles, and I would sprinkle on some salt and eat them by the handful. A dinner of pot roast or chicken and sweet corn could be followed by *shiski*, Slovak fried cakes coated with sugar and raisins. Grandma would brew beer on the back porch and store it down in a cool, mysterious cellar among heaping sacks of potatoes.

Baths were infrequent, and taken in a large galvanized tub on the linoleum-covered kitchen floor, the water carried in by the bucket and heated on the wood-burning stove. During the brutal winters, we slept in a four-bed, unfinished attic, beneath thick eiderdown quilts with the heat rising from the stove downstairs to help keep us warm.

Pitching hay, tending the animals, and doing chores built my own muscles, although I often wished Grandpa was more reasonable about using labor-saving devices. It was a nineteenth-century existence. The one job that made me cringe, but built character, was helping clean the two-hole outhouse. And each spring, Dolores and I were banished to the attic while Grandpa and Dad butchered a squealing calf so we would have meat to take home for the summer. To this day, Dee cannot eat veal.

Perhaps the best thing on the farm stayed out an old shed. There among the tools, covered with a horse blanket, sitting on blocks and smelling of hay, was a Model A Ford with spoked wheels and a rumble seat, a car that would become a major part of my life.

MY MOTHER AND FATHER, Rose and Andy, both grew up in the Chicago area and met at a dance to which they had gone with other dates, but switched partners shortly after being introduced. Mom became a June bride in 1925. Money-conscious, responsible, and trained to work hard by their parents, the young Cernans saved up enough to buy a house on Eighteenth Avenue in Broadview, Illinois, in 1928, and the next year, Dee became the first baby born in that new suburb. A few years after that, just as economic times were really getting tough in America, I entered the world, an unplanned Depression baby. The last thing anyone wanted at the time was another mouth to feed, but, particularly since my sister said she spent cold, hard cash for me, the family was sort of stuck.

My father had been working for an enameling business headquartered in Kansas, and with the aftermath of the Depression, the business folded, Dad lost his job, and then they lost the house. Forced to move, we rented a house on Twenty-third Avenue in nearby Bellwood, and my main memories there are from the time when I about three years old. Dee survived a bout of scarlet fever. For my part, Dad kept a propane gas stove in the workshop to heat his soldering iron, and such stoves were not as safe then as the sort we routinely use today on camping trips. This one exploded. I caught fire and Dad flung me outside, where he rolled his burning son around on the grass to smother the flames. I emerged without a scar, managed to survive the rest of our year-long stay on Twenty-third Avenue and at that point, when I was about the age of four, we moved for several years into another rental house at South Twenty-first Avenue in Maywood, paying the astonishing sum of thirty-five dollars a month.

THERE WERE NO ADMIRALS or generals in my family to guide my footsteps toward military ambition. My mother's father had been an Austrian Army conscript way back in 1853, and few relatives wore uniforms during World War II. Dad was too young for the first war and too old for the second, so soldiering had almost no impact on me as a child.

In 1941, when Pearl Harbor was attacked and the U.S. entered World War II, I was only seven years old and in the second grade at Roosevelt Elementary School. The war meant new jobs for both of my parents. Dad was working for the American Can Company, and when it opened a depot to make torpedoes for the Navy, he went to the new operation on a split-shift schedule. Mom took a job with Jefferson Electric in Bellwood. Every day she would sit on a stool before a large bench and patiently stretch thin strands of wire with her slim fingers before tightly winding them around a ceramic core to make a transformer. At the end of the day, her heavy gloves, and the skin beneath, looked as if they had been sliced by sharp knives.

I was constantly called upon to help my father in his big garden and the garage, where he taught me how machines worked, how to plant tomatoes, how things were put together. He could do anything from repairing a toilet to overhauling an engine. If Dad picked up a hammer, Gene picked up a hammer, and I was always pushed to always do my best at whatever I put my hand to. If I bent a nail while pounding it carelessly into a board, Dad would make me pull it out, straighten it, and drive that same nail back in properly. If you're going to do it, do it right or not at all, he insisted.

THE WAR YEARS PLANTED the germ of an important idea when the family went, as we did frequently, to one of the nearby suburbs to see a double feature at the movie theater. I found myself paying attention to the Movietone news, a black and white tapestry of world happenings that is not that much different from many of today's television news programs. What fascinated me were reports from the war in the Pacific, battles at magical places like Wake Island, Midway, and Guadalcanal. Brave pilots of the U.S. Navy flew out to attack the foe, shot their way to victory, and then flew back to a bobbing, weaving aircraft carrier, the speedy Hellcats and gull-winged Corsairs nosing over slightly when their tailhooks caught the landing wires on the huge, flat deck. Now that looked like fun. I pushed my feet on the seat before me in the theater, pulling back imaginary controls, fighting my way to a safe landing along with the pilots on the screen, and it dawned on me: *That's what I want to do!*

Eventually, the war ended when I was eleven years old, and life returned to a state of chaotic normalcy around Chicago in 1945. The improved economy boosted our family income enough to move us into a little two-story house at 939 Marshall in Bellwood, which would be our home for many years. The Georgian-style house cost 6,500 dollars, was no more than eight-hundred square feet, not including the basement, and had a single bath. Dee and I shared a room upstairs, and for the first time, did not have to sleep in the same bed. From my youngest days and until she got married and I left for college, neither of us had a room of our own. Later, spending time cramped in small spacecraft would be a piece of cake. At least the other astronauts didn't crowd up the place with a frilly dressing table topped by a big round mirror and laden with exotic creams, fingernail polish, and tubes of eyeliner and lipstick.

Since I couldn't be out there saving the world for democracy, I discovered sports. For a nickel I could ride the "el" to Wrigley Field and watch the Chicago Cubs play. They won the National League pennant in 1945 and I became a fan the next year, going with a winner, so much so that I can still name the starting lineup for the 1946 team, and still suffer the annual heartbreak of watching the Cubs fold, because they haven't won a pennant since. On the streets and empty lots, I began to play football, basketball, and baseball and discovered I was a pretty good athlete, although I had to work at it because so many other guys seemed to have much more talent.

On October 14, 1947, a young hotshot test pilot named Chuck Yeager, flying far away over the flat California desert, first cracked the sound barrier. Down in Texas, Wernher von Braun was writing *Space Flight, a program for international scientific research.* Both events were to have an impact on my life, Yeager's accomplishment by opening a new age for jet planes and von Braun's work by formalizing a plan to explore space. I would, in years to come, get to know them both.

I did my seventh and eighth grade work at McKinley School in Bellwood and entered Proviso High School in the adjoining suburb of Maywood in 1948, a gawky kid who played clarinet in the band at my mother's insistence. For my first two years, I would play football in the freshman-sophomore game, then dress in my band outfit and tootle away at halftime of the varsity game that followed. Dad's interest was primarily on my report card, and his dream was for his son to attend the best engineering school in the country. The Massachusetts Institute of Technology was the premier engineering school, but was financially unreachable, and he pointed me toward Purdue, in nearby Indiana, as a solid substitute.

By this time, while playing organized school sports, I had also discovered girls, which meant I needed some wheels, which meant I needed money. As a kid, I had worked part-time for years, from being a stock boy at Jefferson Electric to delivering the newspapers—the *Chicago Tribune* and the *Daily News*—to collecting scrap. Now in high school, I started making some big-time money. I might bring in as much as twenty-four dollars on a weekend of caddying for golfers, carrying two bags per round out at the Medina Country Club. The answer to my transportation dilemma was the Model A Ford that had been sitting up on blocks out in Grandpa's barn. When I turned fifteen I got my driver's license and my life changed. That 1931 Ford coupe needed a complete makeover; I plunged into its guts under my father's guidance to learn how the antique four-cylinder engine worked, and got an early introduction into engi-neering. It had pistons as big as dinner plates. There was a rumble seat. Spare tire on the driver's side. A windshield that could be pushed open. Mechanical brakes. I installed a radio found in a junkyard, polished the car to an ebony sheen, put on mud flaps and painted the bumper silver and whitewalls on the tires. Soon, I had guys hanging all over it and a girl or two at my side as I swept majestically around the school and to the drive-ins and teen-age hangouts. I could nurse twenty-five cents worth of gas for a week.

The academics of high school were easy for me, but a big decision came as football season started in my junior year, when I had to choose between playing the clarinet at halftime of the varsity game or being in the game itself. I couldn't do both, and the choice was easy. It was difficult to be an athlete, but impossible to play the clarinet. Mom didn't like it, but I became an end on the varsity football team.

Once I made the squad, I learned a major lesson, again guided by my dad. The other guys might be bigger, more experienced, and have more natural ability than I, but he advised me to stick to it and do my very best on every play. He was right, of course. I was never the best player, not a gifted athlete, nor the most skilled, but I worked harder than most and listened to the coaches. By my senior year, I was on the varsity bas-ketball, baseball, and football teams, made an eighty-yard touchdown run against our cross-town rival New Trier, and was elected president of the Letterman's Club. Dartmouth even dangled a football scholarship my way and Duke showed some interest.

In the class two years behind me was a sixteen-year-old giant who dominated the football field and could throw a pass sixty yards on the fly. Ray Nitzchke would earn football fame as a linebacker with the Green Bay Packers. And a few years ahead of me, one of Dee's classmates was a pretty girl named Carol Laria, who would become the talented singer and actress known as Carol Lawrence.

The Korean War started as I became a high school senior, and had an immediate impact. Dee, who had just earned her teacher's degree, married Jim Riley, a close friend who grew up only two doors down from us in Bellwood, and Jim soon shipped out to Korea. Dee moved back into our room for the duration.

The idea that I might become a foot soldier in Korea hardly entered my mind because I had other plans. I wasn't going to dodge Korea, but if I went, it would be as a naval aviator. To carve a route to flying and to respond to my father's demand that I pursue higher education, I applied at the start of my senior year in high school for a Naval ROTC scholarship.

I passed with a high score and signed up for the NROTC program at Purdue University, a full-ride scholarship plus spending money, three summer cruises and graduation in four years as an ensign in the regular Navy. The Navy, however, said the Purdue slots had already been filled, and offered me the same deal at the University of Illinois. My father wouldn't hear of it because he felt Illinois wasn't a top engineering school.

The Navy then offered a partial scholarship at Purdue, a program with a pittance of financial help and a commission in the naval reserve. I didn't want it, because I knew my entire family would have to work hard to pay for me to attend Purdue as an out-of-state student. But at Dad's insistence, I reluctantly agreed, knowing that not only would I get a degree, but I could still get a commission in the Navy, albeit in the reserves, and maybe somehow could spin that into my dream of flying.

In June of 1952, I graduated from Proviso High ranked fourteenth in a class of 762. Without studying much, I managed to win bronze, silver, and gold scholarship awards and membership in the National Honor Society. I was off to Purdue, which would be the doorway to my dream of flying airplanes from the decks of carriers, although I had never laid eyes on an aircraft carrier, nor had I ever been in a plane.

4

Wings of Gold

AMERICA WAS BECOMING A nation on wheels, and I was part of that mechanical revolution. I sold my Model A, inherited the old Chevrolet, and headed for Purdue, in West Lafayette, Indiana, 150 miles down U.S. Highway 52. I took to university life, and my first real taste of personal responsibility, like a fish to water.

Money was tight and I felt an obligation to my family to help pay for my education. I lived in a dormitory during my freshman year with an old football buddy, and for the first time was not sharing a room with my sister. To offset the costs, I worked in the dining hall and won a small academic scholarship, for the NROTC payments would not begin until I was a junior.

In my second semester, I pledged the Phi Gamma Delta fraternity, and the "Fijis" provided structure and a sense of community, giving me a center, a home. I moved into the Fiji house in my sophomore year and my roomie was Bill Smith, a sandy-haired guy who had played football for Proviso rival New Trier High School. There were seven men for each woman on campus, because girls weren't attracted to Purdue's primary fields of engineering and agriculture. But being a fraternity man gave me an edge: Smitty says I fell in love so often that he would just ignore me when I returned from a date, enchanted with the latest lady in my life.

I went out for basketball and baseball, but quickly learned I wasn't good enough for Big Ten varsity competition, no matter how hard I tried. But I could play intramural sports, and that schedule was almost as difficult, since the players included former high school all-state athletes and borderline varsity jocks. On the Fiji and NROTC teams, we would frequently play not only other Purdue squads, but baseball and basketball teams from similar programs in other universities.

Many Purdue students were older guys who had seen combat in Korea and were back in school on the GI Bill. One of Smitty's best friends from New Trier was Jan Sharon, who happened to be the girlfriend of one such former serviceman. This fellow was a year ahead of our class, and so modest that you would never know he had flown seventy-eight missions in Panther jets off the aircraft carrier *Essex* and won three air medals. His name was Neil Armstrong.

Years later, when Neil was a top test pilot for the experimental X-15 rocket plane at Edwards Air Force Base, Smitty dropped by for a visit and soon found himself beneath the house with the quiet aviator, wrapping pipes with insulation tape. Smitty, by then an aeronautical engineer, was naturally curious about the plane, which was the hottest thing in American skies, and asked, "So, Neil, you're flying the X-15 now?" Neil kept wrapping the pipes and said, "Yup." End of conversation. Neil was not one to worry about impressing people with mere words, content to let his work speak for him. In fact, he was so quiet that when he made his historic first step onto the Moon and said, "That's one small step for man, one giant leap for mankind," those of us who knew him were not surprised that he had come up with such a memorable phrase. The real surprise was that he said anything at all.

Purdue eventually would be able to list among its alumni both the first and the last men to walk on the Moon. Neil graduated in 1955; I finished in 1956; in the Class of '57 was the affable Roger Chaffee; ahead of us all, in the Class of 1950, was Gus Grissom, and one year ahead of Gus was Iven Kincheloe, the test pilot who set a world altitude record of 126,000 feet with the experimental Bell X-2. In coming years, many other pilots and engineers would discover that a main pipeline into the space program ran through West Lafayette. Obviously, the school's engineering education was pretty good.

The early semesters at Purdue were only slightly tougher academically than high school for me, and I breezed through them, keeping my grades high in the demanding electrical engineering major. While *I Love Lucy* was capturing the hearts of the growing American television audience, I missed out on her comedy because the Fijis stressed academic excellence and the brothers voted not to allow a television set in the house for fear that it might distract from our studies.

I thought I had it made, until I had a real wake-up call one day in a theoretical circuits course. I suddenly realized that the work before me seemed strangely difficult, as if written in gibberish. I blinked. I didn't understand it! *My God, could I get a C in this class? Even a D?* For someone who had always gotten good grades easily, it was a moment of reckoning, and I had to recognize that I was definitely in a new world. *If I get a D, is it possible to fail?* That certainly was not an option, not when my parents were working so hard to send me to school, not when a failure would disappoint my dad and also end my dream of flying. I realized that it was time to get down to business, and learn how to learn.

TODAY, WE LOOK BACK on the Eisenhower years as a pleasant time, for we saw Ike's famous grin as a beacon of better times. But there were dark aspects as well. The French were decimated in a sweltering valley called Dien Bien Phu in French Indochina, which we would come to know as Vietnam. At home, the Communist menace seemed to bloom around us, our fears amplified by the rabid campaign of Senator Joe McCarthy.

Far out in the Pacific Ocean, American experts assembled a sixty-five-ton device with the benign name of Mike in the Eniwetok atoll, and at dawn on November 1, 1952, Mike, the first hydrogen bomb, exploded, and a fireball four miles across blazed like a sun while a monstrous mushroom cloud rose twenty-five miles above where an island used to be. Before long, the Soviet Union announced it also had a hydrogen bomb. The world had been violently ushered into the thermonuclear age. I had no idea that in only a few years, I would be flying a plane that carried a weapon of similar destructive force.

If the time following the Great Depression had been my cradle, then the Cold War became the crucible in which my military career was forged. At the time, however, global events seemed so far away that they weren't a part of my life, even when I would don my midshipman's NROTC uniform and put in long hours studying naval science and history. But lying on my bed in the Fiji house at 640 Russell Street about two o'clock on some mornings, I would hear the ominous drone of B-36 bombers from the Strategic Air Command lumbering through the night sky. We figured they carried the Big Bombs, but although the thought didn't change my life, the real world was tapping at my door, for Midshipman Cernan wanted to be a naval aviator.

In my junior year, the Navy finally started paying the promised scholarship money, the princely sum of twenty-seven dollars a month, and some help with the cost of books. At the end of my junior year, I was nominated to be president of the Fiji house. The seniors were still allowed to vote, and a couple of the guys didn't want a Catholic to lead Phi Gamma Delta at Purdue. It was the first time that discrimination had affected me, but it rolled off my back, and although I lost, the brother chosen to be president dropped out of school and I ran the fraternity anyway.

Then I got the same sort of treatment, minus the religious bigotry, when my grades and service record put me in line to become commanding officer of Purdue's NROTC unit. Because I wasn't in the regular Navy program, and ticketed only for a reserve commission, I had to settle for being executive officer in my senior year. That set me to wondering about whether I had a realistic chance for flight school.

Of course, such discrimination was hardly in the same league as that being addressed that year by the U.S. Supreme Court in its mighty decision to end segregation in public schools, but for the first time in my life, I felt discriminated against. It just made me more determined than ever.

LIKE THE OTHER RESERVE midshipmen, I was required to make a cruise during the summer of my junior year. I took a train to Norfolk, Virginia, and found the cruiser *USS Roanoke* waiting like a gray giant, with guns as big as telephone poles. I saluted the flag on the fantail, then the Officer of the Deck, requested permission to come aboard, and for the first time felt a solid steel deck beneath my feet. I soon realized that as huge as the ship seemed, something was missing. The *Roanoke* had no planes! The cruiser might be my home for a while, but it was *not* My Navy.

I was sick as a dog during the first few days at sea. I never realized that on the ocean, something as big as the *Roanoke* could bob like a cork. Try going to sleep with your stomach churning in a swinging hammock with only four inches between your nose and the bulging body of a guy equally seasick in a hammock right above you. Most of us midshipmen spent the first few days at sea barfing over the side of that mighty warship, to the amusement of the experienced chief petty officers who became our friends and mentors.

As we maneuvered around the Caribbean, we visited Puerto Rico and took shore leave in Havana in 1955. The Cubans were not exactly friendly, since an American sailor had recently urinated on a statue of their leader, the dictator Fulgencio Batista, amid the bright lights of the gambling casinos. In the distant mountains, Fidel Castro was brewing revolution.

While I went about the routine midshipman's duties of learning what made a ship like the *Roanoke* tick, my eyes constantly drifted up to watch real Navy pilots landing real Navy planes on a real Navy carrier that was steaming nearby. Not long now, I thought. I figured it was high time for me to go up in an airplane.

AFTER TAKING A TRAIN to Chicago for some vacation time when the cruise ended, my dad bought me a fourteen-dollar ticket back to Purdue aboard a chunky DC-3 of Lake Central Airlines. My first flight sure was not the thrill I had anticipated: I sat in a cramped seat, just another passenger along for a routine ride aboard a plane that was considered old even at that time. Then a fraternity brother took me up in a little Cessna 152, and as soon as the engine revved and the wheels lifted off, I knew I had made the right choice for a career. Now I could look out of the small window at passing wisps of clouds, could see the spinning propeller pull me along and hear its strong, sweet murmur as the wings flexed overhead. When my friend let me get my hands on the controls, it was as if I became part of the aircraft. Ordinary people might be pinned to that distant grass, but the skies were going to be mine.

By my senior year, a sense of rebelliousness was creeping into the culture. In Montgomery, Alabama, blacks led by a young minister named Martin Luther King were boycotting the public bus system. Elsewhere in university America, a group of "beats" were growing beards, reading poetry, and generally acting pretty strange. Hairline cracks were appearing in the firm base of the Ike years, but did not really have an impact on my life. I had worked too hard and was too close to my personal goals now to drift off in some other direction.

As classes wound down, I received job offers with tempting salaries, for a good Purdue engineer could pull down about $380 a month. That was fine if you wanted to be an engineer, but my Navy dream was alive and well.

With a bachelor's degree in electrical engineering and a 5.1 grade point average on a 6.0 scale, I graduated from Purdue on June 6, 1956, and was commissioned as an ensign in the United States Navy (Reserve). Two weeks later, I reported to Pensacola, Florida, for duty aboard CV-48, the *USS Saipan*, a boxy old carrier the Navy retired from fleet duty and reassigned for use in training. To my eyes, that antique flattop sparkled. I owed the Navy three years of service—my mandatory two-year obligation, and an extra one tacked on for signing up for flight training.

I became part of the *Saipan*'s crew for the next eighteen weeks, until I could start pre-flight school in October. Meanwhile, after learning that pilots aboard the *Saipan* who were assigned to nonflying duties, such as operations or maintenance, had to have at least eight hours a month to qualify for flight pay, I cadged rides in their backseats as often as I could. A bonus came my way during those weeks when some of these career officers encouraged me to apply for the regular navy, which I did, and was accepted. That dropped the "Reserve" notation and I no longer seemed like a short-timer. It felt good to write USN behind my name, but a long naval career didn't seem likely, for only graduates of the Naval Academy at Annapolis were destined for an admiral's flag in those days.

I served as just another ship's officer and when the *Saipan* would put out into the Gulf of Mexico, I spent hours on deck watching student pilots try to land, not all of them doing it well. That was me up in those cockpits. Those guys were doing what I would hopefully be doing in about another year, driving a prop-driven T-28 down to the deck and snagging a *Saipan* wire with a tailhook. That year loomed like an eternity, and time moved as slowly for me as for a kid waiting for Christmas.

While I was still taking instruction in ground school, Soviet Premier Nikita Khruschev scorned America with his infamous "We will bury you" promise. I was a military officer now, and his challenge seemed personal. I looked in the mirror and saw a slim, crew-cut young aviator-to-be, complete with flight suit, the patch of my training squadron stitched on my sleeve, and carrying a bad-ass attitude. I was ready to jump in my jet and go show Khruschev a thing or two. There was a slight problem, however, for I didn't yet know how to fly.

Once it began in January, 1957, flying was very easy for me. My dad had taught me about engines, Purdue had taught me how to learn, sports taught me how to compete, and pre-flight taught me about aircraft. I thoroughly understood the machines that were taking me off the ground. Without realizing it, I was finally putting my engineering education to work. I now understood how planes flew, how they sounded under various conditions, and was aware enough to let the systems talk to me. For some of the student pilots, flying was equivalent to working in a sweatshop, as if they were at war with the plane. Some would wash out of the program and the marginal skills of a few others eventually got them killed. Getting ready for a mission one day, I watched in fascinated horror as one trainee bellyflopped onto the runway and his plane exploded. The pilot died because he forgot to lower his wheels before landing.

For me, flying just felt natural. Less than a month after I began in January 1957, after a grand total of eleven hours of training, I looked around the cockpit and realized there was no instructor in the backseat of my little T-34 single-engine plane. It was time for me to solo, to take her up by myself, to be in total control. I took off with a big grin, just wanting to get lost in the sky. It's a euphoric feeling that everyone should experience.

When we had logged thirty hours, the Navy split up the students, and sent those of us who qualified for single-engine training to Whiting Field to fly the T-28, a high-powered 1,425-horsepower plane. We moved forward inch by aerial inch during the next six months at Whiting, learning the intricacies of flying—formation, gunnery, and cross-country navigation, much of it at night. This was the first time that we had a real taste of the risks involved in military aviation, for there was the occasional crash, a midair collision, or some student just might not return from a night flight. Guys who had become friends died, and you felt they or their machines must have somehow screwed up. *That's not going to happen to me.*

After some 100 hours of cockpit time, I was transferred over to Baron Field to get ready for the carrier, and we learned to land a plane within the lines of a deck painted on a regular runway. That way, if a student went off the "deck," he was still on dry land. Normally, after Baron Field and carrier qualification, I would be shipped off to Corpus Christi, Texas, for advanced training that eventually would lead to flying jets. This was what it was all about, the goal for which I had waited so long and trained so hard.

Only a week before I was ready to go back aboard the *Saipan*, this time as a pilot, an unexpected opportunity fell into my lap. The admirals had gotten tired of spending a million dollars and eighteen months to train a naval aviator only to have him put in a mere year and a half of active duty before retiring to a cushy airline job. So a peculiar order came down from the Pentagon demanding a five-year commitment from anyone wanting to be a naval aviator. It was as if a paper scythe sliced through the corps of pilots. Aviators who were about to win their wings were suddenly faced with having to put in an extra two years, while others just starting to train could not even see the end of a five-year requirement. It was just too much of a commitment for some. The Navy later estimated that it lost almost half of its potential aviators.

I didn't really care, because all I wanted to do was fly. I was young, eager, had no wife, no kids, or anything I really wanted to do more than be a naval aviator, so I said "Yes" and signed the papers. Many others did not, however, and the Navy ran out of students at the Memphis Naval Air Station. When they came around asking for volunteers, I saw an opportunity. The downside was that I would bypass going out to the ship, when landing on a carrier had been what I really wanted to do all along. Nevertheless, it was a shortcut to getting my wings and I took the chance.

Ordinarily, I would have continued to fly the prop-driven T-28 for another six to eight weeks of advanced training to learn instrument and all-weather flying, then slowly move into jets. But less than a month after going to Memphis, I was in the cockpit of a jet fighter, an old T-33 Shooting Star, which rushed me quietly and quickly right upstairs, bursting through the clouds to the blue skies at thirty thousand feet. Going to Tennessee was one of the best decisions I ever made. There was a certain urgency now, for only a month before getting my wings in Memphis, a 184-pound shiny steel ball with four long prongs that looked like metal whiskers sweeping along behind it was launched by the Soviet Union and became the first man-made object ever to reach orbit. They called it *Sputnik*, and every time it passed over our country, transmitting beeping radio signals from outer space, it told us that the rules of the Cold War had changed. I would sometimes stand out in the darkness, look up into the Tennessee night sky, and watch for the little sucker, knowing I could never see it out there, a faint speck among the stars. *How did they do that?* Proving it was no fluke, the USSR launched *Sputnik 2* into orbit on November 3, 1957, with Laika, a dog, as a passenger. So three weeks before I was even given my Navy wings, a Russian mutt had flown farther, faster, higher, and longer than anyone in history. I had never even thought about a dog going into space, much less a man, and certainly not me.

As my dad watched with pride, Mom pinned the wings of gold on my dress blue uniform on November 22, 1957, only ten months after I had begun to fly, instead of the normal eighteen months. I had won the prize, but the game wasn't yet over. I was a Naval aviator, but hadn't yet finished flight training, nor had I landed on a carrier.

WHILE THE SOVIET UNION was successfully launching satellites, the United States was trying, and failing, to get into the space race. While the Soviets launched in total secrecy, we broadcast everything live on grainy black and white television and watched our first attempt to fling a U.S. satellite into orbit blow up right before our eyes.

Success finally came when we turned to our Germans. Von Braun had been saying for years that he and his team could put up a satellite, and do it before the Russians, but he was hooted down by rivals. The Air Force wanted control of any space program, as an extension of its aircraft testing at Edwards Air Force Base. So did the Navy, which was preparing its Vanguard rockets. The Germans, unfortunately, worked for the Army. Jealousy ruled.

Using the Jupiter-C, a missile that was a close cousin to the V-2 rockets they built for Hitler, the German engineers answered the call. Almost four months after Sputnik broke the barrier, *Explorer 1*, only seven feet long and carrying eleven pounds of scientific equipment and two radios, went into orbit from a little-known spit of Florida coast known as Cape Canaveral. The United States was in the game.

YOU AIN'T NUTHIN' BUT a houn' dawg! I must have heard Elvis Presley's newest hit song fifty times as I drove from Memphis back to Pensacola after Christmas of 1957. I disagreed with Elvis, for I felt myself to be quite a bit more than any dog, even Laika, who had died in orbit after a last meal of lethally drugged food. I not only had my wings, but had attained the exalted rank of lieutenant (junior grade), which meant I was no longer a lowly ensign, although I was still damned close. The promotion is so automatic that you can't avoid it unless you die. Nevertheless, I proudly wore the new emblem of rank, a single silver bar, when I went home to Bellwood for the holidays.

On the serious side, my dad's health had begun to deteriorate and I was worried about him. I wanted my parents to know that I truly appreciated everything they had done to make my dream come true. "I'm doing my best to make you proud of me because I owe it all to you and Mom," I wrote from Pensacola.

I STRAPPED ON A single-seat F9F Panther, a Korean War vintage aircraft that wore patches over old bullet holes, and for the first time was given the controls of a strange plane that did not have a backseat. They gave me a plane, a book about how to fly it, a bit of classroom instruction, stood back, and said, "Okay, it's yours." That's when you knew you had arrived as an aviator. I had reached another plateau, and although I still had not landed on a carrier, I was getting closer.

Gone were the days of a T-28's growling propeller and the poky pace of training aircraft. The Panther was a real jet fighter, and I was surprised by how quiet it was. The howling engine was far to the rear, only a muffled whisper inside my flight helmet. This sleek, dark blue machine responded to my slightest touch and moved as if it were a part of me. The cockpit was right on the nose of the aircraft and gave me the sense of gliding through the sky. I found I could use gentle, fingertip control, not realizing at the time how important that sense of instinctive flying would be when I found myself atop a Saturn V rocket or landing the lunar module on the Moon. The real kick at the time was knowing I was riding the tip of a very deadly arrow.

Danger was always present in such an unforgiving profession, and even during advanced training, some young pilots died while trying to master the same sort of birds I was flying. I didn't let that bother me because I had the confidence that I could handle this airplane business. Crashing only happened to other people, generally because they did something foolish. Hell, I guess we all made mistakes, but some of us were just luckier than others.

My flying record was spotless, right up to the final flight of my training command career. Every flight was graded, and a poor performance was scored as a "down," with the chance to fly the mission again. From the first time I crawled into a cockpit, I had never even come close to a "down." Those were for lesser mortals, or so I thought. That changed on the final flight, when four students, one named Cernan, took our Panthers up on a routine gunnery mission, the target being a long banner towed by another airplane. Since we were feeling pretty good about ourselves, we decided to shoot that bastard to ribbons, and shredded that long piece of cloth in a record shoot. We zoomed over, under and around the in-structor's tow plane, firing live ammunition and bouncing him rather wildly. Being a Marine, the man had absolutely no sense of humor and was not impressed with our outstanding work. He gave us all downs and ordered us to refly the mission the next day, which let us go cavorting through the skies again. This time we were more courteous, so as not to upset him.

I graduated third in my class and the Navy offered me a choice of assignments. I selected single-engine jet attack because I wanted to fly low and fast and drop bombs on things, and picked the West Coast because touring exotic Asia sounded pretty neat.

In February, 1958, I threw everything I owned into the trunk of my

Chevy convertible, tuned in some rock and roll and headed across the country for San Diego, home of the Miramar Naval Air Station, Fightertown U.S.A. The place would be known to a future generation by two words: Top Gun. On arriving, looking up to see Navy fighters and attack jets climbing into the blindingly bright California sunshine or circling to land, I realized I probably would not be the king of the skies out here. A rookie with absolutely no seniority, my initial job was the boring one of Squadron Duty Officer, a housekeeping post to answer telephones, shuffle papers, and make sure the roof didn't fall in. On my very first day, it almost did. The first earthquake I had ever experienced rumbled through, shaking the hangar, making the runway ripple and scaring the hell out of the Squadron Duty Officer. It was an omen of things to come, a warning that my life would not be routine, and God's way of saying, "Welcome to the real world, you nugget."

5
Albino Angels

I AM A TOUGH GUY, cracking through the California sky at 500 knots, only fifty feet above the lizards and the cactus on the desert floor, totally focused on putting the nuclear bomb strapped to the belly of my FJ4-B Fury precisely on target. That means hitting the checkpoint at 300 knots, building steam to 500 and hauling back on the controls, the pressure of four times the weight of gravity pushing me against the seat like a pancake and monkeying with my eyeballs. I head straight up in an Idiot Loop, punch the button and throw the bomb. Roll the Fury into a dive and push the throttle through the firewall, forcing the airplane to go faster than its designers could have imagined. Then I hug the ground and burn out of there as the bomb loops over the top of its own parabola and begins its lethal fall back to Earth. My job now is to outrun the shock waves and blinding light of the coming nuclear blast, rings of immense power that could shake me out of the sky. Will I make it? Who knows? Thank God, I never had to find out.

Such was the life of an attack pilot during the Cold War. On this particular day, zooming through the clear blue in southern California, it is only a practice run, the bomb a dummy and the path to the bull's-eye marked by two-by-two timbers stuck into the rocks and sand. Each stick is twelve feet tall and buried two feet deep, leaving only ten feet sticking up. I head into my bomb run, and slip groundhog low to improve accuracy and, in the event of a real attack, evade radar. If they can't see me, they can't shoot me. I'm flying so low that when a pole appears, I jump the plane over it, like taking hurdles on a running track. It's fun, but a little dumb, something only a kid just out of flight training would do.

The jet is pure, smooth speed and the ground swishes past in vague patterns of brown as I watch my instruments and adjust for a buffeting wind. *Thwack! Jolt!* Going exactly 500 knots, my highballing Fury tears a foot off the top of one of the marking posts. I feel the slap and know I have hit something, but the plane is still flying and no warning lights flash, so I rise to a safer altitude and head off to land at El Centro, where the purring Fury puts me down safely.

The ground crew and other pilots walk out for a look as I unstrap and climb out with great nonchalance, and they shake their heads in amazement. One of the nose gun ports is clogged solid with a chunk of wood jammed in so tightly that it might have been carved to the shape of the hole. A gash has been ripped down the right side, from nose to wing, metals panels have been peeled loose, and powdery sawdust leaks from beneath them.

I had come within six inches of jamming that post down the throat of my engine, which would have resulted in a catastrophic explosion. This was the sort of thing that happened to other pilots, never to me. It didn't take long for me to realize that I had done something really dumb and should be lying dead in the desert, entombed in a pile of flaming wreckage. It is okay to make a mistake, but unacceptable to be stupid.

My squadron buddies hustled me off to the Officers' Club for some serious drinking and gave me a crude scarlet banner bearing the legend: "Order of the Bent Pole—Limited to Living, Low-flying Aviators." Naturally, I laughed it off because the unwritten law was to show absolutely no fear. In the past months, I had convinced myself that I was invincible, invisible, and bulletproof. I was still a gung-ho flier, but from that day on, I carried a new respect for my dangerous profession.

SAN DIEGO, 1958. I'M in heaven. Hot Mexican food and cold *cerveza*, surfboard dawns and tanned California girls. *Sure, baby, I fly jets.* They didn't need to know I was only a nugget, a rookie who had just almost busted my ass.

When I arrived at Miramar Naval Air Station, I still had not landed on an aircraft carrier, a rare situation that was cured when I was assigned to Attack Squadron VA-126, call sign, Tough Guys. After practicing on runways bearing the painted outline of a carrier deck, they put me in an A-4 Skyhawk and told me to fly out to the *USS Ranger*, the third supercarrier ever built, with plenty of space on that angled deck. So why did CVA-61 look so small from my cockpit? And why did it keep jinking around like that? How can a big carrier bounce around in still water like a toy?

On my first approach, the ship seemed to fall into the trough of a wave. I stayed with the voice of the landing signal officer, my eyes on the meatball, a dancing ball of light that showed my glide slope, and reduced my speed to just above a stall. Suddenly, the *Ranger* ramp flashed beneath me, the tailhook snagged a wire, and I jammed the throttle to full power as the Skyhawk smacked to a jerking, twisting stop, angry at being told to fly while being held motionless by a steel cable. I was thrown forward against my harness hard enough to rattle my molars, having gone from 125 knots to flat zero in a blink. Good job, Cernan, now go out and do it eleven more times.

Freed from the cable, I taxied forward, the deck crew hooked the plane to a steam catapult, and I tossed a salute to the Cat officer, the traditional signal that the pilot is ready to go. A burst of power snapped my head back, the catapult flung me back to 125 knots and the *Ranger* was instantly at my six o'clock. By the end of that day of shipboard takeoffs and landings, I had my carrier qualifications and could hold my head up in righteous pride. Now I was a real Naval aviator. *Hey, baby, I fly jets.*

I was so wrapped up in my own world at Miramar that I was hardly aware that the outer space satellite derby was accelerating. Rocket launchings had become commonplace.

In November of 1958, the National Advisory Committee on Aeronautics (NACA) was converted into a new set of initials and NASA, the National Aeronautics and Space Administration, was born. That same month, I was reassigned to VA-113, the Stingers, part of Air Group 11 on the *USS Shangri-La*, to fly Skyhawks, the deft little single-engine attack planes we affectionately called Scooters, which had the singular purpose of delivering bombs and rockets to the enemy.

I set out on my first cruise in the western Pacific, known as WestPac, in March 1959, sailing away on a boat laden with thousands of men and more than fifty aircraft, to help patrol a world in which worrisome things were happening. Some five thousand American Marines had gone into Lebanon to brace the elected government; rebels led by Fidel Castro were fighting their way toward Havana, and a guerrilla war was taking root in the newly divided Vietnam.

So we went to sea as Cold Warriors, to hone our deadly skills and show the flag, just as the old American gunboats had done on the rivers of China. In the Straits of Formosa, parallel to the coast of China, we frequently encountered flights of Chinese MiGs heading the other way, passing close enough to see their pilots. We were all armed to the teeth and ready for a fight. A few years ago, in a much-altered world political climate, I flew into Shanghai for the first time, arriving at a military airfield aboard a commercial passenger jet. I looked out the window during the approach and recognized some landmarks. I'd seen this place before! I realized that I was landing at Ground Zero of one of my targets back in those nasty, nuclear days.

ON FIRST ARRIVING IN the wardroom of the *Shangri-La*, I looked around. Several squadrons of pilots were aboard, flying planes bearing names such as Demons, Cougars, Skywarriors, Skyhawks, Skyraiders, and Tigers. Fifteen to eighteen pilots in each squadron, top of the line stick-and-rudder men, and we knew some of us would never reach port again. Maybe an ejection seat would malfunction, or a catapult might lose power and the pilot would ride his plane into the water just ahead of the charging carrier, or someone would simply fly into a mountain or the water. You could not declare yourself safe until you landed on the carrier, taxied to the elevator, rode down to the hangar deck, then, finally, climbed from your plane.

Life settled into military routine once we were out in the Pacific, and I gained more experience with each passing day, flying over open oceans and safely coming back to the ship. Land or splash, that was the choice, and a splash was usually followed by a quiet memorial service on the flight deck, frequently with no body recovered. Complicating matters a bit was the fact that the *Shangri-La* wasn't the same sort of supercarrier as the big, fat *Ranger*. She was a 27-Charlie class, a made-over straight deck carrier that now had a truncated, angled deck. The landing area was shorter than a football field, looked absolutely minuscule in dirty weather, and was damned near invisible at night. Take a deep breath and follow the meatball.

Skip Furlong and Fred Baldwin, squadron buddies from Miramar, were also aboard the *Shang*, and we forged firm friendships as we shared the dangers of carrier aviation, drank Flaming Hookers and raised general hell in ports of call from Tokyo to Singapore and other Seventh Fleet playgrounds.

One reason my confidence was so high was that Zeke Cormier taught a couple of us how to really fly. Not how to merely pilot a plane, but how to slide our powerful Skyhawks through the heavens and paint the sky with bright, aerobatic patterns.

Zeke was the air group boss aboard the *Shang* after a tour as skipper of the Navy's legendary Blue Angels flight demonstration team and that handsome Italian stud looked as though he had stepped right out of a recruiting poster. He wanted to do more than fly practice missions, so he pulled together three of us nuggets (who didn't know any better than to go flying with Zeke) and created the Albino Angels. Zeke in the lead, me on one wing, Baldy on the other, and Dick "Spook" Weber, a skinny and pale aviator, in the slot. Zeke taught us the fancy moves, and we soon were flying precision demonstrations throughout Asia. At first the Navy loved it, but eventually ordered us to change our name to prevent conflict with the Blue Angels. So we performed instead under our squadron colors, the Stingers, and still had more requests for appearances than we could fill.

Flying on Zeke's wing was easy, for he was one of the smoothest pilots ever coined. No sharp jerks, no funny twitches, slick as glass, and by staying locked to his wing, I never knew if I was upside down or rightside up. Coming out of a loop, if he had flown into the water, we would all have flown into the water, still in perfect formation. He could have put us through the eye of a needle, and at times he did, trailing colored smoke and making people wonder if we were really that good or only insane.

ON MY TWENTY-FIFTH BIRTHDAY, I got up early and attacked Hawaii. The *Shang* was participating in an Operational Readiness Exercise that pictured an invasion of our fiftieth state, and four of us Stingers were rousted from our tiny cabins at three-thirty A.M. and briefed for a six A.M. flight. It was chilly and bouncy when I catted off into total blackness, unable to see the distant horizon. As dawn broke crystal clear, I dropped my dummy bombs on a small, uninhabited island that was the designated target, and with plenty of fuel left, flew over the lush green islands on my way home, an aerial tourist in a million-dollar trolley, looking at the pristine beaches and turquoise water. I got a lump in my throat as I swept past Ford Island and the old Battleship Row, which bore the brunt of the Japanese attack on Pearl Harbor in 1941. Only a third of the *Utah* stood above the water, and we could see the eternal oil slick seeping from the doomed *Arizona*, which went down with some 2,000 sailors aboard. This was history that had been made in my lifetime, a reminder of the horrors of real war.

*   *   *

SOME INTERESTING THINGS WERE happening out in space, and finally they were significant enough to register on my personal radar scope. In September, 1959, the Soviets launched *Luna 2*, an 860-pound projectile that hit the Moon so hard it dug a crater ninety feet wide. Crude but effective, it was the first object built by man to actually impact the lunar surface. The following month, they guided *Luna 3* into orbit around the Moon to photograph the far, unknown side. We had been surprised again, for these were not little Sputnik basketballs, but some pretty sophisticated machinery that was probing the universe around us, and it had Russian writing all over it.

The United States balanced that with the introduction on April 2, 1959, of a group of seven American pilots called the Mercury Astronauts—Scott Carpenter, Gordon Cooper, John Glenn, Gus Grissom, Wally Schirra, Alan Shepard, and Deke Slayton. Every military pilot in America wished his name was on that little list of four naval aviators (one of them a Marine) and three Air Force pilots. These were the guys who would take us into space.

I was fascinated by their assignment. How did one get to be an astronaut? For that matter, just what the hell *was* an astronaut? According to the papers, an applicant had to be a graduate of test pilot school, have two years of experience as a test pilot in at least twenty major types of aircraft, own at least 1,500 hours of jet time, be not over forty years of age as of 31 December 1959, stand not more than five feet, eleven inches tall, weigh no more than 177 pounds and hold a bachelor's degree in engineering or the equivalent.

Out of the many requirements, I met only two—I wasn't yet forty years old and I held the right kind of degree. Not the cloth from which astronauts were being cut. The Original Seven were all veteran test pilots, qualified far beyond my own modest accomplishments at that time. I was interested, but thought that by the time I earned those kind of credentials, the pioneering in space would be over. I had joined the Navy to fly, and the idea of riding a rocket ship into space had instant appeal. A new dream formed inside my crew-cut head.

THE *SHANGRI-LA* RETURNED TO San Diego on the second day of October, 1959, and tied up at North Island while the air group flew into Miramar. My squadron was about to change boats. The *Shang* was transferred to the East Coast and our air group went to the *USS Hancock*, known to sailors as the *Hanna-Maru*. But first there would be some most welcome shore leave to push away the military stress for a while, and I chose to go back home for Christmas.

I was in the ticket line at the Los Angeles International Airport, just behind a gorgeous, blond young woman dressed in the powder blue uniform and red beanie of a Continental Airlines stewardess. Damn, she's good-looking, I thought, squaring my shoulders and straightening my uniform. But before I could even tell her about how I was invincible, invisible, and bulletproof, she received her tickets and, without a glance, left me standing there, heading for Chicago, away from her. Luckily, I had overheard her mention to the clerk that she was picking up tickets for a girlfriend and herself, and she spelled her last name A-T-C-H-L-E-Y. I asked the stewardess on my own Continental flight if she knew a stewardess named Miss Atchley. She did, and I learned my mystery girl's first name was Barbara.

Now I had a mission that had nothing to do with the Navy. I telephoned Continental, but the airline refused to divulge any information about their employee. Two weeks later, I was in Pasadena to visit my old Purdue roomie, Bill Smith, and his classy, auburn-haired wife, Lucy. "Smitty," I declared when he answered the door. "I'm in love!" He rolled his eyes because he had heard me say that so many times before. "Yeah. Sure you are," he replied. "Come on in."

I sat on the couch and to Lucy's amazement, described my search for the lovely Barbara Atchley. Bill got tired of listening and took me downstairs to examine his 1955 Thunderbird, which had been in an accident. As we talked about cars, Lucy suddenly threw open a window and called out, "Geno. Geno. I've got Barbara on the line!" I stared at Smitty, who stared back at me and we both turned to stare up at a beaming Lucy. She had telephoned Continental and told a monstrously effective lie, a sad tale about a long lost friend from back home and how Barbara needed to be contacted immediately. Continental called a puzzled Barbara, who called Lucy, who explained the ruse and persuaded her to talk to me.

I chugged a beer for bravery and dashed upstairs, not knowing what I was going to say, and when Lucy gave me the telephone, I was as nervous as if I were trying to land on a carrier during a storm. My words stumbled out in rush, but she didn't hang up, and eventually agreed to meet me. "What a snow job," Lucy said, grinning.

Barbara recalls that when I gunned my convertible up the sloping drive-way at her house in Redondo Beach, late for our first date, my mufflers rumbled and she thought, "Oh, God, he's a hot-rodder."

One look at this gorgeous Texas blonde and I knew it was time for me to do some growing up. Her mother, Jackie Mae Atchley, was there, as was her younger brother, and it felt as if I had stepped right into a new family. At our first dinner together, accompanied by Lucy and Smitty, Barbara had the first martini she had ever tasted and told me her background. She was born in Corpus Christi, moved at the age of two months to Baytown, near Houston, where she graduated from Robert E. Lee High School and worked as a secretary until she became a stewardess for Continental in June of 1959 and moved to California. One of her main runs for Continental was to Chicago, which led to me to describe my family and life. It would not be too long before Barbara would use one of those flights to meet my family, and my parents instantly fell in love with her. "Son," my astute Dad observed, "That woman is built like a brick shit-house."

My roommate, Fred Baldwin, began dating Barbara's roomie, who was also named Jackie, and the four of us soon burned up the 120 highway miles between San Diego and Redondo Beach almost every weekend. Baldy and his Jackie were secretly married in 1960, violating the airline's rule requiring a stewardess to remain single. When Continental discovered the situation, she was fired, and a stern supervisor demanded to know if Barbara, too, was married. No, she firmly replied. Not yet.

BY THE TIME THE *Hanna-Maru* left for a WestPac tour on June 9, 1960, Barbara and I were very seriously in love. But the job intervened, as it does with all Navy families, and I went to sea for the better part of a year, wearing the railroad tracks of a newly minted lieutenant, confident at the controls of my aircraft, and able to razz the new nuggets in the wardroom.

Zeke had left for another assignment, so the remaining Stingers drafted another flight leader and continued barnstorming across Asia when we weren't flying missions. The precision work had a separate and deadly serious purpose, which was to refine our techniques to better do our true jobs in case we came up to the deck one morning and found our Scooters standing there on their stilt-like wheels with the red-shirted ordnance loaders hanging big nukes on the belly racks. Sometimes, as part of a readiness exercise, we would actually carry that big silver bomb—without the igniter—because Those Who Knew wanted our minds to be comfortable with the bomb in case we had to do it for real.

The nukes were so heavy that they were the only bomb the A-4 could carry on those days. Bearing a full load of fuel in addition to the bomb, I needed a maximum velocity catapult shot to help me stagger off the deck. With one of those bombs hooked to my plane, the price of poker became very high indeed, for the A-4 was a finely designed little aircraft built for the purpose of delivering a terrifying weapon to a target. It would probably be a one-way trip for a pilot like myself, who would be aiming the sharp point of a nonreturnable nuclear spear.

Such thoughts weighed heavily on me one day when I was on shore leave in Japan, visiting both Hiroshima and Nagasaki, the only two cities ever hit with atomic weapons. The serene parks were quiet, and monuments to the attacks were draped with colorful chains of paper cranes, considered a sacred bird by the Japanese, folded by schoolchildren who clustered about me, chirping greetings, not knowing who I was, since I was in civilian clothes. Looking out over the rebuilt cities, over herds of happy kids, I considered the enormity of the responsibility that I held, and of what my government was asking me to be ready to do.

Catastrophe seemed awfully close in those days, and we weren't flying those exercises just for the hell of it. The month we deployed, an American U-2 spy plane was shot down over the Soviet Union and its pilot, Francis Gary Powers, was captured. Aggressive as ever, Khruschev used the incident to humiliate President Eisenhower at a Paris summit, a disarmament conference folded in Geneva, and the hot border between East and West Berlin crackled with new incidents.

I left Nagasaki and Hiroshima disturbed by the magnitude of the destruction, thinking about what it must have been like in those two cities fifteen years earlier. However, I departed determined, more than ever, that I didn't want that sort of thing to ever happen to New York, Chicago, Bellwood or any other American city. That was why I was part of the massive retaliation strategy that declared any nuclear attack on the United States would be answered with equal, probably superior, force. There was no question in my soul that if the ultimate war came while I was aboard that carrier, I would fly my mission.

Somebody had to drop the Big Bomb, and that somebody was me.

*   *   *

BARBARA WROTE ME EVERY day, just as I always had a packet to dispatch to her. I would pour my feelings into tape recordings that went out through the mail. When she returned such tapes, her voice soothed me and I counted the days until the cruise was over. My parents were worried that she was not Catholic, but Barbara agreed to convert.

Religion had taken a curious twist in November of 1960 while I was still at sea. A young senator from Boston, John F. Kennedy, used the new power of television debates to narrowly defeat Richard Nixon and become the first Roman Catholic ever to be president of the United States.

And out on the new High Frontier, as we called space, the Russians increased their menagerie, putting two dogs and six rats into orbit aboard *Sputnik 5*. The U.S. launched the first successful weather satellite and the first camera-equipped spy satellite. Such technological marvels were stunning.

Grandpa Cernan, living alone since the death of Grandma, fell to the ground while patching the farmhouse roof and died, at the age of seventy-five, still without electricity in his home.

As my second WestPac tour ended in March, 1961, I was ready for some peace and stability, ready to let someone else live on the edge of the nuclear razor for a while. I was ready to ask Miss Barbara Atchley to be my wife.

6

Two Commander Shepards

THE BRIDE AND GROOM both wore white on that bright Saturday afternoon of May 6, 1961, when Barbara and I were married in the tiny chapel at Miramar, she in a flowing veil and gown, and me in my dress uniform with buttons of brass and wings of gold. As we walked from the chapel, beneath an arch of swords held aloft by my Navy buddies, she kept a close eye on Baldy, who had threatened to goose her with his gleaming blade.

The day before the wedding, at Cape Canaveral in Florida, a square-jawed, crew-cut naval aviator named Alan B. Shepard, jammed into an incredibly tiny Mercury spacecraft, waited through a stop-and-go count-down, waited so long that he wet his pants, then finally blasted off for a sixteen-minute suborbital flight.

On the last day of January, NASA had sent a chimpanzee named Ham on a suborbital ride, but only a couple of months later, Soviet cosmonaut Yuri Gagarin, strapped into a cannonball-shaped spaceship called the *Vostok 1,* blasted off from Earth and became the first man in space, flying a single orbit during a flight of 108 minutes. That was Sputnik all over again.

A week after Gagarin's historic flight, a CIA-sponsored plot misfired and an ill-prepared force of Cuban exiles, expecting U.S. support, landed at Fidel Castro's favorite fishing spot, a place called the Bay of Pigs, and were slaughtered. Two weeks after that, civil rights activists started riding buses into the South to protest racial discrimination in America and were met by an astonishing amount of violence. Turmoil surrounded us. Then came the flight of Alan Shepard and the dreary headlines changed overnight. Now we had an astronaut who had flown, too, and everything else seemed to dim in the glow of Shepard's success. Big Al made Americans feel good about themselves, and the future, again.

While trying to keep my mind on the thousand things that needed to be done before the wedding, I had stayed glued to the television set, mentally putting myself inside that little Mercury capsule and imagining the wild, thundering ride of Alan Shepard. If someone had tapped me on the shoulder at that moment and told me that the next time Alan flew in space, his backup would be a veteran astronaut named Gene Cernan, who had two flights of his own under his belt and had gone to the Moon, I would have laughed out loud. I am proud that this genuine hero became a lifelong friend.

AFTER OUR WEDDING AND a reception at the Admiral Kidd Officers' Club, Barbara and I honeymooned in Mexico, taking wild, puddle-jumper flights from Tijuana to Mexico City to save a few bucks, then spending the difference on bottles of tequila. On reaching the hotel, we discovered that our room had two single beds, and that just wouldn't do. I called the front desk immediately, and moments later a bellboy showed up and, with a big smile, shoved the two small beds together. One bed, he said, with a polite bow and a sweep of his hand.

Then there was the frightening bus ride along twisting, narrow roads into Acapulco. We sat in the front seat, away from the live chickens carried by passengers in the back, and watched in horror as the driver waved and flirted with every woman he passed along the way while seeming to take aim at livestock, people, and vehicles that shared the narrow road through a mountain pass. Somehow, we survived our honeymoon.

Back in California, we made our home in half of a rented duplex cottage in Del Mar, which Barbara described as a little dollhouse. It was right on the cliffs, and had a spectacular view of the Pacific Ocean, so each evening, golden sunsets streamed right into our living room. The owner, Clara Cook, who lived in the other half, took us beneath her wing and became a kind of surrogate grandmother.

Not long after we returned, President Kennedy made a nationally televised address that challenged the entire nation and shook pilots like me right down to our flight boots. Within three weeks after Shepard flew for sixteen minutes, JFK declared the time had come for America "to take longer strides" in space.

"I believe this nation should commit itself to the goal, before this decade is out, of landing a man on the Moon and returning him safely to Earth," Kennedy told America. "We choose to go to the Moon in this decade . . . not because this will be easy, but because it will be hard, because that goal will serve to organize and measure the best of our energies and skills—because the challenge is one we are willing to accept, one we are unwilling to postpone, and one we intend to win." Pretty brave words, since we had very little manned space experience. His statement did not use the word *science*, a fact that would assume great importance later in my career. One thing was certain—that pledge by JFK changed my life.

I NEEDED TO MAKE a major career decision. My five-year commitment was almost up, and there was a chance that I might leave the Navy entirely. At his inauguration, Kennedy had made his stirring call, "Ask not what your country can do for you, ask what you can do for your country." Well, I had already done a bunch for my country and was willing to do more, but the question was, "Do what and for how long?"

Then the Navy came through with a terrific offer. I could attend the Naval Post Graduate School at Monterey, California, and earn a master's degree in a two-year program, with an option for a third year at a major university. And still fly Navy jets! Not the high performance operational aircraft that had spoiled me as a hot pilot, but still, jets is jets and I could make the minimal eight hours a month to maintain my flight pay.

They wanted a two-year commitment for every year of school, which would keep me in for another six years. With the five I already had logged, that would give me at least eleven years and I would be well along the track to becoming a career Naval officer. I always believed in setting goals that I could reach, challenging but reasonable five-year plans, and this was right in the ballpark. After getting an advanced degree in aeronautical engineering at Monterey, I would have a good shot at an assignment to the Navy's test pilot school at Patuxent River in Maryland. After that, I could return to the fleet and be in line for a squadron command of my own.

And who wouldn't like to live in the Monterey-Carmel area, one of the most beautiful places in America? Barbara and I closed up the house at Del Mar, had a farewell bash with the squadron at Miramar and drove up the winding coast, the top down on the convertible, surrounded by California's natural beauty.

The summer of 1961 was exciting, particularly for a pilot with an itch to fly high and fast. Astronaut Gus Grissom rode his *Liberty Bell 7* on a fifteen-minute suborbital flight that ended in near disaster when the hatch inexplicably blew off after he landed in the water. The Mercury spacecraft sank and Gus almost drowned. Naturally, the Soviets trumped us again, and Cosmonaut Gherman Titov orbited the Earth seventeen times in a day-long mission. Our answer was to send up another chimp, Enos, who made it into orbit.

As I settled into schoolwork, the Cold War whirlwind intensified. The Communists built the Berlin Wall to divide Germany and American and Soviet tanks faced off at Checkpoint Charlie. In Asia, where the *Hanna-Maru* was heading, General Maxwell Taylor asked that America send a task force of 8,000 men to Vietnam. I felt a tug of guilt. I was still a Navy attack pilot, and things were really heating up. Where should I be? I concluded that the Navy would find use for a new and improved Cernan in the future.

THE MONTEREY PENINSULA WAS God's country, a place where tall redwoods, blue oceans, and cool summer breezes made life special. The school had the air of a college campus instead of a military base. In fact, the Naval Post Graduate School was in the old Del Monte Hotel, and we didn't wear uniforms.

There was some drab government housing available, but Barbara and I wanted something with more personality, and on a drive through a little tree-filled canyon on the highway to Salinas, we discovered a new development called Fisherman's Flats. There we found a quaint little house with three bedrooms, a bath and a half, and a combination dining and kitchen area. It was only 1,206 square feet in total area and sat on a quarter-acre of land. I had stashed away 100 dollars in savings bonds every month for almost five years, so we put down 4,000 dollars and got a mortgage for about 15,000 dollars. The monthly payments were about 105 dollars.

Throughout our marriage, we never lived on a military base, and cultivated neighbors and friends who were civilians. When Barbara took a job as the office manager at the Walter Colton Junior High School, she widened our circle of nonmilitary acquaintances, but I was pleased to find that an old shipmate had also been accepted at the school. Skip Furlong and his wife, Ry, soon became our closest friends.

We were all in the same boat. Young, ambitious, and with not a hell of a lot of money. We had only about twenty dollars a month to spend on entertainment and used a lot of that for a nice dinner once a month at one of those cozy restaurants along Cannery Row. Every weekend there was a party at somebody's house, and we all thought that drinking Beefeater gin on the rocks was the epitome of class, because we normally drank wine so cheap that we bought it by the gallon.

The school turned out to be damned difficult, and I hit the books harder than I had ever studied in my life. I would go to class at eight A.M., stay there until five P.M., come home and have dinner with Barbara, then study until midnight or one o'clock in the morning. Aeronautical engineering, the Navy way, was a bitch.

Still, it seemed as if we were living in the epicenter of paradise.

LIKE MOST OF AMERICA, I was swept up by the excitement of the space race. Because of the three-hour time difference between Florida and California, an early morning launch at Cape Canaveral meant that I might study all night so I could watch the rockets go up on television in the predawn hours in Monterey.

On February 20, 1962, I was on the sofa with Barbara as the third Mercury flight was launched and John Glenn became the first American to reach orbit. When he got into space and Mission Control said everything was fine, Barbara asked me, "Would you like to do something like that?"

"Hell, yes, I would," I replied, then reality set in. I was still too young, and not yet close to having the necessary experience. We thought little more about it.

My feelings of not yet being qualified for such an assignment were confirmed in September 1962, when the second bunch of astronauts was chosen—civilians Neil Armstrong and Elliot See, Air Force pilots Frank Borman, Jim McDivitt, Tom Stafford and Ed White, and Naval aviators Pete Conrad, Jim Lovell and John Young. I noticed the selection criteria had changed slightly, and that NASA now wanted fliers who were under thirty-five years of age, held at least a bachelor's degree in a physical or biological science or engineering, had test pilot experience, graduated from a military test pilot school or had equivalent credentials. I was okay on age and education, but still years away from that coveted test pilot certificate.

The new group, collectively known as the Next Nine, would fly into the history books. Meanwhile, I was still just another anonymous student studying for difficult examinations, and joining the rest of America in watching space stuff on TV.

Scott Carpenter went up on *Aurora 7*, but didn't pay close enough attention to business and overshot his landing area, a mistake that cost him any future ride in space. Then the Soviets flew Andrian Nikolayev and Pavel Popovich on *Vostoks* 3 and 4, and Wally Schirra orbited for us aboard *Sigma 7*. The race was definitely on and the launches were huge events, but spaceflight didn't seem to be in my future.

Fatherhood, however, was. Barbara delivered a beautiful baby girl on March 4, 1963, a child with huge blue eyes the size of silver dollars, eyes that darted around the room, taking in everything, as if she were asking, "Where am I? What am I? Who am I?" We took Teresa Dawn Cernan home from the hospital right after I persuaded the Bank of America to approve a 200-dollar short-term loan to help cover the 207-dollar bill. Ten days after Tracy was born, Gordon Cooper flew the final Mercury mission, a twenty-two-orbit marathon.

The end of my two years of school at Monterey was nearing, and my grades had earned the option for a third year of advanced study at Princeton, which could add an Ivy League degree to my resumé. But first, there was an intern's job with Aerojet General in Sacramento in the summer of 1963, where I worked on advanced liquid rocket propulsion systems. Rockets meant spaceflight, and that seemed to be a growing field.

I was at work one Friday afternoon while Barbara was in Texas visiting her mother, who had moved back there from California, when a telephone call came in from a Commander Shepard, with the Navy's Special Projects Office in Washington. Shepard? Commander Alan Shepard, the astronaut? No, he replied, somewhat testily, "Not *that* Commander Shepard. *Everybody* asks me that." Then he got down to business.

The commander explained, in wonderfully vague Potomac River bureaucratic terms, that he and the Navy had spent more than six months combing through the files to collect the names of certain officers who just might, perhaps under proper circumstances, be qualified to participate in a special project, and that my name had been among those selected. "Well," he concluded, "do you volunteer?"

I didn't know what the hell he was talking about. My warning antenna went up. What kind of special project? Why me? This was awfully murky stuff and the unspoken rule in the military was to never volunteer until you knew the facts. "Volunteer for what?" I asked.

Commander Shepard sighed, apparently aggravated. It was clear that he was talking to a moron. "Well, for the Apollo program, of course! We want to recommend you to NASA for further evaluation." NASA had asked the military services for a new list of prospective astronaut candidates, and the Navy selection board had included my name.

There was a moment of silence on my end while my heart jumped into my throat. I hadn't even applied. Last time I looked, I wasn't qualified. But this guy was saying the Navy was recommending me to NASA for astronaut training. Was he talking to the right Lieutenant Cernan? It took a moment for the meaning of his question to sink in, then I came out of my fog and shot back with snappy military enthusiasm, "Well, yes sir! Not only that, sir, but hell, yes! Sir!"

Shepard brusquely informed me that my verbal reply was not good enough. "We have to know in writing by Monday morning at nine o'clock." He hung up.

Stunned, but thrilled at the proposal, I hustled over to the nearest Western Union office and sent the busy man a telegram. Then I called Barbara with the news. I had made this potentially life-changing decision without asking her, and as I dialed, I wondered what her response might be to a such a large step that had already been taken. She was excited, although I could detect some deep apprehension. After getting over her initial surprise, she told me just what I wanted to hear: "My God, Gene, we've got to try for this."

An astronaut? Me?

7

Max and Deke

A HURRICANE OF NASA paperwork enshrouded me. It ranged from highly technical details to questions so personal that before anyone from that agency had even met me, they would know my life's story. It turned out this was only a preliminary culling of more than 400 military and civilian candidates.

Three of my classmates, Dick Gordon, Bob Schumacher, and Ron Evans, had also been volunteered. Bob was a good friend, but I didn't know the other two guys very well, having shared only a few classes with them. That would change in the future, in ways none of us could ever have imagined. Finally, I finished the last sheet and returned the whole pile to Houston.

Barbara and I left on a vacation that was originally planned as a visit to her mother in Texas and my mom and dad in Chicago over the Fourth of July. Accompanied by Tracy, who was just beginning to stand up on her own, and Venus, our cocker spaniel, Barbara took a cheapie National Airlines night flight from San Francisco to Houston. I tied up some loose ends in California and hit the highway in our new 1963 Chevrolet, the sensible, family-style sedan that replaced my 1956 bachelor ragtop. As the miles clicked by, I listened to "Puff, the Magic Dragon" and "Rhythm of the Rain" on the radio while I thought about this possible new assignment. Since I would be meeting Barbara and her mother in Baytown, I thought I should swing through the outskirts of Houston and take a look at the new Manned Spaceflight Center under construction in Clear Lake.

Cape Canaveral in Florida was our gate to the heavens, Langley Field in Virginia was the home of the Space Task Group and convenient to Washington, and major contractors were located in California, Missouri, and New York. Twenty-three cities had competed to be the home of the MSC, a prize federal project if ever there was one, but only one of them had Lyndon Johnson of Texas, who just happened to be the vice president of the United States of America and chairman of the President's National

Space Council. So LBJ twisted the appropriate arms and came up with a thousand acres of scrubland two dozen miles southeast of Houston. NASA got a new home and Texas got 60 million dollars worth of Moon money.

The concrete, steel, and glass were being planted fast: instant buildings and test facilities that gleamed in the hot Texas sun when I rolled through, looking at where I might someday work. A couple of years in scenic Monterey had spoiled me. Where we only had to open our windows to stay cool on the hottest summer days in California, this Texas heat felt like a blast furnace. The sun was a hammer, Houston was its anvil, and my car didn't have air conditioning. To say I was overwhelmed would be an understatement. I cruised slowly down the Old Galveston Highway and through the new developments being built to house the hundreds of engineers and technicians swarming to the MSC. The subdivisions bore chic names such as Timber Cove, El Lago, and Nassau Bay, but were really just converted mud flats sweltering in that awful heat, with cows still grazing on future expensive residential lots. How could I ask my family to endure this barren land of old pastures and distant horizons? Barbara was a Texan, so I thought she might be used to this kind of weather, but when I reached her mother's house, which was cooled only by an ineffective attic fan that rearranged the hot air, I found that my wife was as miserable as I. Visions of our pleasant home in Monterey swam in the heat like a mirage, and I thought that not making the cut as an astronaut, and having to live around here, might not be so bad after all. We couldn't get out of Texas fast enough.

We drove to Chicago to introduce my parents to their newest granddaughter, then set out for California, again beneath a merciless sun. Temperatures topped 100 degrees across Iowa. All we could do was roll the windows down, drive like hell, and pray that we could reach the cool shelter of the Rocky Mountains before we melted into the asphalt beside some Nebraska cornfield.

SOMETIME LATER, A LETTER from NASA arrived in Monterey, inviting me to fly down to Houston for an interview, and I learned the original list of hundreds of candidates had been cut by more than half. Somewhat surprised to still be in the running, I set out on a Secret Agent mission that seems awfully naïve today.

To keep the press off the scent of who might be astronaut candidates, Dick, Ron, Bob, and I all flew out of San Francisco on separate planes, wearing civilian clothes and using assumed identities, pretending not to know each other. Strange people met us in Houston, using the utmost stealth, and hustled us to private rooms at the Rice Hotel, where we were all signed in using the name of Max Peck, the hotel's general manager. Naturally, as soon as I walked into the hotel bar, I recognized friends, settled in for a drink, and easily guessed that some of those other slim, crew-cut young men nearby—all of whom were also named Max Peck— were also pilot types. Some secret.

This was somewhat like my early days at Miramar, when I had my wings, but had not yet landed on a carrier. I marveled at the backgrounds of many of the other candidates. *What am I doing in this group?*

Dick Gordon, for instance, was more than just a student at post graduate school. A well-known test pilot, he already had substantial pull inside the program and had just missed the cut for the second group of astronauts. His ex-roomie aboard the *Ranger* had been Pete Conrad, one of the Next Nine, and his instructor at the Navy's test pilot school had been none other than Al Shepard. When Dick won the coveted Bendix Trophy for setting a transcontinental speed record of two hours, forty-seven minutes, he received a telegram of congratulations from the pilot whose record he broke, Marine Colonel John Glenn.

There were other fliers among the current candidates who also held altitude records and speed records, some test pilots with impeccable credentials like Mike Collins, who also had just missed on the earlier cuts, and guys like Buzz Aldrin, who held a Ph.D. from MIT in space rendezvous theory. And most of the Air Force guys had gone through Chuck Yeager's astronaut charm school at Edwards AFB. It was easy to feel somewhat insecure in this group of pilots. What could I say: I'd had two WestPac tours and was now studying in Monterey? I felt my chances of being chosen were pretty slim.

They hit us with another blizzard of paperwork, which now included questions about space travel and orbital mechanics. Although I didn't know much about those subjects, I wrote essay-length answers in longhand to every query. If they were looking at how a candidate handled the unknown, I must have rated pretty high, for I didn't know much at all.

Then came the personal interviews, and for the first time I met real astronauts, the men from the headlines. At a long table with a couple of civilians sat Deke Slayton, Wally Schirra, and Alan Shepard, and I felt like I was in the middle of history. These guys were our heroes of the space age, and I basked at being admitted to their presence, although

I felt like a prisoner before the parole board. They were all quite pleasant, except for Shepard, whose cold eyes seemed to look right through me.

What did they want? Was it how I dressed, how I looked, how I spoke? Was this a trick question? Everything I said was going to be evaluated and I didn't know what they wanted. There was no use trying to bullshit about my record, because they had it all right there before them. My best shot was to answer the questions as honestly as I could and hope that was good enough. For instance, someone asked how many times had I flown over 50,000 feet. Hell, for an attack pilot like me, who spent his life below 500 feet, that was halfway into space! So I flipped the question and answered, "I've flown real low, and if you're going to land on the Moon, you gotta get close sometime." I remember they smiled a lot. Except for Shepard, who seemed to have ice water in his veins.

A few cocktail parties later, after a chance to meet some of the other astronauts and shake hands with the famous John Glenn, I returned to Monterey.

Another letter came, advising me that I had made another cut. We were down to thirty-six candidates now, a couple of those "can't miss" dudes were out, and I was still in.

Exhaustive medical tests followed at Brooks AFB in San Antonio, and NASA scratched off four more names, including Bob Schumacher, my friend from Monterey, who was found to have some minor heart defect. Such a totally unfair and illogical decision demonstrated why pilots don't trust doctors. He was cleared to fly Navy jets in combat, but wasn't up to the mark for astronaut training? However, the incident also showed just how thorough the screening had become. Receiving a B instead of a B+ in some college course years earlier might be reason enough to pick the other guy. It was said that the odds of anyone becoming an astronaut were about 3 million to one and I believed it. But, damn it, my odds were getting better.

After the physicals, the field was down to only thirty-two, and for the first time, I began to feel that I just might have a chance. Still, Barbara and I didn't get our hopes up, because too many variables were involved. *Hey, Cernan, you're close, but don't start counting any chickens yet.* Instead, we revised our plans for Princeton. If I started classes there and got called to be an astronaut, we would have moved all the way to New Jersey for nothing. So we chose to stay in Monterey, where I could take my third year at the Naval Post Graduate School and finish my thesis on using hydrogen as propulsion for high energy rockets. We kept our fingers crossed on the astronaut front, but were comfortable knowing that if I wasn't selected, the worst that could happen would be that I would earn my master's degree.

Then strange telephone calls started coming in from friends and old acquaintances, some of whose names I had forgotten over the passing years. "Geno. Is everything all right? Are you in some kind of trouble? Some FBI agent came around asking questions about you." NASA was doing a thorough background check, talking to everybody from ex-girlfriends to college professors. Bankruptcies and class records, scholastic honors and parking tickets, military awards and disciplinary records, everything was grist for their mill, and Lord help you if you were dirty. I was forbidden from telling anybody what was really going on, to keep the press off the scent.

We knew the final notification would come in a telephone call. If Deke Slayton, who was head of the Astronaut Office, was on the line, you were in, but if Warren North, Deke's assistant, was on the other end of the line, you were out. To keep the telephone free, friends stopped calling and the days passed like a sludge of time. Word could come at any time. And when the telephone did ring, we were afraid to answer it. What if it was Warren North?

Eventually, the phone rang about three o'clock on an early October afternoon, and Barbara answered, her stomach turning. She told the questioning NASA operator I wasn't there, gave them the number of the school. Then she sat down and tried not to think about the question that wouldn't leave her mind: "Did we make it?"

Ron Evans and I were in the same class when the message came through that we both had calls from NASA waiting on telephones in separate rooms. Wishing each other good luck, we closed the doors and picked up the receivers as gently as if they were made of scalding metal.

My heart almost stopped when I heard the gruff voice of Deke Slayton. "Geno?"

I braced ramrod straight, snapping to attention for a man sitting behind a desk hundreds of miles away. "Yes, sir! Deke?"

"Yeah. Hey, Geno," he said, "If you're still interested in coming to work down here, I've got a job for you." Somehow, I must have replied in the affirmative, but I was so elated that I don't even remember hanging up.

Still, it was a bittersweet experience, because I soon saw the face of a very dejected Ron Evans, who had received the dreaded call from Warren

North. He missed the cut and my heart bled for him. No fortune-teller could have predicted that, in not too many years, Ron and I would be together in a rocket ship, flying to the Moon.

Word spread quickly across the campus. Dick Gordon had made it, too, and it was time for some serious celebrating. Before I could even call Barbara, I was swept out the door, down to the bar at the old Mark Thomas Inn and was getting falling-down drunk without buying a drop of booze. Among those buying were Ron Evans and Bob Schumacher.

Several hours passed before I telephoned a very angry Barbara, who had been on pins and needles since answering the call from Houston. She could have killed me, but didn't. Instead, she hurried over to join the party, while my buddies shouted, "He's going to Houston! He's going to Houston!"

WHEN NASA ANNOUNCED THE names of the fourteen new astronauts, our telephone rang constantly, telegrams poured in, and postal workers staggered to our door carrying bags laden with more letters than we had ever received in our lives. In a blink, I'd gone from being Just Another Student to Genuine American Hero and I had not yet done a damned thing in the space program.

We felt like a couple of goldfish in a glass bowl. Everyone was watching us. Newspapers wanted interviews, and neither of us had ever before even met a reporter, much less talked to one who would write stories about us. Thankfully, our old friends provided the stability we needed. To them, we were still just Barbara and Gene, a young couple with a baby daughter, trying to live on the salary of a Navy lieutenant.

ON NOVEMBER 22, 1963, I was in class when a messenger brought a note to our instructor. He read it and turned pale, then announced that President Kennedy had been assassinated in Dallas. I hurried home and found Barbara standing in our living room, curlers in her wet hair and an electric dryer still humming, idle by her side, watching television like a statue. We fell into each other's arms and wept. Only the previous week, thinking that we might some day meet the president and Mrs. Kennedy, Barbara had joked that our daughter Tracy was the same age as their little son, John-John. Now Kennedy was dead, and we all felt an emptiness, no matter what our politics.

The 2,000 officers and enlisted men of the NPGS turned out the following day for a memorial service, a sea of dress blues and white hats lined in ranks around the tall mast on which an American flag was lowered to half-staff. Rear Admiral Charles Bergin, the superintendent, said the gathering was to pay our last official respects not only to a fallen president, but to "a sailor who has given his life in service," for Kennedy had been a PT boat skipper in World War II. As I stood in solemn silence with my schoolmates on that chill November afternoon, I had to wonder how the death of this president would have impact on the space program, for a ship without a captain is a ship adrift.

WE HAD TO FIND a place to live in Texas, and the Navy made a plane available for Dick Gordon and me to fly down to Houston. I found a nice little brick house to rent on Huntress Lane, in a subdivision near the space center, then Dick and I met back at Ellington, and started the long flight home. When we landed at a naval air station near Phoenix to refuel, everyone in Base Ops was watching a blaring television set as reporters explained that a Dallas nightclub owner had gunned down Kennedy's alleged assassin, Lee Harvey Oswald, while he was being led from the county jail.

What the hell was happening to our country?

8

Any Astronauts Around Here?

THE MERCURY SERIES WAS named for the mythical winged messenger, and the two-man program which was about to begin was appropriately known as Gemini, for the constellation of stars that is the sign of the twins. The three-man flights that would lead the charge to the Moon bore the name of Apollo, the Greek god of the Sun. None of my group would fly a mission for another two and a half years. The last member of our group would not ride until almost six years had passed, and four would die before they flew. Only four of us would ever walk on the Moon.

We all moved to Houston as 1964 came around—myself, Lieutenant Alan L. Bean, Lieutenant Roger B. Chaffee, and Lieutenant Commander Richard F. Gordon, Jr., all from the Navy; Marine Captain Clifton C. Williams, Jr.; Air Force officers Major Edwin E. "Buzz" Aldrin, Captain William A. Anders, Captain Charles A. Bassett II, Captain Michael Collins, Captain Donn F. Eisele, Captain Theodore C. Freeman, and Captain David R. Scott; and two civilians, R. Walter Cunningham and Russell L. Schweickart.

As we pulled into Houston, we entered a bubble of protection against unpleasant news from the outside world as the United States grappled with civil rights and social upheaval at home and Vietnam and the Cold War abroad. In a time of brewing trouble, a simultaneous need grew for heroes who could be keepers of the faith and bearers of the flame. As new astronauts, we didn't realize it, but that would be us.

Barbara, Tracy, and I arrived about the middle of January, following a private graduation ceremony in the Office of the Commandant of the post graduate school. Another student might have just gotten a diploma through the mail, but for a new astronaut, things were handled differently.

It was hard for me to believe in those early weeks that I was actually walking the halls of the Manned Spaceflight Center with the famed Original Seven. I'd met them during the interviews and at a few parties, but now they were all around me every day, and I was bursting with questions that I didn't dare ask. I felt like an imposter.

Talk about hero worship. I even got each of them to autograph their book *We Seven*, then added a personal inscription and sent it to my dad as a Christmas present. "If God is willing, maybe someday I can become part of this 'We,' " I wrote. "If I do, all the thank you's in the world would not be enough to repay you for your part in this accomplishment."

THE PACE WAS QUICKENING in the space race, and the Russians were still leading. Shortly before my astronaut class came on board, Soviet cosmonaut Valentina Tereshkova became the first woman in space, successfully making an epic forty-eight-orbit voyage. I would eventually get to know Valentina, and found her to be charming and delightful. They had wanted another "first," and she was it, although she was not really qualified for such a mission, because she had been trained as a parachutist, not for spaceflight. Zero gravity made her violently ill the whole time she was in space and for days afterward.

In our own program, substantial questions needed to be answered. The death of JFK had left a great and unknown vacuum of leadership, and Lyndon Johnson, a politician through and through, had assumed the presidency. Now that our champion was gone, would President Johnson carry through on the pledge to put a man on the Moon? As I settled into my new job as an Apollo astronaut, none of us knew whether there would ever even be an Apollo program.

The pioneering Mercury series had ended seven months earlier, in May of 1963, and Apollo was too far in the distance to see. So NASA was building a bridge between those two programs, a system of two-man flights called Gemini, to test vital concepts en route to Apollo. Could we walk and work in space? Could we find and rendezvous with other spacecraft? Could rockets be built to safely cross the unknown gulf between the Earth and the Moon? At the time, none of those things had been done.

Although it wasn't apparent right at first, some of my heroes were already fading as the astronaut lineup changed. Of the famed Original Seven, all but Slayton had flown during Mercury, and Deke was grounded because of a minor heart fibrillation. For the past two years, he had been head of the Astronaut Office. John Glenn, who had gained fame as our first man in space, was leaving and had politics on his mind. That left five of the Mercury astros still on flight status—Al Shepard, Gus Grissom, Wally Schirra, Gordo Cooper, and Scott Carpenter.

Now that I was part of the program, I had a different perspective on them and sized them up as possible flying partners, an exercise that made me look behind the hero headlines.

Gordo was a pleasant, easy-going guy who was one helluva pilot. Many stiff NASA officials thought the drawling Oklahoman was too much of a maverick, a view that eventually affected his assignment to flights.

Gus was a hard guy to get to know. Other than giving a routine greeting in a hallway, he didn't appear to be close to many people, and wasn't much interested in us new guys at all. Either you were his friend, or you were not; Gus went out of his way to show he was a Big Dog and screw you if you didn't like it. My gut feeling was that after his Mercury flight, when the spacecraft sank and he almost drowned, Gus always ran a little bit scared.

Scott was the only multi-engine pilot among the elite cadre of veteran jet pilots, and it was whispered that he didn't volunteer for the space program, his dynamic and attractive wife did. Scott was just glad to be around, and was physically fit to an amazing degree. But he screwed up his own Mercury flight by joyriding, not paying enough attention to the job, missing his retrofire cue and splashing down several hundred miles from the target area. It became pretty obvious that Scott would never fly in space again.

Wally, an excellent pilot, was everybody's pal and the mother hen for the newest class of astros. Sky Ray, as we called him, a nickname coined from an airplane he once flew, enjoyed taking long, "well-deserved" coffee breaks much more than spending time in the simulators. He was very good at this astronaut game, and behind the irreverent humor was a complex perfectionist. There was no pretense at all in Wally. I liked him.

Al, the first to fly in the Mercury program, was the best of the bunch. He was a natural choice to progress straight through Gemini and into Apollo, and a good bet to be the first man on the Moon. Al was a total mystery. He could be warm and personable one moment and the steely-eyed commander the next, the broad smile suddenly vanishing. It seemed wise for a rookie like me to steer clear of Alan B. Shepard.

In my opinion, Shepard, Schirra and Grissom were sure to command future missions, and Cooper was still a probable. Carpenter was all but gone. So the Seven really were only four, which loosened things up slightly for future seat assignments, but not much. No seats would be coming to any members of my group for a long time. The entire Next Nine stood between the Original Seven and us.

MANY PEOPLE BELIEVE SOME master personnel plan was behind the selection of Neil Armstrong to be the first astronaut to walk on the Moon. It isn't true, and the saga of Al Shepard explains why.

Shepard, just as he had been in the Mercury program, was first in line for a Gemini flight, where he was to be paired with Tom Stafford, from the Next Nine. In the middle of 1963, before the assignment became official, Shepard experienced some dizziness and doctors reached a tentative diagnosis of an inner ear problem known as Meniere's disease, and temporarily grounded him. Al returned to flight status a few months later and was assigned the Gemini premiere, but the doctors brought him in for still another examination and found the ear condition had worsened. This time they vetoed Al not only from venturing into space, but even restricted his normal flying. Under the decision, if he wanted to fly at all, he had to have another qualified pilot—maybe even one of us rookies—go up with him because he wasn't "medically safe." That was not only sticking a knife in his back, but twisting it. My God, we thought, if it can happen to Shepard, it can happen to anybody.

At the time, the existing roster of astronauts to fly on Gemini included Wally Schirra as commander of the second Gemini flight, and Gus Grissom was to be the backup commander to Shepard. With Al out of the picture, who would take over? Deke assigned Grissom to command the first manned Gemini mission and made Wally the backup for Gus. That simultaneously removed Schirra from command of the second flight. Wally was not pleased. His fun-loving temperament wore thin. He hated backing up anybody.

That decision also posed the question of what to do with Tom Stafford, Shepard's partner. Stafford was considered the strongest man in the program on rendezvous techniques, and NASA wanted to get him up fast. Grissom's partner, and Stafford's backup in the original lineup, was Frank Borman. It made sense to promote Grissom and Borman as a unit, so Stafford was bumped, but that still wasn't the end of an episode that took on the mind-boggling confusion of the Abbott and Costello "Who's on first?" routine.

The egos of Grissom and Borman were too big to fit into a single spacecraft, and Borman was being slotted for an important later mission anyway. He was scratched from Grissom's crew in favor of the more low-key John Young, who had originally been Schirra's crewmate. John could get along with anybody and was a damned fine pilot. There were another dozen or so pieces to that puzzle, but this single confusing incident illustrates the quirkiness of the entire crew selection process.

As a newcomer, it was difficult to analyze where I fit into the process. With few exceptions, Deke always made the final call on who flew, when, and in which seat, and we studied his choices with great care, looking for some pattern. But there wasn't one.

TEN MANNED GEMINI FLIGHTS were planned, with two astronauts each, meaning a maximum of twenty seats were available. With Shepard out of the lineup, there were three Mercury astronauts still able to go, and if all of the Next Nine won flight assignments, that meant twelve of those seats were taken right off the top.

Assuming some of the more experienced guys would fly twice, moving up from pilot to commander roles, our new class of astronauts should not expect to find many empty chairs at the Gemini table. But the juggling of Shepard-Grissom-Schirra and Stafford-Borman-Young on the very first mission gave us hope. As the old saying went, "One never know, do one?"

In the midst of all this, top management posts also were changing. Slayton resigned from the Air Force, went full-time with NASA and was promoted to be assistant director of the Manned Spaceflight Center for Flight Crew Operations. While a lesser man might have resigned in pique after being grounded in 1962, Deke rode out the storm and created a unique leadership role for himself in the space program. More than a boss, he became the trusted "Godfather" to the corps of astronauts, respected by all, including NASA senior management.

One of his first acts was to pull the newly-grounded Al Shepard over to replace him as head of the Astronaut Office. That ice-cold, abrasive son-of-a-bitch did not take the doctor's decision with the grace of Deke Slayton, and seemed to consider his prime directive to instill the fear of the Lord into each and every one of us, because we might fly in space and he could not. Deke and Al could play the good-cop-bad-cop roles like a couple of New York homicide detectives, Deke instilling confidence and Al demanding more than your very best. The result was a better program.

*   *   *

OUR CLASS HIT THE ground running, with a brief orientation followed by a punishing twenty weeks of classroom lectures, technical assignments, and exotic field trips. We were only rookies, but had survived the extraordinary selection process. This was heady stuff, being exposed to rockets and the question of what we might find out there in space. Instead of seeing it from the wrong side of a television screen, we were actually walking around the Cape, examining the launch facilities and standing before the huge rockets that could take us into space. Often, NASA had us in hand seven days a week and we discovered that perpetual travel was part of the job. I found it an exciting time, for the people were brilliant, the work fascinating, and the ultimate potential reward—to walk on the Moon—almost unbelievable.

But while everything had been planned in detail for the new astronauts, NASA did not have survival handbooks for our wives. That was a dreadful oversight, and one for which our families paid a heavy price. I guess NASA thought that since we were mostly military families, we were used to the long separations and tightly structured environment of service life, and that wives historically learned to make do with the hardships. They were wrong.

Almost as soon as we settled into the rented little brick bungalow at 1922 Huntress Lane, a new house with no trees to break the Texas sun, Tracy came down with a 106-degree fever and an illness so severe that we had to bathe her in ice, and Barbara caught a bad cold from the abrupt change from cool Monterey. Many years would pass before I learned that Barbara was so frightened to be alone in the strange surroundings that she would stay awake, crying, half the night, startled by the slightest noise and afraid that someone might break in.

She didn't tell me about it then, or perhaps I just wasn't listening. There is no doubt that I was so overwhelmed and excited, caught up with being an astronaut, that when I came home for a weekend, all I wanted to talk about was our training and the program. It was, "My God, let me tell you what I did," rather than asking, "What did you do this week?" Looking back now, I realize my family suffered because of my tunnel vision.

Slowly, Barbara and the other astronaut wives who were enduring the same sort of shock reached out to each other and friendships formed. Just as Deke was our godfather, his wife Marge became the den mother for the wives. And the initial impression we had of Houston gave way to the pleasant discovery that down in Texas, people hadn't forgotten how to say "please" and "thank you" and would go out of their way to lend a helping hand. There was air conditioning to dispel the heat and Tracy found other kids with whom to play. It took a while, but we survived.

Of course, one thing that eased our situation and made us take a second look at any difficulties we might have to endure was the kid glove treatment we received. The best windfall was the famous contract with Field Enterprises Educational Corporation and Time, Inc., for exclusive rights to our stories. With the blessing of NASA and the White House, the publishers had made the deal to pay the Original Seven an astounding total of 500,000 dollars, to be split equally and spread over several years, a fortune in those days. When the Next Nine came aboard, the pie was cut into thinner pieces, but was still a chunk of money. And when we joined the team, the funding was again reapportioned in equal shares and each of us received 16,250 dollars each year. On top of being astronauts, now we were rich! Known as the *Life* contract because most of the stories and pictures appeared in that weekly picture magazine, those dollars looked pretty nice to a young Navy lieutenant and his family who had been living on an annual salary of 10,835 dollars.

Then General Motors offered a deal that allowed us to choose a new Chevrolet, any style, color, or model, run up 3,000 miles on it, then buy the "used" car at a brass hat price. The next year, I would sell it and buy still another new one. American General Mortgage chipped in with the offer of a fantastic four percent mortgage rate. Being a hero had definite benefits. People wanted to show their appreciation and support, and making special deals available to us was a way in which they could do so.

We socked away much of the extra cash in a trust fund for Tracy's college education, but had to use some of it to buy new clothes. The sudden social obligations that accompanied being an astronaut required my wife to have some extra dresses in her closet, and I had to buy my first civilian tuxedo.

We went for the car deal, too, but somewhat reluctantly, dumping the 1963 Chevrolet and buying a 1964 Chevrolet model of the same car, but with air conditioning. We felt that grabbing a Corvette off the showroom floor right at first was a little ostentatious. I also didn't know if Deke or Al might put a black mark by my name if they saw an unproved astronaut zipping around in a 'Vette. Eventually, I did succumb to the Corvette fever, and every year would pass my "old" one along to my buddy Skip

Furlong, who was able to drive a hot sports car with only a few miles on it at a bargain price before passing it along to someone else. Trickle-down Corvettes.

OUR NASA STUDIES PUT a heavy emphasis on basic sciences, primarily geology that would hone our skills at being able to deal with what we might find when we finally reached the Moon. We all had highly technical backgrounds, but damn it, we were pilots! It was an image thing, and we didn't want to be known as scientists. Our attitude was that there was nothing we could not do, including collecting the right kind of lunar rocks. You want a geologist, okay, you got one. Me. Eventually, we proved our point. Eleven of the twelve men who explored the Moon were pilots, and we brought home a treasure of scientific knowledge.

Our classroom lectures were backed up by field trips to such desolate regions as the volcanic territory in Arizona, Alaska, and Iceland. One of our instructors from the U.S. Geological Survey was a stocky young geologist named Jack Schmitt. Jack would become the twelfth man to walk on the Moon, where we would spend three days together.

I looked at a hell of a lot of rocks, crunched through the lava beds and wondered what all of this could possibly have to do with flying in space. Still, I worked hard to master the subject, for things were so competitive that we wanted to excel in every part of our training. No one knew what Deke would look for when he assigned the seats on future missions.

There was a unique bit of training to expose us to jungle and desert survival techniques. We accepted this as a necessity, in case we missed our landing point, although it did little to build confidence in the idea that NASA always knew where a spacecraft would come down.

In March, shortly after Tracy celebrated her first birthday, helicopters sprinkled the damp jungles of Panama with fledgling American astronauts, dropping us off in pairs. Carrying minimal survival gear, only what we would have available on a space flight, we were to live off the land for up to a week.

Naturally, they gave us instructions on how to do that. One was to chop down a palm tree and hack away the top to recover the juicy and tasty delicacy known as hearts of palm, which usually show up only in a pricey hotel salad. I ate so many of the damned things during those few days in Panama that I haven't been able to look at one since.

Another piece of advice was to catch and cook an iguana. Easier said than done. After a few days, with hunger gnawing at my stomach, those big lizards started to look like chicken-fried steak and gravy. The iguanas apparently knew that too, and it was "catch me if you can."

Donn Eisele and I found a stream for a water supply, then built a shelter and tied the ends of our parachutes to trees for hammocks. We had been warned not to sleep on the ground. A log served as a makeshift table, resting on the stump of a palm tree between us. In the middle of the night, we were startled awake by a background buzz, as if a hive of bees had taken flight. We stared into the darkness as the noise became louder and closer, changing into a rhythmic, pushing sound, like a herd of animals was moving through the wet foliage. *What the hell?* We snapped on flashlights and saw the front edge of a huge carpet of ants advancing out of the trees, a writhing mass of insects that covered everything in its path, millions of snapping pincers chomping steadily and loudly. The carpet marched forward, devouring everything before it, going directly between Donn and me. When they reached our little table, the ants went up and over the stump, entirely obscuring the legs and top. Thousands of ants crossed it like a bridge. A large spider that had spun a web in a corner was surrounded, and dropped away from danger on a line of silk, only to fall into the thrashing horde on the ground and vanish. Donn and I remained very, very still. We had nowhere to go, so all we could do was pray for the strength of the parachute cords holding us off the ground as the ants marched on. It was ten minutes before the last rippling end of that monstrous carpet vanished back into the jungle, leaving an empty streak ten feet wide that stretched across our clearing. Not a leaf or blade of grass was left and the crude table was stripped bare of bark, polished by the passage of insect feet and jaws. In our hammocks, we listened to the army of ants munch and march into the distance, masters of the jungle.

THE SPACE CENTER WAS a magnet for development. There was nothing much to support civilization in this semi-swamp we now called home, except for a single gas station along the main drag and a Sears store that was a thirty-minute drive away. But bulldozers were pushing back the Texas scrub to chase out the water moccasins and copperheads, and in their wake carpenters, plumbers, and electricians flocked in to build new houses. Ole Lyndon had dropped a full-employment bomb on Houston. All them Moon people gotta live somewhere! They gotta eat! They gotta shop! Moon people sure as hell don't want to drive twenty-five miles into Houston for bacon and eggs!

Two nice neighborhoods existed in the immediate area, both filled with the program's early arrivals. Timber Cove, the first one built, was home to six of the Original Seven. Al and Louise Shepard lived in downtown Houston. Then there was El Lago, where most of the Next Nine owned houses. The newest developments being carved from the chaparral were the little settlements of Clear Lake and Nassau Bay, which became the residential zone for many of my group.

Barbara and I used part of the *Life* check as down payment on a single lot, then hired an architect and started to build our dream home, a low, cream-colored, ranch-style house at 18511 Barbuda Lane in Nassau Bay. It was about 3,000 square feet and cost 33,000 dollars, with a mortgage low enough for us to handle on my regular pay.

Our neighborhood was one of the most unique in America—all Program. The nearby homes not inhabited by other astronauts were occupied by engineers and managers and their families. Eventually, tour buses loaded with out-of-town, camera-clicking sightseers added Nassau Bay to their route. Even after I had flown in space, I might be home mowing the lawn or planting a tree, wearing a sweaty T-shirt and torn shorts, and some bus driver would pull over and call out, "Hey, buddy! Any astronauts live around here?" I would scratch my head, point down the road, then vaguely reply, "I think a couple of 'em live over yonder somewhere." Neighbors such as Roger Chaffee, Mike Collins, Dave Scott, Al Bean, Rusty Schweickart, Dick Gordon and Jim McDivitt would pull the same scam. If we weren't in space suits, no one recognized us.

MONTHS SLID BY AND training increased. We were adored by the outside world, but inside the space program, we were still the freshman class and the pecking order meant that we had to wait our turn to fly. One thing the earlier astronauts were happy to relinquish was a duty called "the week in the barrel." Every politician and civic group wanted an astronaut as a guest speaker, and Deke fought a major battle to convince NASA that we were training to fly to the Moon, not to give speeches. The compromise was that each week, one astronaut was on public relations duty—having his week in the barrel. The Public Affairs Office lined up speaking requests in order of importance and the astronaut would make the required appearance, give media interviews, and generally show the flag. Those of us doing the talking usually were the ones who knew the least about what was going on.

My first time fell during Connecticut Aviation Week. A NASA protocol officer escorted me to the function and handed me a prepared script to read. The governor of Connecticut pointed with pride to the crew-cut young man at the head table, beamed as he introduced "Astronaut Gene Cernan," and I stood up amid a roar of applause. They might have thought they were looking at a confident and cool star voyager, but my knees were knocking so hard I thought the audience could hear them. I grabbed the podium with white knuckles. *What am I doing here? I haven't even flown yet!* I stumbled through a few sentences and saw the words before me blur. The audience didn't care about this technical gibberish. It was boring! I looked at them for a moment, stopped reading and slowly moved the papers to one side. The protocol officer had a heart attack, because he no longer knew what I was going to say. Hell, neither did I.

But I figured these people had come to this big luncheon to hear an astronaut, I was the only astronaut around, and, although I didn't know much about the program, I knew a lot more about it than any of them. I started to talk as if I were among friends who had come over to my house for a visit. My knees stopped shaking as I told a few stories, laced in famous names like Shepard and Glenn, explained what we were going to do with Gemini and Apollo, and how we were going to get to the Moon. They loved it. *Do you really know Al Shepard and John Glenn?*

I came away from the event with an increased level of confidence. The secret was talking *to* the people, not *at* them. I would never read another NASA-prepared speech.

BACK IN HOUSTON, JUST as I had once looked at the Original Seven, I soon assessed the Next Nine, and found as profound and talented a group of pilots as I have ever seen, all top-notch aviators.

Ed White came across as an All-American, clean-cut straight arrow, the poster boy for the program. He was our Yuri Gagarin. Ed was damned good and we could have picked no better person to be the first American to walk in space.

Jim McDivitt was extraordinary, a nice guy with such immense leadership potential that he was selected to be the commander of his very first flight, *Gemini 4*. Jim didn't talk much. He let his work speak for him.

John Young was a gung-ho, let's-get-on-with-the-job kind of flier, who became a close friend when we went to the Moon and halfway around the world together. John could drive engineers nuts with his "Young-grams," fiery missives that he would write for the record when he found something he didn't like.

Pete Conrad, a tough little gap-toothed guy known as Tweety, was on fire all the time, hell-bent on getting the job done. Pete was the last guy you would ever expect to have a Princeton education and be from a mainline Philadelphia family.

Frank Borman was very solemn, and had leadership stamped all over him. Competence was never a question with Frank, because he operated on a higher level than most of us. He wasn't really one of the guys, and somewhat holier-than-thou, but Frank was born to lead.

Neil Armstrong was still the friendly and unassuming guy I knew vaguely from Purdue and through Smitty.

Tom Stafford and I, as different as night and day, became like brothers because we spent so much time together training for and flying a pair of space missions. T.P. is a brilliant guy from a little town in Oklahoma who thinks as fast as a computer and is usually right. His habit of trying to speak faster than he thinks earned him the nickname of "Mumbles." When things went wrong for us on *Gemini 9* and again aboard *Apollo 10*, I was glad that Thomas Patton Stafford was at my side.

Jim Lovell is known to the world today as commander of the hard-luck *Apollo 13*. Usually happy and friendly, his leadership qualities manifested themselves at exactly the right time on that mission. The hit movie did not exaggerate Jim's ability, even if Pete Conrad had given him the intimidating nickname of "Shaky."

The last was Elliot See, a slight Texan who was a naval aviator and then a civilian test pilot for General Electric, where he helped develop the famed Phantom F-4 jet fighter-bomber of the Vietnam war era. My future was going to be linked to that of Elliot, in a dreadful way.

My conclusion was that Borman and Stafford were at the top of the heap in expertise, followed closely by McDivitt, then Lovell and Conrad. Armstrong, the sleeper, would become the most well-known of all. The Nine were very, very good and were going to make history.

9

The Suit

THROUGHOUT OUR CLASSROOM STUDIES, each new astronaut was assigned to a specialty to support the pair of unmanned Gemini test flights that would lead to the Grissom-Young mission of *Gemini 3* that was scheduled before the end of 1964. Because of my academic background, I drew the job of monitoring the propulsion systems, which took me into the strange land known as Mission Control.

The first two Mercury astronauts had ridden an old Redstone rocket, then the others graduated to the more powerful Atlas, a stubby 75-foot-long warbird with three engines powered by kerosene and liquid oxygen. Convair started developing the Atlas way back in 1946 as an intercontinental ballistic missile capable of carrying a nuclear warhead to a target 9,000 miles away. That was strong enough for the lightweight missions of Mercury, but Gemini demanded a bigger horse.

The answer was the Titan, the largest ICBM in the free world when it became operational in the early 1960s. Standing ninety feet tall, the Titan was a liquid fuel rocket capable of producing the immense thrust needed for its nuclear mission, and that capability was adapted to the peacetime job of shoving a spacecraft into orbit.

On April 11, 1964, we had the first unmanned test launch using the Titan as a Gemini booster rocket, and I was in Mission Control, connected by an intercom headset to the flight director, whose position was known as "Flight." It was as if I were a single cell in a gigantic brain. Flight was linked to about two dozen serious-looking men at a number of similar consoles, each representing a specific part of the mission—medical teams, spacecraft environment, electronic systems, etc.—and each of them was connected to a support team that monitored every aspect of the spacecraft and mission. Flight's questions required instant answers.

A couple of consoles were occupied not by engineers and technical wizards, but by astronauts. One was the capsule communicator, the CapCom, who relayed messages from Mission Control to the crew in the spacecraft. Only CapCom or Deke talked to the astronauts on board. When we were strapped in those seats, ready to launch, we wanted another astronaut on the other end of the radio, someone who really understood us and our mission, and was ready to speak up for us loud and clear. Another astronaut was assigned to monitor the rocket's fuel tank pressures, keeping close watch on dials identical to those inside the spacecraft. That position, called "Tanks," was me.

Gus and John were in Mission Control for the test launch, sitting at my elbows, watching the pressure gauges along with me as the Titan was fueled on Launch Complex 19. The pressure needed to force that fuel from the tanks to the engines, where it would burn with enormous energy, was critical to getting the rocket off the ground. Exceed the low pressure red line and danger was instant, possibly terminal, and reason for me to take action. I was ready, if necessary, to give the order— *"Flight! Tanks! Abort!"*—and shut down the whole show. Gus and John were not only interested in the tank pressures for the test, but also in how the rookie handled the situation. After all, they would soon be atop one of those cooking rockets and if I made the wrong decision, the results could be devastating. On this day, the Titan worked as advertised and *Gemini 1* climbed gracefully into orbit and successfully passed its tests. Tanks walked away a happy man, confident at having reached a personal milestone, for this had not been a simulation or a practice, but the real thing. NASA penciled in *Gemini 2*, another unmanned mission, for July 14, then announced that *Gemini 3*, with Gus and John aboard, was to get off the ground in November.

THINGS WERE LOOKING PRETTY good as I headed out for my desert survival training, with the same drill as before, only this time I was partnered with Alan Bean. Get out of a helicopter, survive for about five days and walk to a rendezvous point. That was harder than it seemed, for the desert of northern Nevada is as bleak a place as you will ever see, and the only things we were allowed to carry were items that would be aboard a spacecraft—some small rations and water, iodine tablets to make water drinkable, a compass, parachutes, a machete, fish hooks and so forth. I knew right away the fish hooks wouldn't be of much help out here. At least in the jungle I had a water source and could find things to eat. In this dusty hell, I could only burrow into the sand like an animal during the day, and string my parachute over the hole to break the merciless sun and provide some shade. We walked toward the rendezvous point only during the cool hours of the night. There was no food or water other than the meager rations from the spacecraft, and I got so hungry that I would have welcomed even a hearts of palm salad. One day I spied a visitor to our campsite, a large rattlesnake. Normally, a sensible person would avoid a big diamondback, but who was normal after a few days of 130-degree heat? This time it was the snake that got scared and took off, pursued across the burning sands by two skinny, hungry astronauts named Cernan and Bean, clad in filthy long underwear and waving machetes like madmen. He got away, and we returned to our shady hole in the ground, where I dreamed of my grandmother's kitchen and rattlesnake kebob.

THE WEEKS SLID BY faster, and *Gemini 2* ran into repeated delays, including a lightning strike and violent visits to Florida by Hurricanes Cleo, Dora, and Ethel. That pushed back the whole schedule, erased any chance that *Gemini 3* would fly before the end of the year, and there wasn't a damned thing we could do about it. Meanwhile, Deke announced that Jim McDivitt and Ed White would be the prime crew on *Gemini 4*, with Frank Borman and Jim Lovell as their backups. We rookies understood clearly that Gemini seats were becoming scarce.

The first hint about who was going to get a flight usually came from Deke, but a NASA technician might suddenly appear in your office and tell you to go up to Worcester, Massachusetts, and get fitted for a suit. The news that you would get a space suit tailored to your exact measurements meant you were in the pipeline for a mission or a backup spot, and the official announcement would be made at an appropriate time. All very low key, of course. Wouldn't do to get excited about just going up to Wooster and setting the seamstresses and tailors loose on your body.

BY NOW, WE FOURTEEN had been working in extraordinarily close quarters as we barreled through months of training. Quirks, gut feelings, and performance divided us into groups. We all worked together, but friendships were being formed, and the little things counted.

It came together for me when Deke and Al told us to submit a peer review, judging our classmates in a confidential memo. This required some soul searching, for I was one of the younger astronauts and somewhat unsure of where I stood. Not that I would let anyone detect even a glimpse of self-doubt. On any official list of the Fourteen, I would automatically put my name on top of the stack, no matter what the category. I expect the other guys did the same.

My real list was different. There were four guys who clearly were head and shoulders above us all in flying experience—Dave Scott, Dick Gordon, Charlie Bassett, and Mike Collins. In my opinion, these veteran test pilots probably would get the first mission assignments.

And at the bottom of my list were Rusty Schweickart, Walt Cunningham, and Buzz Aldrin. They were all experienced pilots, but were collectively considered to be our scientists. Rusty was an irreverent intellectual, like a little red-headed kid with a sharp needle, looking for a balloon to pop. Aldrin was known as "Dr. Rendezvous" because that was the only thing he could talk about, even over a cup of coffee. Cunningham seemed determined to be different from the rest of us, whether reading the *Wall Street Journal* while we busted our asses during a classroom lecture, or driving a Porsche instead of a Corvette. That irritating habit may have cost him a trip to the Moon.

The remaining seven of us were bunched in the middle, in no particular order, and I honestly didn't know where Gene Cernan fit into the scheme. Probably below Bassett, Collins, Gordon, and Scott. Certainly, I hoped, above Aldrin, Schweickart, and Cunningham. Maybe right smack in the middle of the pack. Realistically, a Gemini seat seemed to be just out of reach and moving the other way. Some hero.

As GEMINI 2 WAS having postponement problems, the United States officially opened the Pandora's box we would come to know as Vietnam. In July, U.S. destroyers claimed they were attacked by North Vietnamese boats in the Gulf of Tonkin, and that gave President Johnson and Congress a reason to beef up our presence in Southeast Asia. LBJ was running for re-election against Republican Barry Goldwater and his bellicose political posturing put American armed forces in harm's way to a degree we never expected.

Baldy, Skip, and some of my other squadron mates would be in the thick of it, but they weren't worried about getting shot at. Just the opposite. They were more concerned that this little dustup wouldn't last long enough for them to get in their licks. A few wallops of American air power in North Vietnam should be all that was necessary. Baldy and Skip would later explain how pilots maneuvered to get assigned to an early strike, because they feared if they didn't get on the first missions, the shooting would all be over before they got into combat at all. They were wrong. Vietnam would soak up American planes and pilots like a sponge absorbs water.

IN AUGUST OF 1964, Barbara and I drove down Nassau Bay Drive to Cape Bahamas, turned right on Barbuda Lane near the Nassau Bay Yacht Club and pulled into the driveway of our new custom-built home, a small bungalow of brown stone that seemed to be a slice of heaven. Over the years, we put in a sloping front lawn, added a garage built around a tree on the right side, poured a concrete patio, and added a chest-high barbeque. A kidney-shaped swimming pool, a walk-in bar, a row of six pine trees along the drive, and flower beds made us feel we were living like movie stars as the neighborhood grew and prospered. A thin wood fence separated our house from the home Roger and Martha Chaffee built next door. Children were everywhere and would grow up going through public schools together.

It seemed that we were living a charmed and protected existence, but that illusion of safety and isolation was shattered about eleven o'clock on a warm October day.

Ted Freeman, one of the more quiet members of our group, was making a routine flight out of nearby Ellington Air Force Base in a T-38, a plane with which he was more than familiar. He had actually been a test pilot during the development of the T-38, knew every switch and gauge in the aircraft and could have flown it with his eyes closed. As he was setting up a routine landing approach, a goose smacked into his canopy, cracked it, and pieces of the heavy plexiglass were sucked into his engines. The plane fell lower and lower as Ted fought for control, then finally gave up and punched out. His parachute didn't have time to open properly, the plane crashed, and the first American astronaut died. He would not be the last.

The death of a friend cast a sour mood over the entire program. We had always expected that someone would get killed along the way to the Moon, but being done in by a bird almost within sight of your house? There was nothing for us to do but pay our respects as Ted was buried at Arlington and get back to work.

Plenty of work was ahead for us, too, because the Freeman tragedy wasn't the only black day in October of 1964. The Russians were at it again, and while we were struggling to get a second unmanned Gemini test ready, they somehow stuffed three cosmonauts into one of their space cannonballs and kicked them into orbit. The Soviet plan to send up three men had drawn criticism within their space program, particularly from one top engineer who wouldn't be quiet about the potential danger. They won his silence by naming him to be a member of the crew. That same engineer then eagerly flew a mission he was on record as saying should not be flown.

Voskhod 1 actually was nothing more than another Soviet publicity stunt, for it brought nothing new to the tricky business of rendezvous and docking that would be needed for a trip to the Moon. Unknown to us, the Soviet leadership was in turmoil and the flight may have been a last public relations ploy within the Kremlin. A month before Johnson beat Goldwater to keep the White House, our old nemesis Nikita Khruschev was overthrown.

Both Kennedy and Khruschev had been enthusiastic supporters of the space programs of their respective nations. LBJ had moved swiftly to adopt JFK's goal of putting a man on the Moon, but now we in the space program could see that his interest was becoming more focused on Vietnam and his expensive Great Society programs. Therefore, we wondered if the new Soviet leaders would have the same commitment to space as had Khruschev. Indeed they did.

THE NEW YEAR OF 1965 dawned and we finally got *Gemini 2* off on a successful test that lasted only eighteen minutes in the middle of January, with me still reading Tanks. My job was done the moment the booster rocket burned out, and I could sit back and watch the real pros in Mission Control do their thing. The place hummed like a machine, and the big room was filled with a confidence that they could solve any problem.

The next month, Deke announced that *Gemini 5* would have Gordon Cooper in command and Pete Conrad as pilot, with Neil Armstrong and Elliot See as backups. Four more seats gone and none of the Fourteen were in any of them.

The question of whether the Soviets had lost momentum when Khruschev was toppled was answered when *Voskhod 2* launched on March 18. It was also built like a steel bowling ball, but had a huge, collapsible tube, not unlike a giant vacuum cleaner hose, sticking out of one side. Hatches at both ends made the screwball thing into an airlock. Cosmonaut Alexei

Leonov, one of the gutsiest men alive, pressurized his primitive space suit, even using a simple rubber band in the process, then opened the spacecraft hatch, wiggled into the tube, closed the hatch behind him and vented the airlock. When he opened the other end, he popped out like a cork. For twelve minutes, Leonov walked in space, the first person ever to do so.

It would be many years before we learned that he almost died before pretzeling himself back into the *Voskhod*. He became stuck when he re-entered the elephantine tube head first and was unable to turn around to close the outer airlock hatch, which had to be tightly shut before he could pressurize the airlock and reopen the spacecraft hatch. Only by partially depressurizing his suit was Alexei able to free himself enough to squirm back to safety. Nevertheless, the Russians had trumped us once again.

Not only was the public relations value of the mission immense, but we knew the Russians needed spacewalks in their plan to get to the Moon, and they had just shown that it could be done. Had I known what was in store for me, I would have paid more attention to Alexei's little journey.

I was Tanks again on March 23, 1965, for the long-awaited Grissom-Young flight aboard *Gemini 3*. It was a successful mission, although only three orbits, and proved that the hardware worked and a pilot could actually maneuver a spacecraft. That delighted the technical side, but the mission made a publicity splash of its own. John Young and Wally Schirra conspired to smuggle aboard a corned beef sandwich from Wolfie's deli at the Cape, and when John surprised Gus with it, sharing a bite, crumbs started floating around. The sandwich was hurriedly packed away and the loose bits gathered before they could short out a circuit. Nothing can be taken aboard a spacecraft without fully being tested for how it will impact the entire mission, not even a sandwich from Wolfie's. The press played the story as large as they played the mission itself, and Grissom, Schirra, and Young all caught official hell about it. Then, thankfully, the episode passed.

THAT SUMMER, THE FIRST official American combat troops went into Vietnam when Marines stormed ashore at Da Nǎng, where they were greeted by ice cream vendors and news photographers. The total number of U.S. troops in Vietnam would reach 200,000 by the end of the year, and the bloody battle of the Ia Drang Valley proved those little guys could fight us to a standstill. Viet Cong and North Vietnamese attacks against Americans were answered with a massive bombing campaign called Operation Rolling Thunder, which would drop the equivalent of eight hundred tons of bombs, rockets, and missiles on North Vietnam every day for the next three and one half years.

A Navy pilot, Lieutenant (junior grade) Everett Alvarez Jr. from the *Constellation,* was shot down during the first attack wave and hauled to the prison that became known as the Hanoi Hilton. He was only the first of some 600 American aviators who would be captured and held as prisoners of war in Vietnam for many long years. Another POW taken during the initial attacks was my friend Bob Schumacher from the Naval Post Graduate School, who could just as easily have been safe with us in Texas as part of our class of astronauts. Fate plays tricks.

In Houston, Tracy turned two years old in 1965 and Barbara had not only settled into the community, but was proving to be more than an obscure astronaut wife. She could play the space game as well as anyone, and was a full partner in my career. In March, she came to the Cape for four days right after the *Gemini 3* launch and I had a chance to give her a guided tour of my home-away-from-home, the mystical sandy city where the rocket men worked.

But she could not be there for the launch because of an unspoken and unwritten rule: Astronauts' wives were to be back home in Houston, running the household and smiling for photographers. It was unfair, but there were several reasons behind it.

First, there was Deke, who believed that having your wife around divided your attention. Since we never knew what Deke was really looking for in choosing which astronauts would fly, none of us wanted to jeopardize our chances by crossing invisible lines.

Then there was the idea of "protecting" the wife. If there was a catastrophe on the launch pad, NASA didn't want the wife there to witness the tragedy. They must not have realized that she would be just as upset by watching it on a television set in Texas.

And another reason was established in the early days, even prior to the Mercury flights—sex. There were plenty of pretty women imagining love with a space hero, and some of them would give anything to sleep with an astronaut, a temptation that some astronauts found too great to ignore. Before rock concerts became movable feasts of sex, drugs, and rock and roll, the astronauts were the best show in town. We were attractive, hard-partying pilots, and magnets for the ladies. Any astronaut who wanted sex could easily obtain it by leaving his hotel door open, for the odds were that a beautiful girl might close it behind her within a few minutes.

The wives stayed in Texas, and Florida was an off-limits playground filled with Cape cookies. If you wanted to bring your wife and kids to Florida, you had to get advance approval from Deke and let the other astronauts know. Everyone handled the situation differently, some abstaining altogether, but the opportunities were sure there. One of the guys thought that any girl, upon reaching her eighteenth birthday, had earned the right to share his bed, and he intended to accommodate as many as possible. Another astronaut's death presented a protocol problem, for while the wife stood beside the grave, a buddy discreetly escorted the long-time girlfriend to the funeral.

In the mid-sixties, it was all kept under wraps. No astronaut had ever been divorced, so such a scandal promised an unknown impact on a flying career. Both wife and husband could lose the perks. Over a drink, astronauts might commiserate about marriage woes, but the advice was always the same: Stay together! Don't put Deke on the spot!

The wives heard the rumors, but some simply didn't want to know about the Cape cookies. Barbara was in that faction. Around our house, the subject just was not discussed. That was the safest route through a potential minefield, but times were changing.

GEMINI 4 FLEW IN June, a four-day journey for McDivitt and White, highlighted by Ed's walk in space, which was captured for eternity by a series of magnificent photographs. He was such a physical specimen that he made the so-called Extra Vehicular Activity (EVA) seem almost like fun. Bobbing along and drifting in the emptiness, tethered to the spacecraft by an umbilical cord that fed him oxygen and electricity, Ed could squeeze a little handheld maneuvering gun and get a squirt of power to change his position. His spacewalk ended after twenty-one minutes, then Ed reluctantly returned to the hatch area. It may have been easy until then, but getting back into the tight confines of the Gemini spacecraft proved to be damned difficult, and the unanticipated hard work exhausted him, despite his physical fitness. The lesson was promptly ignored in the wash of wonderful press coverage that accompanied our first spacewalk. Just as with the Leonov spacewalk, I wish everyone had paid closer attention to what had really happened out there.

*   *   *

ALONG CAME ANOTHER NEW group of six astronauts, and they were not entirely welcome. These guys were all pure scientists, and most didn't know beans about flying. The entrance of Owen Gariott, Ed Gibson, Duane Graveline, Lieutenant Commander Joe Kerwin, Curt Michel, and Jack Schmitt rang our chimes. It seemed to us as though NASA was caving in to the scientific community, bargaining for dollars and support by promising a ride for some guy toting test tubes. Flying in space was still risky and unknown and even top pilots ran into trouble out there. Hadn't *Gemini 4* just failed a tricky rendezvous, even with an expert like Jim McDivitt at the controls? We didn't want anyone on board who couldn't handle the flight side of the equation, for if an alarm came on, there would be no time to ask some professor to carry his share of the load.

Graveline was possibly the worst choice ever in the astronaut program, the result of the National Academy of Sciences not doing the in-depth background checks that NASA had always demanded. The problem had nothing to do with his qualifications as an Air Force flight surgeon, but with his domestic life. No sooner was he selected than his wife, tired of his fiery temper at home, filed for divorce. Deke canned Graveline so fast that he wasn't around when the others got together for the traditional group photo.

Now we knew how Deke would react to a divorce. It didn't worry me in the least, because my marriage was solid.

I RAN TANKS AGAIN on *Gemini 4*, the first flight to be handled out of the new Mission Control in Houston instead of from Florida. It was an important task, but I was restless. I didn't want to still be sitting in the Tanks chair when some scientist waltzed in and snagged a ride because of political maneuvering. Those Gemini seats were vanishing fast enough as it was.

The splashdown of *Gemini 3* back in March freed the backup team of Wally Schirra and Tom Stafford to rotate to prime for *Gemini 6*, with Grissom and Young turning around to be their backups. Zap. Four more seats gone, and the Gemini series was at the halfway mark. Not even the top guys in our class had yet gotten a ride—time was running out and I was still warming a cushion in Mission Control. I had been in the program for a year and a half and didn't have a clue about my future.

*   *   *

TRAINING CONTINUED NONSTOP, ALTHOUGH we weren't quiet sure for exactly what. We all went up to Boston for some MIT familiarization on computer guidance systems, then over to Bend, Oregon, for more intensive geology training. If and when we got to the Moon, we would have to be on intimate terms with what we found on and beneath the surface, and I found myself becoming more comfortable with the technical jargon and theory of how mountains were formed, the composition of a valley and what a single rock could tell me. While we were out there, Deke herded the Fourteen into a motel room and actually smiled, his wrinkled face looking like an unmade bed. It was a silent signal, for he only smiled when he had good news. And he did. "Some of you are going into training immediately for upcoming Gemini flights," Deke said. We inhaled in such unison that we probably sucked all the air out of the room.

Deke said Frank Borman and Jim Lovell, both from the Next Nine, would be the prime crew for *Gemini 7*, but that Mike Collins would be paired with Ed White as their backups. A ripple of cheers went around the room to congratulate Mike, but by now we were hanging on Deke's every word.

He announced that on *Gemini 8*, Dave Scott would be the prime crew pilot and fly with Neil Armstrong in command. Their backup crew would be led by Pete Conrad, flying with his friend Dick Gordon. And aboard *Gemini 9*, Charlie Bassett would fly in the right seat, with Elliot See as commander on the prime crew. No backup crew was announced.

No argument from anyone in the room. Dave and Charlie had worked their butts off and deserved the first prime crew missions for our class. Mike and Dick also deserved to be the among the first of our group to enter the flight pipeline.

The rotation schedule that was blossoming indicated that a backup crew would rotate into the prime crew slots three missions later, so Mike would probably be on the prime crew for *Gemini 10* and Dick Gordon would slide into a *Gemini 11* prime slot. All four of my top selections had grabbed the first rides of our class, so Deke must have rated the guys about the same way I had.

We slapped them on the backs, bought them beers, and after they went home, those of us still groundbound realized that an alarming number of seats had just been yanked off the table. If the three-mission rotation scheme held true, we could now project the prime crews all the way through *Gemini 11*, and there were only twelve missions in all, only ten when the pair of unmanned tests were subtracted. Guys like John Young and Ed White were coming around for another turn, and the big bow-wows like Schirra and Grissom probably could bigfoot their way onto any flight, if they chose. Since none of our group could expect a command position, we concluded that the *Gemini 9* backup pilot slot was the only prize left for us. Whoever got that job could rotate onto the prime crew for the last mission, *Gemini 12*.

Fortified by booze, someone brought things into even clearer perspective: Forget Gemini for a minute, because it's more than that now. As we sit here nursing our beer and wounded pride, all those guys who had already flown, those with a ton of experience, and the ones already in the pipeline, were lining up for the early Apollo missions!

When Gordo Cooper and Tweety Conrad flew on *Gemini 5* in August, I was to be on Tanks again. Hoo-fuckin'-ray.

I SHARED AN OFFICE in the new MSC complex with Neil Armstrong, but he was so busy training for his upcoming flight with Dave Scott on *Gemini 8* that I rarely saw him. I was already fully trained for my own job, reading those damned Tanks dials, so I was busy flying my desk, using my Purdue education and astronaut training to weave a chain of paperclips while I considered my dilemma. I had done the survival school, I had done Tanks, I had helped design the Agena rocket to be used as a rendezvous target, I had done every damned thing asked of me. I wanted to fly, but here I sat.

One day, there was a light rap on my door and a tall, thin technician from the flight support division stuck his head into my office. "Geno," he said, "Deke wants you to go up to Worcester to get fitted for a suit." The magic words! He may have said some other stuff, but I don't remember anything but a warm, fuzzy feeling settling all over me as a silly smile came to my face.

Report to wardrobe! I got the part!

10

Crash

THE FORMAL ANNOUNCEMENT CAME November 8, 1965: Tom Stafford would be the backup commander for *Gemini 9* and I was the backup pilot. The good fortune that won me that particular seat was critical. If the three-mission rotation held firm, bagging that backup pilot's seat on *Gemini 9* meant I probably would rotate to a prime assignment on *Gemini 12*. I could almost hear the groans from my nonassigned brethren among the Fourteen. *How the hell did Cernan get into the pipeline?*

By the process of elimination, the backup assignments for *Gemini 10, 11*, and *12* were deadend jobs, for there would be no *Gemini 13, 14*, and *15* flights to which those crews could aspire. At best, they could only hope for some distant assignment in Apollo, where the competition would be absolutely ferocious among the more experienced astronauts.

Elliot See and Charlie Bassett went immediately into full-scale training for *Gemini 9*, and while I continued running the Tanks slot in Mission Control, I also started work with them in that special, tight relationship between the prime and backup crews. Stafford would join us after he finished flying on *Gemini 6* with Wally Schirra. We had to become practically inseparable and almost telepathic in detecting what the other guys were going to do next. Not only would I help Elliot and Charlie get ready for their flight, but I eventually would need every bit of that knowledge when Tom and I rode *Gemini 12*.

Elliot was a short, slight thirty-eight-year-old Texan, a soft-spoken native of Dallas, with blue eyes and brown hair. His boyish looks and quiet, serious demeanor disguised an inner strength. He defied the conventional career path of an astronaut. Instead of West Point or Annapolis or a major university, he graduated from the small U.S. Merchant Marine Academy before also earning a degree from UCLA. After serving as a naval aviator, he joined General Electric at Edwards Air Force Base and was a civilian test pilot for thirteen years, compiling 3,200 hours in jets. Those gleaming credentials got him into the second group of astronauts, one of the rare civilians named to the program. He and his wife, Marilyn, had three kids.

Charlie was part of my group. Born in Dayton, the son of an Air Force officer, he made his first solo flight at the age of sixteen, attended Ohio State and graduated from Texas Technological College. At the age of thirty-four, Charlie was an Air Force major who was considered to be a terrific stick-and-rudder man, and had served as an instructor at Edwards AFB. Married to an attractive wife, Jeannie, and the father of two children, he wore his dark hair in a flattop and had a ready smile.

My task was to mirror everything that Charlie did, and make him as ready as possible to fly that mission and be ready to take his place if something happened to him. We had learned the hard way that astronauts were not invincible. A goose had killed Ted Freeman. Al and Deke were grounded by medical problems. Walt Cunningham almost broke his neck bouncing on a trampoline. Things like that happen in life, and that was what the backup role was all about. But Charlie Bassett was in perfect condition, a pilot in his best years, totally confident and with every reason to remain so.

As WE BEGAN OUR planning, we quickly discovered this was no piece of cake. One internal NASA memo said the flight plan was "*really* ambitious," and the underlined word is theirs, not mine. "*Gemini 9* will be a very exciting mission and, if carried out completely, will provide experience one would not ordinarily expect to get in less than three missions." When that kind of challenging terminology is being kicked around by mission planners, it's time for the pilots to get serious.

Gemini 9 was to fly into orbit aboard a Titan in May of 1966, join up with an Agena rocket that would be launched earlier, light off the Agena engine to push into deeper space and perform several complicated rendezvous procedures. Then the Agena would be abandoned and the crew would move to a new realm of tests. Charlie would do a spacewalk, wear a backpack known as an Astronaut Maneuvering Unit (which everyone shortened to AMU), and fire its hot little rockets to fly around in space on his own, connected to the spacecraft only by a long, thin tether.

The spacewalk, therefore, was of ultimate importance to Charlie and me, and there was precious little information available about what life was really like outside a spacecraft. The Russians weren't talking about what happened with Leonov, and Ed White's success had led us all to a sense of unrealistic euphoria. Had we read some of the conclusions drawn from his debriefing more closely we would have discovered that despite the glorious photographs, Ed overheated so badly getting back into the spacecraft and closing the hatch that he needed several hours to cool down.

But Dave Scott was going to perform a long spacewalk on *Gemini 8*, which, if all went as planned, would provide a lot of new information in time for Charlie's own stroll, which in turn would pave the way for future spacewalks, including mine on *Gemini 12*.

Charlie and I buckled down to work. We planned to overcome the problems that Ed had encountered the old-fashioned way—with brute strength—because we had no other alternative. There was never an official program of physical conditioning among the astros, because Deke expected us to do whatever was necessary to stay in shape. It was part of the job, and you worked out on your own time, whether by playing handball, sweating in the gym, or doing pushups in your hotel. Deke's philosophy was that if you didn't care enough about your job to stay in peak mental and physical shape, you could easily be replaced. Charlie and I hit the weight room almost every day, building our upper-body muscles to gain an extra edge, and before long, we grew Popeye-sized forearms. Each of us strutted through the Astronaut Office squeezing a tennis ball. Toting that fuzzy little sphere needled our colleagues. *Eat your hearts out, I got a spacewalk!*

As if there wasn't already enough excitement, I was promoted by the Navy to the rank of lieutenant commander, selected early, after only nine years in total service and five years in grade as a lieutenant. It was nice that the promotion came for my work as a Naval officer and had little to do with being an astronaut. I was thirty-one years old, and felt that I had earned that new gold leaf on my collar.

SOME GUARDED CONVERSATIONS WERE being held at NASA headquarters and in management offices around the Manned Spaceflight Center. Stunning intelligence reports claimed the Russians were about to attempt another spectacular within a few months, perhaps even a try to get a manned rocket to make a pass around the Moon before we could get up there.

Therefore, the NASA thinkers came up with the idea of beating them to the punch by sending *Gemini 12* around the Moon, if all tests were successful through the first eleven missions. The last five Gemini flight plans already included docking with an Agena rocket, which would go into orbit first. So our engineers figured they could soup up the thrust of the Agena enough to give the final Gemini mission a deep-space capability. In this theory, when *Gemini 12* reached orbit and docked with the improved Agena, the bigger rocket engine would provide enough kick to throw the spacecraft onto a course that would result in a single loop around the far side of the Moon. They counted on the slingshot effect of lunar gravity to fling the spacecraft back toward Earth for our reentry.

People were seriously considering sending Tom Stafford and me around the Moon! Looking back, I'm glad they came to their senses and recognized a really bad idea when they had one. We weren't anywhere near being ready to send a crew on a journey of half a million miles.

HOWEVER, NONE OF US saw another problem that was much closer to home—the Astronaut Maneuvering Unit. When Charlie and I first met the AMU, we looked at each other and raised our eyebrows. Hmmmm.

The Air Force had been developing the AMU toward the time when their mission would be to own the heavens and zip about building space stations, rescuing stranded astronauts and moving between spacecraft. The possibility of using it to send someone scooting off to disable an enemy satellite wasn't mentioned in public because we weren't supposed to be thinking about the militarization of space. The AMU, seven years into the development process, looked like a massive suitcase, three feet high and two feet wide. On Earth, it weighed 135 pounds by itself, with another 31 pounds of fuel and oxygen. It was so big that it would be carried aloft folded up like a lawn chair and attached within the rear of the cone-shaped Gemini spacecraft. Once in the zero gravity, the weight and boxy shape of the AMU wouldn't matter.

The astronaut would spacewalk back there, prepare and check out the AMU, slip onto a small bicycle-type seat, strap on the silver-white box and glide off into space, maneuvering with controls mounted on the armrests.

Charlie and I ran our hands over this conglomeration of valves, levers, dials, and tubing and stopped for a closer look when we got to the so-called propulsion and control system. Nozzles for a dozen hydrogen-peroxide–powered jets were located at the corners of the pack, and were to fire bursts of gas to stabilize and propel us in space. These tiny rockets would spew red-hot exhaust gases, with some located right beside our ears and others pointed down across our butts. One early design even had a rocket that would blast right between the legs of the astronaut! Sure, we said. What the hell. We'll fly the thing.

THAT MEANT THE SEAMSTRESSES and tailors in Worcester had to build Charlie and me a couple of special spacesuits, for the standard Gemini G4C suit sure as hell wouldn't cut it for a spacewalker with rockets firing down around his wazoo.

Here's what we would wear:

1. Long johns. A white cotton undergarment with special waist pockets to hold biomedical instrumentation. Sensor pads would be all over our chests and abdomens.
2. A blue nylon "comfort" layer.
3. A black neoprene-coated nylon pressure suit.
4. A restraint layer of Dacron and Teflon link net, not unlike a knight's chainlink garment, to restrain and maintain the shape of the pressure suit.
5. Seven (count 'em!) layers of aluminized mylar with spacers between each layer for thermal protection.
6. A special layer to shield us from hits by dust-sized meteors.
7. A white HT-1 nylon outer layer.

Now that was just the Kmart blue-light special to protect us from the almost 500-degree swing of temperatures between daylight and darkness in space. What really mattered were the heat-resistant leg coveralls to prevent those rocket blasts from the AMU from cooking us like sides of bacon. The "iron pants" were made up of a thermal insulation sandwich of eleven layers of aluminized H-film and fiberglass topped by a metallic fabric woven from ultrafine fibers of a superalloy known as Chromel R. To prove to Charlie and me that the stainless-steel trousers actually would protect us, an engineer with a blowtorch cheerfully charred a chunk of the material for about five minutes and assured us that while the rockets might be blasting at 1,300 degrees, we would remain a comfortable seventy-five degrees inside our suits. Even in the age of the Nehru jacket and bell-bottomed blue jeans, this was a strange outfit.

FAR AWAY, IN THE Gulf of Tonkin, a surprise was awaiting Ron Evans. Returning from another bombing mission over North Vietnam, he saw the flight deck of the *USS Ticonderoga* grow broad and flat before him, trimmed his F-8 Crusader slightly to match the meatball, and snagged the three wire, safely back in the nest on Yankee Station. After losing out on his bid to become an astronaut, Ron had earned his degree in Monterey and returned to the fleet just in time to be sucked into the raw heat of Vietnam. He had flown more than 100 combat missions and was leading younger, less experienced pilots on those dangerous sorties. The kids were amazed at what this quiet, balding pilot could do.

A messenger was waiting as he climbed from the cockpit, soggy with sweat and exhaustion. The captain's compliments, sir, and would you report to the Ready Room? Lugging his helmet and flight gear, Ron trudged off to meet the boss, running the latest mission through his mind and finding nothing wrong. *Wonder what the skipper wants?* Once inside the room, he plopped into a chair, noticing the smirks of several other pilots. By nature a patient man, Ron figured he'd find out what was going on soon enough. The captain entered and read a teletype message aloud. Lieutenant Commander Ronald E. Evans Jr. had been selected for astronaut training and was to report to Houston immediately! He was to come a complete circle from that Ready Room, for when our *Apollo 17* spacecraft returned from the Moon seven years later, the carrier which plucked us from the water was the *USS Ticonderoga*. The Navy is a small world.

Ron was among nineteen new astronauts chosen this time, and they were a welcome bunch, for unlike the scientists, these guys were real pilots. I eagerly scanned the list of names, was delighted when I saw Ron's, but kept looking for another. For several months, I had campaigned in behalf of Skip Furlong, but he hadn't made the final cut, and the reason was never known. We had drunk many a beer, talking about the day we would be the first men to walk on the Moon together. It didn't work out that way. He wouldn't go at all, and I would be the last. My disappointment was as great as his.

The nineteen newbies meant the publication contract would be cut even thinner, but also meant that they would relieve the rest of us from gofer duties. There would be plenty of fresh astronauts now to go out and talk to the Rotary Clubs while the rest of us worked on getting to the Moon.

THE GEMINI PROGRAM CONTINUED at a rapid-fire pace, each mission proving that still another element of space travel could be safely accomplished. *Gemini 3* had been a pioneer mission to prove the system worked with a crew aboard. *Gemini 4* validated our spacewalk capability, and *Gemini 5* experimented with a long-duration flight and the use of fuel cells instead of batteries for power. The next step was a rendezvous in space, a critical maneuver, for in our blueprint for lunar exploration, the astronauts who landed would have to launch from the Moon, and find and link up with the orbiting mother spacecraft.

That was the job of Schirra and Stafford on *Gemini 6.* An unmanned Agena rocket would be launched first and parked in a drifting orbit. Then a Titan bearing the spacecraft with Wally and Tom aboard would launch, chase down the Agena, and dock with it.

But on launch day, the Agena blew up before reaching orbit, forcing the Schirra-Stafford flight to be scrubbed until a new target could be found.

Gemini 7 was due to be launched soon, with the intense Frank Borman as commander and Jim Lovell as pilot. They had the unenviable task of determining if men could withstand a marathon space flight of some two weeks, which would be about the amount needed during future Moon flights. So a creative mission planner figured that since Borman and Lovell were going to be up there anyway, why not shuffle the schedule a bit and launch *Gemini 6 after Gemini 7?* In that way, Schirra and Stafford could rendezvous with Borman and Lovell instead of with the Agena. *Gemini 7* had a smooth launch on December 4, went into orbit and would circle the Earth for two solid weeks, our longest mission yet.

The irascible Wally now saw his job solely as proving that a pair of manned spaceships could rendezvous in orbit, although they could not actually dock together. The Gemini was designed to join up with an Agena, not another Gemini. He stripped away everything that didn't relate to the rendezvous function, and had no intention whatsoever of spending a lot of useless time in orbit, flying around in circles. Lest anyone complain, Schirra showed them during the next launch attempt why it was best not to mess with him too much. He was a cold-nerved pilot, by God.

On the second launch attempt of *Gemini 6,* the Titan's massive engines ignited, and as the smoke and flame belched around the pad, the damned rocket didn't lift off! Wally and Tom sat through the firestorm, perched on the edge of disaster while the rocket bellowed and shook around them. We watched in awe, knowing that the book called for the crew to bail out of there before the rocket blew up under them. Schirra gripped the orange D-ring that would eject both him and Stafford from the endangered spacecraft, but he didn't pull it! Schirra had balls. He broke all the rules that day, but saved the program from a potential show-stopping disaster. The hot engines shut down, the raging Titan calmed, then Wally and Tom climbed out of the spacecraft and shrugged off the entire episode. Tom, watching the master, had learned a lesson that he would need in a similar situation on a future mission.

Gemini 6 finally went up on December 15, found the long-suffering Borman-Lovell team, waved, flew in close formation, took some pictures, and came straight home. Frank and Jim loitered on, becoming more grungy, irritable, and uncomfortable with every new orbit, and there were 206 orbits—fourteen days. In their cramped spacecraft, they were unable to even stretch their legs.

That flight brought to the fore a problem that would bedevil all space voyagers and intrigue all space watchers—how astronauts urinate and defecate in zero gravity. It's quite unlike perching on a porcelain throne while reading a newspaper.

The recipe for taking a leak in space was distilled to a twenty-step checklist called the Chemical Urine Volume Measuring System, for while we only wanted to relieve ourselves, the doctors wanted samples of each incident. From Mercury through Apollo, the process remained pretty much the same. At one end of the system was the astronaut, who would roll a special latex condom onto his penis. The other end of the condom fit over a valve mechanism the size of a pack of cigarettes that collected the stream of urine. A turn of the valve sealed it off. Once urination was complete, the condom was removed and packed away for future use, and the work began. A sample bag was taken from storage, properly labeled with name, date and time, then hooked to the valve mechanism and filled, faucetlike, with some of the stored urine. The package was restored, then the remaining urine was flushed overboard, creating an impressive cloud of ice crystals.

That procedure was complemented by a special triangular-shaped plastic bag for use during launches and spacewalks. The same open-ended condom linked the astronaut to the bag, which was held in place across the lower abdomen by Velcro straps. When used, the warmth of the urine spread across the stomach, and always caused a worry that the bag had burst.

The best way to defecate was not to do it. For three to five days prior to the mission, we would eat a low-residue diet, staying away from things like salads and butter that are likely to create bodily wastes. During the flight, we would have similar food, such as cheese sandwiches and dehydrated foods to keep us well plugged. On the short missions of Mercury and Gemini, a bowel movement was rare.

In such tight confines, where there was hardly any room to move, much less take off a spacesuit, the work involved for such a bodily function made it damned near impossible for anyone other than a contortionist. Nevertheless, there was a procedure involving what we referred to as the Famous Blue Bags. It involved uncasing one of the especially-engineered blue plastic sacks, peeling away the covering of adhesive tape around the neck and carefully placing it over the strategic portion of your butt. A soft glove, similar to one used in a regular kitchen, was attached inside the bag, to allow you to carefully wipe by using a tissue that was also included on the inside. The tricky part was pulling off the bag and sticking the top together before losing any of the the contents in zero gravity. It didn't always work, and more tissues were used to capture floating particles. Of course, the doctors wanted samples of every bowel movement, too. Things were somewhat better on Apollo, mainly because we had more room to work in the bigger spacecraft and could slip down into the lower equiment bay to peel off the suits to do our business. An expensive device that looked something like a sewer pipe with a potty seat never flew.

The same sort of basic procedures were used in the lunar module during stays on the Moon. The one place I drew the line was on wearing Moon diapers, huge boxer shorts with ample built-in storage space to be worn under the space suit in case the astronaut had to defecate while on a Moonwalk. They made us take them along, but they couldn't make us wear them.

Dealing with bodily functions was a necessary part of any spaceflight, and wasn't usually a problem. Vomiting was just as bad, and diarrhea was the worst. It was just something else with which we had to deal in this peculiar line of work.

Jim Lovell said many years after his flight that being cooped up in *Gemini 7* for such a long mission was akin to spending two weeks in a latrine, particularly after one of the urine collection bags burst.

A PROBLEM HAD SLOWLY become apparent concerning Elliot See's flying abilities, no matter what his credentials were on paper. More than one astro who shared a T-38 Talon jet with him came away knowing he wasn't the best of the best. Deke later wrote that he considered Elliot to be a tentative, "old-womanish" pilot. Yet Elliot had worked smoothly with Neil Armstrong on the backup crew for *Gemini 5*. They were both civilians and were drawn together. The big difference was that Neil flew better than most everyone else in the program, had piloted the X-15 rocket plane, and actually earned astronaut wings by flying more than fifty miles above the Earth *before* he became an astronaut. Deke apparently figured that by partnering Elliot with Charlie Bassett, any problems in the cockpit would be minimized.

As soon as Tom Stafford splashed down after *Gemini 6*, he joined Elliot, Charlie, and me in preparations for *Gemini 9*. We all trained together in the simulators, worked on the mission plan, studied in the classrooms, and spent a lot of time in St. Louis customizing the *Gemini 9* capsule being built at the McDonnell Aircraft Corporation. This was a real spacecraft, not a hallucination. We could see it, touch it, and feel it. This machine would take Elliot and Charlie into space. I found myself frequently drifting down the line to take a look at where the *Gemini 12* spacecraft was being assembled. That would be mine, and I wanted to watch it go through the birthing process. It was little more than a skeleton of struts and pieces of loose gear on the shop floor, waiting to be molded into a scientific and engineering wonder. Cockpit hatches similar to those on military aircraft were propped open from its bell-shaped titanium hull. Inside would be a maze of electronic gear, including sophisticated guidance and navigation systems and a rendezvous radar. I wanted to personally know every bolt and rivet in the thing and spent a lot of time talking to the precise, dedicated men who were putting it together, for my life might someday depend on the quality of their work.

Since Charlie and I were the ones who would perform the spacewalks, we also found ourselves together in a lot of airplanes and sharing a beer or two in hotel bars, hammering at the mission, always the mission. The two of us became a team, helping the LTV Aerospace engineers in Dallas cobble up an AMU that would fit all of our needs. After work, we would occasionally click our glasses in congratulations, for we realized the rocket pack was a significant challenge that would be a headliner for the space program, and it was all ours. The spacecraft commanders, our seniors in experience, might do a wonderful job with rendezvous or save a lot of fuel on reentry, but the big newspaper ink would belong to the spacewalkers. As rookies, we got a couple of good laughs out of that, and felt confident that if anybody could tame this backpack, we could.

The Bassetts lived about three blocks away from us, down by the lake, and Barbara and Jeannie Bassett were good friends, so throughout the training, we found ourselves spending many off-duty hours together too, sharing dinners and long talks. As the weeks rolled by, the friendships strengthened until we were almost a single family.

AS 1966 BEGAN, THE Geminis were flying about every two or three months. *Gemini 8* was set for March, when Neil and Dave Scott would go up to conduct a rendezvous and docking mission with another Agena, and Dave would do his spacewalk. Then *Gemini 9* would launch in May.

On the last day of February, Elliot, Charlie, Tom, and I climbed into a pair of NASA dual-seat T-38s to fly to St. Louis and spend time in the simulator at the McDonnell plant. The lead plane, NASA 901, being flown by Elliot with Charlie in the back seat, carried a baggage pod, and we all stowed our personal papers and NASA identification badges in it before taking off at 7:35 A.M. from Houston. The weather forecast in St. Louis was about what could be expected for that time of the year: three miles visibility, rain and snow flurries. Not enough to worry four experienced pilots, although the instrumentation could have been better. The automatic glide slope computer was out of service at the airport, which meant we needed to pay closer than usual attention. Tom edged into position on Elliot's wing as we rose up through light clouds over Ellington, into a gleaming blue morning sky. The white helmets of See and Bassett appeared in their canopy like a pair of ping-pong balls in a clear plastic tube.

By the time we approached the Lambert–St. Louis Municipal Airport about nine o'clock, the weather had turned crappy, the winter sky alive with a dirty mix of rain and ragged columns of snow and fog that poked down to within 400 feet of the ground. Our little Northrop jets bounced around as if we were striking sharp corners. We lowered through the muck, wing tip to wing tip, almost losing sight of the other plane in a snow squall.

Once we were on the ground, we wouldn't have to go very far to reach our ultimate destination. The McDonnell Aircraft Corporation was adjacent to the field, and the massive Building 101, where all of the remaining Gemini spacecraft were being assembled, sat only 500 feet from the runway.

Properly flown, we should have emerged from the muck at about 400 feet, with the field spread out before us. Instead, we were still looking at instruments, surrounded by clouds and snow, and I didn't like what I saw. Elliot had miscalculated the approach and we were high, fast, and too far along the runway, with only a glimpse of the ground through the dirty weather. "We don't have a prayer of landing on this pass," I told Tom.

Then, inexplicably and without warning, Elliot heeled his T-38 over into a sharp left turn. "Goddamn!" Tom barked. "Where the hell's he going?"

They were immediately lost to us. We saw only soupy clouds and twisting curtains of snow blowing by our canopy. We had been here many times, and knew we were way out of position to salvage the landing this time. Tom retracted the landing gear and raised the flaps while I told the control tower we would continue outbound and make another approach. Long minutes passed as we climbed and the tower put us into a holding pattern. Our only concern was that Elliot and Charlie might divert to another base to land, taking our clothes and briefcases along with them in the baggage pod. We never saw the crash, explosion, and fire that killed our two comrades.

Reports later said that Elliot continued his snap descent and circled behind the control tower before realizing his mistake. One of them managed to light the afterburners in a futile attempt to pull the T-38 out of its steep turn, but it was too late. The plane slammed into the top of Building 101, skidded to the edge, and cartwheeled into the parking lot, where it exploded and showered debris over a wide area. Both men were thrown from the plane.

Firefighters raced to the blazing wreckage and piled thick foam atop the snow until the tail section stuck up like a thin, scarred monument from the mass of suds. One wing was still on the roof, and other sheared off when the plane hit the ground. A partially open parachute lay on the dirty snow like a crushed mushroom. Somehow the line of Gemini spacecraft in the building escaped damage, although fourteen factory workers were injured.

There was immediate confusion over who had died in the holocaust. Two bodies had been recovered but were unrecognizable, and the NASA badges of all four of us were scattered amid the wreckage. While the fire was being fought, Tom and I were still circling twenty miles away, oblivious to what had happened and annoyed that the tower was being so vague in its communications. They weren't telling us a damned thing, leaving us to loiter around the sky on our own, feeling somewhat ignored. Finally, a near-empty fuel gauge forced a decision and we were allowed to land.

We came in smoothly, and saw no smoke or any sign of the accident. As we rolled along the runway, the tower calmly asked for "the pilots' names of NASA nine-oh-seven." That was our plane. "Stafford and Cernan," I replied. In that obtuse way, Charlie and Elliot were identified. I asked if 901 had diverted to another field, only to receive a cryptic reply to check with the Operations Office at McDonnell. Another nonanswer.

We didn't find out what had happened until we pulled to a stop at the ramp and opened the canopy to find a group of grim-faced men standing there to meet us.

I immediately telephoned Barbara. "There's been a terrible accident, but I'm all right," I said, sucking deep breaths to steady myself. "Charlie and Elliot are both dead. I don't know anything else."

She was still wearing her nightgown when she got the call and slowly sat down in a chair, as if struck dumb. I comforted her as much as possible from a cold telephone in Missouri and suggested that she get down to the Bassett house right away.

It was also one of the most difficult moments for Barbara in all of our years in the space program. Jeannie, a real sweet gal, had been absolutely bubbling with excitement about Charlie's upcoming *Gemini 9* flight and the news that he had been killed left her devastated. Now Barbara was at the front door, to be with her in that most trying of times, and it only made things worse.

For the death of Charlie meant that Jeannie had not only lost her husband, but she had lost her ticket to the party. Barbara felt as if she were a thief, stealing something very important from a dear friend. For with Charlie gone, I would fly aboard *Gemini 9* in his place. The headlines, the applause, and the adulation that had been coming to Jeannie would now shift to Barbara. In one of the tragic truths of the program, she would no longer be a member of that tight group of astronaut wives. Jeannie was now alone, with kids to raise, and there was no role in the space program for widows and orphans. It was simply unfair and terrible.

When I hung up, we hurried to the crash site. I'll never forget that gut-wrenching scene and my feeling that this was an accident that just should not have happened. A few hours later, Deke Slayton telephoned Tom and me, and said: "*Gemini 9* is yours."

It was time for two more NASA funerals, but unlike the furor that would surround *Apollo 1* only a year later, the deaths of Charlie and Elliot hardly caused a blip in the program. It sped forward, with even more intensity than ever to hurry things along. Only three weeks before, an unmanned Soviet spacecraft had made the first soft landing on the Moon. *If they can do it with a robot, can they do it with a live crew?* We had no time to waste.

Within forty-eight hours of the See-Bassett crash, *Gemini 9* was taken from Building 101, trundled past a tall pole on which the flag whipped at half-staff in a winter wind, and sent to the Cape for final preparations.

I had to wear my dress blue uniform again for the sad duty of burying friends. Two years before, I had worn it for Ted Freeman. Now it was for Elliot and Charlie. Of the fourteen men in my astronaut group, two— Ted and Charlie—were already dead, and none of us had yet flown into space. Memorial services were held in Texas on March 2 at the Seabrook Methodist Church and Webster Presbyterian, and both churches were filled to capacity. T-38s flown by astronauts ripped through the sky in the Missing Man formation. Formal burial was at Arlington National Cemetery. It was raining and it was cold, and, lost in thought, I jerked in surprise when the three rifle volleys cracked out in salute. *Onward, Christian soldiers.*

When we returned to work, things had changed for me, and I was struck by the enormous difference of being on the prime crew and being a backup. Before, I had the tissue-thin comfort that I would train hard, but I was not the one who actually had to perform. Now it was going to be me sitting on top of that son-of-a-bitch of an intercontinental ballistic missile and being flung into the heavens, and my tissue defense dissolved like sugar in water.

THE MOMENTUM OF THE program was so great that within a month of the crash, *Gemini 8* went up with Neil Armstrong in command, and Dave Scott, a test pilot who held an advanced degree from MIT, ready to do an extended spacewalk. Although he would carry a hand-held gas-jet maneuvering gun like Ed White did, and not try the rocket-powered AMU, we were confident that Dave would bring back a ton of valuable information that I could use in training for my own spacewalk.

They docked with an Agena rocket, and swiftly were wrapped in monstrous trouble. The linked spacecraft began to yaw and roll, then went into a devilish spin, and it all happened while they were out of communication with Mission Control. The crew had no one on the ground with whom to confer as the situation worsened by the second.

They thought the Agena was causing the problem and Neil undocked the linked spacecraft. That only intensified the trouble, and the little Gemini started to spin viciously, doing a complete 360-degree loop every second. "We have serious problems here," Dave managed to radio when they regained communications. "We're tumbling end over end!" A thruster was firing wide open, rolling the Gemini like a top and the two astronauts were close to losing consciousness. Neil managed to shut down all of the major control rockets, then slowly nursed the spacecraft into stability using only the tiny thrusters on its nose. To do so, he had to burn much of the fuel that was reserved only for reentry.

Nevertheless, they splashed down soon thereafter in the western Pacific, where they were rescued by a destroyer, the only ship close by. Neil likes to say that he set a landing record that has never been broken. The aircraft carrier scheduled to recover them was still waiting in the Caribbean when he hit the water some 8,000 miles away, near Okinawa. Despite the horror show of their ten-hour flight, Neil and Dave accomplished a major program goal by proving that docking in orbit was possible.

Unfortunately, the early termination of the mission scrubbed Dave's planned spacewalk. That removed the possibility of me learning any more about that tricky exercise, an absence of knowledge that would prove very costly when I went outside on *Gemini 9*.

It didn't take long for some of the guys around the Astronaut Office to criticize Neil's performance. *He's a civilian pilot, you know, and maybe has lost some of his edge. Why didn't he just do this, or why not do that? Wouldn't have gone into that spin if he would have stayed docked with the Agena.* Monday morning quarterbacks with perfect hindsight, astronauts who had been on the ground while Neil and Dave were fighting to survive in space, were brutal. Screwing up was not acceptable in our hypercompetitive fraternity, and if you did, it might just cost you big-time. Who knew if the criticism might reach Deke's ears and change future crew selections in favor of the person doing the bitching? Nobody got a free pass when criticism was remotely possible. Nobody.

TOM AND I BEING named to fly *Gemini 9* after the crash in St. Louis was not the only alteration in the crew schedule, and, for one man in particular, that ripple effect would have an historic meaning.

As we moved up to prime, we needed a backup crew. Jim Lovell, who had flown an earlier Gemini mission, and was aimed at an Apollo flight, had agreed to be the backup commander for *Gemini 10* in the interim. Buzz Aldrin, who had not flown at all, was in the deadend slot as backup pilot on that flight. But when Tom and I advanced into the prime crew assignment, Jim and Buzz were also moved forward and became the new *Gemini 9* alternate crew, which put them in line to make the final flight of the series, *Gemini 12.*

There was no doubt that Jim was being groomed to fly in Apollo, but that wasn't necessarily the case with Buzz. Without catching that ride on *Gemini 12*, it is unlikely that he would have flown aboard *Apollo 11* and have become the second man to walk on the Moon.

11

The Mayor of Pad 19

THE MEN OF THE *USS Wasp* watched Tuesday, May 17, 1966, break bright and clear over the Atlantic Ocean as the aircraft carrier cruised lazily some 1,180 miles east of Miami. Before long, a hot tropical sun would dry the puddles of water that had formed on the flight deck during overnight squalls. Crewmen wandered around their planes and helicopters while a troop of civilian photographers and reporters loaded film into their cameras and rolled sheets of paper into typewriters. The *Wasp* had been the recovery ship for four previous Gemini missions and would be on station to pluck Tom and me from the water within a few days. A red carpet was stowed on the hangar deck near Elevator 3, awaiting our eventual arrival.

As the morning sun moved west and hit Cape Kennedy, Tom and I were awakened in the crew quarters, ready to blast off in four hours and twenty-four minutes on America's thirteenth manned space flight.

First thing on our agenda was a twenty-minute medical check, then Deke Slayton and Al Shepard joined us for the traditional launch-day breakfast of steak and eggs turned out by our cook, Lew Hartzell, and some last-minute mission talk. I kept a stone face, all business, but butterflies stirred in my stomach because I realized this was The Day. After breakfast, wearing an orange Banlon shirt and tan slacks, I met Dee O'Hara, the astronauts' unflappable nurse, and we went to a private mass and communion in a small room, conducted by Father Vermillion, a friend who served mass at the modest wooden chapel on Ellington Air Force Base on Sundays. My parents and my sister Dee and her family would attend church at St. Simeon in Bellwood that morning, and Barbara would tie a scarf over her hair and also go to morning mass. God was up to date on my plans.

Still in our civilian clothes, as if we were off for a round of golf, Tom and I climbed into a small van with Deke and left the crew quarters on Merritt Island. Police cars, lights flashing, formed a convoy around us as we departed. Cheering crowds waved as we crossed the causeway that spanned the Banana River, and we entered the Air Force station launch area through tight cordons of security. A line of gantry cranes stood along the beachfront, tall steel symbols of the space business, but all activity had ceased around them, everything shut down to focus on our launch.

The van pulled up at a small trailer beside Pad 16, and as I stepped out, I could see the Atlas-Agena being readied nearby on Pad 14. In the other direction, at Pad 19, was the Titan II, with our tiny Gemini spacecraft perched on its nose. That sumbitch looked *huge*. A few dark clouds mulled against a brilliant blue sky, and whitecaps feathered restless swells on the early morning ocean. I gulped a deep breath of fresh, salt-rimmed air, knowing I would soon be sucking on the canned stuff.

Three hours before launch, a weather briefer said those threatening clouds hanging above our rocket were dispersing and everything was ready for us to go. The sense of reality heightened as medics and technicians stuck the biomed sensors to our bodies, then buttoned, zipped, laced, and snapped us into our bulky suits. Around my neck was a religious medal that I had worn for years, a small silver disk bearing the image of Our Lady of Loreto, and the legend, "Patroness of Aviation, Pray for Me." It had caused quite a furor at one point as the doctors insisted it should not be on my body, but in my small personal pack along with my wedding ring and other personal items. I resisted strongly and finally Deke settled the matter: "If you want to wear it, Geno, then wear it." Case closed.

My legs were pushed into those stiff, metal-shrouded pants, and my arms were jammed into the sleeves of that protective cocoon. I tried to flex my fingers and became aware again of the lack of dexterity in the suit, even when it was deflated. It was thicker than the one Tom wore, because of the extra layers of insulation needed to protect me from the extreme temperatures I would encounter during my spacewalk.

Getting into a space suit was a quiet and technical business. There was no glory, no ceremony, just grunts of effort as we struggled into the custom-made, multilayered garments. I had worn it many times, but to-day it felt different. Every wrinkle, texture, and smell added to the vibrant reality, as if the very weave of this suit was leaving individual imprints on my skin.

A technician handed me a glass of orange juice when Deke came over and said, "Tom, I need to talk to you privately." I glanced at T.P., who shrugged, then followed Deke into another room. I had some concern about this little meeting. Only a few hours before launch and the boss wants a private talk with the spacecraft commander? The subject couldn't be about a rendezvous, the weather, or anything mechanical, because I would have been involved. Since I had spoken with Barbara the night before, I knew nothing was wrong at home. So they had to be talking about me. Maybe some reminder for Tom to remember that I was still a space rookie, a possibility that frankly burned my ass. Rookie, hell! I was an astronaut, and if they didn't trust me, then why the hell was I standing here wearing this stupid suit? When they returned, both acted as if nothing had happened.

"What was that all about?" I asked Tom, keeping my temper under control.

"Everything's fine, Geno. No big deal."

It would be years before they would individually divulge their discussion. It was relatively simple. The spacewalk I was to undertake was very dangerous, and there was a real possibility that once outside the spacecraft, something unforeseen might happen with the rocket backpack or the tether and I would be left hanging there, incapacitated. If that happened, Deke told Tom the only choice would be to cut me loose, close the hatch and return to Earth without me. Talk about a tough decision. My pal Mumbles made exactly the appropriate answer: He was the mission commander and it would be Thomas P. Stafford, not anyone on the ground— not even Deke Slayton—who would decide what to do if such an emergency occurred.

I did not like the idea of becoming Satellite Cernan, but long ago had recognized such a risk existed. I knew Tom would be unable to pull me back inside if I couldn't get myself out of trouble. He would work like the devil to rescue me, but eventually would have to abandon me, for that was the only option. We both knew it. It came with the territory.

THEY CLAMPED OUR HELMETS in place, turned on the oxygen, and we could no longer touch, smell, or hear the outside world. Tom and I became different from any other creatures on Earth that day. We would breathe pure oxygen for the next three hours to rid our systems of the nitrogen that might cause bubbles in our blood during a rapid change of altitude, not unlike the "bends" that can afflict a diver rising too fast through the water.

Now there would be no more communication, not even radio contact, until we were in the spacecraft. For the next forty-five minutes, we lay like shrouded mummies on couches in the trailer, slowly breathing and getting ready for the environment in which we would live for three days. There was a quietness that I had never before experienced. The hiss of oxygen and the steady sound of inhaling and exhaling. That was all. In that special silent time, I was alone with my thoughts about where I was about to go and I could almost hear my heart thump. *I'm going to get on top of a rocket and fly into space and be thrust into history.* If I was scared, I didn't know it, because I was so excited.

They helped us stand, then hooked the suit loops to portable oxygen canisters and, like butterflies emerging from a cocoon, a transformation took place. As we waddled out to the van, we were now dressed like astronauts, space heroes, and as cameras clicked and flashed, I realized the attention of the world was focused on the two of us.

A quarter-mile away at Pad 19, the Titan waited, without life and mysteriously silent, as if guarding a secret. It was much bigger than the Atlas and Redstone rockets the Mercury astronauts had ridden, but it had to carry a lot more weight to a higher altitude. Our Gemini spacecraft seemed to be balanced precariously way up on the very top.

There were no crowds around the bright orange gantry, just technicians doing their jobs and, except for a few smiles and thumbs-up signals, we were ignored. They had seen astronauts before. We rode the clattering elevator up, watching the shiny metal skin of the tall rocket creep down past us, then walked across the gangway, a grid of open metal squares that let us look straight down at the ground far below. We went through a little door into the White Room, the clean area which was the domain of Guenther Wendt, the Peenemünde refugee who was now chief of the closeout crew. Everyone in there, including our backups, Jim and Buzz, wore long white coats and white caps. They looked like morticians.

Getting into a Gemini spacecraft was like putting on a giant steel girdle. There was absolutely no room to spare, not an inch, and as a result, Tom and I were stuffed into a space no bigger than the front seat of one of today's little compact cars, and we had to share even that with an instrument console the size of a small refrigerator. We each had less space than the single astronauts who had flown in Mercury. Even under ideal conditions, getting aboard was a problem.

The morticians guided us through the hatches and we wiggled into the seats, lying on our backs, the bulky suits preventing easy movement although they were still deflated and soft. My pants of woven steel fibers locked my legs into place. Technicians strapped us in, attached the oxygen and communications umbilical hoses to the spacecraft systems and gently armed the dangerous ejection seats. We became part of the machine.

Guenther peered at me through his thick, black-rimmed glasses, and took one more glance around the interior of the spacecraft. When he was satisfied, he patted my helmet and flashed a thumbs-up, part of his traditional good-luck benediction of wishing every astronaut "Godspeed" in his heavy German accent, then my hatch was closed and locked from the outside. Anyone with claustrophobia has no business in the space program. Tom and I were sealed into this coffin-like spacecraft like pickled herring mashed into a can. I wiggled and flexed and shifted, trying to arrange my space suit and heavy pants, long underwear and gloves and boots and helmet to get some sort of comfort. Impossible. Naturally, I developed itches in places that were impossible to scratch. Breathe the oxygen, listen to the radio, and wait. Morning light streamed through our two tiny windows. All we could see was blue sky. Locked into the tiny spacecraft atop a fueled booster rocket, I knew there was no turning back. I was in for a ride. Because of our months of practice, everything looked and felt familiar, but this time it was not a simulation. It was for real.

HERDS OF NEWS REPORTERS were on the lawns in Bellwood and Nassau Bay. A dealer had lent Mom and Dad a color television set for the occasion, and relatives and friends gathered to watch with them. Dad had taken a week off of work so he could have plenty of time to observe the entire flight. At Proviso High, where I had spoken twice in recent months, students filed into the auditorium to watch the launch on TV sets placed on tables.

Barbara, wearing a white dress that accented her tan, settled before a couple of television sets in our house on Barbuda Lane. Her mother was at her side, nervously wringing her hands. Ry Furlong, who was living in Coronado, California, where Skip was on the staff of an aircraft carrier group, and Mrs. Cook, our landlady from Del Mar, had flown in to be with Barbara. Other astronaut wives joined them. My three-year-old Tracy, with a bright ribbon in her hair, spent the idle time coloring with crayons and playing with her best friend, Amy Bean, the daughter of astronaut Al Bean and his wife, Sue. NBC producer Fred Rheinstein had three bottles of champagne delivered to Barbara to be uncorked at the appropriate times—Launch, Spacewalk and Splashdown.

*   *   *

T-MINUS-15 FOR THE ATLAS-AGENA. On the Titan, we were locked and cocked, ready to go 100 minutes after the Atlas launched. Under us, in the belly of the Titan missile, almost 30,000 gallons of chilled, poisonous nitrogen tetroxide and a mixture of Aerozene 50 lay quiet. The fluids were uneasy neighbors, for when the valves opened inside those tanks, the two liquids would spray through nozzles, collide, and detonate as soon as they touched. That controlled explosion would propel us into space. Seconds ticked slowly away, grains of time that seemed as large as the boulders that had replaced the butterflies in my stomach.

But before *Gemini 9* could move an inch, that $13-million Atlas-Agena bird parked only some 6,000 feet away had to fly. The Atlas booster, one of the most reliable rockets in the Air Force arsenal, had taken John Glenn and others into space. It had been around for a decade, and some 300 had been fired, with an impressive 95 percent success rate. Of the last sixty, only two had failed.

THE ATLAS-AGENA PACKAGE WAS streamlined from its sharp nose to the small stabilizing fins, and made up of several distinct parts. The Atlas booster was the bottom section. Attached above it was a twenty-five-foot-long Agena, and atop the Agena was the docking collar to which our own Gemini spacecraft would link during rendezvous. On the pad, the blunt docking collar was covered by an aerodynamic fiberglass shroud to give the Atlas-Agena the sleek, pointed nose needed to get it through the thick atmosphere. Just prior to orbit, tiny explosives would snap two narrow steel bands that held the clamshell shroud together and it would peel away in two sections, exposing the docking collar.

TOM AND I WERE plugged into the audio circuits and listened to the launch team go through the final Atlas-Agena countdown. Sounded good. I ran my eyes along the instruments and dials and kept my hands far from the D-ring between my feet that, if pulled, would blow my ejection seat out of the spacecraft and me along with it. I could yank the thing in case of emergency, but I wanted no part of it, and always thought it was silly to endure the shaking and bouncing of a launch with a hand tightly wrapped around such a trigger. I was aboard this bird to fly, not bail out.

My normal heart rate of between sixty-five and seventy beats per minute stepped up slightly.

The mission plan said that after the Agena reached orbit and kicked away its burned-out Atlas booster, it would return over the Cape on its first loop around the Earth. Exactly ninety-nine minutes and nine seconds after it lifted off, as it coasted above Florida, we would launch to begin an 80,000 mile chase through space, and catch it after three and a half orbits. *Time to GO!* Television cameras flashed images of the two waiting rockets, slender missiles almost side by side, to a worldwide audience and the calm voice of Al Chop in Mission Control reassured the public that all systems looked good.

"T-MINUS-60 SECONDS," BARBARA CALLED out at home when the countdown reached a minute before the Atlas-Agena launch. "Girls, keep your fingers crossed."

Martha Chaffee picked up the count as her husband and my fellow astronaut pal, Roger, watched over my family, ready to answer their questions and calm any fears. Barbara grasped Tracy with one hand and her mother with the other.

"Five," Martha chanted. "Four . . . three . . . two . . . one."

A BURST OF FIRE at 10:15 A.M., a boiling blossom of smoke, a peal of thunder, and the Atlas-Agena lifted smoothly away from the Cape in a swirl of color. The ground shook and I could feel the vibrations of power all the way atop our own rocket, and a muted roar filled my helmet. The silvery target missile climbed straight up, balanced on a flame that glowed as bright as the sun, and dashed away, punching through one of those small white clouds that lingered overhead. I nodded with satisfaction. *Go, baby, go! We'll see you upstairs.*

"LOOK AT THAT ROCKET, Tracy," Barbara said, pointing at the television screen and hugging our daughter. Everyone in the living room cheered and applauded as the Atlas sped away, and the euphoria that automatically grips those watching a launch even captured the reporters on the lawn as the Atlas throttles opened wide and the rocket gathered even more speed. *Go. Go. Go.*

"Daddy! Daddy!" yelled Tracy, bouncing on the cushion.

"No, that's not Daddy," Barbara said.

"Who's in it?"

"Nobody."

And thank God for that.

ONLY 130 SECONDS LATER, one of the two main engines in the Atlas went weird. The bell-like covering that directs the outward thrust of the rocket wobbled, then jerked hard over and, with the engine still thundering at full blast, spun the Atlas into a tumble from which it would not recover. Ten seconds later the engines shut down as planned, the Agena separated, but it was too late, too low, too fast, and all wrong. The whole thing plunged into the Atlantic, leaving a curlicue trail of smoke hanging in the sky like a giant question mark some 160 miles from the Cape. "We have lost it," Al Chop quietly told the stunned television audience. "We have lost the bird."

THAT LEFT TOM AND me sitting atop a loaded Titan ICBM, all dressed up with no place to go, very aware of the latest demonstration of Murphy's Law that whatever can go wrong, will. American rockets could still blow up.

"Aw, shit," Tom said, although the comment was cleaned up by the public relations folks before being relayed to the audience. I was still white-knuckle tense as Mission Director Bill Schneider immediately terminated our mission. The red rug on the *Wasp* would stay rolled up a while longer and Fred's bottle of "Launch" champagne would remain corked.

Tom and I began the laborious chore of getting out of the tight spacecraft as the swing arm reached back from the gantry and clamped to the Titan. We carefully returned the pins back into the ejection seats to render them safe, and Guenther's team opened our hatches. We crawled back into the real world, *verrry* carefully, for that Titan rocket still brimmed with fuel.

Helmets off, we took the long elevator ride back down the gantry. As the body of our Titan slid past, this time going the wrong way, I turned to Stafford. He had been through this disappointing business of postponed launches twice before. "Damn, Tom," I asked, "Do you do this for a living all the time?" I was tired and disappointed, feeling totally empty inside, but there was also a strange sense of reprieve. Whew. Astronauts, of course, keep such thoughts to themselves.

In Bellwood, Mom invited the reporters in to help eat the food stacked in the refrigerator. No use letting it spoil.

Barbara sat quiet and immobile on the sofa in Nassau Bay for a few moments, biting her lip, lost in her own thoughts as the television picture flickered with the image of a rocket that had destroyed itself, knowing her husband was still strapped atop another one. Her mother softly sobbed, and that broke Barbara's reverie. She pulled herself together, transforming into Mrs. Astronaut. Gathering Tracy in her arms, she stepped outside to meet the reporters. "We'll just back up and try again. Gene's a pilot. He knows you get the bad with the good," she said, forcing a smile. Over the past few years, we had become friends with many of the newspeople who covered the space program regularly, and through those growing friendships, the original fear we had of the press eased.

And over at Tom's house, Faye Stafford was the first to speak the word that would become inexorably associated with *Gemini 9*. "I think I'm a jinx," she said, and the press found a news peg.

We returned to Houston for a few days with our families and resumed simulator training while the NASA braintrust held emergency meetings about what to do next. Our flight was postponed for more than two weeks, a delay that had to be examined in the status of the overall man-to-the-Moon program, for time was now a factor. The Atlas problem with *Gemini 6*, the See-Bassett crash, the near disaster of *Gemini 8*, and now the initial *Gemini 9* failure because of another Atlas goof had changed the schedule. Day by day, the entire program was being pushed back. It was finally determined that, barring further major mishaps, we could finish the four remaining Gemini flights by the end of the year and not affect the start of Apollo in January 1967. That was if—and it was a very big *if*—we could launch the remaining Geminis at the astonishing rate of one every two months.

That would leave three years to fulfill the Kennedy pledge of getting to the Moon by the end of the decade. That was not a long time when one considered that the Moon was a quarter-million miles away, we were still barely able to fly in circles around the Earth, and were sometimes unable to get a launch at all. The pressure was enormous.

In addition to the delayed schedule, there was another major problem. The computer hardware needed just to get to the Moon, much less to actually land there, simply did not yet exist. In fact, one of my jobs on *Gemini 9* would be to use a pencil with an eraser on the end, a pad of paper, plotting tables, and a slide rule to figure some of the rendezvous calculations, while Tom made star sightings through sextantlike calibrations out his window. It was not far from the way Columbus plotted his path to the New World. I would have given my right arm to have been able to pull out one of today's laptop personal computers, link to a Windows program, dial up a navigational satellite, tap in a formula, and sit back while an exact course popped up on a liquid crystal screen. A modern handheld computer is 500 times more powerful than the biggest one we had aboard *Gemini 9*. Back in 1966, most computers were about the size of a cow, Silicon Valley was still California farmland, and Microsoft genius Bill Gates was only ten years old!

OUR MAIN QUESTION AFTER the scrub was how long it would take to recycle *Gemini 9*. There was no other Agena ready to fly, and without a target, we could not conduct the important rendezvous tests. But NASA was loaded with creative engineers, and they were ready with an answer before the question was even asked.

After the Agena target vehicle had exploded during *Gemini 6*, NASA had contracted for a cheaper, alternate docking target, and for a million bucks, the McDonnell Aircraft Corporation built a stubby thing with the long name of Augmented Target Docking Adapter. That was shortened to the initials ATDA, and soon became known simply as the Blob. It had been at the Cape undergoing tests for a couple of months.

The decision was to roll out another Atlas rocket and stack the Blob on it instead of an Agena. It was basically a tube, eleven feet long and five feet in diameter. The front end looked much like an Agena, with a docking collar covered by a fiberglass cone that would be kicked off once the thing was in orbit.

The main difference was that the Blob did not have that powerful Agena rocket engine we needed to raise our orbit to a higher altitude, one of our primary assignments. In fact, the only rockets on the ATDA were two rings of small thrusters that were supposed to stabilize it during the rendezvous. But the good news was that everything else remained the same. The launch was rescheduled for the first day of June.

SUMMER RAIN SCOURED CAPE Kennedy on the last day of May as we raced through final items of business, such as meeting with mission officials, working out in the gym, and talking to our families. We went to bed early while pad technicians paid loving attention to our birds throughout the night.

WE AWOKE AT 5:11 A.M. on June 1 to find strings of black clouds hanging like mourning crepe above the dark Atlantic, but the weather people told us not to worry. Those would clear over the next few hours and Hurricane Alma was still too far away to bother us. The prelaunch drill seemed more routine the second time around, and by the time they put on my helmet to start me breathing oxygen, I was settled into a comfortable déjà-vu, having experienced it all before. The delay had increased my confidence.

The mission profile had been altered in one significant way to meet the new circumstances of having the ATDA as our target instead of the rocket-propelled Agena. This time, if the Blob didn't make it into orbit, we would bypass that part of the schedule and practice rendezvous techniques with the burned-out carcass of the Titan booster that would take us into space, then concentrate on my space walk.

Once again, Tom and I rode the elevator up the ten-story length of the Titan and were shoehorned into the Gemini as the dual countdowns were underway. This time, the Atlas worked perfectly, blasted away from the Cape only three seconds behind schedule and headed upward at a dazzling speed. The rocket reached the proper height and speed, the Blob separated on schedule and less than seven minutes after it left the pad, it locked into an almost circular orbit.

Okay. Now we had a target, so let's go get it. We had a launch window of only six minutes, from 11:38 until 11:44 A.M., during which the ATDA made its first pass over the Cape. We intended to catch up with it over the Pacific after about three orbits, then dock over the U.S. in broad daylight.

The radio circuit came alive. Puzzled ground controllers suspected something might have gone wrong after all, for a control board light glowed brightly, indicating the big fiberglass shroud that covered the nose of the Blob might not have fallen away as it was supposed to do. After a quick conference, it was decided that we would proceed with our flight and go take a look at the damned thing to find out what had happened.

The countdown didn't miss a beat. An hour. Half an hour. Fifteen minutes. The ATDA crossed the California coast and was headed toward us. Five minutes. Four.

Getting ready. Getting close. The walls of the Gemini spacecraft were the limits of my existence except for that tiny window that showed nothing but an occasional cloud. I took deep breaths to prepare for the onset of increased G-forces during launch, and scanned the blinking board of lights and dials, passing data back and forth with Mission Control during the final prelaunch checkout. Three minutes. Everything in the green. Two.

A COMPUTER IN MISSION Control fed a routine update to an on-board internal guidance system that would alter our flight path enough to put us exactly on the trail of the Blob. And, somewhere in the bowels of our Gemini spacecraft, the system decided not to accept the data. Before we could react, the computer recycled and offered the information again and our gizmo once more refused to take it. Trouble lights flashed in Mission Control and in the spacecraft.

Tick. Tick. One minute, fifty seconds. Decision.

HOLD! DAMN!

The count was recycled to three minutes and the computers chattered some more. *Goddamn computer glitch!* Hold. Recycle again. The Blob zipped past silently, far overhead, waiting for us to come up and play. There was only that precise six-minute window during which we could launch, and the computers were eating up that precious time. Another signal, a final rejection, and that was that. Our mission was scrubbed for a second time.

We had been so close that I couldn't believe things could come to such a sudden stop.

Mission Control patched me through on a private communication link from the spacecraft to my home in Nassau Bay. Barbara took the call in the privacy of our bedroom, and I could hear her crying. "Well, we're getting closer every time," I joked, trying to reassure her. Our mutual disappointment was almost a tangible thing, linking us over the miles from Texas to Florida, and I sent another bouquet of flowers to help ease her anxiety. I saw the guys unbuttoning the hatches as we spoke softly to each other. In Bellwood, Dad wondered whether I would launch before he used up all of his vacation time.

A clearly worried Faye Stafford had endured enough and refused to talk to reporters. Too many things had gone wrong with her husband's flights. Out in Weatherford, Oklahoma, Tom's birthplace, his mother, Mary, had gotten out of bed early to watch the launch and wanted him to call so she could take a nap. Mary Stafford had come West as a little girl riding in a covered wagon and didn't get excited about little things.

This time, the launch was postponed for only two more days, long enough to refuel our rocket, check the computers, find the glitch, and get us back on the pad. We held another scrub party, this one sort of brief, because the jokes were old and the pressure shimmered before our eyes. We ended up over at Wolfie's deli, where we considered our situation while I munched a corned beef and pastrami sandwich and ate an enormous kosher pickle. Word came that we were rescheduled for 8:39 A.M. Friday morning, June 3, when the Blob would once again sail over the Cape.

Meanwhile, the ground troops tried to figure out what was wrong with that fiberglass shroud on the nose of the Blob. If it didn't fall away, any attempt to dock would be hopeless because we couldn't reach the collar. One idea raised around the conference tables was that since Cernan was going to be doing a space walk anyway, why not let him just mosey on over to that Agena shroud and shake it free? It was seven and a half feet long and weighed 300 pounds on the ground, but it would not weigh anything in space, argued the people who would not have to do the job. Why not just give it a good swift kick and see what happens? I thought the idea was sort of goofy, but if that was what they wanted, I'd give it a try.

ON FRIDAY, WE DID it all over again, and on the way to the pad, Deke handed us a cardboard cutout of a match, about the size of a baton with a red and white tip, saying that we could use it to light the rocket if all else failed. "Let's go do it," snapped Tom, frustrated at being called the Mayor of Pad 19 because of all the time he spent there.

Some smartass had hung a sign on the door of the gantry elevator. "Tom and Gene: Notice the down capability for this elevator has been removed. Let's have a good flight." It was signed by the spacecraft crew. Big grins all around. It was good that we couldn't talk to anybody, and the humor that day was definitely grim.

Jim and Buzz had been at work for about three hours checking every switch in the spacecraft, and declared it ready. They got a shot in, too, and when we reached the White Room, there was a sign over our hatches:

> *We were kidding before*
>   *But not anymore*
> *Get your ... uh ... selves into space*
>   *Or we'll take your place.*
>   Jim and Buzz

I smiled again, thinking that it would be a cold day in hell before Buzz Aldrin flew as the pilot of *Gemini 9* instead of me.

The guys in Mission Control had worked long and hectic shifts since our last try for launch, refusing to quit until our Titan went up to where it was supposed to be. The earlier glitch was traced to a guidance system made up of some 2,000 parts, in which two little modules hardly as big as your fingernail had stopped talking to each other. New units were tested a hundred times to make sure they worked, then were packed inside the spacecraft.

About the time the Blob was crossing the California coast again, on its thirtieth revolution of the Earth, the White Room swung away from the Titan and, for the third time, we were alone up there, a couple of rather insignificant human beings strapped to the nose of an ICBM. We could see only each other, and everyone else in the world was reduced to small radio voices in our ears. I felt good about this one, and morning light burst into the cabin, a good omen.

The countdown moved flawlessly along, and at the two minute mark, where the computer had tripped the last time, Mission Control fired a final update of steering instructions to a much-tested internal guidance system, and the bird once again refused to accept the transmission. *Not again!*

But this time the engineers were ready with an unusual and nontechnical solution. The hell with it. We had taken another trajectory update only fifteen minutes earlier, and that would do the job. No scrub! "For the third time, go!" Tom growled.

The countdown reached ten seconds and I could almost hear an invisible crescendo of stirring background music. *Anchors aweigh!* Five, four, three, two, one . . . and we had ignition!

To this day, I don't really know what I expected. My training told me it might be like a catapult launch on a carrier, swift and violent, but Tom and others who had flown said it would be, well, different, although they couldn't explain how. Just . . . *different.*

On television, everyone saw clouds of flame and smoke boil from the bottom of the Titan, but inside the spacecraft, the instrument panel had come alive. Dials were jumping, lights shone brightly, the computers spat out strings of numbers, and ground controllers spoke rapidly. There was a noticeable shudder as the Titan's fuel spewed into the tanks and ignited, then I felt a faraway bump as the bolts holding the rocket to the pad blew away, and something amazing happened ten stories under my back at 6:38 on a sunny Florida morning.

I sensed movement, a feeling of slow pulsation, and then heard a low, grinding rumble as that big rocket ship started to lift away from Earth in agonizingly slow motion. The Titan, once a silent, sleeping giant, was now fully awake and flexing its muscles, ready to romp toward an incredible 430,000 pounds of thrust and haul ass out of there like a favorite leaving the gate at the Kentucky Derby. The initial slow ascent turned into a sudden vault of speed, and we were away.

The sides of the rocket were washed by a glistening sun as the Titan pushed off, gaining altitude and speed by the instant. In Mission Control, Flight Director Gene Kranz listened carefully as his controllers reported, station by station. "Good. Excellent. Everything is green and go!" By then, the rocket was galloping out across the Atlantic and the forces of gravity stacked like bricks on my chest. My heart was beating a mile a minute and I gritted my teeth. A glance showed that Tom was gritting his, too.

"We're on our way." At least Tom could speak. On the other side of the spacecraft, his rookie pilot could say nothing at all. As I worked at my assigned tasks, I simultaneously felt and saw things I had never imagined. *God, if only I were a poet.*

Now we were a mere dot at the top of a long, white vapor trail that stretched farther away from Earth by the second, wrapped in a dream of pure speed that built faster and faster, the rocket shaking and bucking as it bulled through the atmosphere. I was proud beyond belief. Only a handful of people in the history of the world had done what I was now doing.

We accelerated steadily, a long dart with a tail of fire, going faster as the fuel burnoff lightened our load and the atmosphere thinned at higher altitudes, giving us less resistance. We were really carrying the mail, but I had many technical and pilot things to do before I could enjoy what was happening. About four minutes into the flight, we approached first stage separation, when the two big engines would shut down and fall away, allowing a smaller second stage to take over propulsion. Tom had told me this was going to be a kick. He was right.

We had been pinned to our seats by about four and a half times the weight of gravity when we staged, and all of that power that had been pushing us so hard vanished in a blink. Burning and roaring like a son-of-a-bitch one moment, then, *bam,* shutdown. We were thrown forward against our straps and lost enough momentum so that the gigantic fireball that had been tailing us, and still had motion of its own, wrapped the spacecraft in a black-ringed cloud of orange and red, roiling and writhing flames alive with pulsing smoke, like some kind of deadly Halloween horror. All I could see was fire, and although I knew exactly what it was and had been told to expect it, my first thought was that we were burning up.

Another blink of the eye, and the second stage engine kicked in, hurtling us right through the fireball. Once again, the G-forces built up and we were pinned against our seats as the second stage burned hot and hard, a new hand pushing us, applying ever-increasing pressure. Eight minutes into the flight, we were pulling seven and a half Gs, grunting to expand our lungs against the incredible pressure.

The rocket burned out a moment before we reached orbit and we went from having to struggle against a monstrously heavy weight even to breathe to absolute nothing. Zero gravity. A few nuts and bolts left behind by workers oozed out of their hiding places, dust particles and a piece of string did a slow dance before my nose. My hands drifted up in the weightlessness and my legs, wrapped in those metal pants, became featherlight.

When Tom maneuvered the spacecraft around so that we could see the Earth, I eagerly looked out the window. Below was a distant blue ocean and a checkerboard of white clouds, then the coast of Africa slid beneath us.

I am in space.

Nice to be here.

12

The Angry Alligator

THE SUCCESSFUL *GEMINI 9* launch was doubly welcomed by the space-hungry American public because it was our second galactic triumph in a single week. Only a few days before Tom and I finally went into orbit, the *Surveyor 1* lunar probe touched down softly upon the Moon and radioed back 144 photographs of possible landing sites. So we were at least even with the Soviets again on the unmanned spacecraft front, even perhaps a little bit ahead, for although their *Luna 9* had landed on the Moon earlier, it had transmitted only nine pictures. On the manned side of the cosmic race, Tom Stafford and I were about to dish up a stew of space records.

WHILE I WAS STILL getting used to weighing exactly zero pounds, my family back on Earth was overcome with emotion. At our place in Nassau Bay, Barbara had been up since I telephoned earlier, and was optimistic.

The household was tense as the countdown progressed and Barbara nervously picked at the already raw skin around her fingernails. When the television set showed our Titan hovering in a rolling cloud of smoke and flame, she turned to Roger and gulped, "Is that normal?" As he said everything looked great, the missile moved, then flew. "Olé!" cried out Lynn Gilligan, Barbara's red-haired cousin, who leaped to her feet and flourished an imaginary bullfighter's cape. While cheers and applause rocked Barbuda Lane, the Titan climbed out of the camera's view and Barbara fell against the sofa cushions, able to breathe again. "Tell the reporters I've fainted," she told a friend.

Eventually, Barbara did wander outside and describe the launch as wonderful and beautiful. "I know Tom and Gene are just in heaven now," she said with an unintentional pun. Reporters noted her face was radiant, in sharp contrast to her pallid, concerned demeanor after the second scrub. Tracy was asked if she knew where I was that morning. "Daddy is going to walk and carry a float," she replied with a yawn. She had been taking swimming lessons and compared my rocket backpack to the life preserver she used in the pool. My daughter's analogy was as good as any I have heard.

"Everybody's prayers have been answered," Mom told the press in Bellwood. "They really made it." Some sixteen relatives, friends, and neighbors had watched the event at the house. "This is the biggest thing of my life," Dad beamed, showing off a Gemini tie clip I'd given him. Out came the coffee and strudel, and later in the day, Dad brought cold beer to the press. Dee had let her third grade students at Lincoln Elementary have the day off so she could watch.

Faye Stafford emerged from her self-imposed exile only after the press offered a bribe of helping to find homes for four new kittens—Fuzz, Fritz, Yap, and Doctor Rendezvous. Prescient as ever, she warned that the headaches of *Gemini 9* might not yet be over. "This is just the first hurdle," she said, aware that the Gemini spacecraft was the product of more than 4,000 contractors in forty-two states. Bill Dana, a comedian with an astronaut routine that was so funny that the Original Seven adopted him as the Eighth Astronaut, liked to point out that every one of Gemini's 1,367,059 parts was made by the lowest bidder.

Do you remember riding down an old country road and going over a big bump, how your stomach would surge into your throat for a moment before settling down? Upon entering zero gravity, *Gemini 9* seemed to go over one hell of a bump, but my stomach didn't come back down. Because of weightlessness, it continued to lurk just behind my tonsils and I felt the woozy onset of motion sickness. Of course, I refused to say anything. I wasn't some nugget on a summer cruise! Many years would pass before astronauts would admit, even to each other, that most of us felt the same way during those first moments in space.

We were in an egg-shaped orbit and hot on the trail of the Blob, while far below, newspapers published special editions: SPACEMEN BREAK GEMINI JINX. The distance between us and our target was 640 miles, and Tom adjusted the high point of our orbit to about 172 miles. We aimed to catch the drifting target faster than it had ever been done before, not an empty exercise, for someday astronauts leaving the Moon would have to perform the same sort of procedure. Forty-nine minutes after we took off, we toddled across Australia and did another thruster burn to lift the low point of our orbit to 144 miles.

Neil Armstrong was CapCom for the first part of our flight, and that was a special comfort, because after his brush with disaster aboard *Gemini 8*, no one was more aware of the dicey environment of space. Anything could happen, and it was great to hear his calm voice pass along information.

We closed the gap to the Blob to 460 miles by the time we hit the Florida coast, and both space vehicles were chugging along at more than 17,500 miles per hour. We passed through a day and a night each time we looped around the world, and a full Moon brightened the night sky with an eerie silver glow as faraway stars beckoned. Time ceased to have meaning and Earth hours became like minutes as we hopscotched through time zones and circled the globe every hour and a half. I buried my nose in calculations, figured in data from radar and our primitive computer, then passed the information to Tom, and we edged ever closer to the orbiting bull's-eye.

THE LAWS OF ORBITAL mechanics are almost as strange as the regulations of the Internal Revenue Service. A reader might logically ask why we didn't just zoom right up to the proper altitude, burn to maximum speed and catch the target. That is an Earth solution and doesn't hold true in space. The fact is that the further away something is from the Earth, the longer it takes to circle it. By staying in a lower orbit, we would get there faster, and only then climb to catch the Blob. So we came in low, for this was a rendezvous, not a race.

On our third orbit, after four adjustments to correct our flight path to an almost perfect circle 170 miles above Earth, we were flying through the night sky over the eastern Pacific again when we spotted a tiny light blinking far ahead of us, and we knew it could not be a star, for they don't twinkle above the atmosphere. It had to be the strobe light on the ATDA. We had found the elusive Blob in record time, completing the first true assignment of our mission, and were in perfect position, 15 miles below and only 126 miles away. We carefully closed the gap and soon were able to see the flashing strobe and some bright blinks from an unknown source. Nothing was supposed to be doing that. Something was wrong.

We maneuvered through a cloud of about a dozen small pieces of space junk that had once been part of the Atlas launch package and had stayed in orbit, flying in peculiar formation with the Blob through the dark sky. Several newspapers ran stories that called the debris "Mysterious UFOs," and for years thereafter, I would be questioned periodically about my "confirmed" contact with unidentified flying objects and mysterious flashing lights in outer space. Several reporters concluded my outright denials only proved that I was part of a giant coverup about what was really out there. Honest, folks, it was just space garbage, not something out of the *X-Files*. Actually, we hoped that two of those pieces of scrap might be the sections of the clamshell-shaped plastic shroud, but when the Sun rose for the fourth time for us that day, it brought bad news. Tom nursed our thruster jets to sidle up and park about three feet from the Blob. It was a sight straight out of some Hollywood special effects laboratory—spinning and tumbling and rolling in slow motion, totally out of control, with the conical nose shroud still attached, the two pieces hanging agape at the front like a giant, open jaw. Tom radioed Houston, "We have a weird-looking machine up here. It looks like an angry alligator."

Such plastic shrouds had gone into space as aerodynamic covers on seventy previous occasions and always had been shed without a problem, opening and falling off in answer to a command from ground controllers. I guess seventy-one straight would have been too much to ask. A pair of thin steel bands held it in place, and only the top one had sheared away, allowing the forward end to spread apart, while the lower portion stayed locked. In the atmosphere, the wind would have swept it away, but in space, where there is no air resistance, the thing stubbornly stayed right where it was. The off-white reflection we had seen earlier was that dirty nose tumbling in the moonlight.

I WAS CONSIDERED TO be somewhat of a chatterbox among the astronauts, and the press noted that Cernan was being "unusually quiet." Of course I was. What was there to talk about? This was another major disappointment and that damned angry alligator seemed to be laughing at us. Unless that stuck shroud could be popped free, it could spell the end for our docking exercises.

Ground controllers sent a stream of signals up to try and open the still-covered collar in an effort to pry off the pesky nose cone. That only pushed out the bottom part of the shroud and forced the other end, which was open, to partially close. Contracting the collar had the reverse effect, and to us, it seemed that those moving jaws were opening and closing. Tom and I held position a few feet from the gyrating thing and talked about our options with Mission Control, where all of those experts were trying to come up with a solution. Eventually we all decided to adopt an alternative flight plan that would have two more rendezvous maneuvers, contain no docking whatsoever because we couldn't reach the collar, and delay my spacewalk for a few hours.

SHROUD BALKS SPACEMEN. Such headlines overshadowed our launch and the speed-record rendezvous, and showed the world the *Gemini 9* jinx was still alive and well, in the form of a big, somersaulting, celestial gator that was chomping empty space. There was some discussion that perhaps Tom could coast in slowly and nudge the Blob with the nose of the *Gemini*. That was discarded because our precious parachutes were stowed in the front end of the *Gemini* and we needed them intact to get home alive.

So there we sat for a couple of hours, watching the alligator, while conferences were held 170 miles below us. One, in particular, posed serious ramifications. According to Deke Slayton, Buzz Aldrin advocated that I spacewalk on over there and snip that spring-loaded metal strap with the surgical scissors from the equipment pack. An experiment on the ground demonstrated the tool could indeed slice the holding band, but also showed that the Blob bristled with dangerous, sharp edges. Deke said top officials in the program "were just aghast" at the idea, which didn't take into consideration the substantial risks of the explosive bolts holding the band together, the tumbling spin of the Blob, our almost total lack of spacewalk experience, or the fact that the band, under tension from a spring, might snap apart, whip back and puncture my suit. It was another recipe for turning me into Satellite Cernan. Deke would write that after that episode, he had a tough time persuading Bob Gilruth, the head of the Manned Spaceflight Center, to allow Buzz to keep his place on *Gemini 12.*

The angry alligator kept its snout while we backed some thirteen miles away and began a second rendezvous exercise. This time we pretended the radar system did not work and we had to rely solely upon our eyes, the stars, the computer, and my trusty pencil and pad, just to prove that it could be done that way. On some other day, some other mission, such a move might save the lives of other astronauts. It turned out to be a bitch of an exercise that demanded unimagined mental and physical effort. Merely finding a dot in the universe without the help of radar was an overwhelming problem with millions of possibilities. Travel on the wrong path for just a little while, and you would never locate it. Eventually we did find the gator, still snapping, and cozied up close once again as we talked to Houston and, privately, to each other on the intercom loop.

Something unexpected was taking place in our little Gemini. After so much hard work getting ready for the mission, the tension of the launches, the actual flying into space, and a pair of tough rendezvous problems, Tom and I were exhausted. We were in perfect physical shape, but felt as if we had been run over by a truck, and the constant dashing through daylight and dark had ruined our body clocks. We barely knew what day it was anymore. Mission Control, reading our medical sensors, recognized that we were tired and told us to get some sack time. We had a big Saturday ahead that included my spacewalk.

We were more than ready to take their advice and Tom goosed the jets to put some space between us and the Alligator, because we didn't want it tumbling nearby while we slept. We parked ninety-two miles away, put the shades over the windows, and chowed down on some yummy chicken and dumplings, a dehydrated meal packed in a toothpaste-like tube. Squirt in water, shake it into mush, then squeeze the goo right into your mouth. No crumbs that way. Not much taste, either. Then I anchored my weightless arms beneath my suit hoses and tried to sleep, tranquilized by music from the Serendipity Singers. It was only five o'clock on Friday afternoon.

The interlude of rest for us also meant a respite down in Texas for our wives and families. Everybody could exhale now and eat some of the food that covered the dining room table. Faye came by to visit Barbara, for they were the only women on Earth at the moment who could understand what the other was going through.

Tom and I officially woke up seven hours later when Mission Control piped up "The Lonely Bull" by the Tijuana Brass, and we still felt like hell. Mexican trumpets blaring in our ears might have contributed to the problem. We had tried to unwind and relax, but our sleep had been more like a period of idleness, and full-Moon madness shone upon our tiny orbiting home, still zipping around the Earth at almost 18,000 miles per hour. My body was cramped into an uncomfortable area that contained absolutely no wiggle room, imaginary ants crawled behind my eyeballs, and my brain felt as responsive as a wad of cotton. A glance at my Omega

Speedmaster watch, still set to Houston time, showed it wasn't quite midnight on Friday, the same day we had launched.

The third and final rendezvous was going to be the toughest, for we were to simulate the procedures an Apollo command module pilot might have to employ to rescue a lunar vehicle stuck in a lower orbit. We would fly nose down and come in from above, trying to find our target, the Blob, hidden somewhere in an impossibly bright background of the blue seas, white clouds, and brilliantly sunlit land masses of Planet Earth.

We could use the radar, but we had serious doubts about some of the data being churned out by the computer. So this tricky bit of navigation would also have to be done by the complicated, slow, and mentally demanding process of manual calculations. When we looked for the target, the mental perception was that we were falling straight down to Earth, and we did not even see the gator until we were within three miles of it. But we got the job done, completing an unprecedented third rendezvous within twenty-four hours.

But the exercise took much longer than anticipated and burned fuel at an alarming rate. Even the spacecraft seemed tired. We had almost 685 pounds of fuel at launch, but only fifty-two pounds were left, barely enough to finish the mission, and we had a complex spacewalk and reentry still to go.

Our physical condition was deteriorating even faster than the fuel, so Tom and I cut off communication with Houston to discuss it. We felt like we had spent the past day digging ditches with teaspoons rather than doing glamorous space stuff. We could barely keep our eyes open and were panting from the exertion like dogs on a hot summer day. Tom took the bit in his teeth and, as the commander, keyed the mike about dawn on Saturday morning and shocked the hell out of everyone listening.

"Right now, we're both pretty well bushed," he told the ground controllers, in his flat, unemotional Oklahoma drawl. "We've been busier'n left-handed paper-hangers up here. I'm afraid it would be against my better judgment to go ahead and do the EVA at this time. Geno and I talked it over and we think it might be better for both of us to knock it off for a while. Perhaps we should wait until tomorrow morning."

We were trying to give the flight directors information they needed, saying, *Let's consider the variables and modify the flight plan to meet changing circumstances.* The original mission profile had been discarded long ago. Our comments, which seemed so natural coming from test pilots examining all options, took on an entirely different meaning for some people on the ground. For the first time in the history of the U.S. space program, a pair of astronauts was questioning an assigned duty!

That furor rumbled like an earthquake. Since NASA wasn't a military operation, we weren't guilty of mutiny or disobeying a lawful order or anything, and everyone agreed that we were in the best position to assess what was happening in that spacecraft. Still, wasn't this like, well, *quitting?* Astronauts don't quit. Locked inside *Gemini 9*, Tom and I were just too damned tired to care.

Mission Control huddled. If Stafford and Cernan said they were too tired to safely continue, then the ground troops would support that decision. Neil's cool voice came up, "It's the ground recommendation that we postpone the EVA 'til the third day. Would you agree with that?"

"We agree heartily with that suggestion," Tom replied. We asked for a rest period, waved farewell to the gator, pulled a safe distance away and dropped off to sleep like a couple of babes.

While we dozed for ten hours, the people running the show stayed busy analyzing what was happening and keeping critics at bay. There was not a hint of criticism anywhere within the program. Gene Kranz told the press it was not unusual for astronauts to get tired early in a busy flight, and our astronaut brethren ringed us with solid support, shooting withering looks at any doubters. If Stafford and Cernan say they are tired, then they're probably close to collapse, the astronauts said. Test pilots don't do something like this without a damned good reason, and you back up your pilots. Neil told the press, "It is the responsibility of a command pilot [to make such a decision] when he feels he is biting off more than he can chew. I'm glad to see Tom use exceptionally good judgment." A NASA doctor added, "It's a red-letter day when you can get an astronaut to admit he's tired."

The semi-comic air that had gripped everyone with the saga of the angry alligator gave way to serious consideration that *Gemini 9* might be headed for failure. Fatigue was no laughing matter.

MISSION CONTROL SPENT HOURS wrapped in meetings to decide if the spacewalk should be canceled because of our physical state. "Obviously, if the crew is not ready, we would not do the EVA," said Gene Kranz. The doctors said part of the problem was that our waking and working hours had been completely turned around. The current situation showed the spacecraft low on fuel, the docking with the Blob was impossible, a strenuous spacewalk lay ahead, and we were already exhausted. After only one day in orbit.

It was time to revise the game plan again. When we finally woke up on Saturday, the ground controllers had decided to abandon any further work with the alligator, and said we should spend the day drifting in space to conserve fuel, perform some minor experiments, take some pictures, and, primarily, rest. The two-and-one-half-hour spacewalk was postponed until Sunday morning, and we would come home Monday.

OUR WIVES, KNOWING US as never-give-up types, had been concerned about the growing physical exertion and told the press they were delighted when the flight was rearranged for us to get some sleep. Barbara and Tracy picked roses in the backyard on Saturday morning and went to mass that afternoon. Faye Stafford and her daughters, Dionne, eleven, and Karin, eight, went shopping.

But they all remained tense and uncertain. In both homes, speaker systems relayed the voices of Mission Control and *Gemini 9*. While others watched television, our wives kept their ears tuned to the scratchy voices of their husbands coming over the squawk boxes, listening for clues no one else could understand. They were not happy with what they heard, for they knew not only our voices, but our moods and habits. We might be able to outfox the doctors, say we were feeling terrific and were ready to rip, but we couldn't sell that line to Barbara and Faye. They knew we were approaching our physical limits.

13
The Spacewalk from Hell

THE FIRST STEP INTO the void of outer space was made by Soviet cosmonaut Alexei Leonov, on March 8, 1965, as Nikita Khruschev demanded still another space spectacular, no matter the risk. The first American to walk in space was Ed White, who went outside the *Gemini 4* spacecraft on June 3 of that same year, because we didn't want the Soviets to do something that we couldn't.

The classic photographs of Ed are among the most famous in history. A man in helmet and protective suit, one hand grasping a wandlike device that squirted jets of gas to propel him, he seems to be having a good old time floating out there above an incredibly blue Earth, connected to the spacecraft only by a crinkly umbilical cord.

The twelve-minute Russian accomplishment, as usual, was shrouded in secrecy. The American version lasted twenty-one minutes and, as usual, was trumpeted by a blaze of publicity. Although we did not realize it at the time, neither spacewalk was what it seemed. Alexei eventually became a close friend and, although he never admitted it publicly, confided in me about his fight for his life during his brief spacewalk. Ed, a man of considerable strength, was barely able to get back into the *Gemini 4* capsule, and was exhausted by the time the hatch was closed.

More than thirty years later, it can be safely said that we didn't know diddly-squat about walking in space when I popped my hatch open on *Gemini 9*, exactly a year and two days after Ed had romped outside for a few minutes. It's a sobering reflection when I think about it now, and I thank God that I lived through the experience.

IN THE SPACE PROGRAM, everything was designed to advance in baby steps. A test with minimum expectations would be conducted; then another a bit more complex, and so on until the ultimate goal was reached.

Each Mercury flight had extended our knowledge a little further, and the whole reason for Gemini was to lay stepping stones toward Apollo.

This careful method had gotten us safely to where we were, but political considerations and the pace of new and untested technology were starting to bend that rule of caution.

One of the first examples of how things were moving too swiftly came with my spacewalk. Ed's only jobs were to test the spacesuit, a hand-held propulsion device, and the umbilical cord that fed his life-support system from the spacecraft to his suit. Now we leaped to an unrealistic schedule of two and a half hours of hard work for me. Had Dave Scott been able to conduct his *Gemini 8* spacewalk, we would have known much more, but that had been scrubbed when the mission was terminated.

My journey was loaded with experiments and tests. The highlight would come when I strapped on the rocket-powered backpack and scooted around the universe on my own. Good idea, but faulty assumptions, overly ambitious goals, and the hurry-up attitude known as "Go fever" were about to send me walking into an unknown and dangerous environment.

FAR AWAY FROM THE angry alligator, Tom and I spent almost four hours Sunday morning preparing for the spacewalk. Going carefully through an eleven-page checklist, we dropped to a lower orbit, and I pulled a boxy chestpack from a shelf above my left shoulder, strapped it on, and plugged a twenty-five-foot-long umbilical into the middle. The umbilical would feed me oxygen, communications, and electrical power from the spacecraft, and relay information from medical sensors that could be monitored on the ground. Getting the umbilical out of its container in zero gravity was like setting free a twisting garden hose that wanted to worm its way throughout the small cabin. Then we helped each other lock on our helmets, shut the visors, pull the heavy gloves on over silk ones, and pressurize the suits, which went from soft to rock hard around our bodies. When I pumped my suit up to three and one half pounds of pressure per square inch, the suit took on a life of its own and became so stiff that it didn't want to bend at all. Not at the elbow, the knee, the waist, or anywhere else. It was as if I wore a garment made of hardened plaster of paris, from fingertip to toe.

My unique suit had been rather unyielding to begin with, for a very good reason. An astronaut inside a spacecraft did not need the same amount of insulation as someone doing a spacewalk. Out where I was going, the temperature in unfiltered sunlight would be many times hotter than any desert at high noon on Earth, while the nighttime cold could freeze steel until it was as brittle as glass. Without those multiple layers of protection, I could be broiled or frozen in an instant.

We finished emptying the oxygen from the spacecraft and made sure the suits were not leaking as we rode through the night sky, coming toward a dawn that would allow my spacewalk to begin over the United States, for better visibility and communication with Houston.

Mission Control ran a final check of all systems and sent up permission for me to open the hatch. During our thirty-first revolution of the Earth, Sunday morning in Houston but still night for me, I grabbed the big handle right above my head and gave it a twist. I remembered before launch how it had taken several men to wrestle the heavy hatch closed, but in zero gravity, it moved smoothly, reacting to gentle pressure. "This is *Gemini 9*. We are now going to walk," I told everyone.

When the hatch stood open, I barely pushed against the floor of the spacecraft and my suit unfolded from the seated position. I grabbed the edges of the hatch and climbed out of my hole until I stood on my seat. Half my body stuck out of *Gemini 9*, and I rode along like a sightseeing bum on a boxcar, waiting for the Sun to come up over California.

And, oh, my God, what a sight. Nothing had prepared me for the immense sensual overload. I had poked my head inside a kaleidoscope, where shapes and colors shifted a thousand times a second.

"Hallelujah!" was the best I could muster. "Boy, it sure is beautiful out here." I did not have the words to match the scene. No one does. Outer space was dead and empty while simultaneously alive and vibrant.

Since we were rushing along at about 18,000 miles an hour, we hurried the dawn. Pure darkness gave way to a ghostly mist-gray, then a thin, pale band of fragile blue appeared along the broad and curving horizon. It changed quickly to a deeper hue over narrow bands of gold, and then the Sun, a brilliant disk, jumped up to ignite a sky where night had ruled only a moment before, and its rays slowly erased the darkness on our planet below. Blue water shimmered on both sides of the Baja peninsula beneath California and the deserts of our Southwest shone like polished brass. An ivory lacework of thin, soft clouds stretched for miles. This was like sitting on God's front porch. The heavenly canopy surrounding me was still soot black, but stars could no longer be seen, and the subfreezing cold of the space night yielded to new, broiling hot temperatures. We crossed the coast of California in the full flare of the morning Sun, and in a single glance, I could see from San Francisco to halfway across Mexico.

Time was my friend for allowing me a few moments to absorb this panorama, but it could also be an enemy. I had to tear myself away from sightseeing and get to work. While Tom held my foot to anchor me, I positioned a sixteen-millimeter Mauer movie camera on its mount and retrieved a nuclear emulsion package that recorded radiation data and measured the impact of space dust. Then I stretched forward and planted a small mirror on the nose of the spacecraft. Using it, Tom could watch when I started my trek back to the AMU.

After that, I prepared for my first big chore, evaluating something called "umbilical dynamics." I did not have the sort of space gun for mobility that Ed White had, for my job was to determine whether a person could maneuver in space just by pulling on the long umbilical tether.

So I pushed off and rose like a puppet on a string. I had been weightless for two days already, so that sensation wasn't new, but now I was moving away from my security blanket, the protective shell of *Gemini 9*. Instead of being trapped inside a claustrophobic spacecraft, I was suddenly surrounded by the limitless universe. Only two other men had ever experienced such a sensation. I did not feel lonely, for I knew the whole world was keeping up with my every move.

Some NASA shrinks had warned that when I looked down and saw the Earth speeding past so far below, I might be swamped by space euphoria, as if I was in a headlong fall. Ridiculous. My world was relative not to the Earth, but to the spacecraft, and we were bulleting along at exactly the same velocity. There was no disorientation whatsoever, and we never worried about space euphoria again.

My only connection with the real world was through the umbilical cord, which we called the "snake," and it set out to teach me a lesson in Newton's laws of motion. My slightest move would affect my entire body, ripple through the umbilical, and jostle the spacecraft. We were forced into an unwanted game of crack-the-whip, with Tom inside the Gemini and me on the other end of the snake.

Since I had nothing to stabilize my movements, I went out of control, tumbling every which way, and when I reached the end of the umbilical, I rebounded like a Bungee jumper, and the snake reeled me in as it tried to resume its original shape. I hadn't even done anything yet and was already losing the battle. There had been no advance warning on the difficulties I was having because everything I did was new. I was already beyond the experiences of White and Leonov, moving into uncharted territory. Nobody in history had ever done this before.

I felt as if I was wrestling an octopus. The umbilical cavorted with a life of its own, twirling like a ribbon, trying to trap me like a cord winding around a window shade. "Boy, that snake is really running around up here," I said. I was looping crazily around the spacecraft, ass over teakettle, as if slipping in puddles of space oil, with no control over the direction, position or movement of my body, and all the while the umbilical was trying to lasso me. I wasn't lost in space, but I was absolutely helpless. Without a stabilizing device, I had no control over the umbilical, and it pretty much did whatever it wanted. "I can't get to where I want to go," I told Tom in exasperation. "The snake is all over me."

It was not like hauling along on a taut rope, for I had to pull slowly, exactly through my center of gravity, and that was impossible. Even something as mundane as trying to unbend a kink in the umbilical would dangle me upside down or backward, and I was continuously tumbling in a slow-motion ballet. The only time I had any control at all was when I could grab tight just where the umbilical emerged from the hatch, as if holding a dog on a short leash. Otherwise the thing was rubbery as a worm and as stubborn as a curlicue telephone cord. It was flat-out mean.

I fought it for about thirty minutes before deciding that this snake was perhaps the most malicious serpent since the one Eve met in the Garden of Eden.

HAVING ALREADY SET A record time for being outside a spacecraft, I needed a rest. I grabbed a small handrail and pawed my way back to the open hatch, a drowning man reaching for a titanium beach. Once stabilized, I took a deep breath. And burped. The briny taste of that big green pickle I devoured during the last scrub party five days ago returned and would haunt me for the rest of the spacewalk.

My aimless roller-coaster experience with the umbilical complete, I passed my conclusions on to Tom and Mission Control. Future spacewalkers, when they were out where the only rules were push and pull, action and reaction, needed some means of propulsion for control, and the spacecraft needed more points and rails to grab. Without such tools, they, too, would flop around like a rag doll.

I took a short break before moving to the rear of the spacecraft, where the backpack was stowed, and again was faced with the enormity of what lay before my eyes, a feast for the senses. When viewed through the spacecraft window, outer space had been only six inches wide and eight inches high, but now . . . wow!

The naked Sun, an intense ball of gleaming white fire, stared at me, a tiny interloper in its realm. The view of Earth was incredible from my treehouse in the galaxy as my home planet swooshed beneath my boots. The blue horizon had vanished at sunrise and now was merely a tissue-thin curved band of cerulean color terminating in black space. From up where there was no weather, I looked down on the tops of thunderstorms and the giant cottony fingers of Hurricane Alma. In the open seas, I could make out the V-shape wakes of ships, and on land, the dark grids of major cities. Mountain ranges spawned graceful rivers that slid toward the oceans, and I could see the Mississippi wiggling down to New Orleans. A rainbow-wide palette of colors presented emerald rainforests and bronze deserts, sapphire water and ivory clouds, and above it all, total blackness. Try to imagine a place with no boundaries, a room with no walls, an empty well as deep and limitless as your imagination, for that is where I was. And it was going to be my home for the next few hours!

The clock was ticking and I needed to reach the rear of the spacecraft while I still had sunlight, then check out the backpack and strap it on during darkness. Then I would exchange the umbilical connected to my chest pack for the power and oxygen contained within the AMU, and tether myself to the spacecraft with a 125-foot-long piece of thin nylon line. So the next time the Sun popped up, Tom would flip a switch, the single bolt holding the backpack to the Gemini would shear, and I'd be off, rocketing around on my own, the first human to be an independent satellite. Master of the Universe.

BUT FIRST, I HAD to get to where the backpack was folded up like some bizarre bird in a nest. My space suit fought my every move, and I needed both flexibility and mobility, the two things it did not have. It was blown up like a balloon figure in the Macy's Thanksgiving parade, and tried to hold that shape, no matter how I sought to bend it. Push in on a party balloon and it will resume its original shape when your finger pressure is removed. Same thing in outer space. A diamond-shaped web of material had been woven within the suit for additional strength, giving it all the flexibility of a rusty suit of armor. Just to bend my arm required exerting muscle strength to hold the new position. My heartbeat increased with the effort, and I was breathing hard, trying to find leverage. I was thankful for those long hours I had spent in a gym, building muscles and staying in shape.

The bell-shaped Gemini package was made of two sections. When the second-stage rockets tore away after launch, we were left with the reentry module, which was our living and working environment, and behind that was a larger section like a caboose on a train. Designed to connect the reentry module to the rocket, the aerodynamic "adapter section" contained things like fuel cells, oxygen tanks, and mechanical apparatus. When the booster rocket was kicked away, a recessed area was exposed at the bottom of the adapter section, and in the middle of that inward curving base was my rocket pack.

I worked my way hand-over-hand along a small railing, stopping periodically to hook the umbilical through small rings similar to the wire supports that hold a TV antenna cable stretched above a rooftop. By putting the umbilical through one of those "eyes," my line of life support would be steady and out of harm's way. Or so I thought until I found a nasty surprise waiting at the end of the adapter section. A jagged, sawtooth edge had been left all the way around when the Titan ripped away, something nobody had thought about when planning my spacewalk. With careful fingers, I positioned the supporting wires just above the razor-sharp metal to prevent it from slicing my lifeline or my suit. A space suit with a hole in it can quickly become the shroud of a corpse.

As I swung around the rear of the adapter and vanished from Tom's view in the mirror, the Sun blinked out and we entered darkness over South Africa. I unfolded the restraining bars alongside the backpack, and clicked on a pair of tiny lights for illumination. Only one lit up, providing less help than a candle. I raised my golden outer visor and grabbed the bars tightly.

Lord, I was tired. My heart was motoring at about 155 beats per minute, I was sweating like a pig, the pickle was a pest, and I had yet to begin my real work. I held on for dear life to those two thin metal bars as I was hauled through space at the incredible speed of some five miles per second.

BARBARA HAD GOTTEN UP early that morning and, after some coffee, stood before her closet, planning what to wear. The women of America would be eyeing what Mrs. Astronaut wore when she stepped to the microphones to say how proud she was of her husband. She chose a pink sweater and pants, then swept her ash-blond hair into a pyramid of curls. Tracy was also dressed in pink, matching her mom, and they were camera-ready knockouts.

Many astronauts and cosmonauts had gone up in rockets, so a launch, even one as troublesome as *Gemini 9*, had become somewhat routine for the nation's huge audience of spaceophiles. Only two, however, had ever walked in space. I had coached Barbara as much as possible on what to expect, but since I really had no firm idea what it was going to be like, both of us had to accept the unknown. Roy Neal of NBC, an old friend, had come by for a visit and she confided, "I'm so scared." Roy took her by the hand and replied, "Let me tell you something, and never forget it. The more times they fly, the more they learn and the better chance they have of success."

When I opened the hatch, all she knew was that her 176-pound husband was out there seeing and feeling things about which mankind had only dreamed. Roger Chaffee spread out charts and briefing papers in the living room that morning, ready to explain every detail and answer any questions she might have, and the Mission Control squawk box relayed our conversations. Martha walked over with her husband to lend moral support, and slowly our living room filled with people. On television, the spacewalk explanations of anchormen were supplemented by dangling puppets that were supposed to represent me.

TOM COULD NO LONGER see me preparing the backpack for the ride of a lifetime, but the communications link through the umbilical allowed me to explain that things weren't quite going as expected. "It's pretty much of a bear getting at this thing," I told him.

The single working light, not much more than a flashlight bulb, was totally inadequate. I could barely see anything at all as I worked through the thirty-five different functions required to make the thing ready to fly, everything from pushing buttons and opening valves to connecting the oxygen supply. My exertions were taking a toll because what seemed simple during our Earth simulations was nearly impossible in true zero gravity. I had done this exercise a hundred times aboard an Air Force cargo plane that could fly a maneuver to create weightlessness for about twenty seconds. *The airplane said I can do this, so why isn't it working?* Sweat beaded on me and stung my eyes. The helmet prevented me from wiping them. Eventually I flipped the final switch and the backpack powered up. Almost time to fly.

An hour and thirty-seven minutes into my spacewalk, as I became the first human ever to circle the Earth outside a spacecraft and see the night on his own planet during a spacewalk, our old nemesis, the Gemini jinx, struck again.

I was having a hard time seeing things, but it took a while to realize that it wasn't just because of the darkness. I was working so hard that the artificial environment created by the space suit simply could not absorb all of the carbon dioxide and humidity I was pumping out. Vision through my helmet was as mottled as the inside of a windshield on a winter morning, and I told Tom, "This visor is sure fogging up." That's when the spacecraft commander became concerned, perhaps thinking about his little chat with Deke about what to do in the event I could not get back into the spacecraft.

Why is floating in space and turning a few dials so difficult? Let me give you a couple of tests. Connect two garden hoses and turn on the water. Now, using only one hand, try to unscrew them. Or, hold a bottle of soda or beer at arm's length, and using a single hand, remove the twist-off top. For extra reality, run a mile before you start so you're nice and tired, do it while wearing two pairs of extra-thick gloves and close your eyes to simulate being unable to see. Stand on your head while doing some of these things to resemble tumbling in space. You get the idea.

The major problem was my inability to purchase any leverage without the help of gravity. A couple of thin metal stirrups designed to hold my feet in place were entirely insufficient, and to get some stability, I slid my right foot beneath the loop and stood on it, hard, with the left. Like an old sailor who always kept one hand on a brace when aloft, I held tightly to the restraining bar with one hand while working with the other. Sheer arm and wrist strength was needed just to stay in place, and I was again thankful for the long hours that Charlie Bassett and I spent lifting weights to develop muscular forearms.

As soon as one end of me was stabilized, the other end tended to float away. The work was more than hard, and I was panting for breath as my heartbeat soared to 180 beats per minute. Since the visor was fogged on the inside, and I obviously couldn't remove the helmet to wipe it dry, my only choice was to rub my nose against the inside of the shield to make a hole through which I could see.

Then the backpack itself was a complex piece of machinery, loaded with valves and levers and dials, many tucked away in hard-to-reach places, forcing me to rely on the reflection in a polished metal mirror on my wrist, and on the reduced sense of touch through bulky space gloves.

When I tried to turn one of the valves, Mr. Newton's laws of motion would go into effect, the valve would turn me equally as hard in the opposite direction, and there I would go again, drifting off into space. Without leverage, just turning a small knob was nearly impossible: *Agghhhh*, my body went the other way until I could snag a new handhold. Then my feet would flip free again. Weariness threatened to overcome me and my body screamed for a rest period, but I could not oblige, for I was in a race with the Sun. This was my only chance and I couldn't afford to quit. At dawn, I was supposed to be wearing this damned backpack, and, by God, I intended to do just that. If my body could hold out. I was sucking oxygen at a fearsome rate, and always at the edge of my mind was that sharp, sawtoothed metal ring around the adapter section, which threatened to prick my suit while I tumbled without direction.

For ease of stowage, the slick arms of the backpack were telescoped and folded, and trying to get them extended into place was akin to straightening wet spaghetti. I pulled, and the arms pulled back. I twisted them and they twisted me. Progress was measured in millimeters and rapid heartbeats. I eventually got them locked into place, turned, and slid my bottom onto the little saddle seat, and strapped in with a common seatbelt.

Although my mask was cold, my lower back was scalding hot. During the somersaults of daylight umbilical dynamics, I had ripped apart the rear seams on those seven inner layers of heavy insulation and the Sun had baked the exposed triangle of unprotected skin. Now I had a major sunburn and nothing could be done about it until I took off the suit, which would be at least another day. I had a lot bigger things to worry about at the moment, so I disregarded the fiery sensation.

Now I had to exchange the umbilical from the spacecraft for the oxygen and power contained in the backpack itself. More twisting and turning, but at least now, being buckled in, I had a bit of leverage, and could make the swap. It was the first time that a human had cut the secure lifeline to a spacecraft. I was now really out there on my own.

By doing so, I lost radio contact with Tom. The communications link that ran through the umbilical was gone, replaced by a little line-of-sight radio in the backpack. Since I was in the rear of the adapter section and Tom was in the spacecraft, the weak signal couldn't penetrate the steel between us. When I spoke, he heard mostly crackling garble and barely heard me report, "I can't see in front of my eyeballs."

He told the ground controllers, who could not hear me, that the workload was about four or five times more than what had been anticipated, that communications had degraded, and I couldn't see through my visor. "If the situation doesn't improve . . . call it a no go on the AMU. Let him stay there and rest a while." Although I knew he was only being prudent, I had hoped he would not say that, because it just gave Mission Control reason to scrub my flight with the backpack.

Prior to switching over from the umbilical, the medical teams on Earth had been able to read data from my body sensors. Now they could not, and being a rather hand-wringing lot by nature, the doctors grew alarmed. They had lost control! They knew I had been panting with exertion, although I had tried not to breathe heavily. The last thing I wanted was for important decisions to be reached because of pessimism around the flight surgeon's console, for I knew my situation much better than anyone on the ground.

Nevertheless, their most recent charts determined I was spending energy at a rate equivalent to running up a flight of 116 steps every minute. My normal heartbeat had almost tripled, and in their expert opinions, things had gone haywire and I was in a zone from which I might not return. Cernan, they declared, was in deep trouble.

I still wasn't ready to admit that, and gulped with a sense of disappointment at the realization of what must be going on in Mission Control. I had come so far and now this unique chance to accomplish something never done before might be snatched away from me. It was ridiculous, I thought, to have worked my ass off to get this far and not go all the way. If they were going to quit, they should have said so back when I was wrestling the snake. *I'm so close!* My determination not to fail could either lead to one of the greatest achievements in space exploration, or it could lead to my ultimate downfall and cost me my life. Tired as I was, I still wanted to go for it.

Sitting on my tiny throne, I rubbed my nose against the mask again to make a hole in the vaporous shield and peeked out. It was still night, and Australia was passing beneath me, lights sprinkling Perth in the west and Sydney in the east, on opposite coasts of that sprawling continent. I knew that on the other side of the world, where the Sun still shone, were my wife, our little daughter, everything that I loved and held dear. Space, for the first time, seemed hostile, as if I had finally met my match. I had to admit to myself that I was barely hanging on, but I still wanted to fly that damned backpack.

Wisdom prevailed on all of us as the Sun came up.

"Can you see out at all, Geno?" Tom's voice crackled, almost indecipherable. "Can you read me okay? Yes or no?" I shouted into my microphone but he could barely understand me, so we had a garbled, stilted discussion, and reached a disappointing decision.

"Okay," he said, "Your transmission is awfully garbled. Okay. Did you get the word? I say it's a no go . . . because you can't see it now. Switch back to the spacecraft electrical umbilical."

It was the correct decision, and Tom wasn't about to reconsider. He passed word to the ground. "Hawaii, *Gemini 9.*"

The tracking station in Hawaii acknowledged.

"We called it quits with the AMU," said Tom. "We had no choice."

"Roger, we concur," came the reply.

"Gene said to pass along that he hated to do it, but he doesn't have any choice, and neither do I."

"Roger. We understand." And that was it for the nonflight of the rocket backpack.

With a sigh, I closed my eyes and turned my helmet to the new morning Sun so the warmth could defrost away some of the moisture on the visor. I had done all I could. I hadn't quit, and had been ready to romp if that had been the decision. Regretfully, the choice was taken out of my hands, and although I didn't particularly like leaving the job undone, I knew it was the right thing to do. It was time to go home.

Only two things left—getting out of the AMU and back into the spacecraft. Unstrapping, getting reconnected to the spacecraft umbilical and climbing out around the adapter section, carefully retrieving my lifeline as I went, was easier than going out, but time consuming. But I wasn't as gentle and precise this time. The AMU no longer had a mission on this flight and I didn't care about the damned thing any longer. Ten million dollars the Air Force had paid to build the gizmo and we were going to kick it into space and let it burn up in the atmosphere without a second thought.

Time sped by as I escaped the clutches of the backpack, and crawled and clawed my way back up the side of the spacecraft. The inflated space suit had lost none of its stiffness over the past two hours and the visor was clouded solid. My last reserves of energy were flowing out like a tide, and my problems were not over. In fact, one of the hardest parts of the mission was just at my fingertips.

THE SPACEWALK HAD BEEN on almost everyone's mind. Professional golfer Bert Yancey was so engrossed watching the television reports in his motel room that he forgot his tee time for the final round of the $100,000 Memphis Open. In Rome, Pope Paul VI offered a prayer for us during his address from the Apostolic Palace. At that point, I appreciated all the help I could get.

In Texas, worry had crept into our living room. Two hours into my spacewalk, Roger was concerned that what he was hearing didn't match the original mission plan. He left the room to talk privately on a special red telephone that was a direct link to Mission Control. When he returned, his face was tight, and he sat down with Barbara to examine the timeline again.

"Gene's got about twenty-five minutes before he hits the dark side again," he told her. "Without the Sun, it will be colder, and his face mask will fog up worse than ever." Then he raised a subject that few had thought about until that point. "That will make it difficult for him to get back into the spacecraft."

Barbara nodded. "How long will it take to get back in?" she asked.

Roger looked her in the eye. "About twenty minutes." A five-minute margin had never seemed so tiny.

Martha edged closer and put an arm around my wife. "Come on Gene," she whispered. "Get back in."

FROM ED'S EXPERIENCE, WE knew that climbing back into the spacecraft was going to be a bitch. Instead of saying it was difficult, Ed should have said it was damned near impossible. If an astronaut was taller than five-foot-nine, he could not stretch out in the cramped cabin without bumping his head or feet. Even without the helmet, I was six feet tall, which meant I was going to have to scrunch down quite a bit to get back inside. I was also exhausted and wearing steel pants. But no Navy mission is finished until a pilot lands on the carrier, and in outer space, the job isn't done until the spacecraft hatch is closed and locked.

After I had left the hatch, we had closed it to about three inches to allow room for the snake to emerge but also to protect the interior of the craft from the direct rays of the broiling Sun. I groped blindly with my fingers to find the hatch. "I can't see," I told Tom, as I hunted for something familiar. My wandering gloves finally wrapped around the hatch and I lifted it open, turned and stuck my feet inside. Tom, who had reeled in the umbilical, now reached over and grabbed an ankle to anchor me and, at last, put an end to my weightless ballet.

But I kicked the Hasselblad camera that Tom had used to take pictures of my spacewalk. The camera floated out before my eyes and I made a grab for it, as if I were a first baseman going after a foul ball. The bulky glove hit it, and as I no longer had the strength to keep my fingers flexed enough to hold it tightly, the camera spun away. There went my still pictures, but I did retrieve the movie camera.

We were over the Atlantic when I began my eerie effort to squeeze into the spacecraft. Tom held my feet as the inflexible space suit fought like a live thing. Trying to bend it was like trying to fold an inflated life raft. Tom was unable to help any more than he was doing, and there was no one else around, so it was me against the suit and the spacecraft. I was panting hard with the effort, still taking care what I said, because the doctors were listening.

I inched lower and forced my legs to bend into a duckwalk position with Tom holding my feet on the L-shaped seat. If he let go so I could try and stick my legs into the well beyond the seat, I would just float away again, so I tried to crouch. Excruciating pain shot through my thighs as I pulled my body lower, pretzeling like a space limbo dancer, and managed to slide my toes, then my heels over the edge of the seat while pushing my knees beneath the instrument panel. My boots were now planted firmly against a steel plate that sealed the front side of the seat, toes pointed down, and my legs were bent in an awful V position as I pressed down even further on them. I had no choice but to ignore the painful cramps.

My goal was to get my butt flat in the seat and my spine against the backrest, but that was impossible because of the stiff, inflated suit. Effort turned to struggle, then to outright fight as I gained territory a sweaty millimeter at a time. My heart rate, which had calmed somewhat, shot up again as I squirmed about, and I was sucking air forty times a minute.

But this is what Mission Control heard. "Coming in, no problem," Tom said. "No problem," I agreed. No use telling the doctors more than they needed to know. They couldn't help anyway.

I got my fingers around the bottom of the instrument panel and pulled again. Another bit of movement as I wedged my knees beneath the panel so I could use them for even more leverage. That was a tight fit when the suit was soft, and almost impossible when inflated. Go like this, *unnhhh*. Like that, *arrghh*. Push and wiggle and push again, try to *ohhhh*, force the suit to bend. It was worse than trying to stuff a cork back into a champagne bottle.

Eventually, I was halfway in and halfway out the spacecraft, still using all my strength to shove my bulk down into the cabin. I forced my shoulders below the level of the hatch, scrunched down as hard as I could, bent my neck and head at an impossible angle, and pulled on the hatch. It hit the top of my helmet and wouldn't close. Sonofabitch! I still was not in far enough.

Tom reached over with his right hand and grabbed a broomsticklike handle with a chain on it that he could pull to lower my hatch further, and with a jolt, jammed it down another few inches. That caught the hatch on the first tooth of a closing ratchet, which was good, but made things worse than ever for me. I was compressed to a point where I had nothing left to bend and the damned door still wasn't secure. Another scrunch, and I was in awful pain. The body just wasn't built to fold like a piece of paper.

Finally, the latches engaged and I pumped the handle until the hatch closed enough so that it could not pop open. Pain clouded my eyes and I was frozen in place by the suit, unable to unfold my feet, which were still tight beneath me. I could not push my torso any lower, and my knees were immobile, pressed hard against the underside of the panel. We got another click. More work, more clicks from the closing ratchet as I ground my teeth. No bones had yet broken, although I don't know why. I'd never known such pain. I gave the handle a last twist, and the hatch finally locked tight.

I might admit that I was crying, but only Tom really knows. "Tom," I whispered on our private intercom, feeling mortally wounded. "If we can't pressurize the spacecraft in a hurry and I have to stay this way for the rest of the flight, I'll die!" I just couldn't remain trapped in that awful position. Air could not get to my lungs, spots danced before my eyes, and incredible agony lanced through me as I clung to the edge of consciousness.

Tom didn't waste a second, and the hiss of the incoming oxygen pressurizing the spacecraft was the most beautiful sound I had ever heard. As the pressure increased, the suit mercifully softened. When I could move my legs, I painfully unfolded my feet and straightened my body, finally able to fit back into the little seat.

I removed helmet and inhaled sweet oxygen. My face was as red as a radish and Tom was shocked by the sight. One ironclad rule of our training was never, ever to spray water inside a spacecraft, because the floating bubbles might short out electrical circuits. Tom didn't hesitate. He grabbed the water nozzle, pointed it at me like a pistol and squirted streams of liquid coolness onto my burning skin. I closed my eyes with relief, feeling saved, resurrected, back from the near-dead.

I had spent two hours and nine minutes in space, and in that time had "walked" some 36,000 miles, making one complete circle of the world and more than one-third of the way around again. The job was done and I lived to tell the tale, although the memory still makes me tired.

When things calmed, we had the rest of the day to relax, which I was happy to do. I was as weary as I had ever been in my life and when I peeled off my gloves, my hands had swollen so much that the metal ring cuffs ripped the skin from them. At that point, I was so elated at just being alive that I didn't care about losing a few strips of flesh.

I was confident that no one could have fared any better on the spacewalk, for the unforeseen problems I encountered would have been the same for anyone. But the fact remained that I had been sent out to do a job and didn't get it done.

I wasn't worried so much about the whole world watching me, because most people wouldn't understand what had happened anyway. The audience that concerned me was my fellow astros, and there was a clear feeling in my own mind that, somehow, I had screwed up, that I had let them down. I had given it my all, and looking back over the years, I now know that the mission had been pretty damned ambitious from the start. But at that moment, I didn't know how to make the guys appreciate the problems. I knew they would never say anything to my face, but sly comments were sure to be made in a few private conversations around the office. *The rookie couldn't hack it. A real test pilot would have found some way to make the thing work.* Did that equate with failure on my part? So much had gone wrong with *Gemini 9*, would this be my one and only flight? Would anybody understand?

Well, at least we were headed home. The mission was about done and after eight hours of rest time, we would get ready for reentry. I settled into a worried sleep, comforted by the thought that I was returning to

Earth a lot smarter than when I had left, and believing that with only a few hours remaining and little to do, not much else could go wrong. Should have known better.

MIDNIGHT IN TEXAS, AND things were quiet. Security patrols kept an eye on the house. Not a creature was stirring, except for one. Barbara couldn't sleep after the excitement of the day, and lay in bed listening to static on a squawk box, the volume turned low. Nothing was going on in space.

She had been relieved when the news came that I was safely back inside and the hatch was locked, and the celebration that followed was tempered by her staying close to the intercom box, listening for my voice. Then most of the visitors went home, the press vanished, Ry and Grandma Cook went to sleep, and Tracy snuggled into her frazzled Linus blanket. Barbara was finally alone.

She walked out into our backyard and stood on the patio we had built together, and looked up at the dark sky. Somewhere up there was her husband, and she could not see him or reach him, nor could he reach her. The scent of roses and gladiola that we had planted surrounded her on that warm night, and she rested her hand over a stack of tan bricks I was slowly turning into a barbeque pit. That was a project to finish in the future, which meant there would be a future. Although I was far away, I was also close, and I was coming home. The heavy, private burden borne by an astronaut's wife was not unlike the uncertainty felt by the wives of the sailors who took the *Niña*, *Pinta*, and *Santa Maria* across unknown seas to find a new world five hundred years ago.

14

Redemption

WE JETTISONED THE AMU backpack before going to sleep to get rid of its package of explosive fuel, which was nothing less than a cache of live ammunition. Then, on Monday morning, we cut free the adapter section, which had been both its garage and our equipment bay, and pitched the spacecraft around so the blunt end faced forward, with the retrorockets exposed. It was time for a rocky ride back to Planet Earth.

Somewhere past Hawaii and heading toward California, while we were still in darkness 160 miles above the Pacific, ground controllers gave us a countdown and we fired the retros at 8:26 A.M. *Pow!* Talk about a kick! After being in zero gravity for three days, it was like being hammered right back to Honolulu. My ever-eloquent commander, Tom, had warned that the retros would be a "kick in the ass," and he wasn't lying. The violent power slammed us so hard that for a moment, I couldn't even speak. It lasted only a few seconds, slowing the spacecraft by a mere 300 miles per hour, but that was enough to let Earth's gravity nibble at us. We released the now-useless retro package and exposed the heat shield beneath it.

Since we were flying with our backs to the shield, our little windows pointed out over the thin nose of the spacecraft, which was angled away from the Earth and toward the blackness of space. A little accelerometer on the instrument panel stirred to show that we were pulling one-half of one-tenth of one G, a pressure so light that we could not yet even feel it, but proof enough that we were slowing down.

As we slapped into molecules of air, the G-forces built rapidly and my eyes were drawn to the new and unparalleled scene forming beyond our window. A streak of orange flashed past, a skinny lightning bolt that instantly vanished into space. From the other side, a green streak zipped by, then, all around us, brilliant stripes of blue, red and purple came faster and faster as the blunt end of *Gemini 9* collided with the thick atmosphere. Traveling at thousands of miles per hour, the friction of the spacecraft crashing through air created a ball of fire, and heat built inside the cabin. The last words we heard before the radio was silenced were: "Have a good trip home."

The computer gave us reentry readings and Tom rolled the off-center spacecraft slightly, fifty degrees to the left, then thirty-eight degrees back to the right, taking numerical aim at the targeted landing zone some 350 miles east of Cape Kennedy, half a world away.

That slight corkscrewing movement made the long tongues of flame trailing along behind us like sleek wings swirl and curve over each other, brightly fluorescent in the darkness. Shades of oranges and yellows and glowing reds, shining blues and greens intermingled, coiling in a colorful spiral. Our movie camera photographed the fire streaking away from the heat shield to join the tail of flame. Individual sparks would land for an instant on the nose, stick and glow like playful imps, then be swept away by the gigantic wind created by our passing. It was goodbye to darkness and hello to a light show that would put a rock concert to shame. Then the fire completely enveloped us, the blaze coating the spacecraft and spreading from the burning heat shield all the way back beyond the nose, merging at some unseen point far behind.

The forces of gravity climbed steadily, past four Gs, past five and going up as we burned our way through the wall of silence. It felt as if the Jolly Green Giant was stomping on my chest. Radio waves could not pierce the blazing turbulence. Fire was all I could see, and the radio would be dead for at least four minutes while we sailed through this 3,000-degree hell. It is claimed that there are no atheists in foxholes. I know there are none in spacecraft plunging back to Earth in a ball of fire, and I said a quick prayer. We had on our gloves and helmets, mine still soaked with sweat from the spacewalk, and lay back, inert, with no choice but to ride out the storm. Ninety-two miles above the California coastline, and sliding down to sixty miles over New Mexico. Our speed over Texas had slowed to a poky 700 miles per hour.

The colors generated by our chariot of fire mesmerized me and I fully understand today why one of my astronaut buddies, Alan Bean, became an artist in later life. The explanation for what we saw lies not in words, but in color.

Tom and I highballed through the atmosphere like a meteoric bat out of hell, finally punched through the fire, and found our planet coming up at us in a rush. The Gemini spacecraft, so light and angelic in orbit, now possessed all of the aerodynamic characteristics of a falling bathtub.

The *Wasp* spotted us on radar seven minutes before splashdown and advised that we were right on track as we deployed a little drogue parachute at about 26,000 feet to gain stability. It was in the nose of the spacecraft, and left us hanging with the heat shield toward the water and our eyes facing the heavens, watching the small parachute with great interest as it shook us like a wet dog. At about 16,000 feet, the wobbling decreased, we jettisoned the drogue, and deployed the main chute. It had a lanyard at each end to tilt us to one side so we could land sitting upright. We slowed rapidly, swinging like the pendulum of a clock.

"Have you got us in sight?" Tom asked the ship. The reply came, "The whole world has you in sight." Television cameras were flashing pictures of our descending spacecraft, dangling below a peppermint-striped parachute.

Splashdown. Just when we thought we had it made, the jinx had one last thrill in store.

The sea was choppy, and the spacecraft had swung to one end of its arc just as the trough of a couple of five-foot waves passed beneath us. On the final swing back, the blunt end smacked a hard wall of the rising sea with a horrendous crash. It was as if we had flown into a concrete cliff—we were almost knocked senseless. By the time we unscrambled our thoughts, water was sloshing around our feet. The private conversation between Tom and I went something like this: "Oh, shit, we've busted the hull! There's water *inside* the spacecraft, slopping all over everything. We gotta get outta this sumbitch!"

We thought the hull of the spacecraft had ruptured and that after three days in orbit we were about to sink like an anchor. Tom was a Naval Academy graduate and I was a naval aviator, but neither of us cottoned to the idea of going down with the ship.

A wave broke across the window and we rocked sharply up and down, while the water inside the cabin churned about like gin being stirred for a martini. If there was ever a "damned if you do, damned if you don't" situation, this was it. If we didn't pop the hatch and get out of there, the spacecraft might become our sealed and sinking coffin. But if we did open it, the next wave could easily flood inside and the only difference would be that we would sink with the door open instead of closed. Then I felt water inside my suit! If there was a rip, and I managed to jump into the ocean to escape the spacecraft, my suit would fill with water and pull me under in moments.

"We're starting to leak water, get the swimmers over here!" we called to the carrier. As the helicopter buzzed close and frogmen leaped into the waves, we realized the water around our feet wasn't rising. *Gemini 9* wasn't sinking after all. The hard landing had broken an internal water line, spilling our remaining supply of drinking water into the cabin. I looked at Tom and he looked back at me. We smiled and gave each other a high five by slapping palms in victory. We had spent three days and twenty-one minutes in space, had flown 1,200,000 miles in forty-five orbits and were on Earth again with the most accurate landing in the U.S. space program's history. We had plunked down a mere half-mile from the aiming point and only three and a half miles from the waiting recovery ship. Pretty close for government work.

THE FROGMEN WRAPPED A safety collar around the spacecraft and a gentle wind from the east pushed us even closer to the carrier. We removed out helmets and gloves and opened the hatches. Sunshine and fresh air. The smell of home.

An aircraft carrier had never looked so good to a pilot. The huge *Wasp* maneuvered alongside, lowered a hook and lifted the charred *Gemini 9* safely on the deck, with us still inside. We stood, waved at the cameras and crossed the red carpet to the cheers of thousands of sailors. My every footstep was squishy, and water sloshed around my ankles as if I were wearing an aquarium on each foot. Our few words of thanks could not be heard over a brassy "Anchors Aweigh" played by the ship's seventeen-piece band.

"LOOK, TRACY," CRIED BARBARA. "Look. Mr. Stafford and Daddy are coming home from space!" My daughter squealed at my TV image. "Daddy! Daddy!" and her grandmother, Jackie Mae Atchley, passed out the tissues. Tears flowed freely in our living room.

Faye Stafford smiled for the press on her lawn and wiped away the worry, now that Tom was safe, but expressed a strange hope for the future: "When I'm reincarnated, I want to marry a nine-to-five postman, not an astronaut."

Reporters trampling the lawn back in Bellwood heard hurrahs from inside the house at splashdown, then my parents emerged. Dad kissed Mom and thrust both thumbs high in the air with a broad smile. "I'm so happy I can't think straight," he said. "My boy's back."

*   *   *

WE WERE EACH HANDED a telephone and the president of the United States, Lyndon Johnson, was on the other end, calling with congratulations from his ranch in Texas. After saying how proud the nation was of the two of us, the president had a couple of words for me. "That little stroll, Gene, was one of the finest chapters in our whole space program," he said, then promoted me on the spot by one grade, to commander. It was tradition that astronauts were bumped up in rank upon completing their first mission, and Tom had been given the silver leaves of an Air Force lieutenant colonel only six months before, when he finished *Gemini 6.* My promotion meant that I had been a lieutenant commander, a rank that I also had obtained early, for only a year, and I was now about six years ahead of the normal pace of promotions. Who said being an astronaut was a dead-end to a military career?

Once Tom and I reached the medical bay, I had my first shower in three days and a chance to scrape off a stiff crop of whiskers and brush my teeth. When the technicians got me out of my suit, they upended the thing and poured out more than a quart of water. The wetness I had felt at splashdown and while walking across the deck had been the river of sweat left over from the spacewalk. In space, it had not evaporated, so when we reached gravity, it ran down my body and into my boots. Then the medics put me on the scales and discovered I had lost thirteen and one-half pounds in three days. Then they were interested in a patch of sunburn on my lower spine. It was hard to convince them that I felt fine, because I was as gaunt as a scarecrow.

After a two-hour physical and wearing fresh blue NASA flight suits, we were finally able to call our wives, but there was no privacy at either end because it was an open radio link. Although the conversations were somewhat stilted, the voices of Barbara and Tracy helped put things back on track for me. *Gemini 9* faded as I talked to my girls.

Throughout the ship, Tom and I were bombarded with adulation. Gotta admit, it was pretty nice. It wasn't just the admirals and captains, either. We shared two huge cakes with the crew and did a quick inspection of the charred spacecraft that had been our home for three days. I shook hundreds of hands, smiled for hundreds of pictures, heard the pleasant thunder of hundreds of cheering voices.

We knew better than anyone that the horrendous mission had been filled with glitches, but it was as if the mishaps of the past three days had not been noticed. These people wanted to hear about success, not failure, and they treated us like royalty. The president, the Navy brass and thousands of sailors thought we were pretty hot stuff. Television sets showed Walter Cronkite saying we had made history. *Astronauts!* Not so long ago, I had been just another unknown A-4 pilot on a carrier very much like this one. Now everybody knew my name. I felt like a real, honest-to-God space hero.

Six hours after we boarded the *Wasp*, we catted off again, this time as copilots in a couple of prop-driven planes that took us back to Cape Kennedy, where we zoomed low over the runway wingtip-to-wingtip before landing just as a thunderstorm settled gloomily over the area. It might have been an omen, for we left the hero stuff back on the flight deck of the carrier.

Laying a bullshit line on the press was one thing, but standing there on the Cape tarmac, his impassive, craggy face watching us climb down from the planes, was our godfather, Deke, who would lead four days of debriefing at the Cape by NASA types who knew the mission plan as well as we did.

Our victorious homecoming was in for a bit of a detour, for the experts would want to know—*exactly*—What Happened Up There. I shook Deke's hand and muttered something about having "some real good data" for him. "Good job, guy," he replied. That was small comfort, for he said the same thing to every returning astronaut.

For the next four days, Tom and I poured our guts into tape recorders, then flew home to Houston, where the Ice Commander, Al Shepard, head of the Astronaut Office, would guide us through another full week of grilling. Shepard, once the most recognized name in America, wasn't impressed by my new celebrity status at all. No matter what I might say, I felt that the spacewalk hung over my future like a guillotine. The only thing worse than facing the music would be to admit to Shepard that I was worried. The man had no time for whiners.

Meanwhile, the top people in the program were proclaiming all the right things to the media. Bob Gilruth, the director of the Manned Space-craft Center, said *Gemini 9* was extremely successful, despite the setbacks, and that you learn a lot from "the unexpected things." Chuck Mathews, the Gemini program manager, summed it up best. "We are in the test-flight stage of space," during which you make mistakes, then learn from them. "Progress is being made," he told everyone, citing our successful rendezvous work and being able to steer the spacecraft in order to land close to a target. But about my spacewalk, they were curiously cautious. The doctors said they were baffled at why astronauts tire quicker working in space than under Earth gravity. They used the plural, but since I was the only astronaut ever to do any work in space, it wasn't hard to figure out who they were talking about.

I also became aware of conversations going on behind closed doors in the offices of my fellow astros. The same guys who had needled Armstrong and Scott for their performance with *Gemini 8* were now riding my ass, intimating that if Charlie Bassett had been out there, or Mike Collins, Dick Gordon or any other highly trained test pilot used to dealing cleanly with unanticipated problems, maybe things would have turned out differently. Cernan, after all, was one of those middle-of-the-pack guys who was jumped ahead for a flight through pure coincidence, and maybe was out of his league.

During the intensive debriefings, the fact emerged that working in space was strikingly different from what had been anticipated, and I came to understand that my spacewalk had been quite unique. Yet the implied criticism ground at me, and the doomsayers even planted a seed of doubt in my own thoughts: *What if the problem really was me?* I was madder than hell, but until some official conclusions were reached, there was nothing I could do but stew in silence.

BARBARA AND TRACY MET me at Ellington when we flew in from the Cape and I swept my little three-year-old up in my arms and kissed my wife. As we drove home through familiar streets, I learned that a leaky faucet needed to be fixed, Tracy had scraped a knee at nursery school, and the lawn was in dire need of some repair work after being ground underfoot by the press. I had stepped out of an Isaac Asimov science fiction novel back into routine household drama, and found the transition soothing. God, it was good to be home.

There may have been some doubt about my work in space, but Barbara had fired a preemptive strike on the day of the splashdown. Looking like the ideal Mrs. Astronaut in a white summer frock, she told reporters that although she had nearly chewed her fingernails off during the mission, both of us were eager for me to go up again. "That's his job. This is just the beginning of our trip to the Moon." Her words and photos of our daughter, dressed in a red, white and blue sailor suit, gave the space agency some good publicity right when it needed it most.

The NASA budget was being trimmed substantially by Congress and some 60,000 people, half of them in research and development, were going to be terminated as federal money dried up for some contracts. Competition for federal dollars was growing and the NASA public image was becoming ever more important, not less. A little girl wearing the colors of the American flag was a pretty nice chunk of feel-good for a nation reeling on other important fronts.

In Mississippi, on the day of our splashdown, civil rights walker James Meredith had been shot and wounded from ambush and a white man was arrested. LBJ was trying to dampen the growing black rage in the nation with new Great Society programs.

In Vietnam, our pilots were pounding the hell out of North Vietnam without making an appreciable dent in Hanoi's war machine. About the time I was undergoing the hero treatment for *Gemini 9*, my buddy Fred Baldwin was shot down twice and badly wounded. Bob Schumacher languished in the Hanoi Hilton as a prisoner of war. Ron Evans, now in astronaut training, didn't talk about Vietnam, and my pal Skip Furlong was about to fly into combat. I was getting my picture in the papers, but it was pretty plain to me who the real heroes were.

With those kinds of headlines, the nation was looking for good news, a job that fell to NASA and the astronauts. Nothing else good seemed to be happening, and we had been doing quite well in the space race—we now led the Soviets in manned flights, thirteen to eight; in rendezvous, five to zero; and the Cernan-White spacewalks logged two hours and twenty-six minutes, compared to the Leonov's twelve minutes.

As the debriefings went on and on, the growing body of evidence showed that we just had not anticipated the problems astronauts would encounter if they tried to work, as well as just walk, in space. I felt a big corner was turned when Dr. Charles Berry observed, "The difficulty of physical labor in a hard-suit environment is one of the big revelations coming out of this flight." Berry and the astronauts were usually knocking heads, so to win his endorsement meant a lot. The emphasis eventually shifted to how to solve the problem, and I was able to relax.

AT THE END OF June, I returned to Chicago and Bellwood in a role I could never have imagined. From the moment I arrived at O'Hare International Airport until we left three days later, I was feted as some sort of legendary warrior back from foreign shores. To say the least, the magnitude of the hometown welcome was a surprise.

With the Chicago fire department band banging out "My Kind of Town," Barbara, Tracy and I climbed from the NASA Gulfstream, were hugged by Mom and Dad and greeted by Richard J. Daley, the mayor of Chicago. A motorcade rushed us to Bellwood, where every one of the fifty-five lampposts in town was draped with bunting and our little house at 939 Marshall was surrounded by a thousand well-wishers. The town had sent away a skinny college kid and had gotten back a space hero, and it was time for a party.

Models of space capsules were everywhere, nearly every house in Bellwood flew an American flag, and almost all of the 23,000 residents waved one. The next day, some 200,000 people stood in muggy weather along a parade route, six-deep in some places, but my most vivid memory was of one little old man wearing an American Legion hat, standing by the curb and holding a tiny flag. I have no idea who he was, but he had taken time to come out, stand in the hot sun, and salute someone less than half his age.

The town renamed a street and a park near my home for me, the Jaycees surprised me with an oil painting of my folks, and a lavish formal dinner capped the ceremonies. But the best moment came when I walked into the nickle-sized kitchen of our house and found two men sitting alone at the table, sleeves rolled up and their shirts stained by sweat, ties askew, drinking beer, laughing and swapping stories—my dad and one of his idols, Hizzoner, Mayor Daley. I loved it.

A week later, there was a replay in Oklahoma, Tom's home state, complete with a stagecoach ride, cowboy boots and Stetson hats. A politician promised not to go to the Moon if Tom promised not to run for office. T.P. said he wouldn't, but I didn't believe him, and neither did a very worried Oklahoma congressman.

Almost every astronaut who flew in those early years received this kind of hometown treatment. Americans were honoring us, but were also honoring themselves. These taxpayers, after all, were furnishing the money to put us in space.

GEMINI 10 LIFTED OFF on July 18 for a three-day flight, with John Young in command and Mike Collins assigned to do a pair of spacewalks and retrieve a scientific package from an Agena. Mike would have a space gun like Ed White carried for propulsion, not have to do deal with an AMU, and make both trips during daylight hours. His first spacewalk was scrubbed before it could really begin when some toxic substance inside the suit's air circuits caused severe eye irritation. On the second one, he got out and over to the target Agena, but was slipping around so wildly that he had to actually reach into the guts of the rocket and grab a handful of wires to stop himself.

Two months later, it was Dick Gordon's turn aboard *Gemini 11*, with Pete Conrad in command, and everyone felt that if anyone could slay that EVA dragon, it would be Dick Gordon. He had trouble with his helmet visor while still inside the spacecraft and overpowered his environmental system even before he got started. Dick went outside already hot and sweaty, then got so tired during the spacewalk that he actually straddled an Agena rocket as if he was sitting on a horse, just to get some rest, while the exuberant Conrad called out, "Ride 'em, cowboy!"

Those guys were two of the best we had in the program, and their problems served to validate mine, which meant I was no longer the only astronaut who had trouble working in space.

Because of our three rugged EVA missions, things changed. NASA engineers reconfigured future spacecraft and installed a lot of new handholds, railings and stirrups into which future spacewalkers could lock their boots. These worked so well that we called them the golden slippers.

And since I had likened spacewalking to swimming in zero gravity, the agency rented a swimming pool as a training arena for astronauts. Among the first ones in the tank, dressed in space suits, were me and Buzz Aldrin, who would do the EVA on the final Gemini flight. Gordo Cooper and I were the backup team for *Gemini 12*.

Deke, however, had some last-minute reservations about Buzz and the coming mission. The AMU was to be tried again on *Gemini 12*, and as the October launch date approached, it was felt that the still-untested backpack remained a big bite, despite the protestations of its Air Force champions. I was the only one who had even strapped into the thing in space.

Deke called me into his office, closed the door and spoke before even sitting down at his desk. "Geno, how soon can you be ready to fly again?"

I thought he might be assigning me to an early Apollo crew. "Just say the word, Deke. When?"

"Right now. Would you be willing to jump from backup to prime? Fly *Twelve* with Lovell?"

My face must have shown my surprise. Putting me aboard would bump Aldrin from the flight. "Can I ask what this is all about?"

"It's the AMU," he replied. "The Air Force is hanging tough on trying the backpack again, and if that's the case, I want you to fly it. Can you do it?"

Buzz was on shaky ground with NASA management because of his decision-making ability. Brilliant as he was, he just couldn't seem to stick to a subject and wanted to reengineer everything, and we didn't have time to reinvent this particular wheel. Combined with reports of his work in the simulators and other training, Deke said that in his opinion, Buzz would not be up to an all-out fight with the AMU.

I had the experience and he wanted me in the driver's seat. When Deke asked if you would take a mission, there was only one answer, and the chance for another whack at that damned Buck Rogers gizmo was not to be passed up. "Yes, sir," I told him, finally believing that Deke's confidence in me had not wavered. "You bet your sweet ass I'll do it."

But before Deke ever got around to changing the crew assignment, the mission changed instead. The hazardous AMU was removed and the spacewalk was downgraded to basic evaluations to see if even the simplest chores could be done in space. Buzz would just sort of move around outside, safely locked into the golden slippers and stuck to the spacecraft by an abundance of tethers, handholds and railings. Instead of handling the complicated AMU backpack, his assignment was to stand, firmly anchored, beside a panel, cut some cables, twist some bolts with a wrench, attach some hooks in rings, tear away some Velcro patches, and other such things.

Gemini 12 turned out to be extremely successful and Buzz posted a spacewalk record of about five hours spread over three EVAs. Thanks to the substantial redesigns brought about through the tortuous spacewalks of Mike, Dick and myself, he wasn't even breathing hard when he climbed back into the spacecraft. In true Buzz fashion, he would openly claim in later years that he had personally solved all the problems of EVA, and that his spacewalk went smoothly because he was better prepared than the rest of us. Quite frankly, we said he was only working a "monkey board." Draw your own conclusions.

15

Annus Horribilis

THE TEN MANNED FLIGHTS of Gemini were spectacularly successful and proved we could meet every major objective for a trip to the Moon. In less than two years we had leapfrogged the Soviets, whose space efforts now seemed rather plodding by comparison. They had still not conducted a true rendezvous in space, had never docked two spacecraft, and had only twelve minutes experience with a single spacewalk. So just as Gemini followed Mercury, the immense experiment known as Apollo was already underway as *Gemini 12* splashed down in the middle of November 1966. But as the calendar turned to 1967, we had only thirty-six months left in which to accomplish the potentially impossible feat of landing a man on the Moon and meeting the end-of-the-decade challenge of JFK.

OVER THE PAST YEARS, I had watched the future bloom at Cape Kennedy spaceport in the form of the gigantic Vehicle Assembly Building. This huge structure was 525 feet tall, 716 feet long, and 518 feet wide, the largest building of its kind on Earth. Just one of its four inner bays could swallow the United Nations headquarters. The VAB was so cavernous that workers on an upper catwalk were in a different atmosphere, at times shrouded in clouds, with rain misting their faces, all indoors. Suffice it to say that it was pretty goddamn impressive. It cost $100 million, sprawled over eight acres and dominated the flat Florida landscape. Inside, technicians had a safe haven in which to assemble and stack the various stages of the monster rockets of Apollo.

Two weeks before Tom and I had launched on *Gemini 9*, the doors of the VAB, each forty-five stories high, rumbled apart and into the sunshine came a big Saturn V, standing straight up on the baseball-field-sized back of a crawler-transporter, the largest tracked vehicle in the world.

The transporter had eight tanklike tracks, two on each corner; each track had fifty-seven individual treads; each tread weighed a ton. As it inched toward the launch site, crawling up a slight incline to the pad, the top point of the rocket, which would be used in an unmanned test, never wiggled more than the diameter of a basketball. There were three successful unmanned test launches of the Saturn V during 1966. The Cape was ready.

Deke had been busier than a baseball manager in a pennant race as he matched, juggled, scratched and added names to and from potential lineups for the initial Apollo flights. Eventually, he settled on Gus, Ed and Roger to fly *Apollo 1*, and after months of rigorous training, they, too, were ready. They were to ride into space aboard a Saturn 1-B rocket, because their closely-defined mission would all be conducted in Earth orbit, so they did not require the immense power of a complete Saturn V Moon machine.

Everything seemed to be in place and a frenetic energy, almost mad and unrealistic, gripped us all. We can do this! We're going to the Moon and we're going to beat the Russians! Go fever reigned.

I was up to my eyeballs in work. Not only had the spacewalk failed to sidetrack me, but I had landed a backup assignment with Tom Stafford and John Young for the second manned mission of Apollo. That announcement, made three days before Christmas, 1966, lit me up like the decorated tree in our living room.

THERE WOULD BE THREE crewmen on an Apollo flight, rather than a pair, as on Gemini, or the single astronaut aboard Mercury, because it actually was two completely new spacecraft, with a myriad of complicated systems. The mission required one astronaut to remain in orbit around the Moon (the command module pilot) while the other two (the mission commander and lunar module pilot) descended to the surface. The command and service modules, which would remain connected until before reentry, were commonly known by the initials CSM, and the spidery lunar excursion module was similarly known by the acronym of LEM. NASA would soon chop the "excursion" part from the LEM's name because it sounded too frivolous, so it became the lunar module, or LM.

With Gus, Ed, and Roger chosen as the crew for *Apollo 1*, Deke originally named Wally Schirra to head the *Apollo 2* prime crew, with Donn Eisele as command module pilot and Walt Cunningham as the LM driver. Devious Deke figured Wally was nearing retirement, so this was, in his words, "not a crew I planned to use on lunar missions," but one perfectly capable of flying a mission that would do nothing more than duplicate the assigned flight of *Apollo 1* and further test the Apollo systems in a comfortable Earth orbit.

That rankled Wally. He was not the least bit interested in repeating what Gus had already done. In fact, he bitched so convincingly that *Apollo 2* was totally meaningless that NASA eventually agreed and scrubbed it entirely. Wally won the battle but lost his war, for in eliminating the unwanted *Apollo 2* mission, he was forced to be the backup commander to Gus for *Apollo 1* in a replay of their Gemini roles. It's a wonder that he stayed with the program after that perceived snub.

By now, we knew Deke liked to rotate a backup crew three missions later into a prime crew assignment, so I was elated at being packaged with Tom and John to back up *Apollo 2* (before Wally's tirades trashed it). Three flights later, we could be aboard *Apollo 5*, and there was a chance that it might make the first Moon landing. Tom and I were among the original candidates to be the first men to walk on the Moon. Instead, when the *Apollo 2* was scrubbed, we became another backup crew for the important first Apollo mission.

Then, just when everything had been going so well, with crews in training for the first missions and the rockets coming down the assembly pipeline, it all went to hell in those few horrible moments at the Cape. Only twenty-seven days after the start of 1967, when every indicator seemed to read *GO! GO! GO!*, that damned fire ate *Apollo 1*, killed Gus, Ed and Roger, and brought the United States space program to a standstill.

There would be no more American flights until investigators found out what went wrong with *Apollo 1*. I wouldn't be flying in space again for a long time to come.

THE TRAGEDY BLOCKED OUR path to the Moon and left us vulnerable. Our secretive Soviet counterparts were presented with an opportunity to reclaim the lead in the space race, and they moved swiftly to capitalize on our loss. On April 23, only a few months after the Apollo tragedy, they launched cosmonaut Vladimir M. Komarov on an ambitious mission that threatened to crush us beneath a public relations disaster.

Colonel Komarov was aboard their newest spacecraft, the *Soyuz 1*, the vehicle their engineers felt could take Soviet cosmonauts to the Moon.

While our program was dazed and reeling, Komarov roared into orbit. Not only was his launch successful, but the mission plan was astonishing. When he sailed over the Baikonur spaceport, a second Soyuz would launch, then the two vehicles would rendezvous and the cosmonauts would do a double spacewalk and exchange spacecraft.

But no sooner had *Soyuz 1* begun its initial orbit than a vital solar panel Komarov needed to provide electricity to his spacecraft refused to unfold. Working with ground controllers, he tried everything he could to pop it loose, but it remained stuck like a broken wing, and, lacking the sort of battery power that we used in our program, his electrical circuits stuttered, then failed. Voice communications deteriorated, dials malfunctioned and the control thrusters would not respond. After only five orbits, Soviet engineers knew Komarov was in grave danger, and called off the second Soyuz launch.

The woozy spacecraft flopped its way around the globe, each orbit rendering it more helpless. Trying to steady his reentry by manhandling the few controls that remained, the cosmonaut plummeted back into the dense atmosphere and somehow punched through the hazardous reentry phase, only to have his parachutes falter. *Soyuz 1* became little more than a big ball of red-hot steel, spinning toward Earth totally out of control at more than 500 miles per hour. Farmers in the Orsk region of Russia were jarred by a thunderous explosion when it struck the ground. The Soviets had failed and Komarov died, and the Soviet space program crashed with him. But in America, we didn't know how large a setback they actually had encountered. From past experience, we knew a cosmonaut's death wouldn't stop them, and thought the Russians probably had something else up their sleeves.

Officially, we sent condolences, while inwardly, we quietly cheered, probably with the same feelings they experienced after the *Apollo 1* tragedy. In later years, as enemy pilots have done after many wars, American astronauts and Soviet cosmonauts would meet, and as we put faces together with names we had long known, and shared stories over brimming glasses of vodka, a mutual respect surfaced which bloomed into friendship. But during those early days, we wanted their damned rockets to blow up! We were at war. If they reached the Moon first, it would be Sputnik and Gagarin all over again, but much worse, and we would be the losers. We were sorry that Komarov died, but he was a warrior and, like all of us, understood the risks of space flight. We had caught a break. Now we had more time, and another chance. We could still beat them to the Moon.

*   *   *

SUDDENLY, SOME HIGHLY TRAINED naval aviators had a lot of time on their hands. While 1,500 investigators crawled through the rubble of Apollo, checking every nut and bolt, panel and gauge, every inch of the fifteen miles of wiring in the spacecraft, it became clear that their search was going to take months, if not years, to complete.

Finally there was an opportunity for us to turn our gaze toward Vietnam, which was running hotter than ever. There were now more than 475,000 U.S. troops fighting over there, more than had been in Korea at that war's zenith, and we had dropped a higher tonnage of bombs on the enemy than we used in all of World War II. General Maxwell Taylor declared we were winning.

Many of us had tasted the hairy furball of guilt because so many others were fighting and we were on the sidelines. It was a crazy sort of mind trip, but we were uncomfortable wearing the hero image while our buddies were bleeding, being captured and dying in a real shooting war for which we had been trained. Antiwar statements angered us.

Private talks around the Astronaut Office, bull sessions over drinks after work and long discussions during weekend barbeques hatched an idea. Why wait around Houston doing nothing? If Pete Conrad, Dick Gordon, Al Bean, myself or any other astronaut was sharp enough to fly spaceships for NASA, we could certainly polish up our carrier landing qualifications and get into that Vietnam scrape, where our military skills could be used during the lull in the space race. Even before we took the idea to Deke, we knew he wouldn't like it, but we had to try, if for no other reason than to ease our consciences.

Deke probably thought our plan was about as dumb as anything he had ever heard, but sticking to his iron rule, he said the door was open anytime we wanted to leave, quite a courageous act on his part when faced with possibly losing a half dozen or more veteran astronauts. But, he added, did we really understand what was involved? "You can go, but I won't guarantee a job when you come back," he said.

The Pentagon hammered in the final nail. We could return to active duty if we wanted to, and even fly, but never—*ever*—would we be allowed into combat. Imagine the propaganda if the enemy captured an astronaut! Our scheme was squelched. Vietnam would not be our war.

In retrospect, I know we didn't have things so bad right where we were. We could afford to be gung-ho for the war, because we weren't going over there. And if put to the test, we probably would have admitted that driving a Corvette and being a Genuine American Hero at home was a hell of a lot better than getting our asses shot off over Hanoi.

NEITHER THE APOLLO FIRE nor the Soyuz crash brought an end to the space race. While the Soviets dealt with their own disaster, we were fixing what needed to be improved with Apollo and getting back to work, determined to prove that the lives of Gus, Roger and Ed had not been wasted. Our commitment was stronger than ever. Despite a renewed sense of urgency, we would take things a little slower now, we would be safer, we would check and double-check and triple-check. But we wouldn't quit. If we couldn't fight in Vietnam, we certainly could fight the Cold War battles in space.

WITHIN FOUR MONTHS OF the *Apollo 1* fire, a nineteen-pound document arrived on Capitol Hill in Washington. The report to Congress, by the Accident Review Board, identified ten possible causes of the disaster, all of them electrical failures in the same general section of the spacecraft.

There had been political concern that a review board appointed by NASA to investigate a NASA accident might cover up the problems with some whitewash, but the board took its work seriously and attacked the management of both the space agency and North American, which built the command module. As the senators and congressmen sharpened their knives, it was clear that heads would roll because of the hurry-up years of Go fever.

Washington would do whatever Washington did, but as far as we were concerned, there was a program to get back on the rails. Frank Borman, testifying before Congress, finally barked at them to "stop the witch hunt," and make up their minds so we could get on with our jobs. Even Congress didn't want to mess with an angry astronaut.

ON A BRIGHT APRIL morning, Deke called eighteen of us into a small conference room in Building 4 at the Manned Spacecraft Center. In our civilian clothes, we looked no different than the thousands of other worker bees at the MSC that day. Father Slayton gazed out over his restless, earthbound flock. A couple of Mercury types were still around, and Gemini veterans were in the majority. A few guys from our group of fourteen who hadn't yet flown were also there. None of the new scientists were present, because they were still off learning how to fly airplanes, and it was too early for the latest group of astronauts to be included in such a meeting.

Deke stunned us. "The guys who are going to fly the first lunar missions are the guys in this room," he said. There was a slight rumble of comments as we digested his statement. Deke had just kicked us all in the ass. It was time to get back to business.

I took a quick look around. I knew these men well, knew who they were, knew their wives and kids, knew what kind of pilots they were and what they could do. Tom Stafford hunched forward and nodded his head. Neil Armstrong, who eventually would be most affected by the announcement, showed no emotion. Mike Collins was there, John Young, Dave Scott, Dick Gordon and . . . What a collection! I recalled those first days in flight school, my first carrier landings, the preliminary meetings with NASA during the selection process, when I had felt tentative, almost inferior to everyone around me. That was no longer the case. My being among these elite fliers was not outrageous at all. There was no doubt in my mind that I deserved to be sitting right where I was. By God, I had earned that chair the hard way. I *belonged* in that room.

Then Deke dropped the other shoe. The fire-delayed first manned Apollo mission would take place after a few more equipment tests. It would be designated *Apollo 7* and the commander was the one and only Wally Schirra. Once again, his CM pilot would be Donn Eisele and Walt Cunningham would be in the LM slot.

The backup crew would be Tom Stafford, John Young . . . and me.

IT WAS NOT IN the cards for 1967 to continue on an upbeat note.

In June, one of the new astronauts, Ed Givens, wrecked his Volkswagen while driving back from a party and died beside a road only ten miles from home. That was a personal jolt, because Ed had been the Air Force project officer who developed the Astronaut Maneuvering Unit, the backpack that gave me so much trouble on *Gemini 9*. We had spent a lot of time together comparing notes about the AMU. Ed was a good guy, and his death hurt. It was time to brush off my dress uniform again and help bury still another friend.

Only four months later, C.C. Williams took off from the Cape in a new T-38, the plane's controls froze and it drilled straight into the Florida swampland. He ejected too late. The entire space community was staggered by the loss of the gregarious C.C., everybody's buddy who, someone once said, stubbornly refused to allow anybody to *not* be his friend. His young wife, Beth, was expecting their second child soon. I was the godfather of their first daughter. Roger Chaffee's death had been a body blow to me, and now the death of C.C. Williams truly broke my heart. I was tired of losing friends.

C.C. was the fourth member of our group to die, and the fifth astronaut to perish in a single year. Add Komarov, and we lost six spacefarers in 1967. It was such a rotten year that Barbara couldn't write our friends a traditional Christmas letter. It was all just too damned sad.

HOPING TO ESCAPE SOME of the stress, Barbara and I accepted an invitation from friends to go on a deer hunt at a ranch in Llano, Texas, during the holidays. We flew up in a little Cessna 172 the day after Christmas. No sooner did we get there than I received a long-distance telephone call from my sister, Dee.

Dad had gone into the hospital earlier in the day and died a short time before she found me. It was after dark at the ranch, so we lit firepots on the grass strip and flew out of there, back to Houston. Flying to Chicago the next day, I felt spiritually empty, as if I had nothing left to give. I walked back to the little restroom on the airplane, locked the door to ensure privacy, and wept for my father. Like the flight from California to Houston after the Apollo fire earlier in the year, this was going to be another long trip home.

Dad had made so many of my accomplishments possible and gave me a moral and personal compass that I still follow. He was faithful to Mom, and never mistreated her, Dee or me. I respected and loved him, but like many fathers and sons, we had a hard time with any sort of intimate communication.

He had been ill with diabetes for years, and although Dad took insulin, he refused for a long time to change his habits of smoking and drinking. My visits had become infrequent because of the demands of my job, so when I was able to come home, Dad would pull out a bottle of scotch and insist on having a drink with his only son. He was visibly sick, and we both knew it wasn't good for his health, but he was so proud that I had become an astronaut that I felt refusing to have a drink with him might crush whatever spirit was left in that frail body. It was his way of telling me how much he really cared. He was my father, a good man, and I loved him. I'm sorry he didn't live long enough to see me walk on the Moon, but I like to believe he knows I went, and that I thought about him while I was there.

AVIATORS ARE A SPECIAL breed, and we believe that death should not rule life. Snarly old Gus Grissom once said, "If we die, we want people to accept it. We hope that if anything happens to us, it will not delay the program. The conquest of space is worth the risk of life."

A generation before Gus ever wore a space suit, eighteen-year-old John Gillespie Magee, Jr., joined the Royal Canadian Air Force to fight in World War II and was killed in an aerial dogfight. He once zoomed up to 30,000 feet and was inspired to write a poem that became the pilots' anthem. I dug it out at the end of 1967 to comfort me and rekindle my faith.

Oh, I have slipped the surly bonds of earth
    And danced the skies on laughter-silvered wings;
Sunward I've climbed, and joined the tumbling mirth
    Of sun-split clouds,—and done a hundred things
You have not dreamed of—wheeled and soared and swung
    High in the sunlit silence. Hov'ring there,
I've chased the shouting wind along, and flung
    My eager craft through footless halls of air . . .
Up, up the long, delirious, burning blue
    I've topped the windswept heights with easy grace
Where never lark, or even eagle, flew—
    And, while with silent, lifting mind I've trod
The high untrespassed sanctity of space,
    Put out my hand, and touched the face of God.

16

Phoenix Rising

WALLY WANTED TO CALL it the *Phoenix*, a most appropriate name. In Arabian legend, that regal bird would end its 500-year life on a pyre of flames, and a new one would rise from the ashes. For ancient Egyptians, it represented the Sun, which dies each night and is reborn with the dawn. The name was a perfect fit, for Schirra's new bird had risen from the ashes of the doomed *Apollo 1*.

Colorless NASA technocrats never liked personalizing spacecraft with names. Imagination wasn't their strong point, and they decreed that the mission of Saturn rocket number 205 and Command Module 101 (it would not carry an LM) would be known as *Apollo 7*. The United States was ready to fly again.

Throughout 1968, almost the entire program had the singular goal of getting Wally, Walt and Donn successfully launched. There were 33,000 people on the NASA payroll and 383,000 in private industry working on Apollo, and their collective sweat could have floated a battleship. If commitment was rocket power, they could have sent *Apollo 7* out to the far reaches of the galaxy on a voyage similar to those of the *Enterprise* on the popular new TV show *Star Trek*.

Wally was hell on wheels, the congenial, joking backslapper transformed into an intense, disliked, tail-kicking bastard. Being the commander of the first flight back into space, he carried a big hammer and wasn't afraid to use it. Wally was in the face or on the ass of everyone charged with building the new Apollo spacecraft, and let them know instantly if he or a member of his crew was displeased. "You don't have to fly it," he would bark. "We do! And the last guys who tried it were cooked alive. That ain't gonna happen on my watch, brother." Donn and Walt assumed some of their commander's irksome manner.

In a distinct reversal of character roles, no-nonsense Frank Borman became the peacemaker. Borman, assigned to work with the management team building the command and service module for *Apollo 7*, saw that

Wally's badgering had become counterproductive. Frank told Deke that Schirra had pushed far enough, everyone was fully aware of his wishes and the blizzard of demands was getting in the way of the job. Make those guys back off so North American can finish building this thing or it may never get into the air, Borman told Deke, and Slayton did. It would not be the last time Wally and Deke squared off on the flight of the *Phoenix.*

The new spacecraft eventually emerged, completely redesigned and incorporating thousands of changes that cost a half billion dollars. The whole interior had been altered, right down to new paint and fabric that would resist burning even in 100-percent oxygen. The hatch that could not be opened by the *Apollo 1* crew was reengineered so that it could now be popped in only three seconds. Instead of pure oxygen, the astronauts would operate in a much safer nitrogen-oxygen environment before launch. The squat command module, shaped like a paper drinking cup and weighing 11,000 pounds but measuring only thirteen feet in diameter, was transported from California to the Cape for final checkout and preparation. Eventually, even Wally agreed that it was safe, sound and capable. A launch date was set for the fall of 1968, and the training tempo increased.

Simulation time was at a premium, for the *Apollo 7* crew wasn't the only one in the pipeline, although they had priority on the available facilities. As their backups, Tom, John, and I had to hone our skills as well, for we not only had to help prepare the prime crew, but were getting ready for our own flight on *Apollo 10.*

Deke had made more crew assignments, and those guys also were training. *Apollo 8* had Jim McDivitt, Dave Scott, and Rusty Schweickart as prime and Pete Conrad, Dick Gordon, and Al Bean as backups. Right on their heels would come *Apollo 9,* the flight of Frank Borman, Mike Collins, and Bill Anders, who were backed up by Neil Armstrong, Jim Lovell, and Buzz Aldrin.

The mission plan read like this:

Apollo 7 would get us started again and fully test the command and service module systems in an eleven-day Earth-orbit mission. It would be launched aboard a Saturn 1-B rocket.

A few months later, *Apollo 8,* McDivitt's team, would take the first ride aboard a giant Saturn V, and haul the first lunar module aloft. Once in Earth orbit, they would separate the LM from the command module, fly the lunar lander as a separate spacecraft, and rendezvous again with the mother ship.

Then *Apollo 9*, Borman's crew, would carry out the same mission, but in a much higher orbit, about 4,000 miles from Earth, to simulate deep-space conditions.

If all of those tests went well, there was a good chance that *Apollo 10* would fly all the way to the Moon. And land on it! Tom Stafford and I might fly our LM right down to the lunar soil and take some pretty historic steps. Nothing was set in concrete, of course, and the flights of Neil Armstrong on *Apollo 11* and Pete Conrad on *Apollo 12* also would receive heavy consideration for the first landing, depending on timing, circumstance and the success of the early missions.

Nothing I could do about that, so I just concentrated on my new job of being a lunar module pilot, although I had never seen one in the flesh. So a couple of months before *Apollo 7* flew, when I was about as proficient as possible on running my side of the command module, I stole some time to visit Bethpage, New York, home of the Grumman Corporation, where the LMs were being created.

LM-4 WAS A GOOFY-LOOKING thing. Twenty-three feet tall, it squatted on spidery legs on a vast shop floor, leering at me through triangular eyes, with a body that resembled a squashed cigar box wrapped in crinkly gold foil. More like a two-eyed, one-horned, flyin' purple people eater than the spacecraft that could get me to the Moon. Other lunar modules, in various states of construction, hung from overhead beams, clung to frames that jiggled them like milk shakes, or lurked elsewhere on the floor, skeletons awaiting skin.

Inside, the contraption wasn't much better. Tom and I would stand in a space about the size of a telephone booth, with tethers holding us in place, while we piloted the lunar lander by looking out a window, reading computer numbers and playing an electrical concert on a pair of complicated instrument panels and thruster controls.

I was used to flying planes and spacecraft made of sturdy steel, things that clanged if you hit them with a hammer, strong and heavy craft proudly turned out by what aviators called the Grumman Iron Works. What a contradiction this LM was. The squab's skin was made of metal so thin as to be almost transparent. Grumman, instead of piling on the steel, now copped a 25,000-dollar bonus every time they shaved a pound from the lunar lander, and by God, they hadn't left much at all. What little remained looked downright scary. A dropped screwdriver could punch cleanly through it. The two glass windows were shaved so thin that they bulged out when the spacecraft was pressurized. Looks are deceiving. History would show the fragile, bug-like lunar lander would do everything ever asked of it, and along the way, prove to be a lifeboat that saved three astronauts.

I came away impressed by the infectious enthusiasm of the Grumman folks. I mean, these guys actually *kissed* each lunar module they built before sending it away to NASA. If they were willing to fall in love with a machine, I was willing to fly it.

My attention on that first trip had been solely on *LM-4*, the lunar lander that would go up on *Apollo 10*. Had I been blessed with foresight, I would have wandered down the assembly line to spend some time at the station where another lander, the spindly *LM-12*, was in its first stages of creation. *LM-4* will always be special to me, but *LM-12* would be my home on the Moon.

THE FUEL THAT WAS going to get us to the Moon was not Aerozene 50, nitrogen tetroxide, liquid oxygen, hydrogen or Wheaties, but money, and that was getting scarce. NASA requested a budget of 4,324,500 dollars for fiscal 1968, but Congress approved only 3,970,500 dollars, the lowest figure in five years, and Apollo was yet to fly its first manned mission. There were distant rumblings that the cash might not be there to fund all of the planned flights through *Apollo 20*. Astronauts, however, didn't worry much about federal budgets. Our world was solely the space race, which was once again white hot. Go fever was back, and there weren't enough hours in the day to do all the required training, much less try to solve the problems of a messed-up world.

North Korea seized the *USS Pueblo* in January and television coverage of the infamous Tet offensive of February poured bloody Vietnam into America's living rooms. Martin Luther King was assassinated in April, and his nonviolent philosophy was buried with him. Inner cities burned. Bobby Kennedy was shot to death in June while on his way to the Democratic presidential nomination. American students rioted. Soviet tanks crushed a brutal path into my ancestral homeland of Czechoslovakia. The bad news steadily leeched away the federal dollars that supported the space program.

About the only thing on which most Americans could agree was that we had to—we *must*—beat the Russians to the Moon, and we astronauts were totally consumed by getting Apollo underway. The immense and growing pressures for us to succeed left little time to read a newspaper or listen to a television news broadcast. Bedtime reading was a mission plan. Stealing time to see our families on a weekend made us feel like thieves. Even our bull sessions after a twelve-hour day in the simulators were about the mission. Always the mission.

THE FIRST TEST LAUNCH of an unmanned lunar module and command module package aboard a Saturn V rocket was conducted successfully; Yuri Gagarin died in a plane crash, only seven years after he became the first man in space; a whole load of new astronauts came aboard in Houston, so many that I couldn't remember all of their names; and the Soviets were recovering their space confidence in the fiery halo of powerful new rockets. *Zond 4* flung an unmanned spacecraft a quarter-million miles from Earth in a flight that was frighteningly close to our plans for Apollo. A few months later, *Zond 5* carried another unmanned Soyuz spacecraft around the far side of the Moon and the voice of a cosmonaut was heard sending back computer readings. It was only a tape recording, but it shocked the hell out of us. The Bad Guys were back, and owned the first unmanned spacecraft to fly around the Moon and return.

NASA chiefs huddled over how we could respond to the new threat. Would the Russians actually get there first? Could they? We knew they had bounced back from disaster once before, in 1960, when an unmanned rocket filled with a million pounds of fuel detonated like a bomb on the launch pad and killed more than sixty of their leading rocket engineers. Now they also apparently had recovered from the Soyuz tragedy and were ready to fly again. The squeaky, tape-recorded voice of a cosmonaut lurking near our Moon was intolerable!

Yet our sophisticated Apollo package still wasn't quite ready. I was spending hours, days, weeks in the simulators, learning to fly something that had never been flown before, reacting to emergencies dreamed up by the fiendish engineers who conducted the tests. I would crash and burn on their make-believe Moon because I didn't make the right decision fast enough. Have a cup of coffee and do it again, because you wouldn't get a second chance if you screwed up once you were there. Do it again because the Russians were doing the same thing.

Then came the test of *Apollo 6*, an "all-up" tryout of the Saturn V and most of the gear that would take Apollo to the Moon, except there would be no crew and no lunar module aboard. The big rocket was tested harshly in advance, passed continuous reliability checks, was examined in every nook and cranny, because we couldn't afford another failure. If ever a bird was ready to fly, *Apollo 6* was it, and the mission was simple—just to test the spacecraft during the reentry to Earth. We just assumed the damned thing could at least get into orbit.

On April 4, 1968, it launched spectacularly from the Cape, and developed serious pogo problems, severe oscillations comparable to the violent bouncing of a giant pogo stick, in the giant first stage booster almost immediately. It shook so hard that the adapter section connecting the rocket to the service module blew off during the ascent. Nevertheless, the first stage shut down on time and the second stage took over, only to have a pair of its trusted J-2 engines shut down unexpectedly in quick succession. In a manned launch, such a malfunction would cause an automatic abort and the escape tower would snatch the command module away from the wobbling bird and plop the astronauts into the Atlantic.

Next, the computers went screwy because of all of the contradictory information being fed into their little electronic brains, and the rocket slowed dramatically while being ordered to burn its remaining engines even longer to make up for the missing power of the lost J-2s. It was off-course, higher than it should have been, and overcorrected, actually pointing straight down at one point, then cartwheeled around, flying almost backward until it snaked into a crazy, egg-shaped orbit. It was amazing that it got there at all.

On the second orbit around Earth, Mission Control hoped to run the rest of the mission without a flaw and ordered the S-IV-B third stage to fire. It didn't. Instead, the command and service module's single engine ignited, kicked away from the rocket, and whipped into a weird orbit of its own. It eventually was pulled back through reentry by gravity and splashed down in the Pacific. The engineers said they could easily fix the things that went wrong, but the bottom line was the vital test of the Saturn V didn't work worth a damn.

In retrospect, we probably should have stopped everything right there until we could get a perfect test flight, but the Russians were spooling up their Soyuz and Zonds and Protons and N-1s and God knew what else, and the decision was made. While the flight of *Apollo 6* had been about as lousy as it could get, it was still good enough to give the green light to

Apollo 7, which would go into Earth orbit on a Saturn 1-B, not a Saturn V like the one that had just caused so much trouble. *Go-Go-Go* was again the thumping heartbeat of the program.

FAMILY TIME BECAME EVEN more precious than simulator access. Tracy turned five, and I wasn't there. A special time for the two of us might be stealing a few hours on Saturdays, riding horses in dusty rural areas that would later be covered by Houston concrete. Even today, with Tracy a grown woman and the mother of three little girls herself, I consider our time together valuable beyond words, feeling I have to make up for all of the times I missed so long ago.

Barbara and I tried to make the little time we had together count, getting down to the Bahamas, visiting Las Vegas for a celebrity golf tournament, and having trackside seats at the Indy 500. Even then, we would go as invited guests and be surrounded by other people, and it was not the same as spending time alone. The program didn't take into consideration the overwhelming problems it created in personal lives. The strain began to show on Barbara as well as me, as much as we fought the separation blues, because it was part of the price to be paid for what we were doing.

I would come home so tired that it felt as if I were hauling a backpack full of rocks, hardly in a mood to cheer her up. The constant travel and training, under incredible tension, was taking a physical, emotional, and mental toll. I felt that sleep meant I was wasting time, cheating my colleagues and not carrying my weight, because there was so much yet to learn. Tunnel vision closed in, and missing birthdays and anniversaries and important events somehow became acceptable to me. Sacrifices had to be made, and after missing one birthday or anniversary, it was easier to miss the next one, and the next.

I would give a weak apology by telephone. "I'm sorry, honey, but I won't be home to take you to dinner tonight for our anniversary."

She would offer weak absolution. "That's all right. I understand. I don't mind."

Tension rippled through the telephone line.

When Tracy had a birthday while I was out of town, and I wasn't there to watch her blow out the candles, it was hard for me but harder for her. "Mommy, why didn't Daddy come home? He promised!" There was no worthy answer. My five-year-old daughter couldn't understand why I missed important events in her life, and there would come a point where a wife could not understand it either.

Coming from a background in which family relationships were such a priority, this left me sick at heart, but as selfish as it may seem, there was no choice. I was going to the Moon, damn it!

In October, Barbara was invited to Philadelphia to make her first public speech about life in the space program. She was recognized as a leader among the wives, an inspiration to the new women whose husbands were entering the program, but despite her experience, she was as nervous as a cat when she and Dave Scott's wife, Lurton, flew up to Philadelphia to present a program at an aeronautical convention. She wrote her speech in longhand on pieces of Tracy's lined school paper, tearing up and scratching out and rewriting, putting her heart into it.

The first thing people always want to know from her, she said, was what it's like to be married to an astronaut, and she stepped out of character to deal honestly with the question. Being an astronaut's wife means living alone most of the time, almost losing your husband, because he's away all week, every week, and there are no such things as real vacations to ease the strain. It means putting your own ego on the shelf while the world worships your man. It means that you raise your children alone, learn how to fix the plumbing and change a flat tire, deal with money problems and family emergencies without being able to consult your absent mate, worry whether he is keeping safe, and wait at night for the telephone to ring, to hear your husband's voice, because that's as close as you're going to get for another week. (Betty Grissom, reflecting on the death of Gus, would poignantly write later: "I'm going to miss the phone calls. That's mostly what I had of him. The phone calls.") Barbara said the astronaut wife must wear a brave face for the television camera no matter how she felt inside, must endure the pain of attending funerals and seeing other wives become widows, must hide her emotions and never show a weakness. She probably thought, but didn't mention, that a wife also wonders what her hero is doing tonight in New York, Los Angeles or Florida. *Is he really thinking about me?*

Such a burden could be shouldered, she said, only if you believed in the program as much as your husband did. You belong to a special society in which the normal rules of life do not apply. The wife of an astronaut has a duty to be just as effective in her job as her husband is in his, because neither of you can make it on your own. You're part of the team. That is the only way it could work.

I guess it was one helluva speech, but I didn't realize it. "After three bloody Marys and two tranquilizers, I can do anything," she told me that night. On the telephone. Mrs. Astronaut was showing a previously unseen side, but I was so wrapped up in the program, in the mission, that I was almost oblivious to what was going on in my personal life.

Her strong words revealed that the wives of astronauts were no longer content to be silent partners. *I'm just so proud of him!* Several were using the few hours they saw their husbands each week to talk about the big D—Divorce.

ON OCTOBER 11, 1968, John Young and I, as part of the backup crew, helped strap and lock Wally, Donn and Walt into the command module of *Apollo 7*. We left them there, surrounded by two million functioning parts and sitting atop a column of volatile liquid oxygen.

A little while later, the Saturn 1-B, a rollicking, thundering thing, fired on schedule, shaking the Florida sand as if a giant was stomping his feet, and three righteous pilots took the United States back into space. Twenty-one long months had passed since the *Apollo 1* fire.

For eleven days they did two things extraordinarily well—successfully perform every test assigned and piss off about everybody in the program, from grunt engineer to the flight director. Much of the dispute went out on public radio waves. The cockiness they had displayed overseeing the construction of the command module came raging back as they bitched and growled throughout the flight. Soon, they each caught a head cold, making tempers even shorter. They didn't like the food and considered many of their tasks of the "Mickey Mouse" variety. Wally called one manager an idiot and Donn chimed in that he'd like to have a private moment with the man who made an assignment he considered particularly dumb. They were, at best, putting themselves above the whole program, and at worst, believing they *were* the program. Wally finally tore it by telling Mission Control, "We're not going to accept any new games or do some crazy test we've never heard of before." For a military officer to refuse orders was unthinkable. Donn and Wally got into a spat over a navigational problem and spent a day orbiting and pouting. Walt claimed Donn fell asleep on watch. The guys in Mission Control, tired of the antics and complaints from the Wally, Walt and Donn Show, muttered about letting them land in the middle of a typhoon. All three refused to wear their helmets on reentry because, Wally worried, with their head colds, they risked bursting their ear drums. By doing so, they disobeyed a direct order from Deke, lost his confidence, and came down branded as mutinous outlaws. None would ever fly in space again.

Wally—the only astronaut ever to fly in Mercury, Gemini and Apollo—could have cared less. Once back on dry land, he skated away from the fracas with his usual charm. Donn was assigned to the backup crew for *Apollo 10*, but his wife, Harriet, slapped him with divorce papers because of his fooling around with Florida Susie and he was soon going to be history. Ironically, Walt Cunningham had tried to stay out of the line of fire aboard *Apollo 7*, but reaped the whirlwind of resentment he had created over the years. He was chained to a desk and would later write that he felt the entire crew had been tarred and feathered. *Probably with good reason.*

Nevertheless, the bad boys of *Apollo 7* did their job, particularly by repeatedly firing up the service module engine in a space environment. Damn thing works! The ghosts of Gus Grissom, Ed White, and Roger Chaffee could rest easy now. Apollo was on the road.

THE TOP DOGS OF NASA had been sitting on a secret for more than two months. Armed with readouts that showed *Apollo 7* was a total success, they were ready to answer the Soviets and that pesky Zond. Slight change in plans, folks: *Apollo 8* is going to the Moon.

The first item was to figure out who would be aboard. *Apollo 8* was Jim McDivitt's flight, but he and his crew had trained long and hard to master every facet of their assigned mission, which was to take the Saturn V up with a complete command and lunar module package and wring it out in a full-bore Earth orbit practice run. Deke gave Jim the first right of refusal on the revised mission, and wasn't unhappy when McDivitt turned it down, choosing to stay with his original task. The decision surprised the hell out of me. I thought the whole purpose of being an astronaut was to go to the flippin' Moon, but Jim said "Nope" to the offer of a lifetime.

Deke then asked the next guy in line, *Herr* Frank Borman, and that tightly wound little sumbitch almost left skidmarks up Slayton's back in his rush to the launch pad. On *Apollo 9*, Borman, Mike Collins and Bill

Anders were to repeat McDivitt's CSM-LM workout, but in a deep space Earth orbit, and Frank couldn't dump that chore fast enough.

So the crews of *8* and *9* were flipped, with one change. Mike Collins had inherited a bad back from a ride on an ejection seat years ago and needed an operation to fix his spine. While he was still wearing a neck brace, wondering if he would ever fly even as much as a Piper Cub again, Jim Lovell took his place on the new *Apollo 8* crew. Mike was devastated when he learned that he would miss the first Moon trip.

The choices made at that point also contributed to the string of historic circumstances which led to Neil Armstrong taking the first steps on the Moon. McDivitt's backup on the original *Apollo 8* was Pete Conrad, who would have rotated three missions later to command *Apollo 11*. Instead, when Jim passed on the Moon ride, and was bumped back to *Apollo 9*, his backup team, with Pete in command, shifted back along with him. Pete eventually commanded *Apollo 12*. Neil, who was Borman's backup on the original *Apollo 9*, moved ahead by one important notch when Borman did, and three missions later, he flew *Apollo 11*.

VIETNAM DID IN PRESIDENT Johnson, and Richard Nixon squeaked by Hubert Humphrey and George Wallace in the November presidential election. But as 1968 neared its end, Lyndon was still in the White House and decided it was high time to party with his space boys from back home in Texas. Bring in that Borman and his group, Schirra and his people, and the cowboys who would ride that *Apollo 9* rocket. And make sure to invite those three young fellas that got named to the prime crew for *Apollo 10*—Stafford, Young and Cernan. Moon people.

On December 9, a galaxy of astronauts showed up at 1600 Pennsylvania Avenue for a get-together that some have compared to the infamous open house when Andrew Jackson's buckskin friends rode horses in the hallways, shot long rifles from the balcony, and spat on the floor. It was nothing of the kind. We didn't have our horses, the Secret Service wouldn't let us shoot anything, and most of us probably didn't spit on the floor. Matter of fact, as astronaut parties go, it was pretty tame.

Long after midnight, when LBJ had gone up to bed, the ebullient Vice President Humphrey kept the Marine band playing and the drinks flowing. When it finally came time to leave, the guests paraded from the main floor of the White House down an elegant marble staircase to the lower level entrance that led out near the Rose Garden. Barbara started down the stairs, deep in conversation with someone, and I decided to take a quicker way down—the banister. As Hubert laughed and clapped and stunned Secret Service agents and Barbara, livid with embarrassment, looked on, I threw a leg over the long, highly polished railing and slid down with a loud war whoop. A young Marine guard tossed me a crisp salute as I dismounted at the bottom, slightly drunk but still standing, an astronaut who had made a remarkable landing. Barbara chewed my ear all the way back to the hotel, but I still think it was a good idea. Andy Jackson's friends would have been proud.

THE DAY BEFORE CHRISTMAS, *Apollo 8* reached a crescent Moon, burned into an orbit only sixty-nine miles above the surface, and Borman, Lovell and Anders became the first humans to so closely examine the cratered lunar landscape. At 8:11 P.M. Houston time, after being in orbit all day, they came chugging around the far side again, reestablished radio and television contact as they approached Earthrise, and on Christmas Eve on Earth, read from the Book of Genesis. "*In the beginning . . .*" It made us feel as though we were all present at the creation of a new age.

But they weren't out of the woods yet. They still had to come home, and that lone chance rode on the single engine burn that would propel the spacecraft out of lunar orbit and safely on its return path to Earth. It was called Trans-Earth Injection, or TEI, and would have to be performed behind the Moon, out of contact with Houston. If the engine worked correctly, the spacecraft would emerge from behind the Moon at nineteen minutes past midnight on Christmas Day.

Although there was nothing I could do to help, I had spent most of the day at Mission Control, enraptured by the experiences being reported from the circling *Apollo 8*. Then Barbara and I went to midnight mass in the little chapel over at Ellington AFB.

The whole world was on edge as the time approached for the TEI burn, because everyone was aware the lives of three astronauts were at risk as Christmas began. We entered the chapel, but I couldn't keep my mind on the service, and even when I genuflected, I stole glances at my watch. As the time neared for the guys to reestablish contact, I couldn't take the tension any longer and quietly left the service and slipped outside. Under the circumstances, I didn't think God would mind. In the darkness of the parking lot, I turned on the car radio, leaned against a fender and looked up to where that fingernail of a Moon hung in the night sky.

It would be some twenty minutes after the burn before they could re-establish radio contact. If it went much beyond that, then we would know the TEI burn had failed and our guys would be stranded in lunar orbit. I looked again at my watch as the time came and went, and sweated it out like everyone else. Then the radio crackled—Jim Lovell's voice saying, "Please be informed there is a Santa Claus." *Yes!* They had done it!

The first flight to use the full-up Saturn V rocket was an historic success, and *Apollo 8* snapped the Russian's back like a dry twig. We had won the race to reach the Moon, although the actual landing was yet to be accomplished.

My interest was drawn to something else. The victory over Moscow was sweet, and the Bible readings were a masterful touch, but I was fascinated by the photographs *Apollo 8* made of the blue Earth coming into view over the barren lunar horizon, the famous Earthrise photos. We had seen similar shots made by orbiting cameras, but these were more real because they had been made by people, not machines.

I couldn't wait to get out there and see it for myself.

The Magnificent Beast

DON RICKLES, WHO MADE his living needling the high and mighty, did me no favor one evening during his freewheeling comedy act in Las Vegas. Alan Shepard was in the audience, laughing as Rickles skewered everyone in sight, and when the comedian spotted the first American astronaut to ride a rocket, he couldn't resist a wisecrack. "Alan!" he called. "My pal Gene Cernan is going to fly around the Moon. What you did, in my business, would be called an opening act!" The broad smile slid from Shepard's face like snow from a hot rock. Thanks for insulting my boss, Don.

Knowing celebrities, I was to discover, had its ups and downs. This was definitely a down, but Rickles had become a good friend and Alan would get over the jab.

Barbara and I were being drawn into a world vastly different from the ones in which we grew up. Soon, we were receiving backstage passes in Vegas, attending Hollywood parties, going to trendy dinners in New York, and swapping stories with politicians, movie stars and social lions. We fell into the swing of things pretty easily and discovered that behind the hype, some celebrities were pretty nice folks. Singer Wayne Newton, when he heard that Tracy was learning to ride, presented her with a beautiful Arabian colt, just as a gift between buddies. I played golf with Bob Hope, cooked pasta with Frank Sinatra, and found real friendship with Ronald Reagan, Phil Harris, Connie Stevens, Baron Hilton and even my personal hero, John Wayne.

Barbara and I spent New Year's Day of 1969 in Acapulco, then flew to Washington for the inauguration of President Nixon. We were back at the White House for the second time in two months, this time as guests of Congressman, later President, Gerald Ford. During the glittering affair of pomp and parties, we found ourselves frequently in the company of a personable couple with whom we struck an immediate chord of friendship—the new vice president, Spiro Agnew, and his charming wife,

Judy. Nixon would soon put Agnew in charge of the Space Task Group, and he became deeply involved with our flying to the Moon business. It wasn't long before neighbors in Nassau Bay would learn that the sudden appearance of security around our house might be because the vice president and his wife had dropped by to play a game of pool on the back porch while I grilled hamburgers. Many things would overtake Ted Agnew during his ill-starred political career, but our personal friendship overshadowed all else.

AT THE BEGINNING OF 1969, we discovered that the flight of *Apollo 8* had disrupted the schedule for landing a man on the Moon. The monumental task President Kennedy laid before us so long ago was still not complete. We might no longer be racing the Soviets, but we were certainly racing the clock. Three hundred sixty-five days until the end of the decade and counting down.

The Borman-Lovell-Anders mission proved we had a rocket booster capable of taking us to the Moon, but the vital lunar lander package had not yet been successfully "man-rated." That was the job of *Apollo 9* in March, and if that mission was successful, then, wondered NASA, what next?

The original plan, scrapped only a few months before, called for Jim McDivitt to test the lunar module on *Apollo 8*, then for Borman to refine those tests with *Apollo 9*, thus opening the door for a Moon landing by *Apollo 10*. Instead, Borman had not even taken a lunar module along on the revised *Apollo 8*'s stripped down hot-rod flight around the Moon. The result was the loss of an important test, and probably doomed any chance that Tom and I would make the first flight to the lunar surface.

By January 1969, a pair of factors forced the obvious decision. McDivitt's crew had not yet tested the lunar module in Earth orbit, and our lander, *LM-4*, lighter in weight than its three predecessors, was still too heavy to guarantee safe margins for a Moon landing. The program was up against an inflexible calendar with no time to spare, and although the next lunar module coming down the assembly line, *LM-5*, would be light enough to make the landing, it would not be ready by the time we were scheduled to fly in May. And any one of literally millions of things might go wrong on either McDivitt's or our own mission, causing the program to miss the deadline. We simply couldn't postpone *Apollo 10* until *LM-5* was ready because too many unknowns remained concerning the lunar module's operational capability. After *Apollo 9* gave it a test drive in Earth orbit, another solid flight test would be required to see how it worked in the hostile environment of the Moon.

The decisions came in late January. *Apollo 10* would be a full-dress rehearsal and do everything but touch down on the lunar surface. Deke gave Neil Armstrong's crew the historic assignment of tackling the first landing attempt, with the understanding that it just might not happen that way. If the command spacecraft or the lunar module didn't work well enough on *Apollo 10*, the schedule could slip again for further testing by *Apollo 11*. Then *Apollo 12*, or perhaps even *Apollo 13*, would get first crack at the landing. Nothing was certain at this point, except *Apollo 10* wouldn't be bringing home any Moon rocks. Looking back from today's vantage point, it was a good decision. Instead of being disappointed, Tom, John and I eagerly embraced our new roles as lunar pathfinders.

IF THINGS WEREN'T COMPLICATED enough, another event shuffled the crew assignments even more. Al Shepard was back in the game.

The guys knew all along that Shepard would do damned near anything to fly in space again, but we never believed he would make it. Too much had happened since his first flight so many years ago, and even if Al did return to astronaut flight status, he would have to pay his dues, get in line behind a lot of very skilled astronauts, serve on a backup crew, and go through the long and tedious process of learning how to fly the technically demanding Apollo spacecraft. In other words, we felt his time had passed. We had not counted on the pull Shepard had within the program, his bulldog determination, or the deep sentiment that the American public held for him.

His inner-ear condition had actually worsened during 1968, almost to the point that he risked falling down while merely walking across the room. Al was desperate for a solution, for now his entire career was in jeopardy, and none other than my pal Tom Stafford came to the rescue. Tom told Al about an operation he had undergone to cure a minor ear problem that almost kept him out of the astronaut program. Al grabbed the idea like it was a life preserver and quietly arranged a similar surgery, then spent long months recovering, and none of us were even aware that it had happened. Next thing we knew, Big Al was back! The doctors cleared him to fly, he was demanding to fly, he was almost *ordering* the National Aeronautics and Space Administration to get its act together, by God, and get him on top of a rocket as soon as possible. Screw you, Don

Rickles. And if the other astros didn't particularly like the Ice Commander busting in at the front of the Apollo line, well, screw them, too.

In another January announcement, Mike Collins, after months of rehabilitation following his neck surgery, was restored to flight status and Deke appointed Mike as command module pilot for *Apollo 11*, taking the slot that Jim Lovell had vacated when Lovell replaced Collins on *Apollo 8*. The crew list for *11* was approved: Armstrong-Collins-Aldrin.

INSIDE THE VEHICLE ASSEMBLY Building at the Kennedy Space Center, a new "stack" was emerging. An army of technicians swarmed over a multistage Saturn V launch vehicle that wore the designation of AS-505, and was known to us as *Apollo 10*. Wernher von Braun's Moon dreamboat was truly a beast of mythic proportions.

The bottom section alone, the first stage S-1-C built by Boeing, was 138 feet high, 33 feet in diameter, and weighed 288,000 pounds, even without fuel. Its five F-1 engines could generate 7.7 million pounds of thrust, with fuel pumps that pushed with the force of thirty diesel locomotives. Three moving vans parked side by side could easily fit into its interior.

On top of that was the second stage, the S-2 built by North American. Also 33 feet in diameter, it was 81.5 feet high and weighed 83,400 pounds empty. After the first stage burned out, five J-2 engines, fueled by oxygen and hydrogen, would fire and churn out a million pounds of thrust.

Sitting above that would be the third stage, an S-IV-B out of McDonnell-Douglas. The diameter narrowed to 21.7 feet, part of the slimming shape of this aerodynamic spire. The S-IV-B added another 59.3 feet to the rocket's height, and weighed 25,100 pounds without fuel.

The purpose of all three stages was solely to provide thrust and, except for their engines, they were little more than gigantic containers of fuel that would be discarded one by one when the gauges read "empty." Fully loaded, they would hold enough propellant to fill ninety-six railroad tank cars. And together, the engines of the first three stages of a Saturn V had the combined power of 543 jet fighter planes crashing through the skies on full afterburners.

Riding atop the third stage would be a 4,500-pound instrument unit built by IBM, the electronic brain that told the big rocket what to do and when to do it.

Another eighty-two feet yet to go. The next section was a flying garage, and tucked inside, its legs folded like a sleeping insect, rested *LM-4*, our lunar module from Grumman. The garage was encircled by four petal-shaped panels that streamlined the rocket even more to a diameter of 12.8 feet, and connected to the bottom of the service module.

That section, 24.6 feet high, held our life-support systems and electrical generating equipment. It also contained a single rocket on its rear end that would be used to alter course and provide the vital burns needed to enter and leave lunar orbit. So important was this rocket to the mission that its fuel tanks were protected and superinsulated to a point where an ice cube placed inside would not melt for eight and one-half years.

The command module would be attached next, narrowing the tower even more up through the crew compartment in which we would live and work. Above that was the docking tunnel and our parachutes. The command module was jammed with 24 instruments, 566 switches, 71 lights and 40 alarm indicators. And over it all would be the tip of the arrow, a pointed, solid-fuel launch escape rocket that would be discarded once we were on our way.

At launch, the Saturn V would be sixty feet higher than the Statue of Liberty and weigh thirteen times as much. Just measuring from the bottom of the lunar module garage to the top of the command module, we could have carried almost the entire Mercury-Atlas package that took John Glenn into orbit. The escape rocket perched on the nose of our Saturn V would develop more initial thrust than Shepard's Redstone. We would leave Earth atop a machine 363 feet tall, and return to splash down in a steel cone less than a dozen feet high.

That was the magnificent beast that could take us to the Moon. When assembled, this wonder of technology would have all the parts and pieces we needed to finally answer the challenge of JFK.

We checked the stack frequently as it came together, and the only major hardware change was a swapout of oxygen tanks from the service module. The old set had to be removed so technicians could have access to a balky fuel cell, and were replaced by a new set of flight-ready tanks. Our units were taken out, refurbished and installed in *Apollo 13*, where they would contribute to a disaster in space. *One never knows.*

THE RUSSIANS HAD COME damned close to beating us to the Moon. In fact, they had *Zond 7* ready to make a circumlunar trip about two weeks before *Apollo 8*, but a problem was detected by the Soviet engineers before launch, and the mission was delayed. In January 1969, the Zond went up as an unmanned test, quickly developed violent pogo problems, and the big rocket literally shook itself to pieces.

Even with that failure, the Soviets still had one last space arrow, a monster rocket known as the N-1, as big as a football field, larger than our own Saturn V and powered by thirty massive engines. At the end of February, the Baikonur launch facility was rocked by the force of this giant unleashing its full ten million pounds of thrust in its first unmanned test launch. If it worked, a cosmonaut or three might well be aboard the next N-1, and could then still aim for a Moon landing before us.

But it didn't work. One malfunction after another occurred in rapid-fire succession shortly after the N-1 took to the skies, and it blew apart in a spectacular detonation that flung debris for thirty miles. The Zond failure and the N-1 disaster meant Moscow was finally out of the game.

So it was up to us to prove that we could really grab the brass ring. Otherwise, what had all the noise been about for the past ten years?

THE FLIGHT OF *APOLLO 9*, the ten-day journey of veteran astronauts Jim McDivitt and Dave Scott, and space rookie Rusty Schweickart, would give the lunar module its first true space test. To avoid any communication mixups with two spacecraft flying at the same time, NASA gave in and let the crews name their ships, and this team called 'em like they saw 'em. The *Apollo 9* command module was named *Gumdrop* and the spindly lunar module was called *Spider*.

The week before our Tracy turned six years old in March, Barbara joined me at the Cape to watch the launch, but when it was postponed, we were invited by Frank Jameson, a friend and the president of Teledyne-Ryan, to fly down for a few days at his place on St. Lucia, in the Caribbean. Since it would be my last chance at some relaxation and some time alone with my family, we accepted.

Even heading to the sunny island, the talk was about our *Apollo 10* mission, scheduled to fly in only two months. I fell into conversation with Dick Iverson, the Ryan vice president in charge of designing the radar that would look for the lunar landing site. At a certain point in space, with the spacecraft oriented toward the Moon at a specific angle and altitude, the radar was to start scanning the surface and find the precise landing area. When we discussed the exact numbers, Dick's mouth fell open in surprise and he stammered, "But it's not designed to do that, Gene!" I stared back blankly. By sheer accident, our shop talk uncovered the fact that something important had slipped through the cracks. The computer software designers for the landing radar apparently had been working from an early version of the flight plan, and when the trajectory for our mission was refined, the changes somehow had not found their way back to Ryan. Our new path would never reach the invisible, but vital, point that the current radar software needed to do its work. Had Dick and I not had the conversation, *Apollo 10* would have had a nasty surprise when it arrived on station. While the rest of us relaxed on a beach in the Caribbean, Dick hustled back to San Diego to resolve the problem.

EXCEPT FOR A FEW minor problems, the mission of *Apollo 9* was charmed. After five days of orbiting Earth, Jim and Rusty floated weightlessly through the docking tunnel from the command module and into the LM, sealed the hatch, ran the checklists and cast the *Spider* into space. It was sobering to remember the only way they could return safely to Earth was to link up again with Dave Scott, piloting *Gumdrop*, for lunar modules were not designed to come back from the Moon alone.

For six hours and twenty minutes, *Spider* flew alone, using its own rockets to go as far as 111 miles from the mother ship. This was what test piloting was all about—taking a totally untried machine out for a spin in which the only two possible conclusions were success or failure.

The lunar module itself also had two separate and distinct halves. The descent stage, with a powerful rocket, would be used to lower the spacecraft from the lunar orbit to the Moon, then become an expendable launching pad for the return voyage. The ascent stage, which contained the crew quarters and cockpit, had a smaller rocket to power the lander back into orbit for rendezvous. That engine was critical, since it was the only way to get off the Moon.

After proving the descent stage worked by repeatedly firing the engine, Jim and Rusty jettisoned it and used the ascent stage rocket to go hunt up *Gumdrop*, orbiting far above them. Taking their time, they worked their way back to the command module, where Dave had been waiting anxiously, prepared to swoop down for a rescue, if necessary. Ever so slowly, the two space machines closed the gap and a loud clap finally signaled that the docking latches had snapped shut. The sudden easing of tension was obvious in the voices of the crew. They were all coming home together.

An important revelation concerning the flight came when Rusty broke the code of silence about space sickness. It had been accepted that everyone felt woozy on getting up there, and, yeah, maybe you might even toss your cookies a couple of times, but you sure as hell didn't tell anyone, and neither did your crewmates. To admit being sick was to admit a weakness, not only to the public and the other astros, but also to the doctors, which would give them reason to stick more pins in us. You also didn't want Deke to think you might not be able to carry out your assignment because of an upset tummy.

In fact, nausea in space had posed some significant problems on earlier missions. Frank Borman finally admitted he was sick as a dog all the way to the Moon, but only Jim Lovell and Bill Anders knew it and they sure weren't going to tell! Rusty, however, was so damned sick that he was almost incapacitated at some points and was forced to admit it. Because of his illness, the mission plan had to be altered. That opened the door for the phenomenon on to be examined closely, which was necessary if we were going to continue probing outer space. Rusty paid the price for us all. Nothing was ever said in public against him, but he never flew another mission.

THE TIME WAS NEARING for *Apollo 10*, and even at this late date, arguments were still going on in management offices about whether we should be allowed to land on the Moon. Proponents claimed that we were already going into harm's way, taking all the risks to fly within 47,000 feet of the surface, doing everything needed to make a landing, so why not take that one final step? Why not just go ahead and do it? The more cautious warned that the lander was overweight, too much was unknown—hell, we'd only just found out by pure chance that the landing radar had been screwed up—and being able to land two astronauts on the Moon didn't mean we could get them back.

TOM, JOHN AND I stayed out of it and kept training. If the mission was changed, well, then we would fly whatever they gave us. But our plates were already pretty full and the current plan was, as I remembered the haunting words from *Gemini 9*, "*really* ambitious." We were to combine the Moon voyage of *Apollo 8* and the lunar module trial of *Apollo 9*, then push the envelope even further, into an unknown realm.

Our pathfinder role meant launching aboard a Saturn V, flying a quarter of a million miles in space, and leaving John in Moon orbit while Tom and I took the lander on a sweeping flight near the lunar surface. No one had ever done that before. So many what-ifs remained that the engineers who ran the simulator tests wore out their diabolical little brains thinking up new disasters that we might encounter. It got to be too much, and a few weeks before our scheduled launch, we had it out with the simulator folks.

"For God's sake, let's be done with this constant testing for failure. You've killed us a dozen times over, blown us apart on launch, left us stranded on the Moon and burned us to cinders on reentry. Enough, already. Let's run some simulated missions where everything goes right! Otherwise, we won't know what success looks like."

TWO NIGHTS BEFORE THE launch of *Apollo 10*, Vice President Agnew came by to share dinner with the crew, and it was clear that he was wrapped up in the work of the Space Task Group. He brimmed with enthusiasm, confiding to us some of the goals they planned to recommend as the next steps in exploring space, including a space station orbiting Earth with room for fifty scientists, a permanent Moon base, and for the astronauts, a manned mission to Mars by the end of the twentieth century. It was a program filled with promise and the vice president was confident that the money would be made available for it. While he visited us, his wife, Judy, shared a private dinner with Barbara over at Patrick Air Force Base. Faye Stafford and Barbara Young chose to remain in Texas.

THE FOLLOWING AFTERNOON, WITH the hours ticking away before the launch, Deke reluctantly granted permission for me to visit my family one last time. "For God's sake, don't let any reporters or photographers see you on the beach! Don't let *anybody* know who you are!" Deke advised, as only he could do. Before he could change his mind, I grabbed my rental car and drove off, sticking to the back roads, until I reached the beachfront house where Barbara and Tracy had been secluded.

I needed their warmth after weeks of sterile, precise mechanical training. A bellowing monster of a rocket seethed with liquid fuel a few miles away, and I would board it tomorrow, but for a few hours, I could stop being an astronaut and just be Daddy and Husband.

For months, I had coached both of them, as much as possible, on our mission to the Moon, by far the riskiest yet in the space program. Barbara was as ready for the flight as she could possibly be, but I was still not certain that I had gotten through to Tracy, who still saw the Moon through the eyes of a six year old.

I felt it was important to always be positive around her, and would never admit to my child that something bad might happen. As she sat in my lap that afternoon, I went through the story once more. "Punk, tomorrow, Daddy's going to the Moon. That's a long way off and it's not someplace that everyone goes. So what if Daddy wasn't able to come back from the Moon?" I was ready to let the question hang there for a moment, but she already had an answer ready. "Well, I'd just fly up there and get you and bring you home," she said. What a kid.

The knots in my stomach loosened and my nerves calmed. Barbara gave me a farewell kiss at the door and a whispered wish to hurry home, and Tracy almost left bruises on my neck with her vigorous hug. Felt good, but it was time to get back to work. I headed off to the Cape, and in the distance I could see our white Saturn V, shining in the spotlights, a bright beacon marking my gateway to the heavens. Just standing there, even when seen from miles away, she already seemed halfway to the Moon.

Lost in thought, my foot was too heavy on the accelerator as I headed up Banana River Drive. The flashing red light of a police car quickly brought me back to reality. *Oh, shit, what now?* I pulled over.

A policeman approached in the evening gloom. "Where y'all goin' in such a hurry?"

He was a young man, quite polite, in the crisp uniform of a deputy sheriff. *Now what?* "Officer, if I told you, you wouldn't believe me anyway."

Thinking he had a wise guy on his hands, he asked to see my driver's license. A long time ago, if you were in the armed forces and stationed in California, your driver's license never expired. So mine stated that it was good forever.

The cop read the front, then the back, squinting at the small type. "This never expires?" he asked incredulously. "Where do you *live?*"

Oops. "Houston."

"This here is a California license."

"Yes, sir. It is. I was in the Navy out there." Deke's words of warning bonged in my head like Swiss cowbells: *Don't let anybody know who you are!*

"You live in Texas and have a California license, and you are drivin' in Florida?"

"Yes, sir, Officer." I was really backing away. On one hand, I didn't want him to recognize me, while on the other, if he did, then he might send me on my way. But Deke said tell no one, and that's what I had to do.

"How about car registration? May I see that, please?" The deputy was more than a little annoyed. *Never know who you might run into around launch time. Some loon always spinning a yarn about why he deserves a good seat for tomorrow.*

I checked the glove compartment. Nothing. "No papers. Sorry. It's a rental car."

"So, how about the rental contract?"

"I left it in my room." I wasn't about to tell him my room was in the astronaut crew quarters.

"Unh-hunh." He crossed his arms, rocked on his heels, looked at me. "So what brings you 'round here tonight?"

"Sorry, Officer, but I can't tell you that." I was trying to play humble.

"You can't? Okay, Bubba, then let's try an easy one." He read the license again, and like many people, mispronounced my name, starting it with a hard *K* sound instead of the soft *S*. "Kurnin, Eugene—That your real name?"

"Officer, I can't tell you that, either." *If it rings a bell, Deke is gonna kill me!*

"Lemme see if I got all this straight. You won't give me your real name or tell me what you're doin' here. You got a driver's license from California that is good forever, but you live in Texas and we're in Florida right now. Don't have no registration or rental papers. Got it right so far?"

I nodded in agreement, knowing the shit was about to hit the fan. "That's about it . . . sir."

"Know what, Mr. Kurnin or whoever you are? I think I'm gonna have to take you to the station."

"Uh, you can't do that either. You *really* can't do that!" This conversation was definitely going the wrong way and visions of the morning headlines danced in my brain: ASTRONAUT ARREST SCRUBS MOON MISSION. "I've got to go somewhere tomorrow and you just can't take me to the police station!"

"Wanna bet?" Cops tend not to like hearing that. "Step out of the car, please."

He was about to reach for his handcuffs when one of the most beautiful sights I'd ever seen appeared. A battered Volkswagen on the other side of the road lurched to an abrupt halt, and a man with thick black-rimmed glasses leaned out the window, sputtering in surprise: "Cheeno! Vaht you doink out here? You should be gettink ready!"

The cop turned as Guenther Wendt hustled over, the Pad *Führer* to the rescue. We had the young cop surrounded and totally perplexed. I pointed toward the distant Saturn V as I explained my dilemma. "Guenther, I've got a real problem here. Would you please explain to this officer why he can't arrest me tonight?"

"And so vy dun't you tell him yourself?"

"Deke ordered me not to."

"Deke? He iss too here?" He looked around, as confused at the cop.

Other people were watching and another cop edged closer. "No. He said I could come out for a few hours to see my family. Guenther, I've gotta get out of here before somebody recognizes me."

Wendt nodded, took the cop gently by the arm and walked away as I leaned on my car. He gestured at the rocket, then back at me, and guttural, heavily accented German words rolled excitedly into the warm evening. In a few hours, Guenther would be locking me into the spacecraft and I'd be heading for the Moon. Finally, the officer had heard enough. He walked back, grinning.

"I've heard a lot of cock-and-bull stories in my life, and if you think I'm gonna believe that one, you're crazy," he said. "Thousands of people 'round here and I'm supposed to believe I caught me an astronaut on the way to the Moon? But it's such a good story, get the hell on outta here." He laughed and motioned me to drive on, calling out, "And go to your Moon!"

As I drove away, I saw the blunt back end of an old Volkswagen, the chariot of my savior from Peenemünde, sputter away down the road. Then I relaxed. Maybe Guenther showing up at just the right moment was more than coincidence, maybe it was a good luck omen for *Apollo 10*. After darkness fell, Tom and I went over to Pad 39-B for a private moment with the dazzling rocket that stretched thirty-six stories tall above us, every inch bathed in light. It weighed a tidy 6,483,320 pounds and spoke with a discordant chorus of hisses and moans and gurgles. Even standing still, a harness of steel locking her to the pad, the Saturn V seemed alive and aware it was about to do something dramatic.

"This is sure different from Gemini," said Tom as we stood before the Saturn throne like a couple of awed schoolboys. I hadn't felt like this before, back when I had wondered about riding the Titan ICBM. That missile had stayed ominously quiet, just an inanimate *thing* that sat still until its hypergolic fuels were flushed together and exploded. Not so with this Saturn gal. In my mind, she had transmuted from metal to flesh and was whispering to me.

On the Titan, we had been atop just two engines. On its first stage alone, the Saturn had five F-1 monsters, each of which was four times more powerful than the Titan's entire package. They would suck up forty-three tons of kerosene and liquid oxygen in a thunderous nine-second firestorm before she kicked loose from the pad.

"You nervous?" Tom asked with a smirk.

"Hell, no," I shot back. "I can't wait."

"Hell, no. Me neither," he agreed with a loud guffaw, and slapped me on the back.

So why did I feel so damned *little?*

18

Burn, Baby, Burn

THE IMAGE-CONSCIOUS NASA PUBLIC relations people who felt that *Gumdrop* and *Spider* weren't really serious enough names for the historic value of *Apollo 9* were even more underwhelmed when we obtained permission from Peanuts cartoonist Charles Schulz to christen the *Apollo 10* command module *Charlie Brown* and call the lunar module *Snoopy.* The P.R.-types lost this one big-time, for everybody on the planet knew the klutzy kid and his adventuresome beagle, and the names were embraced in a public relations bonanza. The intrepid, bubble-helmeted Snoopy, flying his doghouse to the Moon with a red scarf flapping at his neck, became a symbol of excellence, and before the hoopla quieted, that little dog's image was on decals, posters, dolls, kits, sweatshirts and buttons everywhere. The program had never seen anything like it.

A century earlier, even before airplanes were invented, Jules Verne had written his story about a flight to the Moon, and it bore eerie similarity to ours. There were three astronauts aboard, the rocket was a multistage "Moon train," the launch was from Florida, the return ended with a water landing in the Pacific . . . and they would be accompanied by a dog named Satellite. A pretty close guess, wouldn't you say?

OUR EXPERIENCES WITH PREVIOUS flights rendered a comfortingly familiar routine as the time crept closer for our launch, scheduled for 12:49 P.M., Eastern Daylight Time on Sunday, May 18, 1969.

I awoke at 6:50 A.M., forty minutes before Tom and John, in order to attend a private mass with Dee O'Hara and Father Cargill, a close family friend, then joined about ten of my fellow astronauts for the traditional steak-and-eggs breakfast. We had a physical, a briefing, a weather report, then suited up and were driven four-and-a-half miles to the most distant part of the space center, where pad 39-B was located. It was a fifteen-minute ride. Once launched, it would take us only twelve minutes to reach orbit.

By the time we stepped from the van, three hours before launch, we oozed confidence. And why not? We were the most experienced crew in the program, with five Gemini flights between us. We were old friends and had total confidence in one another. Mumbles and Cool John had known each other since they were midshipmen on the battleship *Missouri* twenty years ago and had each flown in space twice, while I had been up once, with the added experience of that hellacious spacewalk. Tom, with whom I was once again partnered, was a rendezvous wizard and a leader in planning the Apollo missions. John had commanded his own Gemini flight and was one of the best in the business at running the Apollo command module. As the lunar module pilot, I knew my Bug inside out. They were both thirty-eight and I was thirty-five. We had been doing these same jobs for the past three years, first as the backup crew to what would have been *Apollo 2* and, after the big fire, as backup to *Apollo 7*. We didn't just know our machines, we had become an extension of them. *Snoopy* and *Charlie* were part of the crew.

When the pad crews looked at the three guys carrying portable air conditioners and sealed tight in our white suits, with the U.S. flag emblazoned on our left arms, we appeared relaxed, jubilant, happy to finally be on our way. We were ready to get atop that big rocket, take those stages one at a time, reach orbit, then haul ass to the Moon.

The Saturn V was cozied against an open-air web of skyscraper-high orange scaffolding, pointing up through a shroud of low-lying mist. Peeling ice boiled off the metal skin.

The elevator door rattled closed and we rose up, higher and higher, and we could see clearly through the wide openings of the safety door. Every inch of the way the rocket beside us hummed and vibrated. Glasslike chunks of ice slid away as her cryogenic lifeblood, liquid oxygen and liquid hydrogen, boiled and bubbled in her guts. *She's alive!* The elevator jerked to a sudden halt at the 320-foot level and we stepped out. "Welcome to the Twelve-Forty-Nine Express!" called a systems engineer.

I shaded my eyes from the glare of the morning Sun with one gloved hand, looked out, and could see down the beach for miles. Cars and trucks were parked bumper to bumper, and hundreds of thousands of people had gathered along the beaches and further inland. American flags, snippets of bright color, fluttered on car aerials and private homes throughout Brevard County. The VIP grandstands three miles from the launch pad were packed, as was every available open space all the way down to Jetty Park, sixteen miles away.

Fifteen hundred media types from all over the world were gathered at the press headquarters, their morning interrupted by the scream of one woman reporter when a four-foot-long black snake slithered up the steps. A NASA public relations man grabbed the harmless reptile and released it in a patch of weeds. The press corps, safe again, picked up their binoculars and listened to Jack King of NASA announce periodic prelaunch updates. "All still going well at this time; two hours, thirty-seven minutes, forty-two seconds and counting. This is Launch Control."

Astronauts Joe Engle and Donn Eisele had spent hours checking the spacecraft, and now wiggled out and joined the circle of morticians. Gordo Cooper had left earlier to join the CapCom rotation with Jack Lousma, Charlie Duke, Bruce McCandless and Joe. Tom Stafford hunched into the Apollo command module first, at 10:06 A.M., and scooted over to the left-hand seat, the traditional position of the commander. I went in next and moved to my right-hand canvas couch, then John settled into the middle position. Soon, Guenther Wendt declared everything ready, tapped our helmets, flashed an optimistic thumbs-up and gave us his traditional Godspeed blessing, then ordered the hatch shut and the White Room closed. He was probably relieved to see that I was there on time and not wearing handcuffs.

We set to work on the enormous checklist, reading data to Mission Control and taking updates for the computer. Check the stabilization and control system, telemetry and radio frequencies, tracking beacons and attitude and guidance system. Arm the pyrotechnics. Check internal flight batteries. Check automatic sequencer. Double-check this. Triple-check that. "We are at T-minus-forty-one minutes and counting. Still aiming towards a final liftoff at twelve-forty-nine P.M. This is Launch Control."

No time to think, just time to do. But we had done it all so often in practice that our fingers and eyes flew over the instruments like expert typists stroking a hundred words a minute on a keyboard. Pressurize the reaction control system. Update the altimeter. Time raced forward. "Vice President Agnew has arrived at the control center. . . . We are at twenty-four minutes, fifty-three seconds and counting; this is Launch Control."

Almost everything that could be done had been done and we prayed for nothing to go wrong, knowing that even the tiniest mishap might jeopardize the mission. Several glitches popped up and were overcome. Tom and I were well aware of our Gemini scrubs and took nothing for granted. The Moon was a quarter of a million miles away, waiting. Remove the external power source and go to fuel cells. Activate rotational hand controllers. Final status check. Guidance to internal. Weather is Go. Rocco Petrone, the launch director at the Cape, says Go. Flight Director Glynn Lunney, at Mission Control in Houston, says Go. "Sixty seconds and counting; we are Go for a mission to the Moon at this time. This is Launch Control."

The master computer took control of the countdown and the second hand raced around the clockface as the tanks pressurized. Access swing arms pulled back and Stafford ran a final computer check. At T-minus-8.9 seconds, the valves opened and the five big engines on the first stage of the Saturn V came alive with a roar, flames belching into a concrete pit and roiling up alongside the rocket. It gulped thousands of gallons of fuel every second, building to over 7.5 million pounds of thrust needed to hoist the 6.4-million-pound rocket and its passengers. "We have ignition sequence start, engines on, five, four, three, two, all engines running."

Three miles down the beach, people in the VIP grandstand saw the ignition before they could hear it, then the unearthly howl rolled across the water and swatted them. Spectators covered their ears; felt their skin pushed by a hot wind and tingle in the shock wave. Queen Fabiola of Belgium grabbed the arm of her husband, King Baudouin, in surprise. King Hussein of Jordan, a veteran of many launches, flinched. Tracy, startled by the deafening staccato, buried her face in her mother's pink skirt, and Barbara felt the blast against her own face. Flocks of herons and pelicans flapped away in panic. At the base of the rocket, nothing survived where the immense heat glazed beach sand into glass.

On top, we experienced a deep, muted growl, feeling it as much as hearing it, as the vibration rolled up the steeple and shook the innards of the spacecraft. There was no turning back now. The giant rocket had come alive and its horrendous might was absolutely scary. I pressed hard into my couch as the seconds ticked off. I held my breath, since I wasn't used to leaving the launch pad on schedule, and I wondered how anything could still be working right down in that pit of roaring fire.

Only a half-second beyond the exact scheduled launch time, the enormous clamps holding us to the pad snapped back and our Saturn stirred, the giant nozzles vomiting fire and swiveling to keep the nose pointed straight up. The rocket gained balance, and after a heartbeat or two, rose from the pad. "Launch commit. Liftoff. We have liftoff at forty-nine minutes past the hour. . . . The tower is clear." Up we went, trailing a thundering jackhammer of incandescent orange-white flame more brilliant than a welder's torch.

The Saturn tore through a coverlet of high clouds that partly obscured the Sun, which glowed no brighter than our rocket, and rolled lazily onto a southeast course that would lead to a parking orbit around Earth. Only a few moments later, we were beyond the view of anyone in Florida. As the roar vanished, Tracy removed her hands from her ears, turned and saw the empty sky. "Mommy," she asked, "Is Daddy on the Moon yet?"

"WHAT A RIDE," I reported to the world as the G-forces pressed me against my canvas couch. "What a ride." The Gemini-Titan package had been a mere firecracker by comparison. In a minute and a half, we soared a dozen miles and were pulling four and a half Gs. The thrill was marred by the onset of the so-called pogo motion, which shook us up and down, as if the gods were mixing martinis. We had expected it. No worries, and the first-stage rockets pushed that incredibly huge load, growing lighter by the microsecond as fuel was devoured, toward a maximum speed of 4,500 miles per hour. After only a few minutes, we were already forty-six miles high, ready for the first-stage engines to run dry and stop, and the second stage to kick in.

We had anticipated the same sort of staging jolt as on our Gemini flights, but this shutdown was unusually violent and we were thrown back and forth against our straps as hard as if we were hitting a wall. The tailing fireball swallowed us whole. John Young later likened the impact to a great train wreck.

Then the second stage fired and we were snapped back into the seats as we blasted through the fireball in a blink. Things happened so *fast* on a Saturn.

But the pogo shaking stayed with us, worse than ever, as another million pounds of liquid hydrogen and liquid oxygen fuel burned hot and hard for seven minutes, and we accelerated with breathtaking speed. We weren't done yet—the spacecraft was talking to us, and we didn't like what it had to say. Low moans and a creaking groan indicated that metal was aching and straining somewhere in back of us, and the pogo wobbling hinted at big troubles brewing down below. What the hell was going on back there? Since we were still flying atop something as big as a skyscraper, we could not actually see what was happening in a place that would be equivalent to twenty stories below us. Anyway, the only available window was in front of Tom, since the others were still covered by a protective shroud that was attached to the escape tower rocket. We were, in effect, blind.

Then the escape tower, which we no longer needed, blew away with a loud thunderclap. It was another Saturn surprise, because even though I knew it was going to happen, even though I was expecting it at that exact time, the detonation was so sudden and fierce that I wondered for a bleak second if it was going to tear the spacecraft off the rocket. It vanished in a moment and pulled the aerodynamic shroud away from our other windows, so John and I finally had views from the spacecraft. I immediately saw something very familiar in my window, and said, "After three years, it seems a long time, but here comes the coast of Africa again and it looks beautiful."

The second stage firing ended at eleven minutes, forty-seven seconds, and left us whistling along at 15,540 miles per hour, not quite in Earth orbit. Despite the rocking and the rolling, it was exhilarating to be back in space again. "Just like old times," quipped John.

We got another stomp when the third stage rocket kicked in for three minutes, long enough to park us in an orbit 116 miles high and at a speed of 17,540 miles per hour. Suddenly, she was riding like a Cadillac. The pogo vanished when we shed the second stage, and we coasted into weightlessness. There was no euphoria this time at the phenomenon of zero gravity, for we had all experienced it before, and were much more concerned whether the violent liftoff had caused damage that might wreck our mission.

At the moment of launch, control shifted from Florida back to Houston, and Glynn Lunney was putting the Mission Control troops through their paces to decipher from the telemetry whether the spacecraft could continue, with particular emphasis on whether the fragile LM had been damaged. The only thing they knew was that something seemed amiss, but the computer numbers provided no clue. Lunney voted with the data, which said nothing was wrong, and when we picked up communication with the Carnavon station on Honeysuckle Creek in Australia, Flight gave us a Go for the burn that would get us to the Moon.

We had circled the globe one and a half times while awaiting the decision, and started the countdown for the last firing that would push us out of Earth orbit and on the path to the Moon—a maneuver known as Trans-Lunar Injection, or TLI. For some crazy reason, we always went into orbit upside down, so now when I looked up out of my window, I saw the the lights of Sydney wiggling far below but over my head. Then the mighty rocket fired and Sydney vanished. The Aussies were stunned by the brilliant new star that lit up their night sky.

Unlike on Gemini, where dawn arrived at a relatively slowpoke pace, we now crashed into daylight, climbing away from Earth at incredible speed. "What a way to watch a sunrise," I marveled. The pogo was gone, but we were getting a new, harder vibration, so strong that it threw us around in our straps. Metal screeched and the instrument panel danced as if on springs while the spacecraft tried to rip itself away from Earth's gravity. We had no rearview mirror and couldn't see anything that might be going on behind us, but it was clear that things were going sour in a hurry. We could *feel* the rocket's agony. Whatever the trouble had been had just gotten worse.

I looked over at T.P. and John. *You hear that? Feel that?* Tom, in the left seat, cautiously wrapped his hand around the abort handle, and I started calculations for that possibility, although the gauges were shaking so hard I could barely read them. Two minutes to go on the burn. *Don't shut down on us now, baby! Don't lose the mission!*

Some astros have described going to the Moon as a natural extension of flying. I'm here to say that ain't so. When you leave Earth orbit, there is a total break from the familiar, from what you know, from what you have always relied upon as a pilot. This brain-scrambling jerking around in space was a quantum leap from test piloting, where the pilot's job is to push an aircraft to its boundaries of capability and look for answers to predetermined questions. Out here, confronting a foreign and hostile environment where there was no horizon, no up or down, and where speed and time take on new meaning, we not only didn't know the answers—we didn't even know the questions.

It seemed as though our spacecraft was trying to shake itself to death. If Tom decided to abort, he would twist the handle, the rocket engine would immediately be silenced, and at least we would be in one piece. *Apollo 10* would spend a couple of days in a coasting orbit that eventually would dump us back into the Pacific Ocean. Quoth the Raven, no fucking way.

So we rode that bucking creature through the entire TLI burn and Tom never removed his gloved hand from the abort handle, even when he admitted to the ground that we were experiencing "fre-quen-cy . . . vibra-tions," pushing out the words a syllable at a time between clenched teeth because of the severe, thudding turbulence. Perhaps remembering

Wally Schirra's coolness in a similar situation aboard *Gemini 6*, Tom delayed the ultimate decision. We burst through to 20,000 miles per hour, and finally up to 24,300, as *Apollo 10* creaked and groaned like an old house in winter. Hell with it, let's give it a shot. *Stay with us now, baby. C'mon. Burn!*

We guessed right. The third stage shut down right on schedule, the bouncing stopped and silence reigned as we slid into a free-coast to the Moon. I was pleased, and relieved, to find myself still in one piece. Wernher's people had built a hell of a machine. Tom slowly released the handle and his familiar Oklahoma drawl drifted down to Houston, aw-shucksing, "We're on our way."

19

There Is No End

SHOWTIME!

The inability of astronauts to really communicate what we saw in space had always been a problem. We were engineers and pilots, and the world was getting a bit tired of hearing us say "beautiful" and "gee whiz," although I believe it would have been equally difficult for poet or plumber to explain such sights. Photographs and black-and-white movies couldn't portray the true grandeur we encountered during our missions, and I had felt selfish after *Gemini 9* for being unable to better share with others what I had seen and experienced.

Apollo 10 was the first to carry a color television camera, and it would add a new and unexpected dimension to space travel. Finally, the taxpayers would get a look at where their money was going. We made nineteen broadcasts during our eight-day flight, for a grand total of five hours and forty-six minutes of air time, about triple the total of all previous telecasts from space. The results were so astonishing that we won a television Emmy award. Color television meant that we could take everyone, at least vicariously, along with us to the Moon.

I cranked up the camera about three hours into the flight when John Young set about our final major chore of the day, turning the command module around and docking with the LM. With a gentle touch, John moved us about fifty feet away from the exhausted third-stage rocket and maneuvered the spacecraft into a smooth, 180-degree half-somersault.

As we slowly rotated, the Earth came into view for the first time on the mission, and it was a unique, jarring sight. In Gemini, we had flown across coastlines, lakes and cities as we traversed around the world, but now as we rapidly moved away from the Earth, we could see entire oceans and continents in a glance. In orbit, the horizon curved like a giant rainbow, but now it closed in upon itself and the Earth evolved before our eyes while we hurtled away from it at about 25,000 miles per hour. Our cloud-wrapped blue globe was surrounded by a blackness of such great depth that for the first time, I realized that I was truly on a space voyage.

Although filled with wonder, there was no time to joyride. The job at hand was to bring the lunar lander out of the spent S-IV-B third stage. The rocket had separated, but still tagged along like a personal satellite because of our matching velocities, with *Snoopy* tucked inside the small storage garage in its nose. Four white panels that had protected it during the liftoff fell away like the petals of a flower as John inched us forward, aiming the nose of the command module at the funellike receptacle on top of the lunar lander. A bright Sun flashed on the metal skin of the rocket, then I zoomed the TV camera in to focus on the lunar module, with resolution so clear that you could count *Snoopy's* rivets. Mission Control went a bit loony. All those guys who had been locked to the ground for so many years felt they were in the spacecraft with us, finally part of the real-time action.

John popped the bull's-eye and the two spacecraft docked. "Snap, snap, snap and we're there," he reported. Then he slowly reversed thrust, pulled *Snoopy* free, and we reluctantly shut down the TV show to get the LM squared away.

I floated up through the tunnel, opened the command module hatch and checked to confirm the integrity of the spacecraft by making certain the latches holding *Snoopy* and *Charlie Brown* together were all locked tight. The sudden change in air pressure when I opened it had torn away some Mylar covering on the back side of the hatch and 14,449 miles from Earth, I found myself in the middle of a blizzard. A flaky wave of insulation spewed out before I could secure the hatch again, and I returned to my seat with itchy white material clinging to my hair and eyebrows like small feathers. I looked as if I had just plucked some chickens.

Nevertheless, we were ready for the next step—getting rid of the now-useless third-stage rocket, which was still trucking along right behind us in airless space. Four-and-a-half hours after our launch, John moved our little Moon train—*Charlie* and *Snoopy*—out of harm's way, and at a signal from the ground, the S-IV-B booster was fired for a final time to hurl itself into heliocentric orbit, which means it will orbit the Sun forever. Naturally, we caught its dramatic departure on TV.

With most of the mechanical stuff done for the day, we decided to have one last television spectacular and show the Earth to its inhabitants. But when we looked out the windows, we could no longer find it. Although we were in sunlight, all we saw was blackness and stars. Charlie

Duke, the CapCom, told us to keep looking. "It's down there some-where," he cracked. "Ask the navigator. He should know." Unfortunately, the navigator was busy catching flying flakes of insulation at the time.

Eventually, the world popped into view and the camera went on, show-ing perfect colors as I was able to put the entire globe into a single shot. The snow-capped Rocky Mountains and the reddish-brown Baja penin-sula below California emerged, a geography lesson from space. The Arctic ice cap, foggy Alaska, cloudy Canada, stormy New England, and the turquoise Caribbean contrasted vividly against the blackest black imagin-able. "Just for the record, it looks to me like a pretty nice place to live," I observed. I was immensely proud of that television camera, because it gave people a slice of ownership in this part of history, and a perspective on their home in the solar system.

Our first day in space ended with a midcourse correction that was so minor it added only thirty miles per hour to our velocity. *Charlie Brown* and *Snoopy* were highballing right down Space Route 1, slowly rotating in the "barbeque mode" to evenly distribute the Sun's heat. We were all tired, and signed off for the night. I was 22,781 miles from Barbuda Lane and headed the other way.

BARBARA WAS ALL CONFIDENCE as she held a late-afternoon press con-ference at a Cocoa Beach motel, giving the reporters some understanding of the thinking of a veteran Mrs. Astronaut, just as Faye Stafford and Barbara Young were doing back in Texas. None of them was a rookie at this game, and my wife's confidence was obvious as she smoothly fielded question after question. "This is our work, our life," she explained. "I have never been concerned about his safety. I know that sounds phony, but it's true." She left unsaid the fact that she knew there was no way that I would turn down such a challenge. I *had* to go on what was perhaps the mission of a lifetime for a flier. Barbara expressed total confidence not only in our mission, but in the future Apollo flights as well, adding that she hoped I would command one of those. Tracy romped around the room, photographers grabbing shots of her smile, which was absent the two upper front teeth. For her, the excitement was over and she was ready to go home, back to Nassau Bay and a litter of new cocker spaniel puppies, one of which she had, of course, named Snoopy. In Illinois, Mom showed reporters the flowers I had sent before launch, which she called her "blastoff bouquet."

*   *   *

GETTING TO THE MOON isn't all that difficult once you are finally on the way, providing the machine does its job, and after the rocky launch phase, this flight was going textbook smooth. Engineers blamed the vibrations and noise on the boosters bleeding off excess pressure, and concluded there was no cause for alarm. Sail on. When we passed the halfway mark, some 125,000 miles out, we played a tape for Mission Control, Frank Sinatra's "Fly Me to the Moon."

We toyed with the television camera some more, showing millions of viewers on Earth what three unshaven astronauts looked like floating around in zero gravity. We ran through every possible checklist and plucked up the loose flakes of insulation. We swapped jokes and dove into our food packets, trying out the latest invention—a space spoon that made food cling to its surface and brought some semblance of normalcy to the process of eating. And we constantly watched as our home planet slowly grew smaller and smaller—beachball, basketball, volleyball. It moved majestically through space with a purpose I could not fathom, spinning on a mysterious axis that I could not see but knew had to be there, and I would spend many hours contemplating the why of it all, only to find more questions than answers.

There was more than enough time for me to become contemplative and again ask myself that question I pondered so often in space: Is it possible that this was really happening to me? Obviously it was, but the power of the situation was simply overwhelming. One result of space travel was that I had become much more philosophical, at times unable even to focus on minor problems back on Earth because they just seemed so small in comparison to what I had experienced and the places I had been. My fellow astronauts who went to the Moon encountered varying degrees of the same disease; we broke the familiar matrix of life and couldn't repair it.

For instance, looking back at Earth, I saw only a distant blue-and-white star. There were oceans down there, deep and wide, but I could see completely across them now and they seemed so small. However deep, however wide, the sea has a shore and a bottom. Out where I was dashing through space, I was wrapped in infinity. Even the word "infinity" lost meaning, because I couldn't measure it, and without sunsets and sunrises, time meant nothing more than performing some checklist function at a specific point in the mission. Beyond that star over there, Alpheratz, is another and another. And over there, beyond Nunki, the same thing. Behind Formalhaut, even more stars, stretching beyond my imagination. Stars and eternal distant blackness everywhere. *There is no end.* I'm not an overly religious person, but I certainly am a believer, and when I looked around, I saw beauty, not emptiness. No one in their right mind can see such a sight and deny the spirituality of the experience, nor the existence of a Supreme Being, whether their God be Buddha or Jesus Christ or Whoever. The name is less important than the acceptance of a Creator. Someone, some being, some power placed our little world, our Sun and our Moon where they are in the dark void, and the scheme defies any attempt at logic. It is just too perfect and beautiful to have happened by accident. I can't tell you how or why it exists in this special way, only that it does, and I know that for certain because I have been out there and I have seen the endlessness of space and time with my own eyes.

It was not by accident that we three veteran spacemen had John Magee's "High Flight" poem aboard *Apollo 10,* for there were indeed moments when I honestly felt that I could reach out my hand, just as he said, and touch the face of God.

ON THE THIRD DAY we outran the Earth's gravitational pull, and the Moon's gravity caught us and dragged us forward like a leaf in a whirlpool. At the appointed moment, we would fire our service module rocket to apply the brakes. The flight controllers had aimed us perfectly from a quarter-million miles away to come within sixty miles of a moving Moon at the tremendous velocity of thousands of miles per hour, an incredibly accurate shot. A slight miscalculation and we could have become just another crater on that harshly disturbed surface or zipped into orbit around the Sun.

To give the ride an even bigger kick, we approached the Moon in its shadow, leaving us in darkness, so we couldn't even *see* the thing. Probably a good idea. Had we been able to eyeball it, the view of something that huge rushing toward us, completely blotting out everything else, would really have made our hearts skip a beat.

We swept into the lunar shadow a couple of hours before we actually got to the Moon and sailed behind it in darkness. Things got sort of quiet in the command module as we attacked our checklist, trusting that sooner or later, we would bounce out on the other side. Even radio waves could not penetrate the mass that separated us from Earth. We were back there alone, and although we couldn't see it, we could feel the overpowering presence of the Moon. I made the sign of the cross and touched the small silver religious medal around my neck.

I was floating upside down, my nose pinned to the window, and suddenly saw a reflection on the tinted glass. Then some light hit my eyes, and I swear my first glimpse of the Moon showed that it was blue! That lasted only a second before the true, grayish-brown colors emerged with more light. "There it is! There it is!" I called, and scrambled into my couch. We were only three minutes from the engine burn that would put us into lunar orbit, and it had to be done during our first pass behind the Moon, with Mission Control still out of contact and unable to help. But how could I ignore such a sight? Of course, none of us could, and the command module revolved slowly, providing astonishing sights through its five windows. But it was now or never, and Tom finally forced out the order for everybody to put his head back in the cockpit and make the burn, and we did.

Once locked into orbit, however, it was a different story. We became like three monkeys in a cage, scrambling to the windows to get a close look at this big gray thing turning below us. We saw scarred mountains and valleys, deep craters and deeper canyons, rilles and gulleys, possible ancient volcanoes that were white on the outside and black inside, and circular craters of all sizes, from baseball fields to Rhode Island. But not a single sign of life.

Then as we came around the corner, we witnessed our first Earthrise. It was breathtaking to watch our planet climb from below the lunar horizon, its sharp colors seeming to warm the bleakness of space. Not only was it overpoweringly beautiful, but seeing the world again meant that we could resume radio contact with Mission Control, where people had been anxiously waiting for us to reappear from the far side. Tom coughed, keyed his mike: "You can tell the world that we have arrived."

20

Hauling the Mail

ON OUR NINTH LUNAR orbit, after a restless period of relaxation, Mission Control piped up Tony Bennett singing "The Best is Yet to Come." We had been snug in our strapped-down sleeping bags but too keyed up to do much more than doze, and for the past six hours had just counted cows jumping over the Moon. While doing household chores like having breakfast, cycling the cryo fans, and giving dosimeter readings, CapCom Jack Lousma read the news from Earth. President Nixon appointed Warren Burger to be chief justice of the Supreme Court. Thor Hyerdahl set off from Mexico to cross the Pacific Ocean in a papyrus boat, while Nigel Tetley's attempt to sail around the world alone ended abruptly when his boat sank in the Atlantic. Yea for Thor. Didn't want to think too much about Nigel. In the Soviet Union, Moscow TV showed a film clip from *Apollo 10*. The Houston Astros won. My Cubs lost. So what's new?

Wearing soft overalls, I floated through the tunnel, popped the lunar module hatch and dove inside, like Alice going through the mirror, right into a completely different world. I was disoriented because the floor was now above my head, so I rolled into a weightless ball, flipped and let my eyes adjust to the new environment until my equilibrium returned. I glanced out the yellow-tinted window, saw a saffron Moonscape, and smiled.

Even before starting to power up the LM, we had to deal with more of those itching, floating Mylar insulation particles that had leaked from the tunnel covering. Some had blocked vents needed to control the air flow in the tunnel and the LM, so we meticulously cleaned the spacecraft to prevent the junk from messing with our delicate instruments and figured out an alternate way to fully pressurize. Then the radar developed a problem. A gauge went bad and the ranging gear didn't want to work. Then communications went on the fritz. And *Snoopy* had yawed three degrees to the left, threatening to bust the metal tunnel latches connecting it to the command module. Each setback brought a jolt of disappointment, because unless everything worked perfectly, *Snoopy* would never fly alone. We fussed with it for three hours, with the help of Mission Control, speaking fluent space-ese as we orbited the Moon.

CapCom: "*Snoopy, Charlie*, this is Houston. We got a little problem with your gyro platform as it appears and X gyro torquing angle is a little large; we'd like you to repeat the drift check. Over."

Snoopy: "Okay, you want to repeat the drift check. Roger. Give us a second here."

CapCom: "Roger. That's on page forty-three."

Snoopy: "When I load in the K vector, I just lead it in verb, in ninety, don't I?"

CapCom: "*Charlie Brown*, Houston. We'd like one more readout of the LM CM Delta P."

Stuff like that. Eventually, we solved all of our puppy's problems, vanished behind the Moon on the twelfth orbit, and again lost communication with the ground. The final words from CapCom were a tonic: "Okay, *Charlie Brown* and *Snoop*, you're going over the hill. You're Go for undocking and we'll see you around the other side."

We were on our own again, this time to perform the perilous procedure of separation, and although we were excited, all three of us were strictly business. Now that we were protected by our helmets and suits, the big gloves made easy tasks complicated. This was no time for a mistake.

Tom was at the commander's position on the left side of the lunar module and I was on the right, both of us standing in zero gravity and anchored to the floor by spring-loaded tethers. Our eyes were on the instrument panels ranked before us and our hands rested easily on the thruster controls. There was no Moon in the small windows, and we relied on the flashing red numbers of the Primary Navigation Guidance System computer—known as PNGS or "Pings"—on a panel between us, to tell us where we were. The Pings was tuned to the positions of stars so distant they appeared stationary and provided an exact navigational reading. At my right hand was another computer, known as the Abort Guidance System, or AGS, and referred to like an agricultural college nickname— "Ags." Technically, the Ags was an auxiliary navigational system for use nearer, or on, the Moon, but its real role was to get us the hell out of there if unexpected trouble cropped up. Pings and Ags were to play a very important role at an unexpected critical moment in a little while.

A final technical matter. One instrument seen on any airplane control panel is a dancing black-and-white "eight ball" that shows the re-

Working on Grandpa's farm.
(Dolores Riley)

My sister Dolores and two-year-old me.
(Andrew Cernan)

A proud Dad holding his only son.
(Rose Cernan)

Mom watches as I receive my wings of gold.
(Official United States Navy Photograph)

Stinger days aboard the *Shangri-La.*
(Fred Baldwin)

Formal portrait of
Lieutenant
Eugene A. Cernan
*(Official United States
Navy Photograph)*

Mom and Dad
beaming after
Gemini 9. (Dolores Riley)

Barbara and I watch Tracy and Doodles bark at each other.
(Lucy Benjamin)

The fourteen report for duty. Left row, back to front: Walt Cunningham, Buzz Aldrin, Mike Collins, Bill Anders, Al Bean, and me. Middle row: Dick Gordon, C.C. Williams, Charlie Bassett, Rusty Schweikart, and Roger Chaffee. Right row: Ted Freeman, Donn Eisele, and Dave Scott. *(NASA)*

At home with flippered Tracy before *Gemini 9.*
(World Book Encyclopedia Science Service, Inc.)

Fighting the Snake
during my spacewalk.
(NASA)

Telling Dad what the spacewalk was really like.
(World Book Encyclopedia Science Service, Inc.)

Tom Stafford
and me after
Gemini 9
splashdown.
(NASA)

Barbara and Tracy
watching the liftoff
of *Apollo 10*.
(NASA)

John Young, Tom Stafford and me, suited up with our
Apollo 10 spacecraft. *(NASA)*

Tom Stafford, John Young and I share a joke with the Vice President Ted Agnew and Snoopy the day before the launch of *Apollo 10*. *(NASA)*

Giving Major General
Georgi Beregovoy a taste
of Houston hospitality.
(AP Worldwide Photo)

Having fun with some new friends,
Barbara Eden, Frank Sinatra, and
Bob Hope. *(Tom Stafford)*

(Lester Nehamkin)

(Paul Marsh & Associates)

A tense moment in Mission Control during the *Apollo 13* emergency. Seated from left are flight controller Raymond Teague, Ed Mitchell, and Alan Shepard. Standing from left are astronaut Tony England, Joe Engle, Gene Cernan, Ron Evans, and flight director Pete Frank. *(NASA)*

The Navy's astronauts, from left: Commanders Cernan and John Young, Dick Gordon, Pete Conrad, Scott Carpenter and Captains Jim Lovell, Wally Schirra, and Alan Shepard meet with the chief of naval operations, Admiral David McDonald. *(Official United States Navy Photograph)*

The spectacular night launch of *Apollo 17*. *(NASA)*

At friends' home with Prime Minister Margaret Thatcher and President and Mrs. George Bush. *(Dan Cook)*

"Ready for action!" —Just like my hero, John Wayne. *(NASA)*

Tracy being interviewed on the *Today Show* while watching Daddy collecting her "moonbeams." *(Fred Rheinstein)*

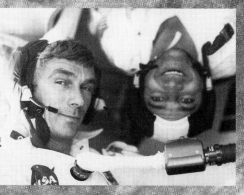

Aboard *Apollo 17*, Ron Evans and I float head-to-head and weightless. *(NASA)*

Inside the lunar module, Jack Schmitt is illuminated by moonglow. *(NASA)*

Welcome Home, Daddy!
(Charlie Wilson)

Working with ABC News during an early
shuttle flight. *(Steve Fen/ABC)*

Jan and I attending a Texas barbecue with Louise and Alan Shepard.
(Brian Payne)

Carrying the Olympic torch with great pride. *(Chilly Newman)*

Jan and me at home in Houston. *(Tracy Cernan Woolie)*

Our wedding weekend in Sun Valley, Idaho. *(Tom McDade)*

Enjoying a moment with granddaughter Ashley at our ranch in Kerrville. (People *magazine*)

The space cowboy trades his rocket for a horse. *(John Van Aken)*

My family of girls. From left: Kelly, Tracy, Danielle, and Jan. *(Gene Cernan)*

lationship between the aircraft and the horizon. When flying level, the black part is the bottom half of the ball, the white half is the top. If the plane tilts, the eight ball tilts at a corresponding angle, a neat piece of information that helps a pilot fly level through darkness, fog or clouds. In space, ours was more complicated, but had the same basic purpose. It was aligned by three gyroscopes and linked to the Pings computer to provide information on how the spacecraft was flying in relation to the lunar horizon. One thing we never wanted to hear was the term "gimbal lock," which indicated the gyroscopes had frozen, rendering the eight ball useless. To cure that, we would have to reload the computers to create a new inertial guidance platform, a procedure that required star sightings, complicated entries, and a lot of time. Usually a gimbal lock meant all that fancy hardware couldn't tell you a thing, that you wouldn't have a clue about where you were or where you were going in the dark heavens, and that you were in an emergency situation and didn't have time to hunt stars and tap computer keys. It meant that you were in deep yogurt.

John Young was alone now in the command module, and took over the separation procedure on the far side the Moon. There was a quiet thud as the docking latches snapped open, and John carefully backed *Charlie Brown* away from *Snoopy*. It was an exciting moment, for John was our only ticket home. Tom and I fired *Snoop*'s small thrusters to gain more distance and adjust our position. Without thick insulation around us, every firing of a *Snoopy* jet sounded like someone was beating on a garbage can with a hammer.

Mission Control waited, waited, and waited. Thirty-six minutes after we had gone dark, Houston got a report from Madrid, where radar was picking up not one spacecraft, but two, coming around the edge of the Moon, flying in formation about fifty feet apart! John grabbed the television camera and gave viewers on Earth great pictures of *Snoopy*'s tin sides glistening in the sunlight and the spidery legs stretched out, comfortable in its home environment above the sandy background of the lunar surface. The guys in Mission Control wore smiles so big they could have eaten bananas sideways.

While Tom and I prepared for our dip down to the Moon, back in Florida, that huge crawler was moving again, this time trundling the *Apollo 11* stack out of the VAB and over to the pad for its launch to destiny. It was nice to know everyone was betting that *Apollo 10* was going to be successful.

*   *   *

SPLIT-SECOND TIMING WAS REQUIRED as *Charlie Brown* and *Snoopy* shooshed along at 3,000 miles per hour, a boy and his dog at work. As we put more distance between the two spacecraft, I was comforted knowing that John Young was up above in our command module. Those CM guys were some of the best fliers in the business. We had worked and trained together so closely that John always knew exactly what we would be doing and precisely where we were. We wouldn't have wanted anyone else as our lifeguard. Ask any astronaut who walked on the Moon about the guy who stayed in orbit and you will hear nothing but high praise. When Deke looked for future Moon mission commanders, the first four astronauts promoted were Lovell, Scott, Gordon and Young, all experienced command module pilots. The show would not go on without them, and our trust in John was total.

EVEN AS WE COMPLETED the exhaustive checklist, Tom and I were only at the beginning of one of the heaviest workloads ever piled onto a crew. The assignments were many, but the goals were only two—reach our objective and survive. We started a countdown to firing the engine on our descent stage for two minutes, only to be corrected instantly by the voice of Charlie Duke, our CapCom, who said Houston determined the burn duration should be only one minute. "Big Brother is watching you," he said. Thank goodness for the guys back in the brain room. Burning the descent engine too long would have been a recipe for crashing straight into the Moon.

"Adios," called John. "We'll see you back in about six hours."

"Have a good time while we're gone," I replied.

John sighed as he drifted alone in lunar orbit, the most isolated man in history. "You'll never know how big this thing is when there's only one guy in it."

Our words belied the serious purpose. None of us knew at that moment what might happen next and whether *Snoopy* and *Charlie* would ever get back together again. There were no guarantees.

The firing of the rocket on our descent stage lasted fifty-nine seconds and shot us away from *Charlie Brown*. John had us on live TV, showing *Snoopy* shrinking to just a tiny little dog running away from home. From my viewpoint, it was *Charlie Brown* that was getting smaller.

The firing was a brake on our speed and dropped us out of the sixty-mile-high orbit and toward the cratered surface, just as we would have to do for a landing on the Moon. Our goal, however, was only to reach another, lower orbit that would sweep us to within less than eight and one-half miles of the surface, and we got there in a hurry. Mission Control heard an elated John Young call out as he watched from far above: "They are rambling among the boulders!"

Down we swooped, lower and lower, and the Moon ceased being a big gray ball, flattened out, and gave us a horizon. It now almost looked as if we were flying over an Arizona desert, but no desert has ever had such terrain. Those crater walls we had once looked down into now took on the distinct and menacing look of an onrushing mountain range, for it seemed like we were below their peaks. Fields of boulders grew in size and shadows lengthened below canyon walls that grew on both sides, their flat tops appearing to be high above our little flying bug.

"We is going!" I hollered to Houston as we made our first pass over the southwestern corner of the Sea of Tranquillity, thrilled at the sight. "We is down among them, Charlie!" CapCom Charlie Duke responded, "I hear you weaving your way up the freeway."

At 100 hours, 43 minutes and 20 seconds into the flight, we would reach pericynthion, a lovely word that means our closest point to the Moon, and I looked along the lashed and whipped lunar surface until I saw the blackness of space. As we dove, I saw something that made my heart flutter. The blue Earth and its mantilla of clouds lifted from behind the Moon, as if God were placing a precious jewel on a pedestal, just for me to view. "Oh, Charlie," I whispered in awe to our CapCom far away. "We just saw Earthrise and it was magnificent."

"They're really hauling the mail," Charlie Duke reported as *Snoopy* lanced across Mare Tanquillitatis. Our verbal reports were short and broken, because there was just so much to see, so much to talk about, and so damned much to do! We were flying over the Moon at an altitude lower than I had sometimes flown planes over my home in Texas, and we were pitched over, face down, the dirty surface rolling past like a rug.

"A fantastic sight. Different shades of browns and grays," Tom said. One of our primary jobs was to photograph the probable landing site of *Apollo 11*, and Tom started to load his Hasselblad camera even as we continued to babble like a couple of excited kids with their noses against the windows of a train. To keep from having to continually press a switch to talk to the ground, we left the communications link open for all to hear. "You can tell Jack Schmitt that there are enough boulders around here to fill Galveston Bay."

Passing Apollo Ridge . . . Sidewinder Rille is hundreds of feet deep and very smooth, the edges are definitely rounded. . . . There are huge boulders around Censorious A. . . . Maskelyne and a string of craters lead right to the landing site. . . . Coming up on Boot Hill and Moltke. "I tell you we are low, we are close, babe," I commented, my voice filled with excitement. *Down there! The landing site!* It was pretty smooth, like a dry riverbed in New Mexico, but with a field of boulders at one end. Duke Island passed on our left, Wash Basin on the right. We were so close that I felt I might have to pick up my feet, lest my toes drag across the mountaintops. It was almost unfair that we could not just sit back and enjoy the ride. So many things to do and so little time.

Tom ran into problems with the cameras that were supposed to map the landing site. "This goddamn filter has failed on me. My Hasselblad just failed. This fuckin' camera." He tried the substitute and it also jammed. Luckily Mumbles's curses were incomprehensible, as the microphone was open to an audience of millions listening in on Earth.

We forged ahead with testing the landing radar, checking the computers, looking for clumps of subsurface magnetic junk that can screw up navigational numbers—trying to expose any little surprises the Moon might hold for the crews that would follow us.

All too soon it was time to leave. We looped *Snoopy* around the Moon once more to the highest point of our orbit on the far side, and made a dive-bomber's steep run back to pericynthion again over the Sea of Tranquillity, preparing to simulate a launch from just about where *Apollo 11* would have to blast off from the surface. This would be when the lunar module would divide in half.

The lower part, the descent stage which had brought us down, would become a miniaturized launch platform, similar to the pads back at the Cape, while the ascent stage would kick the *Snoopy* back into orbit for rendezvous with the command module.

We steadied up for staging. The two halves were held together by four bolts that were to be blown apart by small explosives. About a nanosecond after that, free of the heavy descent stage, the ascent engine would fire and we would zoom away to find *Charlie Brown*, overhead and some 300 miles ahead of us.

Since this was to mirror everything that *Apollo 11* might have to do, we also wanted to simulate an emergency and have the ascent stage guided by the Ags, instead of the more sophisticated Pings. Tom and I had run this procedure a million times in the simulators without a flaw, but in real life, things don't always go the way they do in training.

As we went through the checklist, I reached over with my left hand and switched navigational control from Pings to Ags. We were so busy and familiar with the system that we hardly ever looked at the switches we manipulated. A moment later, Tom reached out with his right hand and instinctively touched the same switch, knowing that it needed to be changed from one setting to another, and moved it back to where it had been a second before.

We thought we were ready to stage, so we prepared to fire the ascent engine and blew the bolts. When we did, all hell broke loose. *Snoopy* went nuts.

"GIMBAL LOCK!" Tom screamed.

"SON-OF-A-BITCH!" I yelled over the open microphone. "WHAT THE HELL HAPPENED?" We were suddenly bouncing, diving and spinning all over the place as we blazed along at 3,000 miles per hour, less than 47,000 feet above the rocks and craters—much closer if you consider those damned mountains that seemed to be grinning around us like gigantic decayed teeth.

Thinking we were in Ags, Tom shouted, "Let's go to Pings," and again flipped the switch, which put us back into Ags. *"Goddamn!"* The computers were by now totally confused and useless. The spacecraft radar that was supposed to be locking onto *Charlie Brown* had found a much larger target, the Moon, and was trying to fly in that direction instead of toward the orbiting command module.

Things went topsy-turvy and I saw the surface corkscrew through my window, then the knife edge of a horizon, then blackness, then the Moon again, only this time coming from a different direction. We were totally out of control. "Okay," I gasped. "Let's . . . let's make this burn on the Ags, babe." We scrambled to stop the gyrations.

Five seconds later, Tom sent a fresh set of heart attacks to Mission Control, where people wearing headsets had jumped to their feet, not believing the onslaught of warnings that were flashing on their computer terminals. "We're in trouble!" he called. Houston didn't know what the hell was happening and things were moving much too fast for them to help.

That old devil Moon whipped past my window again, this time from left to right, and looked awfully close. I stole a glance at the eight ball, which spun crazily as it hunted a nonexistent horizon. Again the lunar surface dodged by, now bottom to top. "What the hell," I called. "Let's get on the Ags. I've got to get this damn thing."

"*Snoop*, Houston," called an alarmed Charlie Duke. "We show you close to gimbal lock!"

Thinking we might have an open thruster, similar to what had happened to Neil Armstrong and Dave Scott on *Gemini 8*, Tom overrode the computers and grabbed manual control of the spacecraft. Then, as swiftly as it had started, the horrifying little episode ended, a fifteen-second lifetime during which we made about eight cartwheels above the Moon, and Tom jerked *Snoopy* back onto a tight leash. Ole Mumbles do know how to fly. After analyzing the data, experts later surmised that had we continued spinning for only two more seconds, Tom and I would have crashed.

Things had been more than a little tense. Hell, I was scared to death. But we got back on track immediately, Tom reporting to Houston that "We've got all our marbles." We reset everything and incredibly discovered we still had enough time to fire the ascent engine on schedule.

Bang! The rocket fired, and we headed up at a terrific clip. "Baby, let's make this one. We're burning," I said, counting the seconds as the rocket thrust us away from that hungry surface. "Seventy-eight to go. Fifty to go. Twenty to go. Ohhh, beautiful, beautiful."

"Congratulations," Charlie Duke reported from Houston. "Looks like you've made the burn."

"Boy, that makes me feel better," I said with genuine relief. The lunar surface was far below, no longer reaching up to grab us.

More than three hours after we had left John, we were hot on his trail. Two and a half hours later, *Snoopy* was tagging along only forty miles behind *Charlie Brown* and edging ever closer. We caught him behind the Moon, and John completed the linkup, the sweet sound of the latches clapping together denoting a successful capture. As soon as communications were reestablished with Houston, Tom radioed: "*Snoopy* and *Charlie Brown* are hugging each other."

It was like being home. We had been standing up inside *Snoopy* for twelve hours and were exhausted, but before we could rest, we had to bid farewell to an old friend. As we slid behind the Moon again, we jettisoned *Snoopy* and sent our loyal pooch into a forever orbit around the Sun, carrying a Stars and Stripes flag and the flags of every state in the nation. Then we went to sleep for nine hours. *Apollo 10* had painted a big stripe right down the middle of the space highway that led from Cape Kennedy to the Sea of Tranquillity.

21

The Gamble

COMING BACK WAS A breeze, after the one critical moment of Trans-Earth Injection, or TEI. The equation was simple: If the burn didn't go just right, we wouldn't get back to Houston or, for that matter, to our planet.

We spent our thirty-first and final revolution around the Moon anxiously hurrying through the checklist, finishing too quickly, for we were left with a half hour in which to contemplate what had to happen next, trying to push away the knowledge that the upcoming maneuver had been done only once before. Silence rang loudly in the spacecraft. No jokes, no comments. No one said a word. After loitering around the Moon for sixty-one hours and thirty minutes, we didn't even look out the windows to see more craters, but were as tensely alert as at any point in our lives. Everything rested on the coming burn. During those very quiet thirty minutes, I closed my eyes, made the sign of the Cross and said a silent prayer to thank God for giving me the opportunity to go to the Moon. "Please take us back to our families," I asked.

The rocket engine fired exactly when it was supposed to, and we were pressed against our couches, counting off the passing eternity of seconds. A stop at any point short of a total burn and the game was over. Two minutes and forty-four seconds later, *Charlie Brown* shot out of lunar orbit. The TEI was perfect and we were grasped by the fist of orbital mechanics, beginning the long fall back to Earth at an incredible and gathering speed.

DURING THE NEXT THREE hours, we watched the Moon change from being so big that it was all we could see to something the size of a basketball, while Earth grew correspondingly larger. "You're coming right down the fairway," Mission Control called up. "It's downhill from here on in." The tension was broken and we let out a cheer.

In celebration, we did something that would be greatly appreciated by the astronauts who would follow us, becoming the first crew to successfully shave in space. On previous flights, shaving with a bladed razor was forbidden because the medics worried that if an astronaut cut himself, he might bleed to death in zero gravity. Another worry was that whiskers might float into the delicate instrumentation of the spacecraft and cause untold damage. Talk about worrywarts. They came up with a little electric razor that was supposed to suck up the whiskers after trimming them, but it didn't work worth a damn and was discarded, so astros returned to Earth after long missions with stubbly chins and looking dirty. The crew of *Apollo 10*, being the sort of trailblazers that we were, carefully lathered up with some thick shaving gel, shaved with a safety razor and wiped off the whisker-embedded cream with a wet cloth, and it worked great. Then we brushed our teeth, something that also was a far cry from the Gemini days when we smuggled along packages of Dentyne chewing gum to freshen our mouths. We felt reborn, and when we took out the TV camera for another show, this time it showed three clean-shaven, pretty happy guys. On a tape, Dean Martin sang "Going Back to Houston."

The fifty-five-hour return was totally without problems and required only one tiny midcourse correction. We came hammering home on Monday, packing a velocity that carried the risk of the spacecraft skipping off the atmosphere rather than plunging through it. We had extra fuel when we left the Moon, and burning it off accelerated us to well over 25,000 miles an hour as we approached Earth, making us the three fastest humans in history.

Our reentry corridor was tiny, only plus or minus half a degree, which would be like a golfer teeing off from the Sea of Tranquillity and making a hole in one at Pebble Beach. We had to be confident that the slide-rule guys would make the shot, because, unlike in the simulators where you got a second chance, we couldn't start this part of the trip over again. It was all or nothing.

After the service module was jettisoned to expose the heat shield, we turned the butt end of the spacecraft toward the atmosphere and began our roller-coaster descent. Poor Tom and John were held captive by their instruments, while I, the LM pilot without an LM and nothing much to do, had a ringside seat for a miracle.

After eight days of weightlessness, the force of gravity welcomed us back to our world, and the G-forces climbed as we punched into the heavy air. Half a G . . . two Gs . . . four . . . six . . . seven . . .

The fireball formed, and I wondered if it would be as spectacular as the greens and blues and reds I had seen on Gemini. I could not have guessed what was about to unfold before my eyes. The different shape of the capsule and our enormous speed drastically altered the formula, and a ball of white and violet flame slipped around us like a glove. It grew in intensity and flew out behind us like the train of a bride's gown, stretching a hundred yards, then a thousand, then for miles and the whole time we were being savagely slammed around inside the spacecraft. White, shimmering flames chewed at the outside of *Charlie Brown*. Then another little round burning ball, a tiny golden sun, formed inside the fire train and stayed perfectly balanced in the furious river that glowed behind our cooking spacecraft, which rode inside a purple shield of pure heat. Everywhere in the South Pacific, we were seen as a brilliant shooting star flashing across the sky.

We came out of it at about 100,000 feet and found the Pacific Ocean painted by the first tangerine rays of dawn, barely light enough to see. The drogue parachutes popped to slow our fall when we hit 24,000, and the main chutes emerged at 10,000, three big puffballs that filled with air and rocked us gently down onto a nearly calm sea some 400 miles east of Pago Pago in American Samoa. The first helicopter to arrive from the nearby *USS Princeton* had a sign painted on its bottom: "Hello there, *Charlie Brown!*" *Apollo 10* had flown for eight days, three minutes and twenty-three seconds.

MANY PEOPLE HAVE ASKED me over the years if I was disappointed that *Apollo 10* did not make the first Moon landing. How could we have come so close and not actually taken those first steps?

Would I liked to have had a shot at it? You bet I would. However, we all believed in the importance of our mission because we knew *Apollo 11* was going to need every scrap of information we could gather if it was to have a successful flight of its own. Our crew had the know-how, but not the right equipment because *Snoopy* was too heavy, and there were too many things still unknown about landing on the Moon before we made our flight.

Really, how could I be disappointed after riding the Saturn V rocket, the mightiest missile ever built, into orbit and then a quarter-million miles from Earth, seeing unbelievable sights, hanging around the Moon for three days, descending to within 47,000 feet of the lunar surface, flying back to my home planet, and making a super high-speed reentry in a fireball to land in the Pacific?

Anyway, I had an idea—I planned to go back.

ABOARD THE HELO, WE changed into fresh, powder-blue NASA coveralls and were given gold-embroidered baseball caps so that when we stepped on deck we would look like clean-shaven, neatly attired astronaut poster boys and protect the image before the television cameras. Actually, not having showered for more than a week and still wearing our rank long-john underwear, we were pretty ripe. The carrier crew gave us a thunderous welcome and we waved confidently as we strolled slowly down a red and blue carpet toward a giant cake. After days in zero G, we were so wobbly that each step along that pitching carrier deck was a little adventure.

With the mission over, I was able to share the excitement that our lunar mission had given people around the world. The crew's cheers were an uplifting reward for taking them along for the trip via the spacecraft's TV camera. When the first Moon-landing crews were immediately put into isolation upon their return, I felt sorry that they were confined, and that they therefore missed one of the greatest aspects of their flights—being able to see the faces and feel the emotions of the people who had actually watched them walk on the Moon.

We stayed aboard the *Princeton* only four hours, and took a congratulatory call from President Nixon, who invited us to the White House for a celebration. We were his first Moon shot, perhaps an omen that his new administration was going to do well, and he intended to get as much beneficial publicity out of the space program as possible. As it turned out, he would need it.

After I devoured my first hot food in a week, eggs over-easy and a filet mignon, we flew to Pago Pago, about an hour away by helicopter, where some 5,000 people waving flags met us. I could see the excitement was not confined to the military, but had also gripped civilians. The outside world was ecstatic. It started to dawn on me that the voyage of *Apollo 10* was really special to all of these people.

*   *   *

BARBARA HAD ATTENDED MASS at Ellington AFB, then visited Mission Control with Barbara Young. Both of them, and Faye Stafford, too, had done their jobs of being thoughtful and brave Mrs. Astronauts throughout the long mission. By now my wife knew what to expect from the press, and what the media expected from her. Barbara felt like an actress who had stepped into a bigger role on the stage, and was able to deliver her lines with grace and style.

Throughout the mission, she carried the banner high and the press fell in love with her and Tracy all over again. Our daughter, romping in muddy cowboy boots and shorts, confided that there was a swarm of bumblebees at her kindergarten.

A friend had coaxed Barbara to play a joke on the press, which would write anything she said, and she decided to wax poetic. "A quote from Kahlil Gibran really says it all," she told the reporters. " 'And when you have reached the mountaintop, then you shall begin to climb. For in that day you shall know the hidden purposes in all things.' " This wasn't the kind of astrowife quote they expected. What about the "proud" and "happy" stuff? She was barely able to contain her laughter as she watched their stunned faces. *Kahlil Gibran?* Finally, she gave them what they wanted, what the country wanted. "I am proud beyond statements," she said. "It was a fantastic voyage."

But Faye had warned Barbara that the second flight would be harder to endure than the first one. Early on, excitement gave way to anxiety, and then to reality, and Barbara found herself alone in a house filled with guests and backed-up plumbing. Late at night, when everyone else slept, she listened alone in the darkness to the squawk box, gripping a cocktail glass to help get through the tense hours.

When I radioed back to Houston that riding around the Moon was a piece of cake, Barbara disagreed, "It was definitely not a piece of cake for me." There was a sharp edge to her comments out of public view. Her mother and Ry Furlong could hold her hands. Dave Scott and Rusty Schweickart could answer technical questions. The wives of other astronauts could lend support, but she had to walk through the valley alone. I was her husband, not theirs, and she couldn't get comfortable. "I knew a million things could go wrong," she told me later. "I didn't know if I was going to see you again."

When we spun out of control above the lunar surface, her nerves, already shot, almost snapped. She turned to Dave Scott and begged, "What are they doing? Are they going all the way down?" Of course, Dave knew only that whatever *Snoopy* was doing sure as hell wasn't in the mission plan, but thankfully the episode was over quickly. By the time we escaped the clutches of the Moon with our TEI burn and were on the way home, lines of worry had deepened around Barbara's eyes.

She played the required role with the press, but would later write to close friends that perhaps she had consumed too much alcohol during the ordeal. Champagne bottles popped open on Barbuda Lane at the moment of splashdown and Barbara led a toast or two to the mission's success while Jackie Atchley watched with disapproval. "I think she's toasted a few too many," her mother observed. Barbara was glued to the TV set for the recovery and when I telephoned her from the carrier, I heard her voice shake.

Far from Houston, in my ancestral hometown of Vyoská nad Kysucou in Czechoslovakia, a small television set flickered in a tiny room crowded with happy Slovaks. One was Imrich Cernan, like me one of the great-grandsons of Andrew Cernan, for whom my father had been named. Imrich held up his glass and also called for a toast: "They have returned to our planet. Let's drink to our cosmonaut!" He later whispered that "now more and more people here claim to be related to Eugene."

IT TOOK A DOZEN hours to fly from Pago Pago to Norton AFB outside of Los Angeles, refuel, and then on to Ellington AFB, where we landed about eleven o'clock Tuesday morning. Deke was there, along with Wally Schirra, Donn Eisele, Jack Schmitt and a flock of other astros and a military band that rocked out "Deep in the Heart of Texas." Hundreds of civilians were gathered at the fences.

I was the first one out of the plane, ignoring the stairs that were lowered from the big C-141 and leaping to the runway to reach my family a few seconds sooner. Tracy, dressed in white, raced to me and I swept her into my arms as she put a tight neck-lock on me, then Barbara was at my side. I pulled her close, too, and we became an island of tearful Cernans. I placed flower leis from Samoa around both of their necks. Damn, it was good to be back. Tomorrow would begin eleven days of intense debriefings, but the rest of this day was mine to enjoy with my girls.

On that warm, starlit night, we walked into our backyard. I picked up my six-year-old daughter, still enthralled by her freshness, and pointed up at the Moon. How could I explain to her this thing that I had done? But she was no longer a baby and would start first grade in September. Maybe she would understand, if I chose my words carefully, for I wanted her to remember this moment.

"Punk," I said, "Mr. Stafford and Daddy flew *Snoopy* close to the Moon. You know, it's real far away in the sky, up where God lives. Your Daddy's gone closer to the Moon than anyone, *anyone*, ever has before."

She considered the information for a moment, twirling a lock of hair with a small finger, and perhaps remembering the times I had disappointed her in the past, replied, "Daddy, now that you've gone to the Moon, when are you going to take me camping . . . like you promised?"

It was as if she had struck me with a stone. Here I was trying to impress my little girl, and she wanted to remind me of something that was much more important than listening to her father talk about going to the Moon. My young daughter had just brought me down to Earth and a world of hurrahs faded to almost meaningless insignificance. She wanted a daddy, not an astronaut. Jesus, I thought, some things in life are much more important and precious than going to the Moon, and I was holding one of them in my arms.

My face flushed in anger at myself. By looking at the Moon for so long, had I lost sight of my family? "Soon, Punk. Soon," I told her and added a hug. "We're going camping real soon." *Damn it, this was one promise I was going to keep.*

ON THE DRIVE HOME from Ellington, Barbara chuckled. "You were a little salty up there, weren't you?"

"What are you talking about?" I didn't know what she meant.

"Do you know that you said 'son-of-a-bitch' on the air?"

"No. I did?" I was mystified. "When?"

She told me the story of how I had cursed over the open mike while millions of people were listening. "You came in loud and clear," she said, and we laughed about it.

"Well, if you say so, I guess I might have. Things got a little hairy for a while."

She was leaning back in the seat, her eyes closed. "I didn't know what was happening," she said, and I heard the pent-up strain in her voice. "It all happened so fast, and nobody ever explained it to me."

Driving through the familiar streets toward our home, I again thought of that swirling Moon just outside the lander's window. "It was touch and go, Honey. *Snoopy* went out of control." Just recalling the moment brought chill goosebumps to my skin. "Goddamn. To tell the truth, I was scared to death."

Barbara looked over, startled, unable to believe that she actually had heard me say that I had been afraid of something. I smiled at her, then added, "But don't tell anybody!"

I didn't know it at the time, but my cursing, done in a very intense moment, was about to ignite a firestorm of criticism.

Much had changed in the past three years since NASA public affairs officers had cleaned up Tom's disappointed "Oh, shits" on the scrubs of *Gemini 9* to read "Aw, shucks." On *Apollo 10*, we spoke as we normally would converse, and the language was sprinkled with some pretty earthy Anglo-Saxon expressions.

In fact, the first time one of us said "fuck" out loud, the young woman typist in Houston taking down the live transcription of our conversation jumped away from her typewriter as if jolted by electricity. NASA told her to make it read "damn." Our astronaut comrades, tired of making treacherous flights and watching every word they said at the same time, were delighted. It was another sign that we were rejoining the real world.

The comments had begun innocently enough with an exasperated Tom answering with "You bet your sweet bippy" when Mission Control asked if the chlorine-laced drinking water tasted foul. Things really became interesting as all three of us got comfortable and spoke plainly. By the time I hollered "son-of-a-bitch" and followed up with "what the hell happened," our transcribers had been treated to more than a few god-damns, fucks and shits and learned that astronauts in space can get royally pissed off. We knew a lot more words than those young typists.

When Mission Control mentioned that the crew would be met by dancing girls in Samoa, Tom asked if it would be a "topless affair." And giving a status report during our final day, I told the ground that all three of us were happy, healthy, hungry and horny. Our CapCom, Joe Engle, replied, "We've got solutions and pills for everything but item four." Without a doubt, *Apollo 10* was suitable for mature audiences only, and other astronauts kidded that our post-flight film was X-rated.

By Saturday, it seemed that everything we had accomplished during the past week was lost in a snit about our language. One headline read:

AIR TURNS BLUE AS ASTRONAUTS BLOW "COOL" IMAGE

The accompanying article said we broke the shackles of having to be super-careful about our language, that no officials had complained, and that other astronauts were saying it was about damned time that we were allowed to be human.

Ah, but nothing is easy. The good Reverend Dr. Larry Poland, president of the Miami Bible College, was most distressed that we had carried to the Moon "language you see written on a restroom wall." The indignant Reverend Doctor wired President Nixon and NASA to demand a public apology and called for Tom, John and me to repent our "profanity, vulgarity and blasphemy." Thousands of people rallied to our defense, claiming that in a similar situation, any normal person probably would have said much worse, possibly even the good Reverend Doctor. Of every hundred letters that poured in, ninety-nine supported us.

NASA caved in to the pressure and I was pinned as the culprit. John wasn't touched by the flame of controversy and Mumbles had garbled his cuss words and the world couldn't understand what he had said. But there was no mistaking what I had said, and an apology was ordered to polish up the astronaut tiara. So I agreed, on the condition that I could do it my own way, and I told a news conference, "For those I offended, I'm sorry. For those who understand, thank you."

The good Reverend Dr. Larry Poland said he forgave us, although that didn't make much difference to me. I never got around to forgiving that self-righteous prig. Bunch of goddamn hogwash.

WHAT'S WRONG WITH THIS picture? Tom Stafford was backup commander for *Apollo 7* and went on three missions later to command *Apollo 10*. Neil Armstrong was backup commander for *Apollo 8* and was promoted to command *Apollo 11*. Pete Conrad was backup commander for *Apollo 9* and commanded *Apollo 12*. Gordo Cooper was backup commander for *Apollo 10* and Alan Shepard was named to command *Apollo 13*.

The three-mission rotation had been junked. Big Al was back in town, and Cooper, the happy-go-lucky flyboy who was one of the Original Seven, was squashed. Gordo did not like it at all, and decided it was time for him to leave.

*   *   *

ALMOST AS SOON AS I got back on Earth, I set my new plan in motion. Even while windows were rattling with applause for our success, huge things were happening within the program. After some long, serious talks, Barbara gave my idea her blessing, but probably thought it was a rather hare-brained, all-or-nothing scheme.

Events were moving so swiftly that, as soon as we splashed down, a sign was hoisted in Mission Control: 51 DAYS TO LAUNCH. Man would walk on the Moon soon, but that didn't mean everything else came to a halt.

Ten more missions were scheduled after our return. Deke was lining up his ducks for future crews and had no hesitation about putting his buddy Al Shepard into the driver's seat on the next available flight, *Apollo 13*. No matter what, Shepard was still one of the best fliers in the business, and if anyone had earned a shot at Apollo, it was Al.

Not everyone agreed. After all, it had been eight years since he had flown on a rocket, and then only for a quick suborbital mission. A lot of time and technology had passed since then. He had never been a backup commander on Apollo, nor even served as a backup command or lunar module pilot, and there were open expressions of dismay, both inside and outside the program, that he might not be ready in time. Flying on Mercury by himself, a quick up and down so long ago, was one thing. Running an Apollo team on a complicated Moon mission aboard a Saturn V was something entirely different. We all knew Al was good, but was he really *that* good? The general feeling around the Astronaut Office was that he should get in line like everybody else.

Deke compromised with headquarters and persuaded Al to slip back one mission to gain extra training time. Jim Lovell was scheduled to command the prime crew of *Apollo 14*. Instead, Deke moved Jim up one flight, with his crew of Ken Mattingly and Fred Haise, to fly *Apollo 13*.

That moved Al back to the open slot on *Apollo 14*, with another four months to prepare. Neither red-haired Stu Roosa, his command module pilot, nor lunar module pilot Ed Mitchell had yet been in space, so the crew was immediately given the nickname of "The Three Rookies," a not-so-subtle needle to Al's ego for having stomped on the rest of us for so many years.

By bigfooting Gordo's chance to fly on *Apollo 13*, Deke and Al had sure put a dent in the three-mission rotation theory, and the question that occupied my mind was, what next for Tom Stafford, John Young and Gene Cernan? Tom was definitely headed in a different direction, either to a new position within the program or a run for the U.S. Senate from Oklahoma. So it appeared that John and I were in line for backup duty on Lovell's new *Apollo 13* team, with John in command and me again in the lunar module seat, which strongly hinted at a rotation to prime crew for *Apollo 16*, when we could walk on the Moon.

It was a nice thought, and a jewel job, and would be the climax for any astronaut's career. It was why we were all here. Only I didn't want it. I had no desire to return to the Moon as an LM pilot. For me, walking on the Moon was not enough!

I have always believed that destiny is a matter of personal choice, where you carefully think out your decision, consider the downside, accept the risk of being wrong, and press on. My goal, something that was the underpinning of everything that I had ever done, was to have a command of my own. Had I still been in the traditional Navy, I would have been campaigning to be skipper of my own squadron, and I now had the confidence and the experience to lead my own team to the Moon.

Deke gave me the opportunity of working with John again, and his eyes widened in surprise when he heard my unexpected answer. "Deke, I've got nothing against flying with John, but I think I've earned a shot at my own command," I said.

He blinked and coughed while his mind assessed what he had just heard. This man who never made promises had just offered me an almost guaranteed chance to fly *Apollo 16*, and I had said, no thanks. "Geno," he said in disbelief, "You're turning down a chance to walk on the Moon?" His voice was like rough sandpaper.

"Yes, sir, Deke. I'd love to walk on the Moon, but I want to do it from the left seat." Despite my preparations for this meeting, my stomach rumbled nervously.

The Godfather put his hands on his hips and leaned toward me, getting into my face like a drill sergeant. "Look, Geno, you know the budget is going to be cut back. There may not be too many more missions and I've got a lot of guys ready to fly. If you don't go with John, I don't know if you'll fly again at all. Take this job on *Thirteen*." He was a good bit shorter than me, but in times of stress, Deke seemed to grow larger than life. You never looked down on Deke Slayton. At the moment, we were toe-to-toe, and if anything, I was looking up at him, a child saying "No" to a a parent.

"I understand that, Deke. I'll just have to take my chances." All of my cards were on the table—it was more important to me to be skipper of my own ship than to walk on the Moon. My astronaut career was on the line and I knew it might very well end with that conversation. It was one of the biggest risks of my life. With so many astronauts competing for the remaining Apollo seats, this was one hell of a gamble. I could easily be punching a one-way ticket to obscurity.

Deke and I stared at each other in silence for a moment, as if he was waiting for me to change my mind. Then he abruptly spun on his heel and almost stomped away, shaking his head in disbelief, perhaps thinking that I was one the biggest dumb-asses in the entire world. He knew something I did not, and would write years later that he thought my chances of getting a command at that point "didn't look good."

A few days after our talk, he posted the *Apollo 13* backup crew. John was the commander, with Jack Swigert as command module pilot and Charlie Duke, instead of me, to fly the LM. On *Apollo 16*, John and Charlie walked on the Moon.

Me? Well, for now, I didn't have a job. Deke acceded to my wishes, leaving me to wonder what the hell I had just done.

22

The Ice Commander

BUZZ ALDRIN HAD WORKED himself into a frenzy with his campaign to be the first man to walk on the Moon. He came flapping into my office at the Manned Spacecraft Center one day like an angry stork, laden with charts and graphs and statistics, arguing what he considered to be obvious—that he, the lunar module pilot, and not Neil Armstrong, the mission commander, should be the first one down the ladder on *Apollo 11*. Since I shared an office with Neil, who was away training that day, I found Aldrin's arguments both offensive and ridiculous. Ever since learning that *Apollo 11* would attempt the first Moon landing, Buzz had pursued this peculiar effort to sneak his way into history, and was met at every turn by angry stares and muttered insults from his fellow astronauts. How Neil put up with such nonsense for so long before ordering Buzz to stop making a fool of himself is beyond me.

Two weeks after *Apollo 10* returned from the Moon and experts reviewed the computer records, NASA declared that *Apollo 11* would launch on July 16. Neil, Mike and Buzz were going to fly one for the ages.

But as their training went into the final phases, Deke was already looking ahead, considering how the three astronauts might fit into his future plans, and he was not really surprised that only one of them fit at all. It was understood that Neil would shy away from the adulation and fame bound to accompany his historic step. What could he, or anyone, ever do to top that performance? What was left?

Likewise, Deke had no intention of giving Aldrin another mission, and Buzz was headed for a hard life, trying to cope with being the second man on the lunar surface. What most people would have considered a great honor, Buzz perceived as a defeat, because he would be *second*. Second. Forever. Neil Armstrong and who? It would send him into a spiral of depression.

Mike Collins, however, was a different story. Mike had fully recovered from his spinal surgery and had emerged as a leader in the space program, with sterling credentials as a test pilot, as a Gemini astronaut and now in training as the CM pilot on *Apollo 11*. Deke badly wanted Mike to command a future mission.

The two of them were flying a T-38, returning from a prelaunch flight readiness review at the Kennedy Space Center when Deke popped the question: Would Mike rotate to be Alan Shepard's backup on *Apollo 14*, and then command the prime crew on *Apollo 17*? Through the intercom of the little airplane, Mike politely declined. The offer would mean another two to three years of hard, continuous training and Mike had decided to spend more time with his family and find new outlets for his talents. Without my knowing it, Mike had been my first hurdle to becoming a commander, but I would not learn of that important conversation until years later. Had I known Mike was the first choice, I might have reevaluated the odds when Deke offered me that LM seat on John Young's crew.

THE ASTRONAUT TALENT POOL was wide on numbers, but not necessarily deep with experience. Some of the older guys like Wally and Gordo were leaving the program and some internal promotions were nibbling at the ranks. Tom Stafford tested the water for a run at a U.S. Senate seat, but instead moved over to Al Shepard's desk as head of the Astronaut Office, which meant I had a buddy in a pretty high place. Jim McDivitt was promoted to manage the Apollo Program Office, and other veterans such as Pete Conrad and Dave Scott and Dick Gordon were up to their eyebrows in training for upcoming flights.

In addition to Mike, I believed there was another astronaut with a high enough rating to warrant an early command slot: Bill Anders, who had made the famous Christmas Eve flight with Borman and Lovell as the LM pilot aboard *Apollo 8*. Borman had hung up his spurs after that mission, Shaky Lovell was to command *Apollo 13* and Bill, an extremely bright guy, was to fly with him again, this time as the CM pilot. That would put him in the pipeline for a command of his own.

Unlike me, Bill couldn't have cared less about having a command. He was a true astronaut, damn it, and his goal was to walk on the Moon. To him, taking the offered CM pilot slot meant that he would just ride in circles around the Moon some more during the flight of *13*, while Lovell, as mission commander, and Fred Haise, who replaced Bill as LM pilot, went down to the surface. Anders felt he had done enough lunar orbiting on *Apollo 8*. And because no one really knew how many flights there would be after *Apollo 13*, Bill thought the chances of his rotating into a command and an eventual Moon walk were pretty remote. So just as I had passed on the backup LM job, and Mike had turned down a future command, Anders declined the *Apollo 13* CM pilot's job. A perplexed Deke Slayton suddenly had to get used to a bunch of experienced astronauts refusing his offers of Moon trips.

Deke asked Anders to help out in the interim by taking a job in Washington with the National Space Council, and Bill reluctantly agreed, with the understanding that he would remain on astronaut flight status and be considered for an assignment that would get him a Moon walk. But once he traded the Banana River at the Cape for the Potomac, Bill lost that particular dream, although Washington rewarded his ability and put him on a different career track. He eventually served as President Ford's Ambassador to Norway and later became CEO of General Dynamics. So another of my potential rivals, another good friend, was also on the sidelines.

With such attrition and crew assignments, I had the feeling that my chances for a command, based on seniority and experience, were improving. Deke wasn't saying anything.

Bill Anders told me a few years ago that shortly after he took the new job, he was seated next to the head of the National Science Foundation during a flight to Washington. The NSF guy held a lot of power in those days, including the ability to influence the NASA budget. While they talked about space during the plane ride, Bill made the offhand comment, "I can't believe you're not putting a geologist on the Moon." His seatmate's eyes lit up as if he had just discovered the meaning of life. Very soon, we would all see the impact of that little conversation.

TOM STAFFORD, JOHN YOUNG and I harvested a bonanza of fame upon our return to Earth. It seemed as if everyone in America wanted to shake our hands and say welcome back, job well done. Except maybe for that Bible-thumper down in Miami.

From the moment we arrived at Ellington, we were showered with congratulations. Kids played hooky from school to get a glimpse of us, and workers took off from their jobs in Houston to join the throng. The excitement was contagious, and Ellington was only the beginning.

At the start of June, we began a whirlwind national tour for NASA that began in California, where Tom, John and I rubbed elbows with the television elite and received golden Emmy awards for the dramatic color telecasts from space. One of the most popular TV shows that year was *Mayberry, R.F.D.*, on which the character of Andy Griffith's son, Opie, was played by a kid named Ron Howard. Our paths would cross a quarter-century later when Ron, who grew up to be a movie director, made the wonderful film *Apollo 13*.

Governor Ronald Reagan declared the Golden State to be ours for a whole week, and we got to say thanks to Charles Schulz for letting us take Charlie Brown and Snoopy to the Moon. San Francisco saluted us with a deluge of ticker tape. Other parades flowed in Oakland, Sacramento, San Diego and Los Angeles, dinners and receptions filled the evenings, and I had a chance to see old friends from my days as a summer intern at Aerojet and a student in Monterey. Barbara and Tracy had a terrific trip to Disneyland, where Goofy and Mickey Mouse played host.

We were feted by Mayor John Lindsay of New York City, then had a marvelous homecoming at Cape Kennedy, and the governor of Florida declared Charlie Brown Day throughout the state. Mission Control had moved to Houston during the Gemini program, and since then, astronauts had stopped returning to the Cape to pay their respects after a flight. But we were allowed to symbolically complete our half-million-mile journey back where we began it. The people responded with almost embarrassing enthusiasm. Schoolkids poured from their classrooms, people stood five-deep along the curbs of Titusville and Cocoa Beach, there were private receptions, and we had a chance to thank the NASA and contractor teams that sent us to the Moon. For some reason, I felt extraordinarily motivated to share our joy with these folks, not knowing then that my efforts were going to pay large dividends a few years later. Talking to some 10,000 workers gathered inside the cavernous Vehicle Assembly Building, I said that "the greatest reward of our flight is coming back here to see you people. . . . You're not on our team, we're on your team." When I found that a twelve-year-old boy on a school tour had gotten sick before being able to see the astronauts, I visited him privately in his room and brought along a NASA doctor to give him a checkup. He was fine, and went home the envy of his classmates. At a lunch, I chatted at length with a seven-year-old girl as well as with officials. This cheerleading not only made the kids feel a part of the Moon program, but would provide me with some needed help in the future.

On to Illinois! Bellwood, which had already turned out a first-class celebration for my Gemini flight, saw Tom and I being paraded through the tree-lined streets once again. Flags and kids, Snoopys and waving neighbors, cheers and hurrahs, then Bellwood handed us off to Mayor Daley, and we shook Chicago. Fire boats in the river sprayed the sky with curtains of water, and a ticker-tape parade through the Loop was seen by about 100,000 people and led to a private reception at the Parker House. I was flabbergasted once again by the salutes. The only untoward event came when Mayor Daley asked me to cut a large cake, and after taking a hack with a large knife, I found the cake was made of plastic.

Back to Houston for a few days, and then to Washington and the White House for the third time in six months, this trip for an intimate black-tie dinner in our honor. President and Mrs. Nixon greeted us at the North Portico, and the president fidgeted eagerly as we arrived in limousines. The *Apollo 10* astronauts were to Nixon what John Glenn had been to President Kennedy, a popular sign that he was leader of a successful cause. As we shook hands, I thought we had found another champion.

Vice President and Judy Agnew awaited us in the Yellow Oval Room on the second floor. Barbara, with frosted hair and wearing a long, lemon-colored gown, gave me a warning glance when I got near my favorite banister.

Another twenty-three of Washington's "A-List" guests joined us for dinner in the State Dining Room, where we munched chateaubriand off the Truman china. The evening ended with Academy Award-winning composer Henry Mancini serenading us with "Moon River."

We wrapped up the tour with a visit to Oklahoma. If Bellwood was running out of things to do to celebrate my accomplishments in space, imagine Weatherford trying to find something new with which to honor Tom Stafford, who was coming around for the third time. They rose to the occasion by almost giving him a deed to the state. Today, more statues in Oklahoma honor General Thomas P. Stafford than memorialize Will Rogers and pioneer aviator Wiley Post combined.

Having pretty much tromped all over the United States, NASA then packed us onto a plane and sent us to Finland for five days. Finland? Same thing over there. Some 200,000 people jammed together in one single event in Helsinki to see us. Space magic was everywhere.

THERE WAS A CERTAIN irony in our visit to the White House. Only two months before we arrived, President Nixon had submitted a NASA budget for the coming year of 3.83 billion dollars, some 25 percent below the peak budget year of 1965. Some champion. Congress sliced it even thinner, to 3.69 billion dollars. The Man-to-Mars program and other plans of Ted Agnew's Space Task Group, which carried a price tag of up to 78 billion dollars over the next ten years, never got beyond the stage of, "Good idea, but we can't afford it."

Even with the glow of Apollo at its brightest—even before *Apollo 11* left the ground—some 5,000 jobs were being pared around Cape Kennedy because of budget cuts, property values in Brevard County were sinking, some small businesses and motels were closing, and the new four-story Apollo office building in Cocoa Beach stood empty. "There's a feeling of panic among some of us now," worried the wife of one engineer who remembered the recent boom times. But maybe those good times would be back. After all, the first Moon landing was yet to be made and plenty of missions were still on the chart, all the way through *Apollo 20*. Beyond that would be *Skylab* and who knew what else? Maybe the magic would return, bringing along those dollars that were flooding out to feed other federal programs, just as a low tide on Florida's beaches was inevitably followed by a high tide.

WHILE WE HAD BEEN in space, U.S. paratroopers carried out meat-grinder attacks on a worthless piece of real estate in Vietnam called Hamburger Hill. American deaths in the war surpassed the total killed in Korea and the massacre of My Lai villagers by American infantrymen came to light. General William Westmoreland declared that things had never been better.

The nation had become sharply divided not only over Vietnam, but culturally as well. On Broadway, a rock musical called *Hair* featured nudity and sex. On campuses, students captured deans' offices. On the streets, long-haired hippies called for open rebellion.

Among the more conservative leaders was the new vice president Ted Agnew, who raised "a cry of alarm to penetrate the cacophony of seditious drivel." When the vice president grabbed the microphone, no one was ever quite sure what he was going to say, and he happily attacked "an effete core of impudent snobs who characterize themselves as intellectuals" and other "nattering nabobs of negativism." Such statements sent him soaring in public opinion polls that soon ranked him as the third most popular man in America, right behind the Reverend Billy Graham and President Nixon.

THE MOST MEMORABLE MOMENT of our generation, and perhaps of our century, came on Sunday, July 20, 1969, the day that man landed on the Moon.

Neil, Buzz and Mike had blasted off from Earth without incident four days earlier, and an incredible sense of worldwide anticipation grew as *Apollo 11* rushed through space. Thanks to the advent of global communications, this would be the most-watched event in history, and when the lunar lander *Eagle* uncoupled from the command module *Columbia,* the world held its breath as the two spacecraft zipped into a tandem orbit around the far side of the Moon. When they reappeared, the impossible would be about to happen, although the men actually flying the machines that day put their chances of actually landing on the Moon at no better than fifty-fifty.

I was in Mission Control, watching and sweating with everyone else, as *Apollo 11* went out of radio contact. Tension gripped the White Team of Flight Director Gene Kranz as they stared at their static-filled television monitors. Kranz had locked the door to Mission Control, and behind the far wall of glass stood a room filled with NASA dignitaries, guests and other astronauts. Inside the control room, you could have heard a pin drop.

Then *Apollo 11* popped around the edge, two radar dots moving above the giant map of the Moon at the front of the room. Radio signals were reacquired, telemetry came alive, and we burst into a frenzy of activity. The *Eagle* edged lower and began its final run. Having flown almost exactly the same mission, Tom Stafford and I knew the Sea of Tranquillity better than anyone else in the room, and were advising the flight controllers on exactly what Neil and Buzz were encountering.

It wasn't going well. Radio communication with the *Eagle* had become spotty, unexpected alarms flashed on, and an overloaded computer gave questionable readings as the lander lowered past 50,000 feet above the surface. But the Mission Control wizards gave Kranz the information he needed to allow the landing attempt. Down they went.

Almost on the surface, we saw the lunar lander had suddenly begun to scoot around as Neil tried to find a clear spot in a field strewn with boulders, then had to dodge a crater the size of a football field. The unexpected maneuvering was burning precious fuel, and CapCom Charlie Duke called out dire readings that showed they were running out of gas. Still sixty dangerous feet above the Moon and only a minute's worth of maneuvering fuel left before an abort would be ordered.

We knew this mission could not be only 99-percent successful. A major glitch or crash probably would be the show-stopper for the lunar exploration program. With thirty seconds worth of fuel left, they were still dangling ten feet above the surface, Neil nursing the controls to counter a slightly backward drift. Buzz suddenly saw the light blink on that indicated long wires trailing beneath the lander had made contact, called out the signal, and Neil hit ENGINE STOP. The spacecraft gently bumped to a safe landing with computer alarms pinging and only about fifteen seconds of fuel left. Armstrong's scratchy voice came down the line: "Houston. Tranquillity Base here. The *Eagle* has landed."

Everybody in Mission Control erupted in cheers and applause, and we pounded each other on the backs as if we had just won the Super Bowl and the lottery at the same time. Charlie Duke happily confirmed, "Roger, Tranquillity. We copy you on the ground. You got a bunch of guys about to turn blue. We're breathing again."

There was not an ounce of "Gee, I wish it was me" in the room at that momentous time. Getting the *Eagle* and its occupants onto the Moon had been such a huge goal for all of us that there was no room for jealousy, only elation. On this particular mission, we were all hitched to the same wagon. I don't think I ever felt as proud in my life as when the three larger-than-life television screens on the walls at Mission Control showed the ragged picture of my spacesuit-clad friend Neil Armstrong emerging from the LM. "I'm at the foot of the ladder. I'm going to step off the LM now," he said, and did. "That's one small step for man, one giant leap for mankind."

We had done it, and the whole world marveled.

A FEW MONTHS LATER, Deke called me over to his office in Building One. "Your gamble paid off, Geno. I'm going to give you a shot. You're commanding the backup crew on *14*." He didn't say, and I didn't expect him to promise, that the assignment also meant that I had the ticket to command *Apollo 17*, but this was definitely a step in the right direction.

Had I not gotten the job, the game would have been over. For now, at least, I was still in the hunt.

The good news was that I had a command, even if it was only a backup command assignment for now. The bad news was that the man I was backing up was the Ice Commander—Capt. Alan B. Shepard.

Deke and I quickly settled on a crew of two space rookies. My command module pilot would be my old comrade from Monterey, Ron Evans, the Vietnam veteran. For lunar module pilot, we chose Joe Engle, a personable guy who had earned Air Force astronaut wings for flying the X-15 higher than fifty miles even before he was chosen for the space program. I liked and respected both men and was determined to make ours the best crew ever.

That left me with the big problem of approaching Shepard. He was pretty snippy with astronauts who thought he wasn't ready to lead the *Apollo 14* mission, and although I wasn't in that group, he didn't know that. Al's hard-ass reputation was well deserved, and my first priority was to crack that barrier between us. Somehow, I had to win the respect and trust of a man I had spent a lot of time avoiding during my astronaut career, even after I had two successful flights behind me. He had always been my boss, and my conversations usually were along the lines of "Yes, sir" and "No, sir." I didn't really know him very well, but reasoned that he must have agreed with Deke on who would be the backup commander of his flight, because if Shepard didn't want me around, I damned sure wouldn't have the job.

So I asked Deke. After all, he knew Al better than anyone in the program. The answer came as an impatient growl. "Just go in there and tell him you're as good as he is," said the Godfather. His iron rule was that any crew could fly any mission, and I better not start showing any weakness now that he had placed a bet on me. I tugged at my forelock and slithered out of his presence.

I took his advice and marched boldly to Al's office. His secretary always kept a cube on her desk with a painted smiley face on one side and a frowning face on the other, pointing the side reflecting her boss' current mood toward the door to warn visitors of what might await them. Today it showed the frowning face. Gulp.

Shepard was leaning back in his chair with his hands crossed on his stomach, his eyes unemotional and flat, like those of a snake about to devour a mouse. He did not leap from his chair and applaud at the news that I was his backup.

"Congratulations, Al!" I blurted with enthusiasm. Nothing but a nod. Sumbitch knew where this was heading, and wasn't about to make it easy for me. Anyway, why was I congratulating him? He already had a job.

I jacked it up a notch. "Al, my crew is going to do everything possible to have your crew ready to fly." He nodded, a flicker of those distant eyes indicating he was amused at my discomfort. *Goddamn him!*

I paused, then words just came flooding forth. "I want to assure you, that if necessary, we're going to be ready to fly, and I'm committing to you right now that I'm going to be ready to fly if you can't." Don't stop now, I told myself, because there won't be a second chance. Anyway, I was on a roll and he could only throw me out of his office once. "I'm going to be ready to do *your* job not only as well as you, but better than you."

Now I'd stepped in it. Sometimes my mouth got in the way of my good sense, and telling the first American in space that I would be better than he is probably wasn't the wisest thing I'd ever said. It was plain that Shepard's backup was never going to fly this mission. There might be two commanders training together, but there was only one Supreme Being, and nothing short of death itself would keep Al out of the spacecraft.

His stare frosted into a silent glare, and I knew there was no in-between with Al—he either liked you or he didn't. For a moment, I thought he might reach in a drawer, pull a pistol, and shoot me on the spot as a warning to future backup commanders about being arrogant. *So, you insolent pup, you're gonna do the job better than me?*

Instead, Al stood up, leaned across the desk and reached for my hand. "Geno, we're going to have a ball," he said. The ice melted, the iron shield collapsed and I was allowed into the sanctum sanctorum of Al's small circle of friends. His cocky fighter-jock smile came through and the sun shone and little birdies sang.

I believe to this day that sinister ole Deke put me in that job as an acid test. If I could win Al's respect, then I could certainly lead a flight to the Moon. If not, well, then I would have written my own epitaph.

23

Secret Mission

THE DIVORCE BUBBLE BURST in 1969 and the debris landed everywhere, upsetting the delicate, invisible support system that had protected astronauts and their families from the ugliness of the real world. So many marriages suffering under so much unrelenting strain for so many years in the public fishbowl could not endure, no matter how much we wished they could.

Donn Eisele's divorce was only the first. His marriage had been unstable even when he flew on *Apollo 7*, and when he was allowed to continue on the backup crew for *Apollo 10*, our wives wondered whether the previously feared consequence of a divorce for an astronaut was less severe than before. Things eased somewhat when Eisele was fired because Deke felt Donn had lost interest in his job, possibly a result of the divorce and remarriage. So maybe, the wives thought, the hammerlike threat still held: An astronaut lost his rocket ride if he lost his wife. Meanwhile, most of the women remained loyal to Donn's first wife and would have nothing to do with the new bride, not because she was a bad person, but because she represented unwelcome change. That schism of hurt feelings ripped the tight social fabric of the community and the tear would never be repaired.

As the year wore on, personal problems that had remained hidden in the astronaut suburbs came to light with shattering results. John Young was splitting up with his wife, Al Worden was also about to divorce, and rumors about other weak marriages spread like bad oil. Al was ticketed to be aboard *Apollo 15* and John was going to command *Apollo 16*, and Deke didn't fire either one of them. They were going to fly. It was the equivalent of a marital earthquake in Nassau Bay, El Lago and Timber Cove. *The women who helped these men achieve their dreams were gone, replaced by pretty young girls! Could this be contagious?*

Barbara and I remained strong, at least I thought so, and before I jumped into training for my new job, we took some overdue vacation time. We went to a ranch in Nevada, where and Tracy and I rode horses while Barbara kicked back and read books or we all went swimming. Then we drove over to San Diego and up the coast to Monterey, returning to Los Angeles for a gala dinner President Nixon gave for the astronauts of *Apollo 11*. When Tracy entered first grade, Barbara and I took a week's holiday in Hawaii with the Staffords. With the marriages of other astronauts collapsing, none of us was taking things for granted.

IT WASN'T JUST DIVORCE . It was clear that the entire world was changing when, a few months after *Apollo 11*'s famous flight, Soviet cosmonauts came to visit. These were the guys who had been our enemies in space, and we were expected to show them around, be buddies, act normal. Actually, the pleasant mutual discovery that none of us had horns or a tail came pretty quickly, and soon we were getting along like a normal, unruly pack of aviators. In coming years, I would become close friends with a number of my Soviet counterparts.

Barbara and I played host for five days to Major General Georgi Beregovoi and civilian Konstantin Feoktistov, the scientist who had been packed aboard the first three-man flight, *Voskhod 1*, back in 1964, to make him shut up about the potential danger of that mission. NASA picked up the bill and we laid it on thick, ignoring the stark contrasts in political beliefs. "Politics baffles us," Neil Armstrong was saying at the time, way over in Pakistan, where the *Apollo 11* astronauts were in the middle of a twenty-two-nation tour.

In San Diego, we took our guests to Sea World, then to a San Diego Chargers football game, where almost 60,000 people stood up and cheered when we were introduced. As I sketched diagrams of what was happening on the field, the confused Beregovoi threw up his hands and described American football as a game of "All fall down, all get up, all fall down." Hot dogs and pizza and a pretty blond interpreter for the general's teen-aged son.

Georgi was an extrovert, a large happy man, and a stark contrast to the thin, wimpy engineer Feoktistov. He drank vodka like a normal person could drink lemonade, and during long evenings of toasting everything in sight, Georgi just got jollier and bearier with every drink and mangled my name, Eugene, into a nonword that was more comfortable on his Russian tongue. "Ou-zheen! One more!" he would call while I was sliding cross-eyed beneath the table. "Come, Ou-zheen, just one more!"

During a party at the swank, cliffside La Jolla mansion of Frank Jameson, the president of Teledyne-Ryan, Georgi put on an apron to help me cook up a mess of barbeque while a Mexican mariachi band honked in the background and his wife, Lidiya, walked into a glass door. Many toasts were drunk to future friendships. "Ou-zheen! One more!" He gamely tried on Mickey Mouse ears at Disneyland and straddled a steer at the Cow Palace in San Francisco.

The business part of the tour came when we took Georgi and Konstantin out to Downey and toured the North American Rockwell operation, where my *Apollo 10* and the *Apollo 11* spacecraft were temporarily stored, and the two cosmonauts were almost reverent in looking over manned spacecraft that had gone to the Moon. Today, *Apollo 10* is in the London Museum of Science, and *Apollo 11* rests appropriately in Washington, at the National Air and Space Museum.

Hollywood chipped in with a huge party at the home of Kirk Douglas, and every star in Tinsel Town wanted to glitter for the men from space. Barbara was seated at a table with two of her favorite movie stars, Glenn Ford and Walter Matthau, and their wives. Clint Eastwood, Goldie Hawn, Dinah Shore, Lee Marvin and Groucho Marx drifted through the crowd, and the Russians chatted without interpreters to multilingual Yul Brynner and actress Natalie Wood, whose last name was once Zacharenko.

Since American movies and music were shunned by the Soviet Union in those days, most of the famous faces were unrecognized by our Russian guests. They didn't have a clue who these people were. Frank Sinatra came through the receiving line, I introduced him to Georgi, who warmly greeted Old Blue Eyes, then whispered: "Who is he?" Comic Dan Rowan bailed out of the line immediately to go get a drink. "Ain't no reason for me to meet them if they don't know Sinatra," he explained.

IN NOVEMBER, 1969, *APOLLO 12* flew with Pete Conrad, Dick Gordon and Al Bean. To those within the program, this mission was as much a challenge as any previous flight. Just because we had landed on the Moon once didn't mean we could do it again. Now we wanted to see just how good we were, whether we could actually navigate up there, and the guys did a marvelous job. Not only did they overcome a lightning strike on their Saturn V during launch, but their lunar module, the *Intrepid*, came to roost on the lunar surface only ten yards from their target, the Ocean of Storms crater in which the *Surveyor 3* robot craft had landed two years earlier. Pete and Al have been known to exaggerate.

But a fickle public was deserting us in droves. What we saw as stupendous stuff from a technical and flying point of view, the people of America viewed now as boring routine. We've already landed on the Moon! We've beaten the Russians! We've seen color television pictures from outer space! Television networks were getting tight with free broadcast time because pictures of guys floating in zero gravity and bunny-hopping around on the Moon were not competing well with soap powder, beer and toothpaste advertisements. That growing apathy translated into a slide in public support, which further jeopardized funding that was already tight, and getting tighter.

By making dangerously difficult missions look easy, we had become victims of our own success. A growing chorus of politicians were hollering for Moon dollars to be channeled toward problems here on Earth, primarily pork barrel problems in their home districts. Why use money to build a space bridge, when a smaller span over Cripple Creek might keep the congressman in office?

NASA decided the time had come to make a deal with that pesky science community, obtaining financial and political support in exchange for putting a real scientist on the Moon. Shortly after *Apollo 12* returned to Earth, such a deal was struck. Dick Gordon had distinguished himself as Pete Conrad's CM pilot and was promoted to backup commander for *Apollo 15*, which positioned him to lead the prime crew for *Apollo 18*. If ever someone had earned a commander's chevrons, it was Dick, with whom I had made a memorable flight from Monterey to Houston to look for housing when we were both young astronauts. Vance Brand, a rookie, was command module pilot on Gordon's crew. At the Manned Spacecraft Center, groans were heard in many astronaut offices when Deke announced that the lunar module pilot would be Jack Schmitt. The geologist! Jack was everybody's favorite scientist, but some aviator had just lost his seat on Apollo.

Deke had been beaten over the head and shoulders by the scientific community so much that he figured this was a compromise that might get him some peace and quiet. Putting Jack on a backup crew guaranteed nothing, and at that point, Schmitt remained a long way from a ride to the Moon. The more vociferous scientists knew that, too, and didn't like his decision at all. Ever more pressure began to build to get their man on a flight. Bill Anders's casual comment to that NSF honcho was starting to bear bitter fruit.

THE YEAR OF 1969 ended with a bang for us, and a grand surprise for my best friend Skip Furlong, when Vice President Agnew invited the *Apollo 10* astronauts along for an official tour of Asia. I was just starting to train for my new *Apollo 14* job, but when the vice president asks, you go. NASA, hungry for help in high places, cleared things in a hurry, granting me some time away from training. *Cernan and the vice president are pals! This might mean more money for the program!* We agreed that Barbara and I would go along for a brief time.

The eighteen-day trip began on Christmas Day and opened up a new world for us. Sailing around the Pacific aboard an aircraft carrier had been much different from being chauffeured around in better-than-first-class splendor as a member of the vice president's official party on a state mission aboard *Air Force Two.* Barbara and I entered fantasy land, with the exotic itinerary of Hawaii, Guam, Manila, Taipei, Kuala Lumpur, Nepal, Afghanistan, Malaysia, Hong Kong and Tokyo, with a side trip for her to Bangkok while I finally got to Vietnam. Kings and queens and presidents and prime ministers and first ladies galore made us feel welcome at every stop.

In Taiwan, Generalissimo Chiang Kai-shek hosted an official dinner for only a dozen people, and unfortunately, his wife was ill and absent from the event. He was so short, a little more than four feet tall, that during World War II, General Joe Stilwell had called him the Peanut. The generalissimo spent most of the evening devoting time to Barbara, who was five-foot-six, and wearing a low-cut, strapless yellow evening gown. Chiang's widened eyes were consistently level with her all-American bosom and Ted Agnew teased her for the rest of the trip about almost causing an international incident.

Saigon was a bittersweet eye-opener for me because I went as a VIP visitor and not as a Navy attack pilot. I joined Agnew for lunch at the presidential palace with Premier Nguyen Cao Ky, and toured the old colonial city in an open jeep with an Army colonel as an escort. I naively asked why he packed a loaded .45 Colt sidearm while riding in the public streets. "Might have to use it," he answered. We flew to an artillery base about 100 miles outside of Saigon and spent the afternoon talking to GIs, making the round trip in a convoy of Huey helicopters so no enemy soldier could determine which one contained the vice president. In Saigon, soldiers carried weapons at roadblocks, warplanes from nearby Tan Son Nhut Air Base soared overhead, and in the distance, one could hear the faint thump of artillery. This was clearly a nation fighting for its life, and I sipped delicious bird's nest soup from a gleaming porcelain bowl while beggars in nearby steamy streets sought handouts from GIs. When we left, I was haunted by the fact that I had never gotten my slice of that war.

As we flew on to Manila, my mind drifted to Skip Furlong, who I thought was up north somewhere, flying combat missions as the skipper of an F-4 squadron. "Would you like to see him?" the vice president suddenly asked.

"Yes, sir. Sure," I replied, thinking he was just making conversation.

"Okay." The vice president summoned a minion and sent a routine inquiry back to his office in Washington. From there, it went to the Pentagon, which channeled it immediately to the Commander of Naval Air in the Pacific. COMNAVAIR zipped it out to Fleet Command in Honolulu, which hotfooted the request over to the Air Group Command aboard the *USS Constellation*, which happened to be tied up at a pier in Subic Bay following a tour of sea duty off North Vietnam. All this within an hour or so. My innocent reply to Agnew had grown in importance along the way up the chain of command into a FLASH message that had set brass hats jumping all over the Pacific.

"Commander Furlong. Commander Furlong. Attention Commander Furlong. Report immediately to an escort at the front door. The vice president requests your presence." Skip was in the base exchange at Cubi Point buying shaving cream when the loudspeaker blared his name and foot traffic froze.

Puzzled, he ambled over to a first class petty officer in dress blues who had been sent to find him. "The vice president of what?" Skip asked.

"Of the United States, sir. The admiral wants you back aboard the boat right away. I've got a sedan waiting outside."

Skip quickly paid for his purchase and climbed into a car for a roaring ride back to the pier.

A Marine guard took him straight up to the ship's bridge and into a grumpy line of authority. The admiral was waiting, along with the chief of staff, the captain of the ship, and the air wing commander. FLASH traffic tended to get attention. "Furlong," demanded the admiral, "what the hell's going on?"

"Sir, I have no idea," my bewildered buddy replied. The senior officers had concluded that Skip, whom they knew only as a pretty decent jet jockey, was actually more than that—he must be involved in some sort of secret spook operation that they, being mere admirals and captains, weren't cleared to know about. *Vice President Agnew himself wants him!*

"Get below and get cleaned up and grab a bag. A helo is en route for you right now."

Skip hustled to his room, put on a clean uniform, packed a small bag, and ran back up to the deck, where a Marine helicopter waited, its rotors turning. Not just any chopper, but the spiffy white-topped kind used only for VIPs. All eyes aboard the *Connie* watched the mystery craft whir away, destination and purpose unknown. Skip unfastened his seat belt and leaned forward so he could talk to the full-bird colonel at the controls.

"What's this all about, sir?" he asked.

The colonel didn't even look at him. "I'm just here as the vice president's pilot, and I'm to deliver you to the Intercontinental Hotel in Manila." End of conversation.

The helicopter swept to a soft landing on a broad green lawn and Skip was met by a pair of Secret Service agents who took him through doors guarded by Marines, never saying a word as they walked along at his side. Up an elevator in a silent ride to a top floor where another plainclothes agent at a desk checked his identification card. The quiet ones took him down the hall, ushered him into a room and closed the door, leaving him alone.

He was in a large, sumptuous hotel room and still had no clue as to what was going on. Two days ago he was flying around Vietnam, getting shot at, and now he was secluded in an elegant hotel in Manila, at the order of the vice president, with fresh fruit and flowers on the table. At least, he thought as he looked out over the sprawling city, it's not a jail cell, so he wasn't being arrested, but there were guards in the hallway.

He turned as the polished brass doorknob rattled and the door opened slowly. I stepped into the room. "Gotcha!" I said.

For the next three days, combat pilot Skip joined the vice president's official party in Manila and attended state functions, parades, cocktail parties, and dinners thrown by President Ferdinand Marcos, and even danced with First Lady Imelda. After a New Year's Eve party at the U.S.

embassy, we were riding back to the hotel in the vice president's limo when, at the stroke of midnight, Filipinos showered the streets with a hurricane of exploding firecrackers. Drove the Secret Service guards bananas.

When his fairy-tale moment came to an end, my buddy was taken back to the *Constellation* by that fancy helo, and every senior officer on the ship was waiting, drooling to know what had happened. "Sorry, Admiral," Skip stonily replied without a smile. "I'm not allowed to talk about it."

Furlong's Mission would stand as one of the great secrets of the Vietnam War.

24

Beep, Beep

THE CLOSEST THE UNITED States came to having a disaster in space happened on the nightmare ride of *Apollo 13* in April, 1971, when we almost lost an entire crew on a trip to the Moon. Jim Lovell, the skipper, and his shipmates Fred Haise and Jack Swigert had left Earth on a mission filled with optimism. What could go wrong? *Apollo 10* had flown almost to the lunar surface, *Apollo 11* had made the first landing, and *Apollo 12* had lent a precision to the whole business of spaceflight and Moon landings. There was every reason to be confident, particularly with Shaky Lovell, making his fourth space voyage, in command.

I had several odd connections to *Apollo 13* before it ever got off the ground. Charlie Duke, who had replaced me as the backup LM pilot for the mission, told Deke only days before the scheduled launch of *Apollo 13* that one of his kids had come down with the measles. Medical folders showed that except for Ken Mattingly, the command module pilot, everyone in the prime crew had the disease as a kid and was immune. Worrywart doctors predicted that Mattingly could get very sick while orbiting the Moon, so Ken (who never did catch the measles) was bumped aside and Jack Swigert was moved from the backup crew to replace him.

Long after they took off, when they were almost 200,000 miles from Earth, a faulty heater shorted out in a shower of sparks. That detonated one of the oxygen tanks, which wreaked internal havoc and blew out a side of the service module that contained the crew's life-support systems. A potential death struggle began in deep space. TV networks, which only a few hours before the explosion had refused telecast time, now stampeded toward the drama of what was happening to *Apollo 13*. I was later horrified to learn that the Number 2 oxygen tank that exploded was one of those that had been replaced on our *Apollo 10* spacecraft.

As for the corps of astronauts, we all jumped into this one together. Any pettiness, bias or personal disagreement, anything not directly connected to bringing *Apollo 13* back safely was put on the shelf, and everyone threw away their badges of difference. Our three guys were in jeopardy far, far away, and we all fought to get them home.

Breathable oxygen soon began to run out in *Apollo 13*'s command module, which was the crew's living quarters, and the damaged fuel cells were unable to generate the electricity needed to run the spacecraft. The command module was collapsing fast, its computers were stuttering, and the three astronauts were forced to seek shelter in the little lunar module, *Aquarius*, which had not been designed to perform in such a crucial emergency.

Mission Control filled with experts. The Grumman people who had built the LM and the wizards who had programmed the computers were all hauled in on emergency status. The Moon landing, obviously impossible, was scrubbed. The goal became something quite different and infinitely more important—keeping the astronauts in that frail spacecraft alive long enough to get home.

Joe Engle and I had been training as part of the backup crew for the next flight, *Apollo 14*, and dove into the gigantic LM mission simulator in Houston to help work out a program for a safe return. For damned near two days, Joe and I ran every possible flight scenario almost nonstop, crashing our butts or spinning out of control with alarming regularity. There simply had been no plan to have the LM do the actual flying in space with the command and service module, a big hunk of dead weight, on its nose. And as we worked, our thoughts constantly turned to Lovell, Swigert and Haise, who were heading around the Moon in a lifeboat instead of a spaceship.

While we were frantically running some new program in Texas, the guys in tennis shoes up at MIT in Massachusetts constantly rewrote the computer software that told the LM what to do in its new, unanticipated role. Spools of revised computer tapes were flown from Boston to Houston, rushed to the Manned Spacecraft Center and loaded into the simulator. Joe and I would then put the latest ideas from MIT through the wringer. More failures, more suggestions, more computer tape flying around the country, more urgent telephone calls, try this, try that. Then the cycle would be repeated. The Grumman guys swarmed to figure out exactly how far the lunar module could be pushed.

The results came together slowly, on an agonizing treadmill of trial and error, while *Apollo 13* sailed around the far side of the Moon, caught the gravitational slingshot effect and headed back toward Earth. It was a miracle that they had survived for so long, overcoming emergency after emergency. Finally, time ran out. Mission Control radioed up the best procedures we all had devised, and then we could only pray. Either it would work or it wouldn't. Somehow, the teams on the ground and the crew in space overcame all the terrifying odds and Lovell, Haise and Swigert lived through the ordeal, successfully returning to Earth.

Many years later, Jim would write a book about his flight, and it was made into the dramatic motion picture *Apollo 13*. Forget horror films. The next time you want to be frightened by a movie, this is the one to see. When I reflect on that mission today, I realize we came within a mere hairbreadth of losing them.

The flight was a crucial moment in the American space program, but in a most peculiar way. Although it reminded us that nothing was ever a sure thing, the salvation of *Apollo 13* should have refocused attention on the positive elements of what could be accomplished. We had done the near-impossible, but the victory carried a risk of also being our undoing, for it gave the naysayers enough ammunition to have an impact on the future of space exploration. JFK had said: "We choose to go to the Moon not because it is easy, but because it is hard." Now the fear of losing a crew of astronauts in space replaced the daring that started the program in the first place, and the brush with disaster took much of the backbone right out of some of NASA's leaders.

The image of a crew lost in space floated before them like a specter, and they concluded that the best way not to have astronauts die going to the Moon was to not send them out there in the first place. Less than two months after Lovell's crew came home, the final scheduled mission of the Moon exploration series, *Apollo 20*, was canceled and the new budget numbers coming down from Washington indicated it wouldn't be the last one to fall.

With the space race over, the Moon conquered, we had become a low priority for federal money and the pessimists were voting to concentrate on some other, safer space goal that wouldn't cost quite so much, nor be as dangerous. Maybe a neat, new, reusable buggy that would fly in careful circles around the world so scientists—*scientists!*—could perform experiments with weightless mice, bullfrogs, seaweed and rocks. Exploration would be left to robots. There was gossip around crew quarters that *Apollo 14* might be the last manned voyage to the Moon, and I wondered if there would even be an *Apollo 17* for me to command.

Just as things were looking bleak, I was notified by the Pentagon that I had been selected early for promotion to the rank of captain. I had reached that rank after just fourteen years of service, and, at the age of only thirty-six, I became the youngest captain in the United States Navy. A four-striper. Never thought I would be one of *Them*.

WHILE I TRAINED THROUGHOUT 1970 as Shepard's backup, some serious politicking began in Houston, Washington and at the Cape over who should fly *Apollo 17*, if there was one. It wasn't an urgent matter, yet, but with future flights undergoing budget surgery, the big question had yet to be answered, and Deke couldn't sidestep it forever. What about the scientist?

I had a terrific team with Joe and Ron, but right behind us was the *Apollo 15* backup squad of Dick Gordon, Vance Brand and Jack Schmitt. The big difference was that Jack was one of the program's acknowledged experts in geology and if NASA had to pacify the scientific community, then Schmitt was the man. Deke probably would have to assign him to a real flight. It boiled down to whether there would ever be an *Apollo 18* or *Apollo 19* on which to stash the scientist. Although still funded and flyable, the life signs for those missions were pretty anemic, and the ax finally fell in September, when two more Apollo missions were chopped. *Seventeen* would be the last stop on the Apollo trail.

The fact that Tom Stafford had become head of the Astronaut Office definitely helped me, but Jim McDivitt, the new chief of the Apollo program section, was a strong fan of Dick Gordon, as was Dick's old buddy and flying partner, the influential Pete Conrad. Deke would hear a lot from all sides in the coming months, and there was nothing I could do about it but keep plugging away at my new job. He delayed a decision, but must have pondered it daily—Cernan's crew or Gordon's crew? My task, while all of that was being sorted out far above my head, was to stay out of trouble, do the best job possible on *14*, and, most of all, not screw up.

RON AND JOE HAD come into the program with the talented 1966 group, both had impeccable credentials, and I couldn't have wished for better teammates on the backup crew for *Apollo 14* than these two Jayhawks.

Ron was from the small town of St. Francis, Kansas, and had taken an electrical engineering degree from the University of Kansas before earning his master's in aeronautical engineering from the Naval Post Graduate School and flying those 100 combat missions in Vietnam. Joe was also from rural Kansas and a graduate from the University of Kansas. He surged through the Air Force and into the elite flying fraternity at Edwards AFB and flew the X-15 into the fringes of space sixteen times before being taken aboard as a NASA astronaut. While at Edwards, Joe had become a protégé and hunting and fishing chum of his boss, Chuck Yeager. They were not strangers to me when we became a crew, for I had gotten to know Ron back during our school days back in Monterey, and had learned to respect Joe's abilities when he was on the support team for *Apollo 10.*

My goal was to weld us together into something more than just a backup crew, for I couldn't help but think ahead to when the three of us just might fly to the Moon together aboard *Apollo 17.* As commander, I had to consider more than switches and numbers—I knew that people problems usually are much more difficult to handle than mechanical glitches, and that any failure on their part would be my failure, too. I had to know what made Joe and Ron tick on a personal level, and to win their trust in me as the skipper of the mission. There was never a question. The two of them swung into high gear immediately and never stopped. In the coming months, we worked closely on an almost daily basis, and spent many of our off-duty hours together, even bringing our wives and kids into our tight circle of friendship.

Joe was a magnificent aviator, perhaps too good, for he would prefer a weekend spent hunting with Chuck Yeager to hanging around the simulators for some extra practice. His ability to fly was unquestioned, but he wasn't as up to speed as I would have liked on the lunar module's quirky systems. Since I was his commander, I felt responsible for his performance and after a long day of work, we would frequently get together at night in a motel room for some extra private tutoring. As time passed, I felt that he needed even more work on the computer software, but didn't really consider it much of a problem because of his genius for flying. If and when we actually took the lunar lander to the Moon, he would be with me, and as a former LM pilot myself, I knew the Bug's systems cold. I concluded that together, Joe and I could handle any emergency.

*   *   *

WE WERE GONE FROM home Monday through Friday, and I missed much of the excitement when Tracy went into the second grade, started in the Brownies and studied for her catechism. Barbara wistfully pointed out that the regimen of the never-ending training grind was growing stale the third time around. In the context of the year's most popular books, my wife felt she had signed on for *Love Story*, but had ended up with *100 Years of Solitude*.

There was still the occasional glittering party to attend, and I noticed several times that Barbara grew somewhat distant when she was introduced over and over as "Gene's wife," almost as an afterthought. She would later tell me that she felt we were at some of those functions only because of my job, and not because the host and hostess liked, or even knew, us. In fact, she felt quite a few were obviously transparent in their friendliness, using us as some sort of party favor for the other guests to admire, much like showing off the quaint oak credenza that Aunt Agnes brought over from England. In retrospect, I have to admit she was right.

Perhaps I was too job-oriented and too self-absorbed at the time to see the strain. The demands on a space wife were getting old for Barbara, and a couple of quick trips to Las Vegas and Acapulco couldn't shake her misgivings. The glitter and the glory were wearing thin for this veteran Mrs. Astronaut. "*. . . and this is Gene's wife.*" I was careful to make sure everyone understood that she was not only my wife, but my partner, and that we had made the long climb up the spaceflight pyramid hand-in-hand. During one dinner at which I was the guest speaker, she was asked to come up from the audience and say a few words. She gave them a big smile when they applauded, then someone asked, "How do you feel about Gene going to the Moon?"

She answered instantly. "If you think going to the Moon is hard, try staying home."

ANY CONCERN I HARBORED about whether I could work with Al Shepard was quickly erased. Instead of being cold and domineering, Al turned that magnetic personality on full force and won us over completely. He was so happy at being able to fly again that he transformed into a human being. There was never a doubt of his leadership ability, nor his flying skills, and he wasn't afraid to delegate authority or to pick my brain over what it was like to fly in deep space. After all, I'd been out there twice, and had gone to the Moon, while he had only that one suborbital flight.

Shepard was a sponge for learning and got to know every inch of his spacecraft. There was simply no end to his commitment to the mission. His crew—Stu Roosa and Ed Mitchell—respected him, and throughout our training he bonded the six members of the prime and backup crews together as tightly as a band of brothers.

As the months of hard work passed, Al and I became more comfortable together and I proved that I was not trying to take away his mission, but was as committed as he to seeing Al Shepard walk on the Moon. When the launch was delayed while the experts figured out what went wrong with *Apollo 13*, we gained even more time and we trained until we were as sharply honed as a bowie knife.

That didn't mean everything was going perfectly, for there was a significant problem that had to be overcome at the last minute involving our lunar module pilots. The brilliant Ed Mitchell was an acknowledged expert on the LM, and Joe Engle could probably have flown a lawn mower, so the fact that we ran into a situation with these guys was both ironic and frustrating. Part of the problem was that they were both so good that their attention wandered.

Deke brought Al and I together one day and laid it out, only a month before launch. He was fed up with Mitchell's penchant for playing around with experiments in extrasensory perception, even wanting to take some ESP tests along to the Moon. Ed just wouldn't let it go, and Deke said he was uncomfortable with the possibility that Mitchell's full attention would not be on the mission.

Deke held up two fingers of his right hand, about an inch apart. "I'm about that close to pulling Ed off the flight and replacing him with Joe Engle," he told us. "What do you guys think?" There was additional tension because Mitchell recently had balked at taking a backup assignment for *Apollo 16*, one of those vital positions that required a lot of anonymous work. Deke told him that after being given a Moonwalk, if he didn't want to rotate to that important but dead-end job (there would be no *Apollo 19* to which he could aspire), then he could just hit the bricks right away and not fly on *14* either. Deke was livid that Ed might not be totally committed to the program. You don't want to help, then don't let the door hit you in the ass on the way out.

Deke's displeasure with Mitchell caught us totally by surprise, and Al said the ESP stuff bothered him, too, but rated Ed a crackerjack LM systems man who was qualified for the flight on every other point. Al didn't want to shake up the crew at such a late date. "My guy can do the job," I told Deke about Engle, although I had to be honest that Joe was not at the 110-percent level of commitment that I would have wished. So we had Joe, the better natural pilot, who was still light on systems knowledge, weighed against Ed, the LM wizard who had developed a rather goofy attitude.

Because the decision to change them would have such an impact on the overall mission, Deke eventually chose to leave things as they were. For many years thereafter, in light of an unknown factor that was waiting just down the road, I would feel guilty about not pushing harder to get Engle aboard Shepard's crew. Because we did not make the switch, Joe would forever lose his chance to walk on the Moon.

IT WAS FORTUNATE FOR the country that Al was next on deck to command a mission. Just as old reliable Wally Schirra had been called upon to restore our faith in Apollo after the big fire, now Al was being asked to rescue that faith once again for a nation shaken by the experience of *Apollo 13.* It was a natural role for the first American astronaut ever to buckle on a rocket. He never doubted for a moment that he could do it, and that infectious confidence spread until we also never doubted that he could do exactly what he said he could.

He even took our good-natured ribbing about his crew being tagged as the Three Rookies. Ron, Joe and I called ourselves the First Team, to infer that we were better than they were. I was always giving Al mock warnings not to mess up, because the First Team was standing right there, ready to strap in and fly that Saturn V if the old man, the fat man, and the cute little redhead couldn't hack it.

Every flight has a personalized crew patch, and *Apollo 14* was no different, except for one thing—we were the first and only backup crew to have a mission patch, too! This loony idea was a "gotcha" on Al, for it depicted a gray-bearded Wile E. "Three Rookies" Coyote coming up from Earth only to find a "First Team" Roadrunner already standing on the Moon, chirping his famous "Beep-beep!"

Every time we would give him a "beep-beep" jab, Shepard would shoot right back, "Beep, beep, your ass!" This time, by God, the coyote was going to win.

25

Fire and Water

As 1971 BEGAN AND the January launch date neared for *Apollo 14*, I was on the top of the world. Everything was going great, and I felt good about my gamble to lead a crew to the Moon. Although the fateful decision on who would fly on *Apollo 17* was still months away, my chances had improved alongside my relationship with Al Shepard. The First Team was doing a super job, we were having fun and clearly were up to the challenge. Deke, the Godfather who knew everything that happened in his kingdom, was obviously aware of how things were going.

I was confident that if Dick Gordon was going to catch me, he was going to have to hurry, but always right there on the edge of my thoughts was the presence of his trump card, the geologist, lurking about like some kind of rock demon. Outside pressures continued to build to have a scientist on the final flight, and the logical assumption was that Deke would not break up a crew. If Schmitt flew, Gordon and Brand probably would fly with him. There was still nothing I could do, nor would attempt to do, about that. My best bet was to stay out of the politics and stick to my job and avoid trouble of any color. We were almost at the finish line, for what could possibly go wrong with only a month left before launch?

Well, on Saturday, January 23, 1971, only a week before the launch of *Apollo 14*, I damned near killed myself.

One of the machines we used for practicing lunar landings was the tiny H-13 Bell helicopter, the little bird seen as a flying ambulance on the television show *M*A*S*H*. It wasn't much more than a bubble canopy with rotor blades, but since it could hover, go up, down, and fly sideways, it was the closest flying approximation to a Moon lander that we had without using the stick-like, rocket-propelled LLTV simulator at Ellington, back in Texas. The prime and backup crews for *Apollo 14* were already in Florida, so I strapped into an H-13 at the Cape on that clear morning, warmed up the old-fashioned 260-horsepower Lycoming piston engine, and lifted off cleanly into a bright sky to log still another hour or so of practicing Moon landings only a few miles from where tourists tanned themselves on sunny beaches.

I zoomed down the Atlantic side of Cocoa Beach, swung across Melbourne and headed back up the Indian River toward the site at the Kennedy Space Center where we did our vertical approach work. The helicopter was somewhat sluggish with its twin fuel tanks filled to capacity and I wanted to burn off some of the heavy load before getting down to work. That gave me a reason to loaf around the sky for a while and invest the extra fuel in some fun flying.

Small boats dotted the clear water below and bright islands mounded here and there on the river. Hardly a ripple disturbed the mirrorlike surface. After so many months of hard work and concentration, I couldn't resist the temptation for a bit of mischief known among pilots as "flat-hatting." So I nosed over and swooped down from a couple of hundred feet to dance the chopper around the island beaches and among the boaters, steadily getting closer to the surface.

The doors had not been attached to the clear canopy, and cool, fresh wind rushed through the cockpit as I zipped along. Many of the people looked up at the chopper and waved, knowing that it probably was an astronaut at the controls, for who else would dare such hijinks in a military helicopter? Was I showing off? Of course! Who wouldn't?

Without realizing the danger, I flew into a trap that was the plague of seaplane pilots. Without ripples, the water provided no depth perception and my eyes looked straight through the clear surface to the reflective river bottom. I had lost sight of the water. But I was in control, or at least I thought so . . . until the toe of my left skid dug into the Indian River.

It was as if a mighty, molasses-sticky hand reached up and grabbed the H-13, yanking the helicopter out of the air. The ever-present gremlin of flight was punishing me for letting down my guard for an instant. I twisted the collective with my left hand and applied more power, pulling back on the controls, trying to get the machine to climb out of trouble. A plume of water erupted beneath the skid, then the canopy struck and a rushing tidal wave filled my vision as the helicopter lost any semblance of aerodynamic design. In a single flashing instant, it went from a speed of 100 knots to flat zero with a lurch as severe as any I had ever felt landing on an aircraft carrier or staging in a spacecraft. I crashed with a spectacular explosion.

Spinning rotor blades shredded the water, then ripped apart and cartwheeled away in jagged fragments. The big transmission behind me tore free and bounced like a steel ball for a hundred yards before going down. The latticelike tail boom broke off and skittered away in ever-smaller pieces, the Plexiglas canopy surrounding me disintegrated, one of the gas tanks blew up, and what remained of the demolished chopper, with me strapped inside, sank like a rock.

Doctors and I disagree to this day over whether I lost consciousness, but I recall settling to the bottom, my hands clutching the controls, still trying to fly the thing. Fortunately, the chopper had not flipped over and I was sitting upright, harnessed securely to the seat, and had not been pinned by the crumbling wreckage or the twisted steel panel of dials near my knees. Streams of bright bubbles rose past my eyes and I realized I was underwater, disoriented and unsure about what had happened. My heavy white flight helmet, buckled tightly beneath my chin, was filled with air and trying to pull away from my head, choking me like a hangman's noose. I unsnapped the strap and the helmet rocketed away from my head, heading for the surface in a rush, as if gravity had been reversed and it was falling upward.

I did a quick internal inventory, and felt no sharp pains of broken bones or ruptured organs, no jagged metal sticking into my gut, but I knew that if I didn't do something quickly, I would drown.

At that point, my training kicked in. *I had been here before. I knew what to do.* Memories came of the old Dilbert Dunker days of naval preflight training and the NASA water survival drills, in which we were taught to escape from submerged planes and space capsules and follow such rising bubbles to safety. Only this wasn't a plane or a spacecraft— it was what was left of a helicopter, and if those big rotor blades were still turning above me, they could chop off my head if I swam straight up. Not that I had much of a choice. Continuing to sit on the bottom of the Indian River was not an option.

Not realizing the canopy all around me had vanished, I undid my buckles and leaned toward where the side hatch should have been. Nothing was there, since the door panels had not been attached and the surrounding Plexiglas was gone. Moving in slow motion as my flight suit and combat boots grew heavy with water, I stepped through the empty space and was free of the helicopter. I pushed off the bottom and swam for the surface, my lungs screaming for air.

The whole river seemed ablaze as I bobbed up in the midst of hellfire and brimstone. The hottest flames I had ever felt burned all around me and the inferno's incredible heat singed my eyebrows and face. When I tried to gulp air, I swallowed fire. Time seemed to stand still as the wall of hungry flames closed about me. The crash didn't get me, I had not drowned, but the fire might finish the job. *Oh, shit, Cernan. Get out of here!*

But where to go? Anywhere! Away! I used both hands to splash at the burning water, to push it back, and then folded over and dove for safety underwater. I could only manage to stay down for a few yards, and when I popped up again, the fire was still trying to roast me alive. More splashing and another dive. And again and again, inching my way from beneath the spreading inferno that glowed bright above my head, daring me to come up for air again.

Even as I was trying to escape the fire, my water-soaked flight suit and heavy boots became anchors. I had survived the crash and was beating the fire, but now my own clothes were trying to kill me. Kicking and swimming became harder and harder, then nearly impossible, and I wondered what had possessed me not to wear a Mae West life vest that day. I broke to the surface away from the fire, but the heat remained overpowering, as if I had stuck my face in front of an open oven. Instead of the cool, fresh air I craved, I sucked rocks of heat into my aching lungs and it felt as though a scalding towel clung to my face, suffocating me.

Treading water and looking back at the crash, it was almost as if I were the survivor of a torpedoed ship and now getting a water-level view of hell. The gasoline fire rampaged and the heat surged across the water like a hot fist, punching me in the face. All I could see of the helicopter were bits and pieces, including one gas tank that was still intact and maybe still three-quarters full of gasoline and merrily baking in the flame. *If it blows . . .* At this point, I was out of options and about out of strength. I had no plan, and the Indian River looked as wide as the Atlantic Ocean. It was only about ten feet deep, but I was only six feet tall. I tried to untie my boots and lose their weight, but could not. One dangled on my foot, making it even harder to tread water.

The crash had been a real fireworks display, with a thunderous explosion and a rising ball of flame and smoke that clearly marked the point of disaster. I had missed the show, since I was inside the detonation and was not a spectator. Boaters surged toward the area to help, looking for me. From out of nowhere came a small fishing craft with only one person aboard, a woman, and she grabbed two handfuls of my soaking, yellow flight suit and helped wrestle me out of the drink. I collapsed on the deck, gasping for breath. I was a mess and disoriented, my lungs hurt with each breath, unable to murmur much more than a feeble "thanks" as she ferried me to shore. When I tried to speak, I didn't recognize my own voice. Words came out in a rattling, deep croak because my throat had been seared and I sounded like a frog.

A Brevard County deputy sheriff rushed me over to Patrick Air Force Base for some initial treatment. While the medics probed, bandaged, stitched and salved, I called Barbara in Houston. She had already been contacted by NASA and was still shaky, having mental flashbacks of the deaths of Charlie Bassett, C.C. Williams and other departed friends. NASA reassured her that I was okay and not seriously hurt, but I had to tell her that over and over again.

Deke dispatched a car to haul my charbroiled butt back to crew quarters, and as I rode those thirty miles, I could visualize the ASTRONAUT CRASHES headlines that were sure to come. For the first time since hitting the water, I had time to think about what the hell I was going to say about the accident. What was my excuse? I'd flown into the damned water! Pilot error, plain and simple. What could be the ramifications? I was still juggling the possibilities as we reached the crew quarters and I rode up the elevator, one soggy, scorched and sorry-looking excuse for an astronaut.

I didn't stop to clean up, but went straight down the hallway to the dining area, looking for Deke. Al Shepard was sitting there having breakfast and those steely eyes took in the soaked flight suit, the bandages and singed hair. I had constantly ragged on him never to stumble in his preparations to fly *Apollo 14*, now my joke had taken a dreadful turn. Al hadn't goofed, I had.

"Okay, Al, you win," I croaked. "It's your flight." Shepard gave me a grin and asked what had happened and if I was okay. Naturally, I said that I was fine. What else could I do? Stand there and cry? So I told him, in froggy *ribbitt* talk, that I had staged Mr. Toad's Wild Ride on purpose. "Things are so damned boring around here that somebody had to do something if we want to get some publicity about *Apollo Fourteen*."

"Right," he said, and continued eating. Other astros had come in to see what they could see, and I damned sure wouldn't show a weakness.

Deke arrived, took me into the adjacent briefing room, and spent a short time assuring himself that I wasn't seriously hurt. I left the bullshit, macho-pilot language at the door and was ready to face the music when Shepard stuck his head in. "Phone call for Geno."

Deke was testy. "No calls right now," he barked. "I don't care who it is. Tell 'em he'll call back."

"Deke, it's the vice president of the United States."

Sure enough, Ted Agnew was on the other end of the line, and wanted to know the same thing as everyone else. "Geno, what the hell happened? Are you okay?" After explaining the accident and thanking him for the concern, I hung up, and Deke got down to business. He was going to have to tell the press, the NASA brass, and the American public what happened, and he immediately offered me an easy way out of this mess. Left unspoken was the fact that he also was going to have to see how it would fit into the matrix for choosing an *Apollo 17* crew.

"So, exactly when did the engine quit on you?" His eyes were steady and his voice firm. All I had to do was agree, say the engine died, that the machine screwed up, not me, and I could walk away from blame. He was presenting an alibi on a silver platter. I had only to pick it up. But I could not do that and live with the knowledge of what had really happened. "Deke, the engine didn't quit. I just flew the son-of-a-bitch into the water."

His expression didn't change, not so much as an extra wrinkle in that craggy face. "Maybe you didn't hear me right, Geno. Exactly when did that engine start to sputter?" Deke knew and I knew that I was at fault, and what was at stake, but he wasn't about to throw me to the wolves. In his eyes, it was his responsibility as well as mine, for he had always vouched for my ability.

"Like I said, Deke. It didn't quit. I just screwed up."

Slayton shrugged his shoulders, shook his head. "Well, if that's the way you want it."

"That's the way it happened," I croaked. There it was, plain and simple.

"Get cleaned up and go see the doctors." He left the room to make his report and face the press. Other astronauts checked in, kidding that I had crashed just to meet the woman in the boat. I told them no woman was worth that. There was a double dynamic at work. They wanted to be sure I had come through it, but they also knew that I had flown into the water. A crash is a crash is a crash, but once they knew I was okay, man, it was time to jump on my ass. *Cernan has really screwed the pooch this time! Remember his spacewalk?* Laugh it off, I ordered myself. No weakness! Don't touch the bandages or feel the burns or even say ouch. Never, never, never exhibit a shred of self-doubt.

Finally alone, I walked back to the showers, stripped off the soaked flight suit and boots, threw them into a pile, and stood beneath a torrent of icy water, letting it pound on my back and neck as I leaned my palms and forehead against the cool tile wall. The irony overwhelmed me. I had flown all the way to the Moon, only to bust my ass in a helicopter back on Earth.

By telling the truth to Deke, had I dashed my chances to fly *Apollo 17*? It was as if I had been on display in a glass cage for years, with everything to lose in a program where mistakes were not tolerated, and now the whole world was about to know that I had fucked up big time. If you were going to command a mission to the Moon, you must make the right decision, do the responsible thing, the right thing, every time, without exception, and I had just done something really dumb—again. I had a vivid flash of memory of that long-ago, ugly day in the California desert when I had won membership into the Order of the Bent Pole—Limited to Living, Low-flying Aviators. Had I been a cat, I would at least be working on life number five or six by now.

I lived through the helicopter crash, but felt I had probably ripped my knickers in terms of accrediting myself as a Moon flight commander. Word about what had happened spread around the Cape as fast as that gasoline fire had out on the Indian River.

Tom Stafford, my mate from *Gemini 9* and *Apollo 10*, called from Houston and I answered the telephone while in my bunk, still tired beyond belief. Tom knew the accident might vault Gordon and The Geologist onto *Apollo 17*, and Mumbles quickly gave me the lay of the land. "You dumb fucking shit, what the hell did you do? I'm out here trying to make sure you command *Seventeen*, and you just may have fucked it all up." For a slow-talking Oklahoman, Stafford sure had a way with words. I had somehow managed to cheat death and he was making me feel guilty for ruining his day.

I wondered what must be going through the mind of my rival for that command, Dick Gordon, who was sitting pretty with a scientist in his back pocket and no helicopter crash on his record. Years later, as we shared a beer, Dick would laughingly tell me, "Geno, when you crashed that chopper, I thought I had it made."

After the shower, I called Barbara again for a long talk. She had recovered better than I, but was still scared, for we both knew the possible consequences of the chopper accident.

"I've blown it," I said in a hushed, coarse voice. It still hurt to talk, but I had to. I was ready to grab a T-38 and fly back home, just to surround myself with Barbara and Tracy and say to hell with the unrelenting, every-minute pressure of the goddamn space program. "I've blown it," I confessed.

"No, you haven't," she softly replied. "Has Deke said anything about *Apollo Seventeen*?"

"Not yet. He's got to make a decision soon, though, and I just made the choice a hell of a lot easier." I was awash in self-pity and Barbara was the only person to whom I could speak of my deepest fear. "I can't see how he can pick me now."

She was silent for a moment. "It's going to be fine, Honey. He knows things like this can happen to anyone. Deke will understand. The important thing is you're okay." But what else could a wife say under these circumstances?

We finally hung up with the situation unresolved, because we weren't the people who could resolve it. That night, the dreaded words *pilot error* kept flapping around the room like vampire bats wanting to slurp the lifeblood out of my career dream. I went to sleep manufacturing excuses to steel myself for what I believed to be the inevitable outcome of my latest misadventure. Hell, I'd already been to the Moon anyway, so losing out on *17* wasn't going to be all that big a deal.

In retrospect, perhaps the best thing I did was level with Deke, to look him in the eye and be honest. I did a dumb thing flying into the water, but salvaged a certain amount of respect by not trying to weasel out of the responsibility, thereby not leaving him on the hook for defending me. Although unbelievable to many people, within forty-eight hours I was back on flight status and ready to fly *Apollo 14*, if needed. As far as Deke was concerned, the helicopter situation was over and done, and things went back to normal. It was just an accident, I lived through it, and the only thing on his mind right now was Al Shepard's flight. He sent me back to work and never mentioned the crash again.

I also caught a break with the calendar. The crash happened on Saturday, a slow time for newspapers and television news stations. The only headline of consequence on Sunday morning was in the *New York Times.*

APOLLO BACK-UP PILOT
IN HELICOPTER CRASH
BUT ESCAPES INJURY

The story was from a wire service, and not an in-depth investigation of what had really happened. By Monday, reporters had other things demanding their attention. *Apollo 14* was still the center of focus at the Cape, the Russians landed a spacecraft probe on Venus, and out in Los Angeles, the demented Charlie Manson and three woman members of his hippie cult were convicted of murdering actress Sharon Tate and six other people. Two days after the accident, I was old news. I wrote a letter of thanks to the woman who hauled me from the river and tried not to think too much about *Apollo 17*.

Today, I sometimes look at a battered flight helmet that sits on a shelf in my office at home. The bottom half is still white and hard, but the top is charred black and melted into strange plastic shapes. When I hold it, soot dusts my fingertips. Someone fished it from the Indian River the day of the crash, where it had floated like a ball in that inferno, and returned it to NASA, who sent it to me. I can only wonder how, and why, I survived.

26

Dr. Rock

"HEY, GENO. LET'S GO out and look at our spacecraft." It was the night of January 30, 1971, only hours before *Apollo 14* was to launch, and Al was too keyed up to sleep. Boy, did I know that feeling. We grabbed a car outside crew quarters, drove over to Pad 39-A, were waved through security cordons, and parked right at the foot of the Saturn V. Arrows of bright spotlights bathed the big bird.

The fueling process was underway, with all the accompanying aches and groans as the missile's thin sides and innards flexed to accept tons of liquid oxygen, which went in at minus 293 degrees, and liquid hydrogen, pumped at an astonishing minus 423 degrees. The icy frosting made it look like a giant's birthday treat, and the Saturn seemed to come to life as we watched, as if it were sniffing the salty breeze and the night skies. I felt humbled by its barely contained strength, and thought incredulously, "There stands the spaceship that is going to take Shepard to the Moon."

His eyes scaled the orange gantry and the entire length of the rocket, as if counting every rivet all the way up to where the command module *Kitty Hawk* rested on the nose, and where the lunar lander *Antares* lay folded inside its third-stage hideaway like a lawn chair stored for the winter. He said nothing, but had to be recalling how much frustration he had endured in the past decade, waiting for this moment to come and wondering if it ever would.

Al was now forty-seven years old, an inch under six feet tall, and still the cocky fighter jock, almost exactly ten years down the road from his famed first flight. He wore his brown hair longer than back then, when he had a military buzz cut, and at 173 pounds, he was only a dozen pounds heavier. Rotary and Kiwanis member, husband of Louise, father of Laura, Julie and adopted niece Alice. Millionaire. Big houses in Houston and at Lake Travis. Investments galore. Ruler of astronauts. Legend!

Tonight, measuring the Saturn with crystal blue eyes, he knew that his earlier flight was the hop of a gnat compared to what lay ahead. Previously, he had flown for fifteen minutes and twenty-two seconds, dashed down-range 302 miles and reached an altitude of a mere 116 miles, barely nibbling the bottom edge of outer space. This rocket was about 100 times more powerful than the primitive Redstone that carried him up in 1961, and this trip was going to be substantially longer, faster, higher and tougher.

Shepard had mastered the Apollo system that was to ferry him, Stu Roosa and Ed Mitchell up to Fra Mauro. Criticism had been sharp: *Apollo 14* was the Kid's Last Flight, and Shepard, it was said, was taking a half-million-mile ego trip. That was nonsense, because after working hand-in-glove with him for the past year and a half, I was convinced the right man was in charge of this mission. Besides, I knew that he really had no choice. This was something he had to do, to fulfill his destiny. Long past the point at which a lesser person would have given up, Shepard's total dedication to getting to the Moon redefined the meaning of the word *commitment*.

If ever man and machine were a match, it was Navy Captain Alan Bartlett Shepard, Jr. and his Apollo Moonship. Yet I could not help but believe that even he was humbled by it all.

Ten years earlier, I had been one of millions of Americans who looked up to this guy as our only space hero. I was a young naval aviator about to get married in San Diego when he took this nation's first manned rocket ride. But after all this time, Al, a decade older than I, still had only that handful of minutes on a rocket, while I had already flown twice, aboard Gemini and Apollo, walked in space, and spent eight days circling the Moon. And all that did was bring me up to his level. So, in what was a very special moment for me, I stood with Al Shepard as his equal.

"This one belongs to Al," I thought, examining the bright, hissing Saturn. "I wonder if I will ever get my own?"

EVERY SPACEFLIGHT HAS SURPRISES, and *Apollo 14* ran into problems as soon as they reached Earth orbit, when *Kitty Hawk* balked at docking with *Antares*. That put the entire mission at risk, for you can't land on the Moon without a lander. Finally, Stu Roosa just rammed the docking probe hard enough to force the metal latches to clang shut and lock, and they were on their way. On the final descent to the Moon, Shepard fought a radar problem that threatened an abort, but there was no way Al would have gone that far and not have landed, radar or no radar, and he put *Antares* down without a hitch.

With the help of a two-wheeled pull cart that increased the amount of rocks they could carry, their lunar strolls brought back a pile of samples from an area where it was believed a meteor slammed into the Moon some 5 million years ago and gouged out a valley 700 miles long. From that boulder-strewn desolation, Shepard and Mitchell picked up clues about the formative stages of the solar system.

Mitchell tried some of his personal ESP experiments, attempting to mentally telegraph symbols on some Zenner cards back to parapsychologists on Earth, with negligible results. Deke wasn't impressed.

Then, to the astonishment of Mission Control, Shepard reached into the cart and converted one of his Moon tools into a six-iron, produced a couple of dimpled balls, and whacked the longest golf shots in the history of the solar system, chortling to duffers back on Earth that balls sailed on for "miles and miles." But I saw a picture later and could swear there were two white spots in the sand only about thirty feet from the LM.

All the way to the Moon and back, even on the lunar surface, whenever the crew opened a box, bag or locker, out would float a First Team mission patch. Ron, Joe and I, as the backup crew, had final access to the spacecraft, and while we set the switches and checked the gauges, we also stuffed our Roadrunner patches into every nook and cranny, setting up a future mini-blizzard of "gotchas" for the Three Rookies. Perhaps the most repeated phrase on the private radio loop during the flight of *Apollo 14* was Shepard's annoyance when still another patch would suddenly appear. "Tell Cernan," he growled, "Beep-beep, his ass."

AL, THE ONLY ONE of the Original Seven astronauts to reach the Moon, got back to Earth just in time, as far as I was concerned. The sand was running out in Deke's hourglass to choose a crew for *Apollo 17* and pressure was building like steam in a closed kettle to put Jack Schmitt aboard the final flight. Astronauts took bets on who would be the commander: me—or Dick Gordon, who had Schmitt, the strong wild card, on his *Apollo 15* backup crew.

I was pleased that Shepard's mission had been so successful, for it reflected on the kind of job I had done in helping him prepare, and I was trying mightily to impress Deke. I had developed a strong relationship with Al during the *Apollo 14* training, but that didn't guarantee anything.

Still, I felt it likely that Al was in my corner, so I probably had Stafford and Shepard leading the charge for me, while Gordon was championed by McDivitt, Conrad and Dave Scott. Anticipation was thick as molasses around the Astronaut Office that summer.

For the time being, Deke stubbornly resisted putting a scientist—any scientist—into a rocket seat instead of a highly trained pilot, and clearly rated Joe Engle above Schmitt. But he nevertheless stalled on announcing, immediately after *Apollo 14*, that the backup crew would rotate to prime three missions later. He was obviously waiting for Dick's *Apollo 15* backup team also to be in the clear. The question was whether NASA headquarters would allow Deke to make the ultimate decision.

It wasn't that long ago that Dick and I had been rookie astronauts flying together to Houston to look for housing, and his family now lived only four doors down and across the street from mine. His youngest daughter once helped Tracy color the walls of her room with crayon scrawls. In fact, there was little that Dick and I could do other than joke about the current situation. "I've got the scientist," he might crow over a cup of coffee. "Too bad," I'd respond with mock sympathy. If I were ever in a tough spot and had to have another astronaut cover my back, I would have picked Dick Gordon. But there would be only one commander on the last Moon flight, so two good friends had to compete for the prize of a lifetime. It was sweat-it-out time.

ONE FINAL PIECE OF important Moon hardware, the Lunar Roving Vehicle—affectionately known as the Rover—arrived in time for *Apollo 15*. It was Wernher von Braun's prediction come to life, an extraterrestrial chariot that would allow astronauts to get away from the lunar module and explore distant mysteries.

The Rover rode piggyback to the Moon, attached outside the lunar module like a piano tied to a moving van, and once lowered, it unfolded like a Murphy bed in a Manhattan hotel room. This was a dune buggy with a future, or so we thought, for if it could handle the rugged lunar surface, there was no reason that a new generation of Rovers might not be driven someday on Mars.

Slightly more than ten feet long and almost four feet high, the Rover weighed 460 pounds on Earth, but only seventy-six pounds on the Moon. It was impossible to have a flat tire, because each wheel was a woven mesh of zinc-coated wire with chevron-shaped treads of titanium. Wire wheels!

Powered by batteries, the individual quarter-horsepower motors on each wheel could zip the Rover along at a top speed of eight miles per hour, with small fenders deflecting roostertails of dust. Instead of leather seats, map lights, and cup holders, the extras on this baby included a mobile television broadcasting unit, a solid-state computer and a gyroscope for navigation.

Despite its versatility and capability, there were limitations. You could not drive the Rover further from the LM than you could walk back breathing only the oxygen remaining in your backpack, and in case of a breakdown, there would be no roadside assistance in sight.

Dave Scott and Jim Irwin gave the buggy its first lunar workout during *Apollo 15*, and it was a total success. Instead of hanging about the landing site, they scooted all around Hadley Rille and Mount Hadley.

Meanwhile, up in orbit, Al Worden examined the Moon's surface from his lofty perch, and discovered a rugged area that contained some of the darkest material ever seen down there. Al knew that scientists back on Earth would want to consider this mysterious place surrounded by tall mountains for future exploration, so he used his powerful cameras to photograph and map out the shadowy patch near the Sea of Serenity, in the upper left-hand corner of the Moon.

Apollo 15 returned as perhaps one of the most fruitful scientific explorations of them all, but its spectacular success would become overshadowed by the extremely poor judgment of the crew. They had hauled a cache of unauthorized envelopes to the Moon, canceled them there, and sold them to a collector in Europe. The incident caused a huge uproar, embarrassed NASA, and the talented Dave Scott, as mission commander, watched helplessly as his star-studded career wrecked on a most unlikely shoal. Nobody ever believed such a thing would happen. A bunch of lousy stamped envelopes destroyed one of the sharpest guys in the program.

The flight also meant that Dick Gordon and his crew had finished their backup jobs and were ready for a new assignment, so the pressure was jacked up another notch on everyone involved in the coming choice for the last ride to the Moon. If this had been a footrace, Dick and I would have been neck and neck, with the finish line just ahead. Deke was out of time and had to make a decision.

In my opinion, the logical thing for him to do under the circumstances was to keep a well-trained crew together. If NASA insisted that the scientist must fly, I would probably have put Dick's entire crew aboard

Apollo 17. Hard choice and tough luck for Geno, but that's the call that made sense.

TRACY, AT THE INTERESTING age of eight, went away for a month to summer camp in the Texas Hill Country in 1971, leaving Barbara biting her nails when mother didn't hear from daughter for days on end. Finally, she gave in to anxiety and called the camp, and a puzzled Tracy explained that she hadn't telephoned because she had just been too busy. I knew exactly what she meant.

That left Barbara with an empty nest on Barbuda Lane, because I was always gone somewhere most of the time. She had created a life filled with motherly duties—the Girl Scouts, the music lessons, and the PTA becoming her own enjoyment. When Tracy was no longer around to supply those distractions, Barbara faced a tough adjustment, and didn't like it very much.

We had been married for ten years, and I had been training almost continuously, on either a prime or backup crew, for eight of them. It was taking a toll on both of us. My ego was being fed, and I thrived in this peculiar social world in which we might not have money but had something better: a mystique that dollars could not buy. People were thrilled at being close to an astronaut, but to my wife, the adulation along the cocktail circuit rang false. After one party, Barbara snapped, "That's the biggest bunch of bullshit I've ever had to sit through, and I'm not going to do it anymore."

To make things even worse, I received a continuous stream of invitations to play in celebrity golf tournaments all over the country, and enjoyed going to great places and meeting interesting people. I had also discovered the joy of hunting out in the sprawling Texas countryside. Although my youthful summers in the woods of Wisconsin had taught me many things, hunting was not among them. I found the solitude of the outdoors a welcome respite to the constant strain of waiting for the *Apollo 17* decision, but both golf and hunting demanded time away from my family.

Not knowing whether I would fly, I continued working long hours in the simulators, for the last thing I wanted was for Deke to perceive that I wasn't interested enough in the job. That kept me busy Monday through Friday, but on weekends, I would take a few hours to go horseback riding with Tracy. Throw in the hunting trips and golf tournaments from Montana to Miami, and time alone with Barbara became scarce. She wrote to friends that she wouldn't mind my excursions so much if I was home during the week, but "that's rarely the case." I had felt for a long time that I had cheated Tracy, but it never dawned on me that I was also cheating Barbara.

UNKNOWN TO ME, DEKE sent his recommendation to Washington: Cernan, Evans and Engle would fly the final mission. Headquarters shot that idea down immediately. Their own decision had already been made, and it snatched the choice out of Deke's hands. It was made very, very clear to the Godfather that the only name they absolutely demanded to see on the crew list for *17* was Dr. Harrison H. "Jack" Schmitt. The Geologist would fly!

Deke fought it, but the handwriting was on the wall and he surrendered to the inevitable, accepting a compromise. Instead of Cernan-Evans-Engle, the crew became Cernan-Evans-Schmitt. Fine, said Washington. They didn't care, as long as Schmitt got the ride.

Barbara and I were at the Las Brisas in Acapulco with Ron and Jan Evans for a brief holiday in October when the call came from Houston and I heard Deke's gruff, familiar voice. "Congratulations, Geno," he said. "*Apollo Seventeen* is yours." Ron walked into the room while I was on the phone and I happily flashed him a thumbs-up sign. Good news.

I started to burble with excited appreciation when I realized he hadn't told me who would be my crew members. Ron pointed a finger at himself and raised his eyebrows in question. "Does this include Ron and Joe?" I asked.

"Well, not exactly. Ron's your command module pilot."

I nodded quickly to Ron and he raised both arms in victory, then swept his petite wife off her feet in a bear hug as I continued talking with Deke.

"What about Joe?"

"I need to talk to you about the rest of your crew."

"Why? What's happened?"

He interrupted curtly. "Look, get back here and we'll discuss it."

The call ended and we were all left standing in a beautiful hotel room, looking out over a sea washed by a warm sun, not knowing whether to laugh or cry. The four of us adjourned to the bar for a few rounds of rum and Coke, elated because we had gotten what we wanted, but disappointed, too. Even without being told, we knew that Deke probably had been forced to shuffle the crew, that Jack was going to fly and Joe was going to stay home.

I was crushed at the thought of my team being broken up. Joe had worked hard for the lunar module pilot job and we had spent so many long months together in the LM simulator that we understood the nuances of each other's personality and the inflections of our voices. We could react instinctively to what the other man did in a critical situation, and I was very concerned that I could ever have that same kind of rapport with anyone for whom flying was not a first love. I was forced to bet my life on a choice mandated by Washington, one of my first bitter tastes of politics.

We left Mexico the next day, and the moment I arrived back in Houston, I went to Deke's office, where he confirmed what I already knew in my gut. I started to argue, pulling out everything I could to persuade him to put Joe back on the team: It was neither fair nor smart to introduce someone new into the mix at this point; I was being asked to fly a lunar lander down to the Moon's surface with a scientist as my co-pilot! Since Gemini, we'd always flown our spacecraft with at least two pilots for a damned good reason. Good God, Jack had never flown *anything* before joining the program. He had done a good job learning how to fly little T-38 trainers, but for Christ's sake, Engle was an X-15 driver!

Deke let me bitch for a while, nodding in agreement with every word I had to say. When I cooled down and ran out of breath, he spoke quietly. "Geno, you don't understand. Jack is going to fly and you've got two choices. Take the flight with Jack as your LM pilot, or step aside and I'll rotate Dick Gordon's entire crew into *Apollo Sevemteem*. You have to decide whether or not you want to walk on the Moon."

Biting my lip for a moment, I considered the inflexible situation. "So there's nothing we can do about Joe?"

"Not on this flight. Don't worry about Engle. He'll get plenty of work on down the road. The question is, what are *you* going to do?"

I could either fall on my sword or accept a decree that I could not change. "What about if we—"

Deke cut me off, his words sharp, and his flat palm slapped the desk with gunshot finality. "No. Not a chance, Geno. It's done. Make up your mind. You want to fly, then you fly with Jack, like it or not. Tell me right now. I've got work to do either way."

There was no alternative, and I knew it. Hell, this was what I had been struggling for all of these years, and truth be told, I would have been willing to fly this mission with Goldilocks and the Three Bears. But what should have been a time of joy carried a big shadow, for I had to tell my friend, Joe Engle, that he wasn't going into space with me after all. Joe took the bad news with grace, having read the tea leaves as well as anyone. It had been no secret that Jack's star had been rising as the Apollo flights were trimmed back, so Joe reluctantly set his sights on the future. By the time he retired, he was a major general in the Air Force and commanded the second space shuttle mission. Even today, I often wonder what would have happened if I had fought harder to have Deke swap Joe for Ed Mitchell on *Apollo 14* so he could have a Moonwalk. Would it have made any difference?

SO WHO WAS THIS guy that had been such a thorn in our sides for so long? This person we called Dr. Rock who had just replaced a true-blue aviator?

Well, Jack proved to be perfectly competent as an astronaut as well as being a genius-type pebble-pusher. When his name was inked onto my crew, he was a thirty-seven-year-old bachelor from the sandy town of Santa Rita, New Mexico, a state he would one day represent as a United States senator. Jack, whose father was a New Mexico mining geologist, had done undergraduate work at CalTech and earned a Ph.D. in geology from Harvard in 1964, a year before he was chosen as a scientist-astronaut.

While still a student, he attended the University of Oslo in Norway for a year, and worked for Norwegian and U.S. Geological Surveys before taking a teaching post at Harvard in 1961. After picking up his doctorate, he joined the USGS Astrogeology Center in Flagstaff, Arizona where he became an expert on lunar field exploration and a recognized authority on photographic and telescopic mapping of the Moon. When astronauts were trained on lunar geology, Jack was one of the instructors, and remained as our in-house geologist even while undergoing flight and astronaut training himself. He was among the handful of experts allowed to analyze the rocks brought back from the Moon.

Doesn't exactly fit the test pilot profile, does he? Word came quickly to me from Dick Gordon that Jack could do the LM job, and I knew Deke would never have accepted him on the crew if Jack wasn't able to carry his share of the load.

Tightly focused and spartan in his personal life, quiet and hard to get to know, he had a passion for thinking. At such times, you could almost hear the wheels turning inside his skull. On a first introduction, he usually came across as unlikeable, and his taciturn nature and brashness made it hard for people to get close to him. He didn't seem to care a whit. That was part of our problem, for Jack just wasn't my kind of guy.

Barbara and Jan Evans had become close friends with Mary Engle during the past few years while their husbands trained together, and the women were heartbroken when I confirmed the crew change. Not only were they losing Joe and Mary, they were getting Jack, a bachelor, in return. Not a carefree guy like C. C. Williams, but often a sarcastic character with a caustic personality who didn't seem to know how to fit in socially. The women groaned in anticipation of the road ahead.

Jan Evans, a feisty little brunette who seldom minced words, summed it up: "We have to put up with *that* asshole?"

But I had no time to worry about social discomfort. My paramount job was to mold the three of us into a team that could fly to the Moon, not to make sure everybody liked Jack, and we plunged into training.

A sense of finality haunted us because everyone was aware that *Apollo 17* would be the last of the historic series. We had a year to go before launch and already a black tide of despair licked at the shores of the Cape and dark clouds of depression hovered over Houston, for when we lifted off, thousands of people would lose their jobs. Apollo was ending! Deke even had a difficult time rounding up a backup crew before volunteering John Young, Stu Roosa and Charlie Duke.

I not only had to get myself and my crew and my rocket ready for a trip to the Moon, but was forced into the role of cheerleader for the entire space program. Downhearted workers thinking about missing a mortgage payment could make mistakes, and that could not be tolerated. In this line of work, defeatism could be a deadly virus, and it was up to me to find a cure.

27

I Can't Walk!

JACK, WHO COULD HAVE a wild idea once in a while, wanted to land on the far side of the Moon. Over the past two years, he argued, previous missions had adequately explored the front side and the final flight should take advantage of an opportunity that would not come again for many years.

Such a dramatic scheme might have been wonderful for a scientist, but it was somewhat lacking in operational common sense, for such a landing would leave us totally out of communication with Houston. Jack suggested putting a satellite into stationary orbit around the Moon, keeping it constantly overhead to bounce radio transmissions to and from Houston. He had gone so far as to identify the hardware needed and even projected the cost, just to prove it could be done.

It was bad timing, and I didn't like the idea. Jack ignored me and took his campaign straight to the top ranks of NASA management, where he pressed so hard that my telephone started ringing and some agitated manager would bellow, "Goddamn, Cernan, get Schmitt in line and keep him there!"

Jack and I had known each other for years but were uncomfortable when we started training together, for our loyalties had been firmly welded to our original crews. He obviously would have preferred Dick Gordon as his commander, and I would rather have had Joe Engle sitting in that lunar module seat. But that was behind us now, so we turned to making the situation work. After all, the consolation prize for having to be together wasn't too bad, because we were both going to walk on the Moon.

After the first few months, the only significant problem remaining between us was that Dr. Rock had not come to grips with the idea that he was no longer one of the top scientists in the Apollo program, but rather just a crew member. He had been a senior member of the planning teams for past missions and thought nothing of taking his ideas and complaints right to the top, disregarding the chain of command and bypassing a lot of people—most importantly, me—in the process.

We knocked heads for a while until he realized that although NASA was a civilian agency, its mission leaders came primarily from the military services, where a commander's word was final. We could discuss differences and problems, but the old Supreme-Being argument had to apply. As commander, I wouldn't have time to debate when a critical decision was needed. I finally made it clear that he was going to work through me, like it or not. Period, end of story, sit down. Jack got the message, subdued his independent streak, and became a solid crew member instead of a rebel.

We became a team, and I found Jack to be a tireless worker. Instead of taking off on a weekend to go hunting, he would curl up with an operations manual or coax technicians into Saturday simulator time. He didn't chase girls and, as far as I could tell, had no diversions whatever. In my opinion, this dour Sherlock Holmes of a scientist deserved every opportunity to solve the riddles that had remained hidden on the Moon for billions of years.

TECTONIC SHIFTS WERE TAKING place both inside and beyond the space community's bubble of life in 1972.

Vietnam, the war that had shadowed my astronaut career, was finally winding down, and it looked as though the Vietcong and North Vietnamese were going to win. At home, students, women and blacks had grown militant, and voices of rage were still heard throughout the land. President Nixon devalued the dollar, froze wages and prices, was overwhelmingly reelected and became embroiled in the Watergate scandal.

Only three years earlier, during my flight on *Apollo 10*, national excitement for space exploration had been at its zenith. Now people responded to Moon trips with boredom, and when the public walked away, politicians walked away. Federal budget cuts poured gloom all over NASA just as the agency was scratching for money to build the space shuttle.

Then there were changes at the very top of the program. The peerless Wernher von Braun left to take a job in private industry, and MSC director Bob Gilruth departed soon thereafter. Gilruth was replaced by the competent Chris Kraft, who had been one of the driving forces behind our exploration of space, and a man for whom I held the highest respect.

Not long after he moved into his new office, Chris gave me some fatherly advice that was part warning, part plea. "Geno, put away that fighter pilot's white silk scarf and just bring your crew home alive. If you run into something you don't like out there and decide not to land, I'll back you one hundred percent."

His comments reflected the feeling of a number of NASA managers who couldn't shake the ghost of *Apollo 13* and were turning conservative, with the shared belief that *Apollo 17* was a gamble they did not need to take. We had whipped the Soviets, already had ten Moonwalkers, and had brought back rocks and pictures and stories. Skylab and a joint Soviet-American orbital venture were being planned, and the distant future belonged to the shuttle. Why risk three more astronauts? Hadn't we done everything on the Moon that needed doing?

I tried to ignore such statements, but worried that the naysayers might gain enough support to cancel *Apollo 17*, and I was not going to let that happen. This was no time to be conservative. We would fly to the Moon, do our jobs, and come home again. If they were looking for anything less, they were looking in the wrong place, for my flight would *not* end in failure.

So Chris's remark had a reverse effect on me. Instead of being cautious, I left that meeting pumped up more than ever and took this situation as just another challenge to be overcome . . . and I love challenges.

I was determined to keep our space banner bright, for *Apollo 17* would cap a historic undertaking in which all Americans could take rightful pride. My most useful tool was the press, and I dutifully mined the contacts I had made among correspondents over the years. If someone wanted an interview, I was ready to talk. A photograph? Where and when? I treasured printer's ink and broadcast time like gold, to get out the message that this mission was going to be something special. I talked so much that Jan Evans appropriately gave me the nickname of "Mouth."

I grew tired of being compared to the tail of the dog, the last thing to go over the fence, so I met with as many engineers and production workers as possible, to spread the Gospel According to Cernan: "*Apollo Seventeen* is not the end, but rather the beginning of a whole new era in the history of mankind. You people who are putting this together are important! We are in a unique moment in history, so let's make the last one the best!" I preached until I was hoarse, and probably bored poor Ron and Jack to tears as they heard the same words, over and over. The job became as much political campaign trail as Moon training as I climbed on chairs at parties, or factory tables, and talked to whomever would listen, trying to boost morale and confidence.

I wanted everyone who made this amazing feat possible to know that what they were doing was special to us, and that we wanted it to be special to them, too. *Apollo 17* was not just another serving of the same old thing, for we were going to places never before seen by man. We were all part of a grand tradition of exploration that would yield results so astonishing and far-reaching that generations might pass before the significance of what we had done would be totally understood.

My task to keep everyone focused wasn't easy. A cartoonist pictured two workers in hard hats on a scaffold, one about to jump, holding a notice that he had been fired. The other guy was on a telephone, asking: "Can we get Gene Cernan up here to give Smith that 'It's not the end, it's the beginning' speech again?" There were a lot of Smiths out there, for some 13,000 Cape workers had lost their jobs over the past several years, and another 900 would get pink slips as soon as we blasted off. Many of the Grumman troops literally worked themselves into unemployment when our lunar module went out the door at Bethpage, and more would be gone at the moment of liftoff. But during one visit there, a supervisor told me, "We're giving you our heart and soul on this one, Geno. This is the best LM that's ever gonna fly."

That was the typical reaction of everyone involved with *Apollo 17*. The workers responded with a dedication bordering on ferocity, proving their professionalism by making this flight one for the record books. The last-but-best determination galvanized us all.

BARBARA WAS SOLIDLY WITH me in this campaign to polish the Apollo image, and masterfully juggled reporters and photographers who went after homefront stories. "If we're ending the Apollo program, let's make it spectacular," she told them, reciting the family refrain. "It's sad to see it all end."

"I never worry about Gene coming back," she replied to the usual questions about how she handled the potential danger. "But I do feel apprehensive with each step of the mission—that A goes right so B can follow. I want the mission to be perfect." She likened *Apollo 17* to reading the last chapter of a good book, and wondered if anyone might ask a question she had not heard before. They didn't.

For every reporter I spoke with at the Cape, she was meeting one in Nassau Bay, and Barbuda Lane sometimes had the look of a media parking lot. Once I telephoned home and she answered with a merry, "Look, sweetie-pie, we're working with the press right now. Can you check back in about an hour?" She was farming the reporters so hard she didn't have time to talk to me? I hoped she didn't tell them about all the Fridays that I would come home after a week of training and plunk a load of dirty laundry on the floor for her to have cleaned and ready before I left again on Monday.

WE NAMED THE COMMAND module *America* and the lunar module *Challenger* to salute the daunting task that lay ahead, and for a mission patch, turned our pen-scratched ideas and goals over to artist Robert T. McCall, who helped us come up with a wonderful design based on the theme of mankind, country and the future. The golden face of Apollo, Greek god of the Sun, was laid on top of a contemporary drawing of an American eagle. Red bars in the wings reflected our flag, and were topped by three white stars representing our crew. A deep blue background featured the Moon, Saturn and a spiral galaxy, with the eagle's wing just touching the Moon to suggest this celestial body had been visited by man. Apollo gazes to the right toward the galaxy to imply further exploration, with the eagle leading mankind into the future.

MISSION PLANNERS HAD BEEN trying for five months to find a landing site that held the most potential for the last flight. The decision, handed down on February 17, was the site Al Worden had spotted during *Apollo 15*, the deep and rugged valley at the edge of the Sea of Serenity, so far off the usual track that it didn't even have a name. Finally, it was given the hyphenated designation of the Taurus-Littrow Valley to represent the huge crater named for the nineteenth-century astronomer Johann von Littrow and the bordering Taurus mountains. Scientists hoped it contained volcano-ejected rocks that had not lain too long on the lunar surface, and therefore might have material from deep within the core of the Moon. The combination promised vital knowledge about both the birth and death of our companion satellite.

Thanks to the previous Apollo missions, most Earth scientists had junked the supposition held for years about the Moon being some sort of battered and forever-cold body. Instead, it was now believed to once have had a churning, hot core that generated seas of molten lava, material that hardened into the lunar crust when the heat flickered out some 3 billion years ago. That led to further inquiry about how the planets throughout our solar system might have been formed. So did Apollo have exploration value? Just consider the implications of fundamental changes in what we believed! An entirely new Moon theory had evolved—that of a heat-born planetoid rich with chemical elements, possibly even subterranean water.

Jack liked the chosen site because of the pure science that beckoned, and for me, the challenge of flying into an unexplored box canyon was a space pilot's dream. Moon mountains as big as the Rockies reared up both north and south of the landing site, while our entranceway from the northeast was guarded by the towering Sculptured Hills. Craters, fields of boulders and debris from ancient landslides pocked the flatland. I had only eight months of training left in which to perfect my ability to fly a spacecraft across 250,000 miles of emptiness, then make a pinpoint landing inside a gorge deeper than the Grand Canyon, pushing the LM's envelope of performance and testing everything I knew as a pilot. By God, I loved the idea!

There was one more surprise. It would be impossible to land on the Moon in darkness, but if the Sun was too high, its furious light would wash out the lunar surface below during our approach. Therefore, it was determined that *Apollo 17* must leave Earth after dark in order to arrive over the landing area, days later, with the lunar morning Sun at just the proper angle to cast the stark shadows we needed to outline the surface details. Ours would be the first and only night launch in the history of the U.S. manned space-flight program, and was scheduled for a few hours after sundown on December 6, 1972. That caused some of the more conservative managers to start worrying all over again. Launching at night would be dangerous, they said, as if launching in daylight was *not* hazardous.

I WAS SMART ENOUGH to give Jack the lead in preparing the mission plan for our three days of work on the surface, since we wanted to maximize his scientific expertise. Quite honestly, it didn't matter much to me. I just wanted to explore, and once in the valley, there would be plenty of geology for both of us. He named craters in the landing zone on a theme of thinkers and explorers, honoring people like Shakespeare and Lewis and Clark. That was fine for the big picture, but I wanted my personal imprimatur on several within the area where I planned to put *Challenger* down. I needed to be intimately familiar with those few craters, so I named them after family members, subtly using nicknames so people wouldn't think me too ostentatious. My aiming points in those final critical seconds would be Punk, named for Tracy, Barjean, for Barbara Jean, and Poppie, for my father.

There was one more important crater, a big one right in the middle of the dusty plain, and we called it Camelot, not only for the mythical kingdom of King Arthur, but also for the storied aura of President Kennedy, who had set our course to the Moon a decade earlier.

Meanwhile, scientists were trying to pack every experiment they possibly could aboard *Apollo 17*, well aware this was their last chance for some live Moon work. I didn't have a dog in that particular fight and let them figure out the gizmos we would take along. I did, however, constantly remind them of the definite limits on what we could carry, and what could be done. From bitter experience, I knew that just because something worked on Earth didn't mean it would do so in space. As commander, I couldn't lose sight of the singular goal of landing on the Moon. Without that, all of the fancy experiments would be meaningless.

A FEW MONTHS AFTER our landing site was chosen, John Young led his *Apollo 16* crew of Charlie Duke and Ken Mattingly to the Moon in April, scoring large for those of us who argue that until mankind personally explores something, the story gathered by remote vehicles ain't necessarily so. Their landing site in the lunar highlands had been chosen because, based on the results sent back by unmanned probes, it would yield a treasure of material from an ancient volcano that had created the rugged terrain. When John and Charlie finally got there, they found no volcano, nor any evidence of a lava flow. All of the probes and experiments and the analysis that preceded them were wrong.

As always, there were problems enough to label *Apollo 16* a cliffhanger of a mission, but the ingenuity of the crew—which at one point included kicking some stubborn instruments to make them work—again made the dangerous enterprise look easy and the blasé television audience yawned.

I wonder how they would have felt if the lunar module *Orion* had missed its landing spot by only fifteen feet and toppled into a huge hole from which it would not have escaped.

LIFE CAN BE SPOOKY among the lunar mountains. For me, it was getting sort of complicated back here on Earth, too.

Summer brought bad news. The *Apollo 15* stamp scandal became public at the worst possible time. NASA had to handle the internal disaster just as the program was lobbying Congress to provide funds for the space shuttle, and press reports about astronauts making money from their Moon trips further eroded support and made my job as chief cheerleader more difficult.

On the other side of the world, terrorists attacked the Munich Olympic games and murdered a number of Israeli athletes while a stunned world watched on television. U.S. intelligence services soon picked up information that a bloodthirsty group known as Black September might be planning something even more bizarre: a strike at *Apollo 17*. Charley "Supercop" Buckley, head of security at the Cape, quietly escalated his protection procedures, but the crew wasn't told anything at the time. Headquarters felt we had enough on our minds without worrying about a bunch of thugs.

Ron, Jack and I had been swallowed whole by flight training, and the physical and mental requirements were exhausting. One day I would be tromping around the Beartooth Mountains in Montana studying geology, and the next I might be floundering in the Gulf of Mexico, practicing what to do if the spacecraft landed upside down in the water. Or I might be driving a Rover near Las Vegas, where the Atomic Energy Commission had tested nuclear bombs and left a desert filled with Moonlike craters. Or I could be back at Ellington, flying practice missions aboard the weird, sticklike craft known as the Lunar Landing Training Vehicle. Test the suits, check out the rakes and drills we would use to collect samples, practice putting a rod of radioactive plutonium into the nuclear reactor that would power the science package on the lunar surface, and spend hour upon hour in the simulators. Hundreds of things, right down to perfecting how to plant an American flag on the airless Moon, screamed for my personal attention, for I had the final buy-off responsibility for everything on the spacecraft. It was frustrating, and something always seemed to come up that no one had thought of before.

By the end of summer, I thought it would be hard to surprise me on anything. But Deke and Charley Buckley managed to do just that one afternoon when I returned to the crew quarters and found carpenters putting the finishing touches on a new door. The old lightweight panel had been replaced by one that looked about the same on the outside, but had an interior that was a slab of hardened steel. "Bulletproof," Charley said.

Deke and Supercop felt the terrorism threat had grown to a point where they had to tell us about Black September. Inside the crew quarters, they explained the situation was being taken very seriously, but also was being kept very quiet. The kooks wanted headlines and we weren't going to give them any. "Geno, everything is under control here," said Deke, without elaboration. I looked at that new steel door and hoped he was right.

Then he brought the conversation up another level. The security experts had concluded that Black September might not try for a heavily protected astronaut or the Saturn at all, but instead might go after the most vulnerable targets—our children. With the kids as hostages, the terrorists would hold some pretty powerful leverage. Barbara and Jan Evans were shocked, almost wide-eyed with surprise and fright, when we broke the news to them.

Ron and I were furious at the idea of faceless terrorists posing a threat to our families while we were on the Moon, where we would be helpless. We didn't know who these terrorists were, so for us to grab a couple of shotguns and try to go out and stop them made no sense at all, particularly when loads of trained cops were already doing that job. The security chiefs proposed that teams of their men be allowed to park outside our homes in Houston twenty-four hours a day, and for plainclothes officers to take our kids to school. We approved the stakeouts, but not right in front of our doors. So until we got back from the Moon, unmarked cars with quiet, armed men inside parked just down the way, watching my house on Barbuda Lane.

But Ron and I refused to further disrupt our children's lives by forcing them to live within a police cordon. They were normal kids—as normal as kids could be who had fathers going to the Moon—and we wanted them to stay that way, so they would continue to ride the school bus. As a compromise, when our children went to school each day, one of those unmarked police cars drove right behind the bus, and Tracy's classes were watched over by well-dressed, polite and very capable federal agents. Amazingly, the press never figured it out.

*   *   *

Our Saturn V, strapped atop the crawler, emerged from the Vehicle Assembly Building before daylight on Monday, August 28, 1972, and trundled out to a nearby area where a news conference would be held that morning. She was pointed straight toward half of a dim silver Moon that sat like a spectator in the predawn sky, waiting for the game to start.

Ron, Jack and I met the reporters and photographers, then rode the elevator all the way up to the third stage as the crawler started its snaillike trip to the launch pad, where technicians would spend the next four months getting her ready to fly. Far below, I could hear the crunch and clank of the crawler's giant treads, and by craning my neck to look straight up, I could see the point of the stack, wrapped in a protective shroud. The rocket gleamed in the morning sunshine. I felt like a tiny bug that had crawled into a metal sandwich. *My God, these things are big!* Our training had passed in a blur, but now I could see all the way to December, and launch day was coming closer with each clank of the crawler's tread. I reached out and touched the chill skin of the Saturn to make sure she wasn't a fantasy.

A few weeks later, Chuck La Pinta, our *Apollo 17* flight surgeon and a good guy, was poking around my body during a routine physical exam and discovered I had a prostate infection. Chuck was a medical anomaly, so he didn't run right out, ring bells, alarm everybody, and report me as being unfit. Instead, he told no one at all, but worked quietly to resolve the problem.

"We'll take care of it here," my nonchalant doctor said with a deadpan expression, humorless eyes watching below the brim of the straw porkpie hat he always wore. I gladly agreed to be treated in secret, because I didn't want some manager to think I was anything less than a genuine, totally healthy astronaut. So I spent many a morning having my prostate digitally massaged by the flight surgeon, a very awkward position for a space hero. The experience was both embarrassing and a little degrading, but I was not going to let something like that keep me from going to the Moon.

La Pinta carried his treatment plan a bit further. "I'll tell you what, Geno. From now until launch, you're to have no coffee, no tea, no beer, no booze . . . and I want you to get lots of sex." Joking was his way of minimizing the situation.

I decided to call his bluff. "Would you put that in writing?" I asked, and without batting an eyelash, La Pinta pulled a prescription pad toward him and scribbled out that I was under doctor's orders to have "lots of sex."

"Okay, now, Chuck," I asked. "Where do I get this filled?"

NO MERCY. STU ROOSA and Charlie Duke killed a six-foot-long rattlesnake on the track behind the simulator building at the Cape, cut off its head and planned a major league gotcha. They coiled the long body of the reptile, which was as thick as your forearm, beneath my desk, with its tail of sixteen rattles sticking up from the middle of a hidden mountain of snake. Then they had our secretary tell me that I had an important telephone call.

I climbed out of the simulator and hurried to the office, noticing that a lot of people seemed to be hanging around for that time of day. They had put my chair almost in the middle of the room, and I plopped into it and pushed quickly toward the desk, picking up my feet so the chair would roll freely.

Just as I reached for the telephone, I caught sight of the curled, scaly monster and my fucking heart stopped. I came out of the chair like I had a rocket up my butt, and slammed flat against the wall clear on the other side of the room, staring wildly at that big damned snake. *Sonofabitch!* I don't think I have ever been that scared in my life.

The whole crew and support team, who were all in on the joke, doubled over in laughter. Gotchas are dreadful when someone plays them on you.

OCTOBER ARRIVED. LESS THAN two months to go before launch, I was very comfortable with where we were. The mission plan looked good and all the hardware and the crew were in top shape, except for my prostate problem, which didn't officially exist. As the days fell from the calendar, I felt that nothing could stop me. Should have known better.

I stepped up to bat during another morale-building softball game at the Cape and slapped a line drive into the outfield, then tried to stretch a double into a triple as if it were a matter of life or death. *Zap!* I could almost hear something snap inside my leg as I rounded second base. It felt like a machete had chopped deep into my lower calf, and I hit the dirt with a roll and a scream of agony. Within sight of my Saturn rocket, and watched by most of our launch team, a tendon in my right leg had given way, and I lay there with my brain storming. *Goddamn, what have I done?*

I had sworn after the helicopter accident that I would never again do anything dumb before a flight, but now I was sprawled on a softball diamond. I didn't even have to be playing in the damned game, and could easily have done my cheerleading from the sidelines. Oh, no, not Superman Cernan. Watching wasn't my style if I had a chance to get involved. Not only was I in the lineup, but apparently was trying to prove that the mission commander could win the game all by himself, when I really should have been protecting my health at all costs. My basic aggressiveness sometimes put me in self-destruct mode. Ass-tronaut.

Unwilling to admit what had happened, I tried to stand and walk through the pain, just pretend it wasn't there, and fell right back on my ass. Ron and Jack carried me from the field, my leg on fire and dangling as if it were about to fall off. *I can't walk! If I can't walk, they damned sure won't let me fly. I've blown it.*

Worse, there was no way of keeping this a secret, and the six weeks remaining before the flight might not be enough for full recovery. Dick Gordon and my backup commander, John Young, just back from his Moon trip, were both ready and qualified to step in and take over. The word spread: *Cernan's done it again!*

Chuck La Pinta once more came to my rescue, still wearing his little straw hat, a most unlikely looking hero. We didn't know how serious the injury was, just that it was serious enough. They loaded me into his car, and as he drove to the infirmary, Chuck laid out the possibilities. None of them sounded good, and I didn't really want to hear the truth. "If it's ripped and we have to operate, Geno, you're through. It will take two or three months to repair," he said. "If it's not ruptured, you're still going to be in bed, then on crutches for a while. No matter what, it's going to take some time."

When the X-rays came back, Chuck clapped them onto a light board and scowled at the results. He had not taken off that silly hat, but was as serious as I had ever seen, and that scared the hell out of me. "No rupture, but it's a pretty severe stretch, really hyperextended. But since it isn't ripped, we've got a chance," he declared. "We don't have to operate, but you've got to sit it out for maybe as long as two weeks." I knew he wasn't joking, although I wished he was just pulling some macabre gotcha.

"There's more. You've got to do exactly as I say and not push things too hard. Try to rush this recovery and you could tear the tendon apart and you'll never get to fly *Apollo Seventeen*. It's up to you."

"You're not grounding me! I can walk!" I was almost shouting in frustration. My dream wasn't going to die because of a lousy softball accident. It just couldn't. I tried to put weight on the leg and it crumbled so fast that La Pinta had to catch me and lift me back onto the examining table. One word from Chuck to the bosses and I was dead meat. I could almost hear the rumor mill grinding, and knew that many other doctors would be tempted to make a big deal out of the situation to get their own names in the papers. Not Chuck.

"Geno, we've got a serious injury here." He wrapped the leg tightly. "But I'm not officially grounding you because I think we can lick it. You work with me, take it slow for a few days, and I'll get you ready on time. Far as anyone else is concerned, I'll tell 'em it's no big deal."

No big deal? *If I can't walk, how the hell can I go to the Moon?* From where I sat, it looked like a pretty damned big deal, indeed.

Chuck downplayed the episode when questioned by program honchos. "Not much to it. It isn't as bad as it looks. A little whirlpool and rest and he'll be good as new." The man was a great doctor, a terrific liar, and an even better friend. The managers had to trust the judgment of the flight surgeon, but no matter what he said, one thing was clear: I couldn't walk.

The mission commander was hobbling around on crutches, his leg unable to support his weight, telling everybody that things were really, really swell. "Just a sprain," I'd say. "Can't hardly feel it. La Pinta insists that I use these damned crutches."

I believe in mind over matter, willed myself to get rid of those sticks in a hurry, and only four days after being injured, I put them away, risking more tendon damage, but having to demonstrate to everyone that I was okay. It hurt like hell, but I swallowed the pain, for I couldn't limp in public. Bad for the image, and I knew I could be taken off the crew with the stroke of a pen if the leg didn't show improvement in a hurry.

"I watched him working in his suit today, and he seemed fine," La Pinta lied to the curious managers at the end of the first week. He had watched me getting into the bulky suit, which wasn't easy to do even on the best of days, and knew the leg hurt because he could see the sweat beading my face. I just bit my lip. The suit techs, also on my team, said nothing.

"What if he rips the tendon when he's on the Moon?" Even Deke was eyeing me, talking to Chuck and thinking about the launch that was approaching so swiftly.

"Don't worry," Chuck reassured the Godfather. "I'm taking care of it. He's good." I climbed in bed at night with ice packs numbing my throbbing leg, feeling disappointment and pressure gnaw at me because so many things seemed to be going wrong—the leg, the prostate, Black September, the worried program managers, and the thousand and one details I had to watch as mission commander. Sometimes I had to ask myself just what Deke was asking Chuck: Could I do it?

"Geno doesn't look so good." Deke, who had pulled my fat from the fire after the helicopter crash, would accept only so much bullshit.

"He'll be okay. Coming along nicely." The doctor's neutral expression gave no clue. I felt a huge debt of gratitude to Chuck and became stonily determined to get well and prove he was right. Now the flight surgeon was massaging my rectum for the prostate and my leg for the tendon every day, keeping his mouth shut about both problems, racing to get me ready to strap on a Saturn, and the clock kept ticking. If I couldn't get into that spacecraft, then his career probably would go down the drain right alongside mine. Defying the odds, we made it work. I remained on flight status, and the leg slowly and steadily began to feel better.

TRACY AND BARBARA WERE at the Cape with me for the month before launch, and I gave them every tour and briefing possible so they could be ready when I stepped into the unknown. Barbara, as a former stewardess, had no fear of flying and always considered it to be just my way of commuting to work. I had gone into space twice before, and thought that she had grown used to the idea of extreme missions. I would learn later that she hadn't.

Tracy was nine, and for the first time, could truly understand what was happening. I gave her a ride in the Rover, let her climb through the simulators, and gently guided her through any questions. I ran a finger along a lunar map. "This is where Daddy's going to land," I told her, pointing to the swirls of Taurus-Littrow. "Here's Poppie's Crater and here's one named for your mom, and right there is the crater that I called Punk, after you."

When I showed her the space suit I would wear, Tracy told me she and her mother had new mission outfits of their own. Her grandmother had made matching gray wool maxiskirts, and Mrs. Eagleton (who had moved into the Chaffee house next door) created large *Apollo 17* patches that were sewn onto them. Blue turtleneck sweaters completed the outfits. In a year when other people were being swept into a unisex clothing revolution aswim in peacock colors, my girls looked great.

On November 15, we went into quarantine at the Cape for three weeks of medical isolation, restricted to the living quarters, the training facility and flying T-38s to keep our senses sharp. Only 109 people were cleared to be in contact with us, to prevent a cold or flu from messing up the flight. Jan Evans and Barbara took the appropriate shots and could be with us until four days before launch, but our kids were off limits. I could talk to Tracy only through a glass partition. Jack, being a bachelor, led the life of an ascetic monk and loved it, spending his private time cuddled with schematic diagrams and tech manuals right up until the last minute.

Apollo 17 seemed to have banished much of the strain Barbara and I had endured over the past few years, and my wife was upbeat and as determined as the bride of any first-flight astronaut. Perhaps we both were looking at the mission through a positive filter that distorted reality, but it seemed that things had come back together for us since I had been appointed to the command. After all, *17* was the last one of the series, and when it was done, I would not rotate to a new flight, at least for a very long time. So after I achieved my long-sought goals of leading a mission and walking on the Moon, there would finally be time for family again, time for our marriage, time for a future together. "I think Gene wants to fly forever," Barbara confided to friend. "But we want him home for a while."

Nothing guaranteed, but maybe, just maybe, the magic of *Apollo 17* might also mend our personal lives.

28

Top of the Pyramid

ON WEDNESDAY, DECEMBER 6, 1972, villages of tents and mobile homes sprouted like multicolored flowers along U.S. 1 and the causeways around the Cape, and the inhabitants basked in an eighty-degree Florida winter afternoon. The schoolkids of Titusville were released early from classes to stake out prime viewing spots for their families. By sundown, about 700,000 people had gathered for the last launch of Apollo, coming from as far away as England and Australia to watch the spectacle.

Americans of all walks of life came together in a common adventure, a Pittsburgh steelworker's kids playing in the surf with the dog of a California hippie couple, while the parents toasted *Apollo 17* with drinks and ate potato salad from the cooler in a VW van, everybody joking with the cops and waving to passing limousines. Some listened to rock music and others sang hymns. Every bus within a 250-mile radius had been rented and hauled in more birdwatchers by the hour, swelling the population of the instant city. We didn't realize it, but the liftoff of *Apollo 17* was one of the early harbingers that a tired and torn America was starting to knit itself back together.

Cash registers chimed all around Brevard County, as the throng of excited spectators rubbed shoulders with early Christmas shoppers. Chamber of Commerce–types hoped the activity indicated the future of a new, post-Apollo community, when tourism, retirees and diversified industry would replace the jobs lost by the ending of the Moon program.

Two Communist Chinese journalists joined the largest press corps to ever cover a launch. A well-known governor, George Wallace of Alabama, crippled by a gunman during his presidential campaign, would be seated in the VIP grandstand near a little-known governor, Jimmy Carter of Georgia. They were among the 42,000 people who actually held invitations, and I had personally invited more than fifty, including not only my mom and sister, but celebrities and friends, such as Skip and Ry, Baldy, John Wayne, Connie Stevens, Bob Hope, Don Rickles, Dinah

Shore, Johnny Carson, Henry Mancini and Eva Gabor. Not only were they invited, but they came, joining the vigil for this once-in-a-lifetime event, this home run in the last inning of a space World Series, the final touchdown in a celestial Super Bowl.

As night fell, high-rollers motored in from luxury yachts anchored offshore to munch roast pig and shrimp beneath a big green-and-white tent that sheltered the Time, Inc. luau from a passing shower. Only two weeks before, the publishing company had closed *Life* magazine, severing the link with the astronauts who had seen their pictures spread in those glossy pages over the years, and who had collected precious paychecks in return.

Dominating the festivities from over there at Pad 39-A, standing proud and majestic against the stage of orange scaffolding at the edge of the Atlantic Ocean, was my Saturn V, whitewashed by seventy-four big xenon spotlights, a silvery needle gleaming in the night. Sheets of ice slid from her sides as workers pumped in the freezing fuel, and she owned the night. The birdwatchers glanced over frequently to admire her sleek lines and to keep a sharp eye peeled, as if she might sneak away unseen.

There was at least one heretic in the bunch: Charlie Smith, age 130, the oldest living American. Charlie had been keeping his guard up ever since he was tricked onto a slave ship as a child. He had seen many wondrous things in his long life and rated the voyage of *Apollo 17* about on a par with the day the preacher ran off with Charlie's money and the deacon's wife. "Ain't nobody going to the Moon—me, you or nobody else," he confidently opined. But he stuck around for the launch anyway.

Far out beyond the bright lights, the steel-drum music and tables laden with shrimp and steak, Charley Buckley's security teams were hard at their stealthy work. Helicopters circled the area, military patrols fanned through the swamps, and undercover cops worked the civilian areas. Security had never been as tight at the Cape, and although we seldom saw our guardians, they watched our every move. Black September was no joke.

FOR SEVERAL DAYS RON, Jack and I had stayed up until the early morning hours, then slept late, adjusting our body clocks for the all-night workload that was coming. I invested most of my hours throughout Wednesday in last-minute drills in the simulators, mostly out of habit, because if I didn't know how to fly these birds by now, I never would. The best part of the last evening was a brief visit with Barbara and Tracy, although we were separated by that damned pane of glass, a space-age sneeze guard.

Late Tuesday night, President Nixon telephoned to wish us bon voyage, but the conversation soon veered off into one of the strangest one-way calls I'd ever had. He wished us good luck and made the usual cheery banter, then his good nature suddenly fell away and was replaced by a sense of morose pessimism.

The president began discussing how hard he was working to obtain peace with honor in Vietnam, and yet the American people didn't appreciate, or even understand, that he was trying to do the right thing over there, and the press was always unfairly attacking him. By calling us, Nixon had stumbled into a protected, safe haven where politics was seldom discussed. Three astronauts about to leave for the Moon had other things on their minds and were about as nonthreatening an audience as he was likely to find, for we had no political agenda at all. He wanted someone to talk to, and that night, it was us.

Ron, Jack and I were on separate phones and we looked over at each other in bewildered surprise as our president rattled on for forty-five minutes about how he felt persecuted and pilloried by the very citizens he was trying to serve. About all we could say was, "Yes, sir, Mr. President." I couldn't very well tell the president of the United States that I felt sorry for him.

I vividly remembered the gregarious and confident President Nixon who had greeted Barbara and me on the steps of the chief executive's mansion three years ago after *Apollo 10*. This voice on the telephone wasn't the same person, but that of a demoralized stranger, almost pleading with us to understand his position, as if he sought our benediction. Nixon sounded like a tired and lonely old man, living an isolated and empty existence in his big white house, more prisoner than president.

I HIT MY BUNK about two A.M., Wednesday morning, and this time I wasn't having trouble adjusting to the idea of riding the Saturn, or even commanding my own crew on a complex mission. Those were matters for which I felt well prepared, and I could now wave them aside, just as Wernher von Braun had brushed away the problems of getting to the Moon at our dinner so many years ago. *Get to the Moon? Oh yeah, sure, we can do that.* What vexed me was more philosophical than tangible, but it nevertheless robbed me of sleep as effectively as a burglar with a gun.

I lay in the darkness, hands behind my head on the pillow, knowing that I would probably be the last man to walk on the Moon for many years to come, since no more manned lunar missions were planned for as far in the future as we could see, a cold fact that seemed truly wrong to me. Therefore, I would be expected to say something appropriate at the conclusion of this epic adventure, and the press was killing me to disclose the words I didn't yet know. Neil had come up with the wonderful "one small step for man" quote, and now it was my turn. Despite all my extemporaneous public speaking, I didn't have a clue. Adios? Thanks for the memories? It really is made out of green cheese?

And the whole first-man-last-man conundrum toyed with me. Would I have rather been first on the Moon, make the historic step and hang around for a couple of hours, or last, when I could spend entire days on the surface, drive the Moon buggy to distant reaches where lunar secrets lurked, and have time to savor those precious moments? Which experience would be richer? A true enigma, but a moot point. My bird was *Apollo 17*.

I took comfort in knowing that, in a few days, Jack and I would pile into the *Challenger*, dive out of lunar orbit and dash through the final 47,000 feet that had denied me a landing three years before. I rested well through the quiet early morning hours, but as a popular new song put it, *Last night, I didn't get to sleep at all.* Under the circumstances, who would?

LEW HARTZELL HAD THE usual steak and eggs waiting when I got up about noon, and after a private mass with Dee O'Hara and Father Cargill, who by now considered himself to be an astronaut because he spent so much time with us, we all caught up on the final briefings while sipping coffee and horsing around. Everything unfolded at a rather leisurely pace in comparison with the hurly-burly of a morning mission.

Our launch window was between 9:53 P.M. and 1:31 A.M., Florida time, and those times were firm, but the weather report was kind of iffy. After the sunny temperatures of the previous afternoon, a cold front had stalked in from the west and a layer of gray clouds flapped high above the Cape like a line of dirty laundry, threatening to spread a curtain of thunderstorms across our sky path. The weather folks said we had a better than 50 percent chance of getting away on time.

The Boeing workers were back on the job after a last-minute settlement of a dispute over wages, which meant there would be no picket lines at the spaceport tonight. We would have gone anyway. A computer failure in the firing room had forced everyone to shift to an alternate system but did not seriously disrupt the countdown. Chuck La Pinta and I grinned at each other as I squeezed my aching butt and sore leg into my space suit. When asked how I felt, I lied a little and he knew it. No biggies. Ron smoked the last cigarette he would have for almost two weeks. Its memory must have haunted him, because one of the first things he would do aboard the recovery ship was bum a cigarette from a sailor.

I took a moment when we were alone to remind Jack and Ron, who had no idea what they were in for, to soak up the experience they were about to have. "We're going to shake, rattle and roll once the flight begins. Just hang in there and do what you've trained to do," I told them. "But I want you to enjoy this, enjoy every second before it's gone. This will be one of the most breathtaking experiences you've ever had, and we won't be back this way again." They didn't know how to respond. I remembered when Tom Stafford had tried to explain the thrill of a Gemini reentry and I was unable to grasp what he was trying to tell me. You can never really understand until it happens. This was just going to have to be a life lesson for my crew mates, something they would have to undergo for themselves.

Before getting into the helmets for the prebreathing session, we joked about how empty our pockets felt, because of the reaction that had followed the *Apollo 15* stamp scandal. We could carry no more than a dozen items of a personal nature and absolutely nothing, zero, *nada*, to indicate we might make a nickel off of this flight. That meant we disappointed a lot of friends and relatives who wanted us to take along some harmless trinket. When a reporter had asked me what I was taking to the Moon, I replied, "Ron and Jack."

Actually, I had an American flag and the mission patches from my previous flights in my personal pack, along with my wings of gold, a special ring of my dad's, and personal mementos for Tracy, Barbara, Mom and Dee. Still, I was disappointed that the new rules prevented carrying little tokens of appreciation for close friends and the people who put that Saturn into the sky.

After suiting up and breathing pure oxygen for the allotted time, we waddled outside, and Barbara and Tracy were waiting beside the stairs so I could get one last hug. Lord, did that feel good, but their presence once again reminded me of the threat of terrorism. The possibility that some nut might try to shoot the Saturn full of holes didn't concern me, because I knew Charley's people were all over the place. But the safety of my family had bothered me from the first day I had learned of the danger, and I constantly wrestled with the possibility of them being threatened while I was on the Moon, a quarter-million miles away. Nightmare scenarios had plagued me for weeks. What would I do if my daughter was taken by terrorists who then demanded that I denounce my country while the whole world watched? Today, it's a question I don't have to answer. At the time, I just didn't know.

WE GOT OUR FIRST glimpse of the gathered throng as our special van made the drive from the crew quarters to the pad. With my big fishbowl of a helmet on, I could hear nothing but the steady hiss of oxygen from my life-support briefcase, but I could see people cheering, a chorus of unheard voices. Bright lights dappled the nightscape as we drove through the darkness, following the familiar road past the VAB, past the press site and along the very track that had ferried the Saturn to the pad. A spotlight beam from a helicopter hovering above improved our driver's vision, for it just wouldn't do to run over a spectator at this stage of the game. Far away, faint fingers of lightning snapped in the sky. I leaned my head forward and scratched my nose on a small piece of Velcro imbedded on the faceplate for just such a purpose.

The routine of getting to the pad, something I knew so well, had assumed an almost religious quality for hundreds of thousands of people this time, and I was moved by the palpable sense of emotion surrounding us. *The last ride of Apollo!* By the time we reached the elevator, I felt absolutely charmed, and was grinning from ear to ear.

My Saturn V sparkled like a 363-foot-high jewel rampant against the night sky, center stage and draped in spotlights. She was no longer a mystery, and it seemed that she eagerly awaited my arrival, not as some cold, distant prom queen, but as a rambunctious and confident go-go gal of the seventies. My partner for the last dance was a confident and happy thoroughbred, trembling and anxious to get on with the mission for which she had been so carefully groomed by thousands of hands and hearts. I could almost hear her giggle, *"Hey, Geno, where ya' been? Lookit all those people down there! Hop on, darlin'! I'm gonna take you to the Moon!"*

*   *   *

THE ELEVATOR ROSE SLOWLY up the side of the Saturn, and the American flag painted on her flank passed before my face and disappeared beneath my toes, then the black letters SETATS DETINU slid by, one by one, bottom to top. Every inch of the rocket was slathered in lights, and frosty bergs of boiling fuel peeled from her skin. I could hear nothing through my helmet, nor could I talk to anyone but myself, so there was no way to share the isolated wonder that I felt at that moment. This wasn't *Apollo 10* déjà vu, but an entirely new sensation, amplified by the darkness, with puddles of light stretching away far below in every direction, even to the east, out in the Atlantic, where boatloads of spectators bobbed and waited. By the time the elevator came to a jerking, shaking halt at the top, it was as if I could see all the way to Miami.

Crossing that open narrow walkway on the access arm from the elevator to the White Room, a temporary protective shroud around the hatchway, was the longest twenty feet of the mission. Alone in a crowd, wrapped in enforced silence so dense I heard my own heart beat, I looked down into a boiling, writhing hell of confusion that fell away to unimagined depths beneath my feet and prayed the steel mesh could support my weight, because it all seemed so damned thin and frail. Tendrils of mist oozed through the tiny open spaces, clawing at my boots. Step carefully. Quickly.

The morticians await, but one is missing. Guenther is not there as the pad crew führer, having been promoted away to more important duties, and I miss him. It is a break with tradition, and somewhat unsteadying. Who's going to tap my helmet and wish me Godspeed? The new guy is perfectly capable, but without Guenther, something seems out of balance.

We stuff ourselves into the spacecraft, buckle up, attach the O_2 hoses and cables, and the radio comes alive in our ears. The hatch is closed and the White Room folds away. We are alone. *We're really going to do it.* Nerves calm as training clicks in, and I can't help but grin as I start the pre-flight checklists. The next few hours fly past.

"TWO MINUTES AND COUNTING," came the announcement from Launch Control, and a hush settled over the eastern edge of Florida. I looked at the clock on the instrument panel and pushed my shoulders and body deep into the canvas couch. I was in the commander's left seat, Ron was in the middle position of the CM pilot, and Dr. Rock, the LM pilot, was on the right. An aerodynamic shroud covered the spacecraft during liftoff, and of the five windows available, only one was uncovered, and it was just above my face. There was nothing to see but some light reflecting off the low haze. We were right on time for the scheduled 9:53 P.M. liftoff, and control had shifted to the electronic hands of the automatic sequencing computer. I scanned the dials one last time. Everything was in the green. *Time to go.*

A hiccup.

A launch computer failed to give the command for a third-stage oxygen tank to pressurize and controllers sent a manual override command. "One minute and counting," came the words through our helmets. "Thirty . . ." I took a deep breath and held on white-knuckle tight. Something was happening, but I didn't know exactly what, and the businesslike voices from Launch Control reeked with disappointment. *Are we going?*

The hiccup grew to a glitch as the automatic sequencer refused the manual command and, without warning, the whole show shut down in a heartbeat, the only last-moment halt in Apollo history. A lifeless computer had decided that we weren't going anywhere.

"We have had a cut-off," announced a stunned Launch Control official. Hundreds of thousands of people along the Atlantic coast let out their breath with a single exhalation, as if the night were deflating like a torn beach ball. Very aware of the trouble my mouth had caused on *Apollo 10*, I didn't shout, "Oh, shit!" but I sure thought it.

ENGINEERS STARTED A FRANTIC race with the clock to cure the problem before the launch window closed, while Ron, Jack and I sat immobile, three guys tightly bound to little couches more than 300 feet in the air, grumbling about electronic gremlins. Although we were atop a fully fueled booster, we were in no danger, but the service tower swung back into place, just in case. I didn't like this. Memories of Gemini scrubs surfaced, but that was then and this was now. I was no longer a twenty-nine-year-old rookie astronaut, so I thought of Schirra, Stafford and Shepard and ordered myself to remain the cool captain, although doubts swarmed in my brain until I started to believe we were not going to launch that night after all. I thought about those thousands of people standing out there in the dark, getting their ankles savaged by the no-see-um bugs and waiting for the big show. I managed to convince myself that if we had a scrub, all my friends, who by now had run out of booze, would leave in a rush and be unable to come back and that I would finally depart Earth watched only by an audience of alligators, mud turtles and mosquitoes.

Now that we had nothing to do, time crawled by as we lay there, wondering about what sort of failure had occurred and how long it was going to last. Was it ground control equipment or the booster itself? Could the problem be found? And, if found, could it be fixed? I dreaded the possibility that one of the morticians would start unlocking the hatch. Jack seemed to be in some sort of trance, perhaps thinking about the fact that he was sitting atop a powerful bomb that was waiting to go off, but more likely just reviewing the thousands of things for which he had prepared during training. I had to hand it to Dr. Rock. He was as ready as any astronaut could be. Unflappable combat vet Ron Evans, so sharp and patriotic that we called him Captain America, didn't think the delay was any big deal and went to sleep, his relaxed snore a deep undertone to the chatter on the radio net. My Lady Saturn continued to hum and mumble as the engineers kept topping off the frigid fuel. I could feel her breathing, and knew she was straining at her leash.

Flat on my back with my legs elevated, pressure built inexorably on my kidneys until I could hold it no longer and peed in my pants. The first American astronaut to fly, Al Shepard, had done it, so why not me? Thanks to Al urinating in his suit, designers had come up with a sort of space-age motorman's friend that let an astronaut relieve himself without a lot of hoo-haw, and I felt the eerie touch of warm liquid flowing through a tube and into the collection bag around my abdomen. I assumed success, but knew that if the bag broke, we would be picking up blobs of urine for the rest of the trip. The bag's contents would be flushed away when we got into space, and the freezing temperature outside the spacecraft would turn the droplets into a cloud of bright, drifting crystals. Some astronauts described those routine dumps, which Wally Schirra nicknamed the Constellation Urion, as being among the most amazing sights they saw on an entire voyage.

After a couple of hours, the guys in Launch Control found a way to outwit the cranky computer, and the countdown was resumed at five minutes before midnight. I almost let out a cheer when they gave me the word. Go in forty minutes. While we were busy with our final readouts, December 7, one of the most historic dates in American history, appeared on the calendar.

"THE ROCKET WAS GORGED with a highly volatile fuel called liquid oxygen, and the three men were waiting for someone to light the fuse. Who on Earth were they? Or, rather, what were they? Why were they willing to do such a thing?" observed author Tom Wolfe, down at the Cape on assignment for *Rolling Stone*, but getting an idea for a book. "The main thing to know is that capsule right now is filled with three colossal Ti*tan*ic egos . . . The main thing to know about an astronaut, if you want to understand his psychology, is not that he's going into space but that he is a flyer and has been in that game for fifteen or twenty years. It's like a huge and complex pyramid, miles high, and the idea is to prove at every foot of the way up that pyramid that you are one of the elected and anointed ones who have *the right stuff* and can move ever higher and even—ultimately, God willing, one day—that you might be able to join that very special few at the very top, that elite who truly have the capacity to bring tears to men's eye, the very Brotherhood of The Right Stuff itself."

Guess who is on top of that pyramid tonight?

THERE WAS A BRILLIANT and frightening burst of orange fire below the Saturn when the five huge engines ignited with a fury that shook the land and sea for miles around, and thick columns of white smoke boiled into the spotlights, instant angry storm clouds that rushed away across the low ground. For nine long seconds, the power built and the thunderclap roar spread over the sand dunes and marshland, making people in the grandstands three miles away cover their ears and shield their eyes as the deafening, staccato blast shoved against their bodies hard enough for them to feel shirt buttons press against their chests.

At 12:33 A.M., the hold-down arms released and Saturn stirred, balanced on a dazzling fireball that grew to the size of an atomic bomb. As a show-stopping spectacular, nothing in the entire space program compared to our night launch. "The clock has started," I told Launch Control. "Thrust is good on all five engines," CapCom responded. Music to my ears. We are on our way!

The vibration wiggled up the tower and shook us as the big rocket came alive, an inferno growing and growling and seemingly out of control. But it wasn't. I held it in my hands. The awakened Saturn would now respond to me, go where I wanted, and do exactly what I told her. I had the power to steer her into the heavens, or to close her down. Prior to the bolts blowing far below, someone else had been making the decisions, but from here on, I called the shots for this shaking and quaking monster, and I happily endured every jolt, for this was the payoff for my big gamble with Deke. For good, bad or worse, over the next thirteen days, I would be responsible for whatever happened.

UP WE WENT, CRASHING through a feathery layer of mist, a beautiful shot in the dark. Into a roll at twelve seconds, G-forces pushing me down while the rocket pushed me up, a soul-searching lifetime as we swept away from the pad, trailing a searing tail a half-mile long and so bright that it lit up the night sky from North Carolina to Cuba.

The reflected fiery light bounced off the clouds and came through my window to paint our instrument panel a violent red. All systems were working perfectly, and Ron yelled "Whoopee!" as Jack cried out, "We're going up! Man, oh man!" This was odd. Ron's reaction was about what I expected, but our quiet, Harvard-trained scientist must have snuck his talkative twin aboard *Apollo 17* while nobody was looking, for the no-nonsense geologist was actually having fun.

At two minutes and forty seconds, the first-stage rockets burned out and we were gobbled up by a fireball the likes of which I had never seen, a maelstrom of flame that toyed with my certain knowledge that we were not burning up. *We're not. This is normal.* The straps holding us to our couches strained as we were slung forward and back, side to side, again and again.

When the second stage fired to take over propulsion, people on the ground saw the separation as the explosion of a minor blue star and we catapulted right through that ominous fireball, stacking on ever more speed. "Four minutes and we're Go here," I reported, with CapCom coming back instantly, "Roger, Gene. We're going around the room. Looks Go here. You're looking real good, Gene. Right down the line."

The escape tower separation, barely noticeable in daylight, tore away in a blinding burst of light akin to the birth of a comet, and yanked off the shroud that covered the other windows. Ron and Jack could now see the enchantment unfolding around us. Soon, Jack would start to jabber like a kid at the circus.

At four and a half minutes, I reported, "Let me tell you, this night launch is something to behold." We rushed out into the star-dotted heavens, dumped the second stage at about nine and a half minutes, then slipped into Earth orbit on the third stage, only a dozen minutes after liftoff, as easily as falling into a favorite easy chair.

THERE WAS NO DIFFICULTY following something that glowed as bright as the Sun at midnight, and down in Florida, Barbara and Tracy watched us leave the planet from a small point surrounded by water. When the brilliant light flared from our engines, schools of startled fish leaped into the air, hung there wiggling and silvery for a moment, and splashed back down, churning the water into a froth. The Earth trembled and false daylight brightened the area like high noon, then swiftly faded back to darkness. This wasn't a launch, it was a dream.

My girls had been surrounded by so many people for so many days, the objects of so much attention, that they welcomed the respite provided by the liftoff, feeling linked through noise and flame to the husband and father in the distant spacecraft that was soaring away from Earth. No matter what happened, we were together. Tracy said she was unafraid and never entertained the slightest thought that I wasn't coming home again, but in truth, Little Miss Astronaut clutched the *Apollo 17* emblem on her gray maxiskirt and cried.

EVENTUALLY, WE FADED FROM view and the excited spectators had a chance to talk about the astounding show. "Your eyes will never see anything like that again if you live a thousand years," said enthusiastic Julian Scheer, a NASA spokesman. Charlie Smith, well on his way to living that long, wasn't so sure. "I see them goin' somewhere, but it still don't mean nothin'." About three hours after launch, we had already made two loops around the world, weightless and preparing for the next step of our journey.

Jack Schmitt happily spent the time giving ground controllers a running account of almost every cloud passing below us, amazed by the difference between textbook theory and real life. If he was so turned on by seeing a rainbow, I couldn't wait to hear him on the Moon. Houston signaled a Go to reignite the third-stage rocket, which only eased us against our seats. This burn lasted a bit longer than normal to make up for the time lost during the delay on the launch pad, but when it was done, we were out of Earth orbit and on our way to the Moon.

Next stop, Camelot.

29

Falling to the Moon

As we began our eighty-six-hour coast to the Moon, Ron freed the command module from the third stage and linked *America* with *Challenger*. The S-IV-B, no longer of any use, was maneuvered away by Mission Control; the big engine fired for a final time and the rocket hurtled toward the Moon, where it would crash like a meteor just before we arrived.

Jack stayed at his window, chattering about the marvelous things he was seeing. "Hey, there's Antarctica. It's all full of snow!" he told a nearly empty Mission Control room at five o'clock in the morning, Houston time. "I couldn't have believed this would be an experience like it is now. Every time you turn around, there is something else to see and wonder what's causing it." For the next two days, he would do a running account of Earth's weather patterns as the globe spun like a blue top, growing smaller by the hour. "You're a human weather satellite," one CapCom needled, but they encouraged him to talk on and on. After all, he was the first scientist to enter what had always been a pilot's domain. Since he wouldn't be able to see the Moon for a couple of days, Jack had planned, with some of his colleagues, to examine the weather patterns of Earth as never before, from Australia to Zanzibar.

We fought our way out of our bulky space suits, which had the effect of adding three more people to the already cramped cabin before we could get them pressed flat, stowed and out of the way. I glanced out the window myself and reported, "Houston, I know we're not the first to observe this, but *Apollo Seventeen* would like to confirm the Earth is round."

The mechanics of the mission were going surprisingly well, with only the amber flicker of a few alarm lights requiring attention as we ran the numbers to make sure everything worked. Then we dug into our meal packs, and while I had half a sandwich and some water, Ron tried potato soup, which oozed out of the plastic bag and hung in the air like globs of glue that he guided into his mouth. Our first rest period began almost exactly nine hours into the mission, and although we had been awake for about twenty-two hours straight, we were too excited to do much more than sleep fitfully.

Back in Florida, Barbara had stayed awake after the midnight launch until we had bolted out of orbit and were safely on our way to the Moon, then she caught a few hours of sleep before getting up about dawn to pack. She, Tracy and Jan Evans and her kids, Jaime and Jon, left aboard a NASA Gulfstream Thursday morning out of Patrick AFB to return to Houston. My wife's immediate plans, she told reporters before departing: "I'm going to take the phone off the hook, take a bath and go to bed."

I AWOKE SOMEWHERE OVER the Pacific, and found the Earth had grown smaller very quickly. The entire long coastlines of North and South America rolled beneath us, and after we had a breakfast of sausage patties, grits and cocoa, Weatherman Jack was immediately back at his window. Southern California was in good shape, but a nasty storm system was reaching into the northwestern United States. Jack finally realized that he was looking at more than just cloud formations and continents, and there was a momentary crack in his scientific mien. "When we moved away from the Earth, how fragile a piece of blue it looked to be, and that impression certainly grows the farther you get from it."

A course correction was scrubbed because of the extraordinary accuracy of our path, and except for a brewing sense of anticipation, things actually got boring as we hurtled away from the planet at unbelievable speeds. Despite conducting a long series of experiments, the biggest moment came when Ron lost his blunt-nosed surgical scissors. "Scissors, scissors, who's got the scissors?" teased CapCom Gordon Fullerton. Chowhound Ron, frustrated, urgently searched the cabin, since the scissors were the only way into the sealed bags of food.

ON BARBUDA LANE, A plywood cutout of a jolly Santa Claus had been staked on the lawn, neighbors had arranged red, white and blue Christmas lights to resemble an American flag, and a bag of mail awaited the busy fingers of Tracy. Another herd of reporters was waiting when my family arrived home, and Barbara told them, "For us, when we came into the program, Gene's goal was to reach the Moon. He's now reaching that goal. This is our challenge, and we've met it. I feel so very proud." Her familiar mask of optimism held firm.

It would be many years before she would lower her guard and write a friend, "I have been asked many times how I felt when he was off on a space trip, and if I told you I wasn't scared to death each time, I would not be telling the truth." The strain this time would be more than anything she had ever endured. Because of the length of the mission, its complexity and its importance, Barbara would soon feel besieged in her own home.

On the private radio loop, I asked Deke an oblique question to be sure the security guards were on alert around my house back in Nassau Bay. "Don't worry, Geno," he said. "Everything is fine on that front." Then I was told that Tracy was listening, and I reminded my daughter from a hundred thousand miles away not to forget to feed the horses. CapCom reported that Barbara suggested putting a nice young female voice on the speaker to tell me good night and say that she loved me. Actually, she wasn't far off the mark. When I turned to that night's page in the flight plan, I found the *Playboy* centerfold, beautiful Miss December 1972, was along for the ride. Our backup crew had been at work.

The next time I awoke, after a full eight hours of sleep, it was late on Friday, December 8, on Earth clocks, and we were all still tired, primarily because of the enforced idleness of the cramped spaceship, where we had little to do other than putter with a seemingly endless line of experiments and listen to the Dr. Rock Weather Channel.

A two-second midcourse correction tacked an extra seven miles per hour onto our speed, then Jack and I went through the narrow connecting tunnel and spent almost two and a half hours inside the lunar module, inspecting the guts of *Challenger* and preparing the systems for our upcoming three-day stay on the lunar surface.

Hours passed slowly as we flashed through the empty halls of outer space. We had a lot of time to kill and grew exhausted doing nothing at all that might be considered exciting.

Our velocity had steadily bled away as our home planet tried to pull us back, and we were only traveling 3,000 miles per hour, a virtual standstill in space speed as we settled in for another rest period. CapCom warned that we might feel a bounce during the night because we were about to rumble across an imaginary speed bump, when we would leave the Earth's sphere of gravity. Soon, the Moon would grab us and draw us forward.

*   *   *

THE NEED FOR SLEEP must have caught up with us, because it took ten tries by Mission Control to awaken us. They repeatedly tripped warning tones on the instrument console, received no response, then played three loud renditions of "I'm a Jay, Jay, Jay, Jayhawk,"—the fight song of Ron's alma mater, the University of Kansas—still without effect. I finally noticed a blinking light on the control panel and snapped, "Hey! We're asleep!"

"That's the understatement of the year," said Gordon Fullerton, again on CapCom duty. We had overslept by an hour. "Ron was supposed to be on watch but claims he fell asleep after a big party," I explained. Actually, Ron had inadvertently kicked an audio connection and disconnected his communications in settling down to rest. It was no big deal, but gave us something to talk about other than the missing scissors, and was the most interesting thing of the day. Funny thing happened on the way to the Moon—not much. Should have brought some crossword puzzles.

It was Saturday, December 9, and we were in the Moon's firm hold, only about 38,000 miles out and drawing closer by the moment. Jack and I slid back into *Challenger* to give the lunar module a final checkout, and found the bug was ready. I looked out of its triangular windows, but still could not see the Moon because of the angle at which we were approaching, sailing easily through an ocean of bright Sunlight. I had experienced this sensation before on *Apollo 10*, and felt comfortable in familiar territory. But I also had a few disconcerting thoughts because I knew what lay ahead. We were close. Although unseen, the Moon would now be very large, lurking nearby like a grizzly bear pawing at the outside of a log cabin door.

Then the Sun disappeared and we were enveloped by Moonshadow. As the light blinked out, our spacecraft, that miraculous product of a program in which safety was a paramount concern, began to seem fragile and vulnerable, and I remembered that the gold outer skin of *Challenger* had a thickness of only one two-thousandths of an inch, not much more than the edge of a piece of paper. The bear was closer. I could *feel* it. For about an hour, things got very quiet as we plunged through obsidian blackness.

Then suddenly, at three days, twelve hours, six minutes and thirty-one seconds into the flight of *Apollo 17*, we crossed out of shadow, burst back into brilliant sunlight, and there it was, still some 10,000 miles away but encompassing our universe, and I let out a shout: "Boy, is it big! We're coming right down on top of it!" The Sun was low on the horizon and blazed right in my eyes, and the Moon blotted out everything else. "I'll tell you, when you get out here, it's a big mamou."

Looking at the Moon from our vantage point was quite unlike seeing it from Earth, when it is so distant. Now it was gigantic, a world of its own, and it forced me to question what I was really seeing. Such scenes existed only in science fiction, for not even the simulators could impart the reality of such a moment. We plummeted toward it faster and faster, and the closer we got, the bigger it grew. There was a faint feeling of vertigo, as if I was falling down a shaft toward the surface, and might soon pancake right into some crater. "I'm considering putting the window covers up," I told Fullerton. Gordy chuckled, "Chicken, huh?" Damned right.

I thought I was prepared for our arrival, that I knew what to expect because I had been up here before, but I really didn't. The dynamics of time and space were unfolding so rapidly that my brain barely had time to register one sensation before having to grasp another that was even more overwhelming, like trying to identify individual cards as an entire deck flutters to the floor.

Dr. Rock was also stunned by the sheer size of the planetoid that he had spent a lifetime studying. Never in his wildest dreams had Jack imagined such a sight, and he momentarily lost his ability to even speak. The Sun illuminated the high peaks and mountains, and the rims of giant craters and surface details emerged, bathed in gold or hidden in deep shadow.

By now we were only 2,600 miles up and coming in like a bat out of hell, trying to thread an orbital needle by hitting an invisible bull's-eye only sixty miles above the lunar surface. I put my eye to the monocular and, *wow!* I could see straight down into some of the craters. High ridges rolled away over the horizon like the waves of an ocean. "I have the feeling someone is watching this spacecraft maneuver and burn across the lunar surface," I said, awed by the majesty of the Moon.

While Jack sat mute, transfixed, and I also gazed in wonder at the unfolding details of this distinct celestial body, Ron was less rapt. He alternated staring at the Moon with poking around the spacecraft interior. "I'll have a hard time eating if you guys take all the scissors with you," he said. Ron had his priorities straight. Food was more important than sightseeing.

*   *   *

WE SWEPT BEHIND THE Moon, and out of contact with Earth, at 3:36 P.M., December 10, Houston time. Almost exactly four years after *Apollo 8* wove man's first loops around the Moon, *Apollo 17* became the eighth and last crew to see it from orbit.

Eleven minutes into that first backside pass, we fired the command module rocket in a 6-and-a-half-minute braking maneuver that decreased our speed by more than 2,000 miles per hour and allowed lunar gravity to capture us firmly in an elliptical orbit that stretched 60 miles by 195 miles. It went smoothly, but only Jack, Ron and I knew that because we were in the silent zone. On Earth, the suspense built for another twenty-two minutes until we came rocking around the front side. "Thumbs up, Houston," I called. "You can breathe easier. *America* has arrived on station for the challenge ahead."

Four hours later, we lit the engine again and dropped into an even lower orbit, of about 68 miles, the area I knew so well from *Apollo 10*. "We is getting back down among 'em where us plain folks belong," I called. For some reason, when I got around the Moon, my syntax fractured. Jack and I went back into the lander, ran the final checks, and pronounced *Challenger* ready to rip.

Ron had not found his scissors, but Jack had found his tongue. Now that we were in orbit, he went on a verbal rampage, words spilling out in a Niagara of information. Earthly clouds and low-pressure fronts were long forgotten. He was pointed the other way now, at the Moon, and was talking rapidly in short stories of science, describing Eratosthenes, dark albedo areas within the ejecta of Copernicus, central peaks like Reinhold and Lansberg, the nonlinear characteristics of ray patterns, the Marius Hills, Oceanus Procellarum, and the irregular swirls in Mare Marginis. Not mere sentences, but whole long paragraphs in a single breath, driving the poor transcribers back in Houston nuts, and we hadn't done a damn thing yet except reach lunar orbit.

We jettisoned the world's largest lens cover, a 170-pound door that protected science instruments and cameras in the equipment bay on the side of the command module. That opened the two cameras and three multimillion-dollar instrument packages, which Ron would operate as he flew in high orbit while Jack and I were gone. The data and pictures he would gather would provide new measurements, draw a thermal map of areas over which he passed, and bounce radio waves into the surface to measure soil composition more than a half-mile deep in a search for water, permafrost or ice. Water on the Moon, of course, would vastly simplify maintaining a space habitat there.

CapCom gave us news from Earth. Ron and I were extremely interested in what our families were up to, and Mission Control passed along the comforting words, laden with import, that everything was still okay around the home front. They had news for Jack, too, and told Dr. Rock that his mother was "pleased as all get out" at what her son was doing. "That sounds like Mother," he replied, brushing it aside. Personal feelings were not going to interfere with his science, and the next thing he said was, "I just got a real good view of Copernicus . . . a big crater eighty kilometers in diameter."

The *Washington Post* carried a front-page photograph of Tracy and Barbara seated on the floor watching television, a small American flag between them as they listened to the squawk box. They made small talk with friends and tensely waited for us to reappear during that first pass around the back side of the Moon, when we had to do the burn to go into orbit. When we reported that all was well, Barbara flashed a thumbs-up sign and cried, "Great." Tracy looked up. "Was the fire okay?" Yes, it was, her mother said. Tracy nodded happily and chirped, "I am going to look up there at the Moon and see if I can see Daddy tonight."

CapCom alerted everyone that it was time for a rest period that would last through almost four lunar orbits, and reminded us that tomorrow would be a busy day.

WE AWOKE TO ARLO Guthrie singing "City of New Orleans." Jack and I had a different destination. We climbed aboard *Challenger* at 8:50 A.M., December 11, Texas time, and donned our suits, zipped and snapped, connected the helmets, and put on the gloves. Many of the items we needed for the lunar landing were crammed inside the spacecraft, and the outer edges of *Challenger* were lined with the folded Rover and other things too large to fit in the cabin. It looked like Fibber McGee's closet on the inside and the Beverly Hillbillies' truck on the outside.

When all was ready, we undocked at 11:21 A.M. "Okay, Houston. This is *America*," Ron radioed. "We're floating free out here. The *Challenger* looks real pretty."

"Checkout is complete," I reported. "We're looking at *America* the beautiful."

Two tiny spacecraft, so far from home, spun around the back side of the Moon in tandem at 12:41 P.M., and Ron took the command module back into a higher orbit while we headed the other direction, lowering our own position another eight miles. As the rocket roared beneath our feet, I recalled that NASA officials had said this flight would be near the limits of our performance capabilities. No problem. All I had to do was make a pinpoint landing in a place no man had been before.

IN TEXAS, BARBARA AND Tracy went to morning mass at Ellington. Ron's wife, Jan, and their two kids, Jaime and Jon, also attended a church service, then as the time neared for the landing, they came over to our house. For the long coast to the Moon, neither family had been glued to the television set, and kept generally abreast of the situation in space through periodic NASA updates. It was a major change from the early days when wives and children hung on every word from space, but of course that was before the missions mounted into long days and longer nights.

Now it was time for the big show, and Barbara found our living room filled with friends sharing the event by television, with twenty-five people munching cornbread and beans as *Challenger* struck out for its flight to the Moon. Barbara and Tracy were on the floor with their fingers crossed, monitoring our chatter on the squawk boxes and following a minute-by-minute flight plan that was unfolded on the carpet. My mom sat beside the television set, and the screen reflected the colored lights of our decorated Christmas tree in a nearby corner. Dave Scott and Alan Bean, Moonwalking veterans, were on hand to answer questions.

Barbara wore a dark turtleneck sweater over her spreading maxiskirt that bore the mission emblem and made sure to smile for the photographer, although some quiet strain, compounded by a lack of sleep, was building on her. She had changed considerably since the flight of *Gemini 9*, when NASA had thrown her out into the front yard to a press corps that was in a feeding frenzy. Just as the space agency had not helped the wives adjust to moving to Houston, neither did it ever say the gals didn't have to meet the press if they didn't want to. It was just something else that was expected to be done without complaint. But by *Apollo 17*, Barbara was far past the novice stage and in much more control of what was going on in and about her house. Still, there were so many people around. So many.

*   *   *

THE LANDING SITE WAS on the northeastern edge of the Moon, so when *Challenger* emerged from the far side, I had only about fifteen minutes for Mission Control to check the LM systems and give us a Go for the burn. Those few minutes passed quickly as Jack and I hurried through the checklists, Houston confirmed everything looked good, gave us a brief countdown and, at the exact designated instant, I fired the descent engine. We started falling out of orbit, and I was barely aware when we dove past my *Apollo 10* floor of 47,000 feet because my eyes were riveted to the instruments as I sought to absorb every nuance of the machine. In order for the push of the rocket to slow us down, its fiery end was pointed in the direction we were moving, parallel to the Moon's surface, and inside the cabin, we were traveling feet first and facedown.

When I stole a look, I immediately recognized the large, undulating area rolling beneath *Challenger*. Thanks to the simulators back on Earth, with their computer-enhanced photos of the approach to the landing site, I knew this place better than I knew my own palm, and there were no surprises as we zoomed toward the jagged highlands that separate the Sea of Tranquillity from the Sea of Serenity. I called out the passing landmarks that verified we were on track to the narrow entrance to the Valley of Taurus-Littrow.

To align the spacecraft for landing, when it would have to touch down on its four thin legs with us facing forward and able to see across the landing site, I rolled *Challenger* over so we were now on our backs—still parallel to the surface, but looking upward. For the next few moments, the windows were filled only by sunlit blackness.

That changed at about 12,000 feet, when I started tilting us upright, and was able peek over the bottom edge of my window. There was the crater Poppie, right where we were going to set this baby down. "Man, Gordo, this is absolutely spectacular." *Challenger* swooped lower, the horizon flattened, and I could see Nansen. I could see the Scarp. I could see Lara.

And I saw something that was a balm for my soul while we whizzed toward the hostile planet. Halfway through the twelve-minute burn I told Jack, whose eyes were also pinned to the instruments, "We're allowed two quick looks out the window. One now and one when we pitch over." Something rather spectacular was out there and I didn't want him to miss it.

He glanced up. "I can't see a thing except the Earth."

"That's what I'm telling you to look at."

"Okay. There's the old Earth." He went back to the instruments. Sometimes I didn't understand Jack, but what else could I have expected from a scientist?

At 7,000 feet I pitched smoothly upright, so the rocket was firing almost perpendicular to the surface and the burn lowered us like a fast elevator. The maneuver also stood us up straight, which helped me regain equilibrium. Earth now dangled like a colorful Christmas ornament smack-dab in the middle of *Challenger's* window.

On that Earth, where most mountain ranges are part of a long, sloping climb to altitude, there is seldom an opportunity to stand at exact sea level and look up at a mountain towering 8,500 feet above you. Even in the Rockies, you're already a mile high before you reach the higher peaks. On the Moon, life is different.

The age-old flutter of exploration excitement gripped me as I realized we were entering the unknown, the *terra incognita* of lore, the sort of place on which ancient mapmakers wrote, "Beyond Here Be Dragons." Down we flew toward crop-duster altitudes, scooted over the domelike Sculptured Hills, some of which were more than a mile high, and roared into the eastern entrance of a crater-pocked lunar valley deeper than the Grand Canyon, surrounded by mountains whose crests were above us. "Oh boy! Come on, baby. . . . Boy, are we coming in! Oh, baby!"

The North Massif rose sharply to our right and the South Massif was on our left, anchored by the debris of some time-distant landslide, a huge shelf of broken and fused rock, while Family Mountain was in blockade position some three miles away at the far end of the valley. In front of Family crouched the Lincoln Scarp like a line of stone infantry, a rupture in the lunar surface eight times higher than any cliff on Earth, where geologists hoped we might find rocks that had come up from fifty miles deep in the Moon. Wonders awaited our discovery. A quick check showed I had plenty of fuel as we danced above the craters, and I blessed those many hours of simulator training. What I saw out there was familiar, not frightening.

I used a small switch on the console for precise changes in vertical speed, altering the rate of descent by only a foot per second and tracking the changing altitude on a gauge known as the H-dot. A small triangle of craters I knew as Frosty, Rudolph and Punk came near, there was

Barjean, and I had been watching Poppie since the first moments. The familiar names and memories provided comfort and drew me closer.

Jack's voice was crisp on the radio in my helmet as he read off the data from the computer and radar. "At twenty-five-hundred feet, fifty-two degrees. The H-dot is good. At two thousand, H-dot is good. Fuel is good. Fifteen-hundred feet, fifty-four degrees, Gene. Approaching one thousand, approaching a thousand feet, fifty-seven degrees. Okay, you're through one thousand, and I'm checking radar altitude and Pings altitudes agree. You're through eight hundred feet. H-dot's a little high."

I had a deadlock visual. I knew exactly where I was, and the LM had become part of me, responding to my wishes as well as my touch on the controls as we lowered closer to the surface. "Hey, I don't need the numbers any more. I got it." It was hard enough to keep my focus on what was approaching and I was too busy to listen to more data, for the numbers didn't tell the whole story. What I saw outside forced decisions on when to slow down, dodge left or right, or maintain a steady rate. *I've got it. I've got it.* Finding a place to land wasn't as easy as anticipated. A boulder the size of a house—that wasn't supposed to be there—loomed right in front of me. I slid over it, only to encounter a deep hole that had remained hidden for time eternal. Hitting either would ruin the entire day.

"You're thirty-one feet per second, going through five hundred . . . twenty-five feet per second through four hundred," Jack reported. "That's a little high, Gene." Jack was one determined LM pilot, keeping his focus and watching the instruments so closely that he never saw the landing. The rocket engine continued its booming growl and the constant vibration felt like big wheels were churning beneath my feet.

"Okay." I adjusted and took aim for my final target, riffling past the edge of Sherlock and toward the hummocky lip of a big crater. "There it is, Houston! There's Camelot!" Trident was out the left window, Lewis and Clark out the right. I couldn't go beyond Camelot because it dominated a low plain we had dubbed Tortilla Flats, where massive chunks of rock jutted out like the points of sharp spears. It was now or never. I tickled the little switch with a single fingertip and *Challenger* responded, moving toward the landing zone as if drawn by a magnet.

This was the payoff, the ultimate dream of any pilot, for I wasn't flying a normal airplane but a spaceship, something much more complex, and this flight would be its only one. Only five other human beings had ever done this. There were no practice takeoffs and landings with an LM, and simulators and helicopters could convey only some of the characteristics. Every normal frame of reference had disappeared, and beyond the thin window, the strange Sunlight was richer, the shadows long and deep, the lack of color absolutely forbidding. Going down to the surface of a foreign planet had dropped me into the Twilight Zone and I was truly in a different dimension, moving the bug across unearthly terrain, with no room for a mistake of any sort and feeling the weight of a watching world.

"Three hundred feet, fifteen feet per second," Jack reported. "A little high. H-dot's a little high."

The dark mantle of the valley just below contrasted with the massifs, shining and bright. The Earth, fighting for my attention, dominated my window as if painted there when we entered the Dead Man's Zone about 200 feet above the Moon. Past that point, if the descent engine quit burning for any reason whatsoever, physics and time would take over and we would fall to the surface and crash before either I or the computer could possibly recover. The emergency Abort button would be useless.

"Okay, nine feet per second, down at two hundred. Going down at five. Going down at five. Going down at ten. Cut the H-dot. The fuel's good. One hundred and ten feet. Stand by for some dust. Little forward, Gene."

I scanned for an empty space in a parking lot of boulders as big as automobiles, and was concerned the powerful LM engine might kick up a cloud of black dust that would blot my view. Instead, there was very little, and I was able to eyeball the landing site. So close to the valley floor, those surrounding massifs seemed damned big! The sheer North Massif to our right stood as tall as eight-and-a-half Eiffel Towers and to the left, the wretched slab of the South Massif would equal the height of about seven Empire State Buildings stacked one atop the other.

A determined Jack stayed with his readouts. "Move her forward a little. Ninety feet. Little forward velocity. Eighty feet, going down at three. Getting a little dust. We're at sixty feet, going down at about two. Very little dust. Very little dust, forty feet, going down at three."

Almost there. I steadied the lander for the final hop as charcoal-gray dust rose up and roiled about the windows, obscuring the view. "Stand by for touchdown."

"Standing by. Twenty-five feet, down at two," Jack said with tense words. "Fuel's good. Twenty feet. Going down at two. Ten feet . . ."

Wire sensors nine feet long trailed from the pads of the lander legs, and when one brushed the surface, a blue light flashed on my console and I shut down the rocket. We dropped the last few feet with a stomach-flipping thud, jolted once and came to rest slightly tilted in a shallow depression. We were only 200 feet from the precise place picked as a target months ago on Earth.

It was 1:54 P.M. Houston time on December 11, 1972, and four days, fourteen hours, twenty-two minutes and eleven seconds had elapsed since we had blasted off from Florida. I paused for a moment and slowly exhaled after making one of the smoothest landings of my career.

More than two and a half hours of unrelenting dynamic action and steely tension had drained my senses since we had undocked from *America*, and now everything came to an abrupt stop. Instant silence reigned. Not a word from Jack, who was as stunned as I, no pounding rocket, no vibration, no noise. Not the song of a bird, the bark of a dog, not a whisper of wind or any familiar sound from my entire life. I was totally enveloped by such a thorough and complete stillness that I have difficulty comprehending it even today. The only sound inside my helmet was my labored breath, and even that slight disturbance seemed so terribly intrusive that for a brief moment, I stopped breathing, too. Then there was nothing at all.

I broke the spell. "Okay, Houston, the *Challenger* has landed!" I joyfully reported and pried my cramped hands from the thruster controls. "Yes sir, we is here. Tell *America* that *Challenger* is at Taurus-Littrow."

Above the South Massif, the Earth stood still in the inky southwestern sky, my silent, guardian star.

30

Down in the Valley

DREAMS REALLY DO COME true. Four hours after landing on the Moon and wearing the backpack that contained my life-support system, I wriggled backward through the tiny hatch, got to my knees on the small porch, and cautiously descended *Challenger's* ladder, a rung at a time, until I stood on the saucerlike footpad. The Sun glared bright all around as I had my first good look at the vast emptiness, while the canopy of sky remained thickly black from horizon to horizon, a contradiction that played *How can this be?* with my logical mind.

No fear, no apprehension, but a tremendous sense of satisfaction and accomplishment welled within me. My size-10½ boot was poised just inches above the surface of this almost mythical land that mankind had watched so closely for uncounted eons and to which we had assigned properties ranging from religious icon and symbol of romance to maker of werewolves and clock for the harvest. Every night of my life it had been up there, patiently waiting for my visit.

I lowered my left foot and the thin crust gave way. Soft contact. There, it was done. A Cernan bootprint was on the Moon.

I had fulfilled my dream. No one could ever take this moment away. "As I step off at the surface of Taurus-Littrow, I'd like to dedicate the first steps of *Apollo Seventeen* to all those who made it possible," I called to Houston. "Oh, my golly. Unbelievable."

My God, I was standing in a place no one had ever been before. The soil that was firmly supporting me was not the dirt of Earth, but of a different celestial body, and it glittered in the bright Sun as if studded with millions of tiny diamonds. The Sun, low in the lunar morning sky, cast a long shadow beyond the parked *Challenger*.

I slowly pivoted, trying to see everything, and was overwhelmed by the silent, majestic solitude. Not so much as a squirrel track to indicate any sort of life, not a green blade of grass to color the bland, stark beauty, not a cloud overhead, or the slightest hint of a brook or stream. But I felt comfortable, as if I belonged here. From where I stood on the floor of this beautiful mountain-ringed valley that seemed frozen in time, the looming massifs on either side were not menacing at all. It was as if they, too, had been awaiting the day someone would come and take a walk in their valley. I wasn't worried about what might happen next, whether some unknown danger lurked at my elbow, nor did I give much thought about how we would get out of this place when the time came. We had gotten here, and we would get home. For the next three days, I planned to live my life to the fullest, to milk every moment of this rare and wonderful existence.

As I stood in Sunshine on this barren world somewhere in the universe, looking up at the cobalt Earth immersed in infinite blackness, I knew science had met its match.

I gazed around to get my bearings. Deep ruts had been cut by giant boulders that had toppled down from the mountains. The Sculptured Hills, over which we had made our approach, looked like the wrinkled skin of a hundred-year-old man. A stony landslide had flowed into the valley, and everywhere I looked were craters of all sizes, a most familiar one only an arm's length away. "I think I may just be in front of Punk," I reported, amazed at flying a quarter of a million miles, then landing beside the lunar crater named for my daughter.

I skipped around to get my sea legs in the low gravity of this strange new world. Learning how to walk was like balancing on a bowl of Jell-O, until I figured out how to shift my weight while doing a sort of bunny hop. During my time of personal enchantment Jack had wormed out onto the porch, looked down and grumbled, "Hey, who's been tracking up my lunar surface?" He hopped off the ladder and stepped from the footpad into a geologist's paradise.

Like me, he was immediately unsteady. We had gone from Earth's gravity to zero gravity during our three days in transit, and now we were in one-sixth gravity, something only ten other humans had experienced. Every step churned up dust as we bobbled about like rubber ducks in a bathtub, already huffing and puffing as our suits lost their pristine whiteness to the sticky, fine-grained Moondust. Me: "Gosh, it's beautiful out here." Jack: "[The soil looks] like a vesicular, very light-colored porphyry of some kind; it's about ten or fifteen percent vesicles." That meant the sparkles on the ground were tiny specks of glass reflecting Sunlight. The Odd Couple goes to the Moon.

* * *

OUR FIRST JOB WAS to unload the Rover, which was carried outside of the LM like a piano tied to a truck. With lanyards, cables and hinges, we lowered it, a puzzle of folded wheels, armrests, seats, console, footrests, fenders, battery covers, and so many other parts that I felt like I was putting together a Christmas bike for Tracy. Jack made the highly technical observation that "It's safe to say this surface was not formed yesterday." I hauled him all the way up here for him to tell me this?

The fine dust clung stubbornly to our suits, visors, gloves and tools as if by magnetic attraction. "Man, it looks like I've been on the surface for a week already," I said, whacking at the stuff with no result. Jack reached for a rock, lost his balance, and toppled into a pratfall. When he struggled upright, he wore another layer of dust and had dropped our only remaining pair of scissors in the melee. We had left one pair behind with Ron, who had still not found his, and now ours had vanished into the lunar soil. If we were unable to cut open the plastic food packets, life might get pretty interesting. We had planned for every other emergency, but no one ever thought of starving to death on the Moon.

I finished assembling the Rover and bounced up and sideways into the driver's seat as a teenager might hop into an open Jeep, turned on the batteries, tried the steering, checked the forward and reverse controls, and goosed it. This was a moment of truth, for if it didn't work, we'd be walking, and our opportunity to explore this valley would be substantially curtailed. The electric motors on each wheel hummed. I fed it more power and scooted away for a test drive around the LM. "Hallelujah, Houston. *Challenger's* baby is on the roll!" A Moonmobile with wire wheels and no top is pretty cool.

A TV camera had not been mounted outside our spacecraft as on earlier flights because of weight considerations, but now we attached one on the Rover, and back in Houston, Ed Fendell, who was known as Captain Video, took over by remote control and became our long-distance cameraman. We could now share our private valley with the world.

Jack fell again while trying to grab another Moonstone. "I haven't learned to pick up rocks, which is a very embarrassing thing for a geologist," he admitted. The thick, clumsy gloves added to our problems and our fingers ached with the strain of holding onto things we could barely feel. Houston advised we were already seven minutes behind schedule, and we hurriedly loaded our lunar farming gear onto the Rover to get on with the day.

The Earth kept drawing my gaze away from the bleak surface, and reality felt like a hallucination. I had already seen it many times, but was still mesmerized by the most spectacular sight of the entire journey. Memories from *Apollo 10* flooded back as I reflected on the rare privilege of standing on the Moon and looking back at the only known place in the universe that contained life. *So perfect.*

I made one more attempt to get Dr. Rock to realize he was on another world. "Hey, Jack, just stop. You owe yourself thirty seconds to look up over the South Massif at the Earth."

"What? The Earth?"

"Just look up there."

"You seen one Earth, you've seen them all." It was typical of his droll humor, but I was almost disgusted with the blasé reaction, because I felt any human being should have been awestruck by the sight. Jack went back to his soil observations, but did launch into a verse of "Oh, bury me not, on the lone prairie; where the coyotes howl and the wind blows free." He might not want to acknowledge our planet in public, but sang out loud and clear to everyone who would listen. Then he found the scissors. We were saved.

A final job before leaving our home base was to erect an American flag, and I hammered in a thin metal staff and adjusted the small arm that would hold the red, white and blue banner out straight. This flag had been carried to the Moon and back by *Apollo 11*, and had been displayed in Mission Control ever since. Now it stands forever in the Valley of Taurus-Littrow, a fitting tribute to the folks who got us there. I told the guys back home, who watched it unfurl, "This was one of the proudest moments of my life. I guarantee it."

JACK AND I MOVED on to position the most sophisticated array of scientific instrumentation ever assembled for a lunar mission. Its heart was the Apollo Lunar Surface Exploration Package, known as ALSEP, which was powered by a small nuclear reactor. It was a complex system that would take a long time to deploy, and we hurried so it wouldn't cut into our available time. While unloading gear from the Rover, my rock hammer, its handle sticking out of my suit pocket, snagged something. "There goes a fender. Oh, shoot!" I exclaimed, being careful with my language.

Here I was in the midst of a high-tech nuclear experiment on the Moon and I come up with a fender-bender. A section of thin plastic fender cracking off seemed insignificant at the time, and I used the only thing available, a strip of good old-fashioned duct tape, to hold it in place.

We both worked fast, but the going was tougher than expected, and we chewed into the four hours that had been allotted for the deployment of the Rover and the ALSEP. Exceed that and the ninety minutes set aside for a journey south to the crater Emory, our first true geologic stop, would be in jeopardy.

I grabbed a battery-powered drill, especially made for Moon work and the granddaddy of today's cordless tools, and bored into the rocky soil to gather subsurface samples and plant heat-measuring devices. I had to grip it tightly and force my whole weight on it, but progress was no better than haphazard. The drill would find easy access for a few inches, then clunk against rock and kick back. My heart rate went up to 150 beats per minute, my hands hurt from squeezing the handle, and dust swirled in a sticky haze. I had to cut three eight-foot holes for the heat sensors, and without warning, the rocky soil of Taurus-Littrow would snare the three-foot-long bits, as thick as candles, with an unrelenting fist, freezing the drill and spinning me around like a drunken sailor. This stuff was tough as nails, and our work was consuming both oxygen and time. "Come on, baby. I'm going to get this thing out," I growled to the scientists listening far away. To pull it out, I used a tripod and lever, pumping it like an automobile jack.

While I tried to drill through stone, Jack did his best to erect the gravity-wave detector, a delicate package designed to determine how the Moon oscillates during an internal quake. The gadget had to be perfectly level to work, a smooth procedure during our Florida practices but almost impossible up here. It gave Jack fits. I was amused to listen to the scientists on Earth snottily hint that the scientist on the Moon hadn't deployed their precious toy correctly. In exasperation, they finally told Jack to use the tried-and-true repair method of giving it a good smack with one of our tools. Even that didn't work. We repeatedly drove back to this site in time-wasting repair attempts before its creators finally gave up.

Directions were coming fast and furious from Houston, where geologists and scientists were packed into a room two doors away from Mission Control. We knew these guys well, since they had trained us and carefully mapped exactly what we would do on the surface. But once we got there and started having problems and making unexpected discoveries, previous

agreements broke down and the teams fought to protect their own turf.
As the debates grew loud, Jim Lovell, who was assigned to filter their
decisions for us, became more of a circus lion-tamer than an astronaut.

Jack was antsy. Fulfilling the instructions of other scientists was sub-
tracting time from his own geologic plans. "I was afraid that would happen, with all those rocks," he muttered, staggering over to where I was
making only slow progress. He jumped on the lever to help yank the
damned drill out of the surface, lost his balance, and disappeared ass-over-
teakettle into a small crater. That brought a chuckle from Houston, but
I was horrified, immediately worried that he might rip his suit and ruin
my whole day.

Eventually, Mission Control gave us the bad news. We were forty
minutes behind schedule, and the first day's geology had to be trimmed.
Instead of the mile-and-a-half trip south to Emory, we would stop halfway, in a boulder field near the crater Steno. Jack was not a happy camper.
Still, he couldn't repress his sheer delight at being up here, and again
broke into song. "I was strolling on the Moon one day . . ."

I joined in for a duet. "In the merry, merry month of December . . ."
I stopped. "No, May."

"May."

"May's the month."

He went ahead. "When much to my surprise, a pair of bonny eyes,"
then lost the verse, trailing off into an aimless "be-doopy-doo-doo . . ."
The whole time, we stayed busy, but joking around was a wonderful stress
reliever. And anytime you put two little boys out to play in a sand pile
this big, they're going to have fun. This was the lark of a lifetime. But
work called.

We boarded Rover again and I floorboarded it, but almost immediately
reduced my speed to a crawl over the thin dark mantle of lunar dirt
covering the undulating plain around the lander. The route was pocked
with craters of all sizes, from tiny to large, and large boulders frequently
forced me to detour. All of the hazards were partially buried, making what
should have been a routine trip a rather risky undertaking.

In addition, my duct tape didn't hold, the broken fender fell off, and
we were flailed with a roostertail of dust that spread before me as thick
as a hailstorm. It was like trying to look through a waterfall of dirt, and
since I was also driving straight into the Sun, I could barely see where I
was going. The wire mesh wheels collected some impressive dents when

I sideswiped a few boulders. The valley would later be determined to be the dustiest visited by any Apollo mission, and it posed a special problem. Jack and I were both grimy beyond belief and our delicate instruments were coated with layers of dust that threatened to cause them to fail. Once we reached Steno, where we hoped to gather some prime samples, we found that time and terrain had again conspired against us and we only made it partway up the crater's rim. Again whipped by dust, we made our slow way back to Camelot to play with the balky ALSEP.

I was going to have to get that damned fender fixed, and there wasn't a repair shop within 250,000 miles.

WE SPENT SEVEN HOURS and twelve minutes on the surface before going back inside *Challenger* to end our first day, filthy and exhausted. We had worked astonishingly hard and had not slept for almost twenty-four hours. The most welcome tool in the entire kit turned out to be a big old paintbrush that we hung beside the ladder to thoroughly dust each other off before climbing on board the LM.

The *Challenger* had changed. It was no longer just our ticket from space to the Moon—now it was our home, our own little castle in Camelot, the only sanctuary we had on the surface of this new world. Bless those guys and gals at Grumman.

We pressurized the spacecraft and it was as if an oil can was suddenly filled with a blast of air. *Bloop*. The pressure forced the thin little hatch cover to bulge, reminding me how fragile the Bug really was.

Stripping off my gloves was a painful process, and I wasn't surprised to discover the knuckles and backs of my hands were blistered with a fiery red rawness. My fingers felt almost broken and I had to flex them to see if they still worked. The gloves were thick, with multiple layers, and when pressurized after we suited up, had become as rigid as the cast on a broken arm. Every time we grabbed something, we fought their stiffness, scraping our knuckles and skin against the unyielding inside layer.

Next, we helped each other wrestle our way out of the bulky suits, which took up an incredible amount of room in the tiny living area. They were wet with sweat, so to dry them, we attached our helmets and gloves to the empty garments and hooked up the oxygen hoses to circulate air. That was like inflating a pair of big balloons and it seemed as if two more guys had just crawled into our lunar pup tent. The backpacks were hung on the walls, but it was impossible to roll the suits up, so we lay them across the ascent engine cover, which pimpled up like a garbage can in the middle of the cabin, and pressed them as flat as possible.

Stripped down to our liquid-cooled underwear, we had a quick dinner, debriefed with the guys on Earth via a private radio loop, and played with some of the rocks we had stowed in the cabin boxes. Several of the twenty samples we had taken were too big for the bags provided, and I turned one over and over in my bare hands, examining it closely. How amazing. Cooled lava that had lain on the surface for at least 3 billion years, scoured by radiation in a vacuum for untold centuries, becoming a rock from another planet, and yet it looked so ordinary, like so many I had seen on our geology field studies to Greenland. Crystalline, with tiny openings through which gas probably escaped during some ancient time, and coated with dark dust that smelled like gunpowder and puffed away at the slightest touch or shake. Ordinary but simultaneously extraordinary. My fingernails were soon rimmed solid with black dirt, as if I had been digging in a garden, because I could not put the rock down.

Jack was frustrated, feeling we had accomplished very little serious geology during our first exploration period because we spent so much time laying out the experiments. If for some reason we had to leave now, we would have only a handful of coarse basalt to show for our years of preparation—mere samples skimmed from the top layer of Taurus-Littrow, and nothing to unlock the true secrets of the valley. I agreed. We had been acting like a couple of robots, the extended arms and egos of other people, responding obediently when they tugged our leash, and not really exploring, which was what we had come to do. As if to mock Jack, the dust from the rocks made him sneeze. I described the fender situation to Mission Control so they could work on a possible remedy. We *had* to find a fix.

THE WEATHER WAS COLD in Texas, with a high of only forty-four degrees and a slight drizzle plinking the reporters outside our house. Christmas decorations glowed in the dampness. When I stepped onto the surface shortly after six P.M. Houston time, cheers and applause erupted, and when a telecast showed me bringing the Rover around the LM, my wife and daughter could actually see me, a quarter-million miles away, driving on that crescent of a new Moon in their sky. Toasts of Cold Duck were raised.

"We finally put him there," Barbara told reporters gathered before the wooden Santa Claus. "Listening to them land today was just fantastic. It's the happiest day of my life." They asked if the waiting was easier the third time around. "The apprehension is there," she replied. "The nervousness, the excitement. You can't do anything about it." The lumps are always in your throat at crucial times, she said, and the lumps got bigger as the years went by. At her side, Tracy rubbed an *Apollo 17* medallion as if it were a magic charm.

Barbara was once again the strong supporting wife who knew her role in the Apollo epic—the one who had to face the media every time she stepped outside, while playing hostess to a gang of friends inside. All of them thought they were helping her through this trying time, but in fact, they were just adding to the pressure. For weeks she had been on display, both in public and private, and while I remained on the Moon and then found my way back to Earth, my wife would bear the burden of taking care of everyone else, presenting herself as the picture of supreme confidence in order to reassure the entire world that things were going well. After a decade of this, it had become too much. She finally asked Ry Furlong to take care of things for a little while. "I've just got to be alone," she whispered to her best friend.

But where? Outside, the house was almost under siege by reporters, photographers, and well-wishers. Two dozen people were milling about inside, discussing the amazing thing that was happening on the Moon and listening to the squawk boxes. Barbara quietly retreated to the bedroom, then to the bathroom, where she locked the door, turned on some music, and stepped into a hot shower just to get some peace. Beneath the steaming water, her formal manner wilted, the pressure overtook her, and her confidence finally broke.

Barbara had toughed it out during the *Gemini 9* spacewalk fiasco and the *Apollo 10* flip-flop near the Moon, but she well knew what had happened to Martha Chaffee after Roger died at the Cape, how Jeannie Bassett was crushed by Charlie's death in the Gemini days, what Marilyn Lovell endured when Jim almost didn't come home from *Apollo 13*, how she herself had felt upon learning of my helicopter crash, and she had consoled too many astronaut widows through the years. No matter what she said in public, Barbara knew in her soul that there were substantial risks on every mission, this one above all, and it was unfair that she was not allowed to be afraid. Even if I died up there, she would still have to walk through the chaos and be the strong, ideal Mrs. Astronaut *(We were all so proud of him!)*.

The accumulated stress of a decade came together in a thunderclap moment of black and bitter despair, and my wife couldn't take it anymore. Barbara slowly curled into a ball and wept, pounding on the shower wall and screaming at the top of her voice in a place carefully chosen so that no one else could hear. Women don't get calluses on their hearts. Thirty minutes later, she returned to the living room, calm and back in charge.

JACK AND I STRUNG our hammocks in an X shape, his on the bottom near the floor where we stood when flying, and mine across the top, over the engine bell. My feet were against an instrument panel, and I took care not to kick any switches while my face looked up the tunnel and the suits poked me in the back. Damn, this thing was small. Memories of the *USS Roanoke*.

We were dead tired, and slid fiberglass covers over the windows to create our own nighttime. I should have dropped right off but could do no more than doze, listening to the quiet, sweet hum of the spacecraft's environmental system keeping us alive, and Jack's steady breathing and occasional sneeze in the other hammock. There was an eerie stillness outside. No hushed breeze or patter of raindrops, no crickets or frogs, not even any air. Every hour that I stayed on the Moon, the sense of absolute nothingness grew. I leaned up and pulled away the nearest shade to see if anything had changed. The motionless flag still glistened in the Sunshine, and the Earth still dominated the coal black sky. No. That's just the way things are here. I put the cover back in place, massaged my sore leg, and tried unsuccessfully to rest.

What a waste of time! My mind whirled as I lay in the hammock, wide awake. I was mentally and physically whipped, but felt I should not be loafing around in my underwear while there was a whole Moon to explore just beyond that little hatchway. We only had about sixty hours left, and time had warped. When we were outside, the hours just galloped away, but inside the spacecraft, the clock didn't seem to move at all, and our rest period passed with agonizing slowness. Eventually, we slept.

EIGHT HOURS LATER, MISSION Control kicked us awake with Wagner's volcanic *Ride of the Valkyries*. It was December 12 at 12:48 A.M.,

Texas time. While we slept, John Young's U-Fix-It Garage in Houston had come up with a way to make a replacement fender. Engineers folded four geology maps into a fifteen-by-twenty-inch rectangle—only about as thick as a kid's Halloween mask—and taped the seams, then used screw clamps from the emergency lighting pack to attach them to what was left of the original fender. John talked me through the time-consuming procedure and it worked, but by the time the Rover Boys headed across Tortilla Flats, we were already eighty-four minutes behind schedule for our second seven-hour trek.

A few geologists believed that from here on, I should just become Dr. Rock's taxi driver and surrender some of my leadership role to Jack. Not bloody likely. I would give Jack great latitude, for I trusted him without question, but there was too much at stake, and my job was to see that everything was completed as successfully as possible. Collecting rocks was important, but we had a lot more than that to do.

Anyway, we had a basic difference. Dr. Rock was a product of Mission Control and the scientific laboratory environment, while I was an aviator. Jack thought that if we got into trouble, the guys back in the control room would bail us out. I knew from too many hairy carrier landings that the people sitting behind consoles were there to help, but the bottom line was that they were not flying the spacecraft. I was the guy sitting at the controls, with the ultimate responsibility of getting our asses back home again.

Besides, just as Jack had become a pretty fair pilot, I had become a pretty damned good lunar geologist, and could look at the stone forest while he was among the pebbles. The result was that we were a doggone good team, Jack precisely analyzing details while I provided a descriptive overview.

We reached our first destination—Hole in the Wall, at the foot of the South Massif—by driving tilted along a steep slope, dodging craters and rocks, with the TV camera capturing the bouncing, rolling terrain. In one-sixth G, the Rover felt like it was about to roll over, so I made sure that Jack was always on the downslope side. For an hour we explored boulders that had tumbled down the towering 8,500-foot mountain in some distant time, giving us highlands material without our having to actually go to the summit. In fact, we had tapped such a geologic goldfield that Houston stretched our time there to the maximum, and it was still frustrating to leave such a promising area.

The dilemma of staying longer at a good site or moving to one that might be even better haunted every Moon exploration, and the scientists in the back room at Mission Control argued heatedly about what should be done. After some portable-gravimeter and surface-electrical-properties experiments we drove off for the next stop, the rim of a small crater a few hundred yards to the north at the base of the Lee Scarp, tearing downhill so fast that I claimed a Rover speed record—almost eleven miles per hour!

Again, we were so far behind schedule that the pressure was on to accomplish as much as possible to make the minutes count. Time was added to some experiments, subtracted from others, and Jack and I lumbered around like a couple of dirty elephants, drilling, raking, scooping up rocks and samples, and getting fearfully worn out by trying to please everybody. A bracket on the TV camera came loose so Jack had to hold it tightly as we drove, cramping his arms even more and limiting his ability to work.

We would travel a dozen miles and visit the craters Shorty, Lara and Camelot before the day was done, and Jack would take such a spectacular, spinning fall while trying to collect samples that CapCom Bob Parker said the Houston Ballet was interested in his services. Again, the pressure of so many experiments cut into Jack's geology quest, leaving him frustrated, but he did have one gigantic moment.

While I took photographs near the rim of Shorty, he looked down at the nearby soil which his boots had disturbed. "Oh, hey!" He bent over for a closer look because he didn't believe what he saw. On the bleak Moon, he was standing on a carpet of color. "There is orange soil!"

I thought he had been sucking too much oxygen. *Oh, my God, my scientist has been here too long and has overdosed on rocks. There's no orange soil on the Moon! There's no color up here at all!* "Don't move it until I see it."

His voice rose as he scuffed with a toe. "It's all over! Orange!"

I stopped what I was doing and bounced over.

"I stirred it up with my feet." Jack's mind was already churning with the immense possibilities of such a find.

I was boggled by the sight. "Hey, it is! I can see it from here. It's orange!" Our gold visors were down, and perhaps the reflection was throwing off our perception. "Let me put my visor up." Nope. "It's still orange . . . He's not going out of his wits. It really is."

The back room in Mission Control almost exploded. This was unexpected treasure, like a Spanish conquistador finding jungle gold. But now that we had it, what the hell were we supposed to do with it?

Jack trenched into the patch as I fetched more supplies and Captain Video homed in with the color TV. Aware of the disappearing sands of time, we stopped talking and worked like a couple of ditchdiggers getting paid by the job. As we bagged and tagged, the guys in Houston debated about what to do next, for they were engulfed by a bonfire of curiosity.

At first, we thought the presence of the multicolored dirt, which ranged from bright orange to ruby red and looked like oxidized desert soil, might indicate the presence of water or geologically recent volcanic activity. Could Shorty, a crater that was 110 meters in diameter, really be some sort of ancient volcano? If the colored soil proved that, then the Moon's internal heat machine had not shut down 3.7 billion years ago as almost everyone thought. This would stand almost every existing evolutionary theory on its ear.

Alas, when scientists eventually examined our find, they discovered the soil to be tiny spheres of colored glass that were not of volcanic origin, and about the same age as other old Moon rocks. The material probably had come from as deep as 300 kilometers inside the Moon in some distant age, spurted out of a surface vent by enormous gas pressures in a process known as fire fountaining, not unlike the fizzy eruption from a shaken bottle of cola. The gas propelled a spray of molten lava thousands of feet into the air, and it cooled into the beads of glass whose coloration was decided by its mineral content.

The theory continued that the droplets of glass lay on the surface for eons until covered by some lava flow from a true volcano, which provided layers of protection from the eternal rain of tiny meteorites that would have destroyed them. Then along came the huge meteor that slammed into the Moon, scooped out the crater we called Shorty and, in doing so, uncovered the colored soil, and it waited on the surface for thousands of years until Jack and I came stumbling along to find it.

So while the orange soil didn't prove the existence of recent volcanic activity and thus alter the timeline of lunar evolution, it did contain chemical elements from deep within the Moon. When matched up with green glass droplets discovered among the *Apollo 15* lunar samples, scientists discovered they contained titanium, bromine, silver, zinc, cadmium, and other such "volatile" elements that were not imported by some stray meteor. Through these discoveries, we obtained information on the internal makeup of the Moon that we never would have had otherwise, and scientists could unlock further Moon mysteries.

In years to come, experts would say the orange soil was one of the most surprising discoveries of the entire Apollo program.

AT THE END OF our second day, our arms were as heavy as lead, our hands were chipped, raw and bleeding, and all we had was a little hand lotion to soothe them. After we had had some chow and settled down, Deke told me on a private radio loop that everything was fine at home. "I talked to Barbara and she said everything is okay," he said. Not a peep from Black September.

I was relieved to put the possibility of terrorism aside for a while, for something else dominated my thoughts that night. I was going down in history as the last man to walk on the Moon for a very long time, and had nothing prepared to say to mark the occasion. The press had never stopped badgering me about what I was going to say when I left the surface, and I had dodged giving an answer, because I didn't know. I had no electric phrase to inspire those who would eventually follow us. I turned to a blank page on my cuff checklist and made a few notes, praying that, when the time came, something would make sense. How could I encapsulate in just a few words all that this meant, the magnificent things that we, as a nation and as humankind, had accomplished by escaping the bonds of Earth and exploring our Moon? What could I possibly say that would have lasting meaning? Frankly, I had no idea, and could only pray that something deep inside of me would come forth to express those feelings. It's tough being last.

THE FINAL INVESTIGATION OF the Moon by the astronauts of Apollo started shortly after Mission Control jacked us awake on Wednesday, December 13, Day Three, with "Light my Fire" by the Doors. Like ordinary commuters, we ate breakfast, dressed and drove to work, although our food, clothes and car were quite different than those of the average person. Bone-tired, we took off for another seven hours, this time for a round trip to the steep slopes of the North Massif, then over to the base of the Sculptured Hills and to the Van Serg crater, chipping and hacking with burning hands and aching arms. The stretched tendon in my leg hurt with every step I took.

Our first stop was a split boulder, about three stories high, that had rolled and bounced down the mountain in a prehistoric avalanche and cracked into several huge segments when it slammed to a rest. Jack was finally in his element and performed a decisive field study of that gigantic stone to piece together its volcanic history, while I huffed my way up a slope and took a set of panoramic photos of him at work. In later years, I would often be asked if getting a scientist to the Moon had been the right decision. There is no doubt in my mind that it was, for not only had Jack carried his load as a crew member, but Joe Engle and I, without having the encyclopedic knowledge of a professional geologist, would never have complemented each other as well. That is no rap on Joe or me, but a simple fact. Jack Schmitt belonged up there, and more than proved his worth.

BACK IN HOUSTON, TRACY had stolen the show. Jim Hartz, host of *The Today Show* and an old friend, had coaxed Barbara into letting our ponytailed daughter go on national television. Wearing her turtleneck sweater and the maxiskirt with the mission emblem, Tracy perched on a stool and watched us on the Moon while the nation watched her. She calmly explained the meaning of the mission patch and confidently chatted about what her daddy was doing at the moment. "It looks like they're having a ball," she said, identifying me as the one with the red stripes on his suit and helmet. When Jim asked if we might find water up there, Tracy giggled, "If they find water, they're in the wrong place."

She broke some hearts when Jim asked what souvenir I might bring home for her. "I can't tell you." Jim persisted and Tracy still refused, saying it was a secret. Jim kept coaxing, smelling a good story, until she finally gave in. "He's going to send me back a Moonbeam," she told an audience of millions. When Jim took her back home, Tracy barged through the front door, locked into a model's pose, and declared, "The star needs a Sprite!"

DUST AND FATIGUE WERE definitely causing problems. Those insistent, fine grains of lunar dirt had worked into the moving parts of our tools, and things were breaking down. Then the makeshift fender gave way and showered us with more dust wherever we drove. And because everything had to be gripped so tightly, our entire upper bodies, particularly our hands and forearms, felt as heavy as granite. The dirt which had once only rimmed our fingers was now caked deep beneath each fingernail, as if driven in by hammers.

Still, at the Sculptured Hills, we ended our rock hunt with a bit of fun. We were now accustomed to the light gravity, and could move around freely, so climbing steadily up the slope was tiring, but presented little difficulty. But instead of walking back down, I went into a legs-together kangaroo bounce and *boing-boing-boinged* my way back to the Rover. Jack pretended to ski, and his radioed comments of *"shoosh-shoosh-shoosh"* mystified Mission Control.

We were exhausted from climbing, digging and hauling rocks, but when we reached the Van Serg crater, Jack argued to stretch our safety margin and stay out longer. But Flight Director Gerry Griffin called it a ball game. It was time to go.

BACK AT *CHALLENGER*, WE dusted each other off, loaded our final boxes of rocks, then Jack climbed the ladder and disappeared into the hatch. By then, we had stayed longer and traveled further on the surface of the Moon than any other crew. We had covered about nineteen miles and collected more than 220 pounds of rock samples and, even before we were aboard, scientists in Houston were crowing that this had been the most meaningful lunar exploration ever. We were living proof that the Apollo program had paid dividends.

While Jack cleaned up inside, I drove the Rover about a mile away from the LM and parked it carefully so the television camera could photograph our takeoff the next day. As I dismounted, I took a moment to kneel and with a single finger, scratched Tracy's initials, T D C, in the lunar dust, knowing those three letters would remain there undisturbed for more years than anyone could imagine.

Alone on the surface, I hopped and skipped my way back to *Challenger*, my thoughts racing wildly as I sought to encompass this experience. Just being there was a triumph of science to be celebrated for ages, but it was more than a personal dream come true, for I felt that I represented all humanity.

There was a sense of eternity about Apollo. Sir Isaac Newton once said, "If I have been able to see farther than others, it was because I stood on the shoulders of giants." Every man and woman who put in long hours to get us to the Moon now stood with me beside the lunar lander in that odd Sun-washed darkness. Every astronaut who had gone into space, who made it possible for me to fly a little higher, stay a little longer, was at my side. These were the giants upon whose shoulders I stood as I reached for the stars. I could almost feel the presence of Roger, Gus, Ed, and all other astronauts and cosmonauts who died in the pursuit of the Moon. We had carried on in their names.

I took one last unfiltered look at the Earth and was enveloped by a sense of selfishness, for I was unable to adequately share what I felt. I wanted everyone on my home planet to experience this magnificent feeling of actually being on the Moon. That was not technologically possible, and I knew it, but there was a bit of guilt at being the Chosen One. I put a foot on the pad and grabbed the ladder. I knew that I had changed in the past three days, and that I no longer belonged solely to the Earth. Forever more, I would belong to the universe. With everyone back home listening, I ignored the notes on my cuff checklist and spontaneously spoke from my heart.

"As we leave the Moon and Taurus-Littrow, we leave as we came, and God willing, as we shall return, with peace and hope for all mankind." I lifted my boot from the lunar dust, adding, "As I take these last steps from the surface for some time to come, I'd just like to record that America's challenge of today has forged man's destiny of tomorrow." As I turned, I again saw the small sign pasted beneath the ladder by some unknown well-wishing worker, a phrase that I repeated every time I entered or left the *Challenger*. "Godspeed the crew of *Apollo Seventeen*," I said, and climbed on board.

Mine would be man's last footstep on the Moon for too many years to come.

BACK INSIDE, WE DID some last-minute cleaning and tossed a bunch of very expensive gear out of the spacecraft. Cameras, tools, backpacks and other now-useless material were flung to the surface. We had to shed weight if we were going to get off the Moon safely. Mission planners had worked out the exact balance needed, and every container of rocks we brought aboard was weighed on a handheld fish scale, calibrated for one-sixth gravity, before being stored. We had just enough fuel to get us into orbit, with almost no margin for error, so the overall weight of the spacecraft, its passengers and cargo of rocks was critical. We threw out nearly everything that wasn't nailed down.

Jack and I were exhausted, so we rested well that night. The next morning, we donned our suits, helmets and gloves, talked with Mission Control, and readied the Bug for departure. Ron Evans passed overhead in *America*, still hard at work and waiting for us.

Houston fed us the computer numbers and we opened the valves and watched the pressure rise on the helium that would force fuel into the ascent engine. When the computer issued its command or I hit the ignition button, the fuel would flow together, instantly detonate and we would vault from the surface, head into orbit, link up with Ron, and go home. If everything worked. Here there was no Rocco Petrone pad crew to assist us, no Guenther Wendt to lock us in and make sure everything was ready, no Glynn Lunney to ramrod the liftoff, no second chance at all. I threw in a Hail Mary and a sign of the Cross, because I needed all the help I could get.

Watches and clocks counted down in synchronized slow motion on two planets. All the valves were open except the final one. From Houston, Captain Video zoomed in with the Rover camera to show the *Challenger* launch.

I rested the tip of my left index finger on the yellow ignition button at 4:56 P.M., Houston time. *Ten seconds and counting.* I turned to Dr. Rock—*five . . . four . . . three*—and said the last words any man would speak on the Moon for the rest of the twentieth century. *Two . . .*

"Okay, Jack, let's get this mutha outta here."

31
The Search

THE QUESTION THAT I am asked most frequently is: "Did going to the Moon change you?" I would like to think that I am the same person I have always been, for I still pull on my pants one leg at a time, bleed red when cut, and have to pay the mortgage when it is due. Just like everyone else. But how could having lived on another planet not force at least some sort of change? Walking on the Moon and walking on Main Street are two entirely different experiences. I can always walk on Main Street again, but I can never return to my Valley of Taurus-Littrow, and that cold fact has left me with a yearning restlessness. It was perhaps the brightest moment of my life, and I can't go back.

Enriched by a singular event that is larger than life, I no longer have the luxury of being ordinary. To stand on the lunar surface and look back at our Earth creates such a personal sense of awe that even Alan Shepard wept at the view. Trying to exist within the paradox of being in this world after visiting another may be why some Moon voyagers tend to be reclusive.

I spent years searching for the Next Big Thing to replace my grand Moon adventure, constantly asking myself, *Where now, Columbus?* I realize that other people look at me differently than I look at myself, for I am one of only twelve human beings to have stood on the Moon. I have come to accept that, and the enormous responsibility it carries, but as for finding a suitable encore, nothing has ever come close.

WE REMAINED IN LUNAR orbit for two more days to finish Apollo's exploration of the Moon. I had reservations about that, but it was a compromise I made with Jack and his scientific colleagues during the final stages of our mission planning. To me, our primary goal had been accomplished, and with immense success, so loitering around in lunar orbit any longer than absolutely necessary seemed to be an undue risk, just waiting for something potentially catastrophic to happen.

Finally, the crucial moment arrived with the behind-the-Moon TEI burn of the rocket engine and we hurled out of lunar orbit. When we came around the corner, headed for home, the first thing Mission Control heard was Dean Martin's voice once again crooning "Going Back to Houston."

The return trip was highlighted by Ron's chance for glory, and Captain America did a terrific spacewalk to retrieve the film and experiments from his days in orbit. We held a televised press conference, but apparently were already yesterday's news, for the networks didn't find time to put us on the air. Our splashdown in the Pacific on December 19, 1972, brought an end to an historical era. We landed in sight of Ron's old boat, the *Ticonderoga*, and after gobbling down a real sandwich, had our physicals and took the traditional call from the president. In two days, we were back at Ellington, where several hundred people braved a stiff December wind to welcome us home. When Tracy grabbed me with a neck lock, I couldn't help but think, "Thank God, no Black September."

Christmas was very special that year, and to make it even more memorable, we had the damnedest splashdown party ever in Judge Roy Hofheinz's top-floor suite of the Astroworld Hotel. My pal Jimmy Demaret stood on the piano to sing carols and the vice president of the United States, Ted Agnew, made the toasts. Bob Anderson, a good friend and the CEO of Rockwell International, which built the command and service modules, invited us to Bimini for the New Year's weekend. Dr. Rock declined, but Ron and I welcomed the opportunity. Our initial flight reports were finished and the holiday would give us our first chance to relax with our families and reflect on the mission.

But just as the good Reverend Doctor Larry Poland bushwhacked me after *Apollo 10*, Senator William Proxmire, chairman of the Senate Appropriations Committee, was hiding in the bushes this time. He was furious about our Bimini trip. He claimed that Ron and I had gotten a free vacation from a government contractor and that Rockwell was somehow profiting from our brief vacation. It didn't take long for NASA to cave in and a few weeks after I had commanded one of the most successful Apollo missions, I received a letter of reprimand. The incident bothered me for a while, but I eventually realized it was just politics, and rose above it.

A few months later we made an extraordinary tour across America—

twenty-nine states and fifty-three cities—where people showered us with appreciation, and then, after being guests at a White House state dinner, the president sent us around the world on a flag-waving tour to ovenlike places I had never heard of before. We visited every nation along the equatorial belt throughout Africa and Asia, including Pakistan, India and the Philippines, where we celebrated July 4 on the balcony of the Malacañang Palace, shooting off firecrackers with President Marcos. Within two years of our trip, almost every president and dictator who hosted us was either assassinated, in exile or headed that way.

The receptions, parades and travel were, however, only a false euphoria, for only one thing was really on my mind: *What now? Where do I go from here?*

I had worked steadily on space voyages since first being assigned to backup duty on *Gemini 9*, living at a breakneck pace that was as if I was getting off one fast-moving express train only to immediately board another. Now the trains had stopped running and I was standing in a deserted depot, with no idea of what to do. Thirteen years of my life had zipped by so quickly that I never caught up with them. I had met presidents and popes, and had friends who were celebrities from all walks of life, but none of them could solve my dilemma. In contrast to my personal quandary, there was a wind shift, a sense of positive change, in the United States. The troubles weren't quite yet over, but things were moving inexorably toward a more tranquil period, and soon, the rebels would become lawyers and accountants. When historians look back, they might see the white spire of *Apollo 17* as a milepost marking when things started to get better. Within a few years, the Vietnam war ended, the prisoners came home, and one of the most divisive periods in American history was over.

THE SPACE CUPBOARD WAS pretty bare after *Apollo 17*. There was no work for me in Skylab, but when there was the long-awaited joint venture with the Russians, known as the Apollo-Soyuz Test Program, I was on the negotiating team representing the American astronauts, away from home as much as ever—if not more—something that Barbara found hard to accept. From 1973 to 1975, I traveled to the Soviet Union numerous times, and to my pleasant surprise, found lasting friends among my once-morta enemies, the Soviet cosmonauts.

I briefly considered vying for command of one the first space shuttles, but while those birds represented the next generation of space flight, I had already been far beyond the Earth orbits in which they would park, so I let them fly without me. I found myself with a great resumé, but was chained to a desk when I really wanted to fly.

I tried to be realistic, aware that there was not a lot left out there for me to accomplish, and finally faced the facts: "I'm not going to Mars. I'm not going back to the Moon, and, truth be told, I'm probably not going back into space again at all." Apollo was over and NASA's golden age of exploration was fast fading into glimmering memory.

The Navy wanted me to take over its tactical space program, a Pentagon slot that carried the two stars of an admiral. It was a dramatic opportunity, but if I was going to return to active duty, I wanted command of an aircraft carrier, not some desk job, even one with a flag attached to it. But because of my early promotions up through the ranks to captain, I was now considered too senior to be a carrier skipper and was firmly snared in my own personal Catch-22.

I retired from the Navy and left NASA in June of 1976, still searching for that next big challenge.

Periodic attempts were made to lure me into politics, once for a U.S. Senate seat in Illinois and several times for Congress in Texas. Such offers were nice ego trips, but I wasn't interested. The kind of campaigning I prefer is speaking to a class of curious students, where I might be able to make a difference. Nothing gives me greater satisfaction than to see a kid walk away with a gleam in his or her eyes, a young face filled with the inspiration and willingness to reach for a dream because of something I might have said.

For I firmly believe that among the elementary school students of today are members of the crew of that first spaceship that will take us to Mars. These kids won't want to just go back to the Moon, where we have already been, nor will they be content orbiting in circles around the Earth for weeks or months. We have already lived on another planet and rightfully can call the universe our home, so they will want to reach beyond that, and Mars is the next giant leap for mankind.

Such a mission most likely will be an international effort, requiring the resources and talents of many countries, and the astronauts who make the long trip will not be confined to pilots. A flight crew of six to ten people probably will include a myriad of disciplines, and extend beyond science, into the arts, so that poet and artist we all want to go into space may finally get a ride.

The crew has plenty of time to mature, for as the twenty-first century dawns, we are not yet ready for the big leap toward Mars. The technology is still evolving, although some of the items on the shelf today can help us get there. Today, a trip to Mars would require many months in transit, then probably a stay of about two years to make it worthwhile, and another seven to nine months to come back home. However, by the time we are able to assemble such a mission, technology will have advanced to give the astronauts new propulsion systems that will speed up such a trip, just as the design of a new sail or wooden hull and crude navigation tools were developed to allow early explorers to cross vast oceans—when the time was right.

The main reason that we will venture back into deep space is simply that we must. It is a necessity, not a frivolous whim, and a lust for science is not enough of an explanation, for we really don't know what we will learn on Mars. We will go because it is logical to do so, and our curiosity as a species will not allow us to remain locked to our home planet much longer. Humankind must explore, for we want to learn what lies over the hill or around the corner. Inspiration, sweat, challenges, and dreams got us to the Moon and they will get us to Mars and beyond. It is our destiny.

MY MOVE INTO PRIVATE industry coincided with the final chapter of my marriage to Barbara. My work offered interesting opportunities, and a different lifestyle, but I found myself away from home as much as ever. The higher salary helped, but did not solve our problems, which had never been about money anyway.

We still lived in the little house in that cloistered environment of Nassau Bay, but were no longer part of the active astronaut corps. New and younger astronauts were moving in with their families, and the rookies would never be so forward as to assume that we might want to attend their parties, or share dinner at their homes and get to know them. It was ironic that to this new generation, we, the most social of people, had become like John and Annie Glenn and Alan and Louise Shepard, whom we had viewed as unapproachable, although they really were not. *Captain Cernan's flown in space three times and walked on the Moon! And Barbara is almost as popular as a movie star! We can't just ask people like them over for hot dogs and potato salad!* It was as if we had been cast out by the clan.

In 1977, we built a new house in the upscale Memorial area on the west side of Houston, thinking that moving might make things better, but of course, it didn't. In 1980, when Tracy was a teenager, Barbara and I separated, then divorced the following summer. Looking back, I can see that, like many of the other wives in the program, she got tired of being Mrs. Astronaut. Those years had brimmed with excitement, but that was yesterday, and she wanted an identity of her own. She once observed, "My name is not going to be in the history books for doing anything, but I know that I did." Actually, all of those incredible wives should be in the history books.

MY BUSINESS INTERESTS TODAY are in Houston, but my heart lies across the state at my 400-acre ranch outside of Kerrville, in the peaceful Texas Hill Country. I fly over there in my twin engine Cessna Golden Eagle whenever possible. It's no rocket ship, but it links me to *Challenger*, *Snoopy* and the aerobatic Stingers, and assuages my continuing passion for aviation. I love being in that cockpit, clipping the wispy tops from mounds of purple evening clouds as I fly to my new Camelot, always with one of my dogs curled up on the floor behind me.

The hours in the air give me plenty of time to reflect on what it all really meant, and the answer remains elusive. Another hundred years may pass before we understand the true significance of Apollo. Lunar exploration was not the equivalent of an American pyramid, some idle monument to technology, but more of a Rosetta Stone, a key to unlock dreams as yet undreamed. Our legacy is that humans are no longer shackled to the Earth. We opened the door to tomorrow, and our trips to another celestial body will rank as the ultimate triumph in the Age of Achievement. And for the price, it was the biggest bargain in history.

Sometimes it seems that Apollo came before its time. President Kennedy reached far into the twenty-first century, grabbed a decade of time and slipped it neatly into the 1960s and 1970s. Logic dictates that after Mercury and Gemini, we should have proceeded to build the shuttle, then an orbiting space station, and only then sought the Moon. As it was, we accomplished the impossible, then started over again. It was as if our young nation had chosen to never again cross the Mississippi River after Lewis and Clark discovered the Northwest Passage.

I often reflect upon that cold winter day when I stood by Roger Chaffee's grave in Arlington, wondering if the final notes of "Taps" were also the death knell of our space program. Now, having been to the Moon, it's clear that we not only survived the *Apollo 1* fire, but succeeded beyond anything we could have imagined, and the question has become, "Why didn't we go on?"

Our nation is impatient and fickle about even the most astounding achievements. After we landed on the Moon six times, perhaps we needed to take some time to figure out what we had learned before taking the next step in space, and Skylab and the shuttle were worthwhile places to spend our space dollars in the interim. Then as the years passed, the aggressive spirit gave way to caution, to not even wanting to attempt such ventures unless success could be guaranteed. The disaster of the space shuttle *Challenger*, seen on television by millions, reinforced that seeming determination to make space travel a no-risk business, which it cannot be. It is sad to think that what we did in the decade of racing to the Moon probably would take twice as long to accomplish today, even if the national will and treasure could be mustered, which is a significant question in itself.

MY OWN FEELING OF invincibility received a large dose of reality in 1990, when Ron Evans died in his sleep. How could someone who had over one hundred combat missions in Vietnam and had gone to the Moon pass away so easily? One of the most difficult things I ever had to do was deliver the eulogy at his memorial service, but I found comfort in the poem "High Flight," knowing that Ron would finally "reach out and touch the face of God." He was a special person with whom I went on the journey of a lifetime.

Although we still do not have a lot in common, Jack Schmitt and I are good friends today, with a mutual respect borne from having shared something truly unique. Looking back, I realize that his assignment as an astronaut placed him in an almost impossible situation, and we sure didn't make it easy for him to break into the fraternity of macho test pilots. Jack is a rare and talented individual who overcame every obstacle to walk on the lunar surface and, once there, proved why science deserves a place at the table of exploration.

OVER THE YEARS, I'VE reached a truce that lets the Moon hold its secrets in exchange for allowing me to live in the present, rather than in the past, through a loving family, good friends, and challenging work. I believe I have been particularly blessed and granted a new life after the old one ended.

In 1984, I met Jan Nanna, a lovely dark-haired lady who claims she first spied me while watching television in her living room as I stepped from the *Apollo 17* spacecraft. "So they finally have a tall astronaut," she said at the time, then promptly forgot all about me and the space program until we met at a party in Houston. We were married in 1987 in a little church in the mountains of Sun Valley, Idaho, and I gained an anchor of stability and a sense of direction in my otherwise stormy and drifting existence, and that resulted in a rich, new way of looking at life.

The marriage also gave me two more beautiful daughters, Kelly and Danielle, and I now have a growing flock of grandchildren, including Tracy's twins. This personal growth has been a joy for me, because while I remain an intense competitor, I am no longer imprisoned by the tunnel-vision mentality of my space days. Jan, the girls, their husbands, the babies, are always at the forefront of my thoughts. Columbus has come home.

As everyone who knows me is aware, there has always been one other important woman in my life. The best part of my early civilian career came when I interviewed a petite Tennessee dynamo who was looking for a job as my secretary. Claire Johnson is one of those steel magnolias from Dixie, and in addition to being my champion, she is very special to me.

MY FAVORITE TIMES TODAY take place at the ranch, whether feeding my longhorns or getting mud-filthy digging post holes. With a fire crackling in the stone hearth at the end of the open porch on a cool evening, Jan and I watch the deer come down to drink from the ponds and graze unafraid among the cattle. Our three Labs sprawl in a lazy pile, and grandchildren prowl about. The feeling is idyllic.

It was on one such evening that I watched the Moon rise full and achingly bright. When I see it like that, I can instantly transport myself back to the valley I once called home, a place where I had a house, a job, a car and commuted to work. The Sun bathes the boulders and massifs, and I again tingle with the absolute stillness and understand the presence of our Earth in the heavens. The crisp memories are not unlike those of childhood, such as the barn and cornfields of Grandpa's farm, or when

Mom and Dad would take my sister and me on vacations to places of which we had only dreamed. Some things are no less real just because they belong to the distant past.

On this evening, as the Moon climbed slowly above the hills, I scooped my five-year-old granddaughter Ashley into my arms, just as I had once held her mother, Tracy, beneath a similar night sky. I thought that now perhaps she was old enough to understand, to remember, and prepared to tell her the story.

But before I could speak, she pointed straight up, and declared in an excited voice, "Poppie, there's your Moon!" She had always called it that, never knowing why.

"Do you know how far away the Moon is, Punk?" I asked.

She seemed puzzled, for a child of that age could not possibly grasp such a distance, so I rambled on, using words familiar to her. "It's way, way far away in the sky, out where God lives," I said. "Poppie flew his rocket up there and lived on that Moon for three whole days. I even wrote your mommy's initials in the sand."

Ashley gazed at it a little while longer, then lowered her eyes to meet mine, and she saw not some mighty suited-up space hero from an age before she was born, but only her silver-haired grandfather. Insects and animals were beginning their night song and a few antelope scurrying among the shadows drew her attention. She wiggled, growing anxious because she wanted to give the horses a carrot before going to bed. But she glanced up again, then back at me. "Poppie," she said, "I didn't know you went to Heaven."

I felt a jolt, almost an electrical surge, as I considered her statement. Her innocent view of life unlocked the riddle that had puzzled me for so many years. My space voyages were not just about the Moon, but something much richer and deeper—the meaning of my life, weighed not only by facts from my brain, but also by the feelings from my soul. For a moment, I was again standing on another world, watching our blue Earth turn in the sable blackness of space. *Too much logic. Too much purpose. Too beautiful to have happened by accident.* My destiny was to be not only an explorer, but a messenger from outer space, an apostle for the future.

Too many years have passed for me to still be the last man to have walked on the Moon. Somewhere on Earth today is the young girl or boy, the possessor of indomitable will and courage, who will lift that dubious honor from me and take us back out there where we belong.

Listen. Let me tell you what it was like . . .

I gave Ashley a big squeeze. She had just bathed and smelled fresh and clean and alive, her baby powder so much more enchanting than the distant, dusty perfume of the goddess Luna. I have a wonderful set of yesterdays. Jan, my kids, and the grandchildren are the promise of tomorrow.

"Yes, Punk." I carried the laughing little girl over to the corral. "Your Poppie went to Heaven. He really did."

Index